This fourth Companion to Ancient Thought is devoted to ancient ethics. The chapters range over the ethical theories of all the major philosophers and schools from the earliest times to the work of the Hellenistic philosophers. There is a substantial introduction which considers the question of what is distinctive about ancient ethics, and an extensive bibliography. This collection provides a sophisticated and accessible introduction to the moral theories of the ancient world.

COMPANIONS TO ANCIENT THOUGHT: 4

Ethics

Companions to Ancient Thought

In recent years philosophers have radically reappraised the importance and sophistication of the philosophical texts of the ancient world. This new series of Companions is intended particularly for students of ancient thought who will be reading the texts in translation but approaching them with the analytical skills of modern philosophy and with an eye to their contemporary as well as their historical significance. Each volume is devoted to a specific field of philosophy and contains discussions of relevant ideas of all the major philosophers and schools. The books do not attempt to provide a simplified conspectus of ancient views but rather critical discussions of the central and therefore representative arguments and theories.

A particular feature of the series is its exploration of post-Aristotelian philosophy, which has been shown by recent scholarship to be both philosophically exciting and historically important.

Already published

1 *Epistemology*
2 *Psychology*
3 *Language*

COMPANIONS TO ANCIENT THOUGHT: 4

Ethics

Edited by Stephen Everson
Department of Philosophy, University of Michigan

CAMBRIDGE
UNIVERSITY PRESS

PUBLISHED BY THE PRESS SYNDICATE OF THE UNIVERSITY OF CAMBRIDGE
The Pitt Building, Trumpington Street, Cambridge CB2 1RP, United Kingdom

CAMBRIDGE UNIVERSITY PRESS
The Edinburgh Building, Cambridge CB2 2RU, United Kingdom
40 West 20th Street, New York, NY 10011-4211, USA
10 Stamford Road, Oakleigh, Melbourne 3166, Australia

First published 1998

Printed in the United Kingdom at the University Press, Cambridge

Typeset in 10/13pt Monophoto Photina   [SE]

A catalogue record for this book is available from the British Library

Library of Congress cataloguing in publication data

Ethics / edited by Stephen Everson.
    p.   cm. – (Companions to ancient thought: 4)
    Includes bibliographical references and indexes.
    ISBN 0 521 38161 4 (hardback) – ISBN 0 521 38832 5 (paperback)
    1. Ethics, Ancient.   1. Everson, Stephen.   11. Series.
BJ161.E84   1998   97-8899   CIP
170'.938–dc21

ISBN 0 521 38161 4 hardback
ISBN 0 521 38832 5 paperback

Contents

I

Introduction: virtue and morality

STEPHEN EVERSON

No branch of philosophy has been more influenced by serious consideration of ancient writings in the past quarter of a century than has moral philosophy – or 'ethics', as it is often now called (a change in nomenclature which is itself a sign of that influence). This has made it more difficult to delineate helpful contrasts between ancient and modern moral philosophy. Had one set out to write an overview of ancient ethics some twenty years ago, it would have been relatively easy to contrast the sorts of issue which concerned ancient writers with those to be found in contemporary discussion. Whereas modern moral philosophers were still largely wrestling with the competing merits of utilitarian and 'deontological' accounts of moral action, the key notions in ancient ethics were rather those of virtue and *eudaimonia* – and although '*eudaimonia*' has standardly been translated by 'happiness', it plays a very different role in ancient ethics from that given to happiness by utilitarians. For the ancients, to give an account of *eudaimonia* was to specify what made a life valuable – and, at least generally, the accounts they offered were far removed from the sort of reductive theories offered by utilitarians in terms of pleasure and pain or the satisfaction of people's desires.[1] More generally, whilst modern moral philosophers focused on the question of how to determine the right action in any given circumstance, the ancients were primarily concerned with issues of character and the evaluation of a person's life considered as a whole.[2]

Ethics is by no means the only area of philosophy in which contemporary

---

[1] Epicurus is exceptional in this respect. Although he seems to accept the status of *eudaimonia* as the final end, he does attempt to provide a hedonistic account of what it is to be happy. In this, he is less radical than the Cyrenaics, who maintain hedonism whilst denying that happiness is the final end. For discussions of the difficulties which are occasioned by the combination of eudaimonism and hedonism, see Mitsis [760], Annas [71], ch. 16, Striker [772] and Irwin [735].

[2] This point is frequently made: see, for instance, Williams [70] and Annas [71].

philosophers have looked back to the work of the ancients, but if recent interest in ancient epistemology and psychology has been encouraged by a reaction against Cartesian assumptions about knowledge and the mind, interest in ancient ethical theories has been in large part the result of a reaction against broadly Humean assumptions about moral psychology and the nature of evaluative judgements. Thus, if it is thought obvious that one's evaluative beliefs are not capable of truth, then the ancient concern to achieve ethical knowledge will seem to rest on a straightforward misunderstanding of the nature of the moral philosopher's subject-matter. Again, if one takes for granted that one's evaluative beliefs are motivationally inert – that whatever beliefs the agent has, it is an open question how he will be motivated to act – then the moral psychology to be found in ancient writings will seem decidedly peculiar. As these Humean assumptions began to be challenged, however, ancient ethical writings became attractive sources for those who wished to see what form a secular moral theory might take when it did not suppose that one's evaluative beliefs could neither motivate action nor be assessed for truth.

As a result of this, whilst one can discern obvious differences between ancient ethics and moral philosophy as it was generally practised twenty years ago, it has become more difficult to draw usefully broad distinctions between ancient and contemporary moral philosophy. Indeed, one construal of the effect of the influence of ancient ethics on contemporary philosophy might be that it has encouraged a flight from 'moral philosophy' altogether – if by that one means the philosophical investigation of moral reasons. Some philosophers have argued that ancient ethical theories are so different from the main traditions of moral philosophy that it is misleading to look to them for views about morality since, for better or worse, the ancients in fact lacked the very notion of morality, that is, of specifically moral reasons for action. Thus, in her paper 'Modern moral philosophy', published in 1958, Miss Anscombe argued that if one wishes to elucidate the 'modern way of talking about "moral" goodness, obligation etc.', one cannot go back to Aristotle, since, whilst he is happy to talk about blame, he does not distinguish a species of moral blame. Indeed, 'if someone professes to be expounding Aristotle and talks in a modern fashion about "moral" such-and-such, he must be very imperceptive if he does not constantly feel like someone whose jaws have somehow got out of alignment: the teeth don't come together in a proper bite'.[3]

---

[3] Anscombe [1933], 2. She does not regard this as a defect in Aristotle, since she recommends abandoning the notion of morality altogether: 'the concepts of obligation and duty – *moral* obligation and *moral* duty, that is to say – and of what is *morally* right and wrong, and of the *moral* sense of "ought", ought to be

More recently, a more generalised version of this concern has been expressed by Bernard Williams – a philosopher who has himself recommended abandoning the notion of morality.[4] Thus, in a brief survey of ancient philosophy, Williams contrasts Greek ethical thought with 'current concerns' and 'the moral inheritance of the Christian world'. The former

> takes as central and primary questions of character, and of how moral considerations are grounded in human nature: it asks what life it is rational for the individual to live. It makes no use of a blank moral imperative. In fact – though we have used the word 'moral' quite often for the sake of convenience – this system of ideas basically lacks the concept of *morality* altogether, in the sense of a class of reasons or demands which are vitally different from other kinds of reason or demand . . . Relatedly, there is not a rift between a world of public 'moral rules' and of private personal ideals: the questions of how one's relations to others are to be regulated, both in the context of society at large and more privately, are not detached from questions about the kind of life it is worth living, and of what it is worth having or caring for.[5]

Like Miss Anscombe, Williams regards this absence of a distinctive notion of morality as an advantage: it is a respect in which – as with its having no need of God – 'the ethical thought of the Greeks was not only different from most modern thought, particularly modern thought influenced by Christianity, but was also in much better shape'.[6]

Now, the force and plausibility of the claim that the ancient writers lacked the notion of morality depends, of course, on quite what one takes that notion to be. Certainly, there is no analogue in the ancient philosophical texts for Kant's way of distinguishing moral requirements as universalisable maxims, for instance, and no support for the idea that one might derive moral reasons from divine edict. If one thinks that only some of the reasons for action are moral reasons, and that those reasons must be distinguishable by reference to some criterion whose nature can be understood by someone

---

jettisoned if this is psychologically possible; because they are survivals, or derivatives from survivals, from an earlier conception of ethics which no longer generally survives, and are only harmful without it' (p. 26). She makes the further claim that 'it is not profitable for us at present to do moral philosophy': 'that should be laid aside at any rate until we have an adequate philosophy of psychology, in which we are conspicuously lacking' (p. 26). There are certainly many contemporary moral philosophers who would maintain that the moral psychology one finds in Aristotle comes considerably closer to adequacy than that which was to be found in the moral philosophy about which Anscombe was complaining.

[4] See his [979], ch. 10. Surprisingly, although Williams there cites Anscombe as targeting 'the moral *ought*' (p. 223, n.18) he makes no reference back to Anscombe's paper in his discussion of the Greeks – but the similarity of concern is clear enough.   [5] Williams [70], 251.   [6] *Ibid.*, 251.

who does not already have a grasp on the notion of morality, then it will not be denied that the ancients lacked the idea of a distinctively moral reason for action. Anscombe indeed links the notion of a moral obligation to a 'law conception of ethics', and maintains that in continuing to make use of it once that conception has been renounced, philosophers maintained 'the survival of a concept outside the framework of thought that made it a really intelligible one'.[7] If this were right, then it would indeed not be possible to find in ancient texts – except, possibly, those of the Stoics – any elucidation of what it is to be a moral agent, that is, an agent whose actions are (properly) motivated by moral reasons.[8] This characterisation of a moral reason is not one which is immediately compelling, however. What makes it dubious is precisely that even those who do not accept that there are moral rules, whether or not of a divine provenance, find it natural to distinguish between moral and immoral actions, as between moral and immoral agents. At least before engaging in philosophical reflection, it seems perfectly intelligible to deny that the proponent of rules of behaviour provides a satisfactory account of moral reasons – that is, to maintain that he fails to delineate how one ought morally to act – and if that is genuinely intelligible, then the notion of morality is independent of the notion of a moral law.[9]

Williams' characterisation of the notion of a moral reason is more difficult to assess precisely because it is more vague – and so, of course, his thesis that the ancients lacked the concept of morality is correspondingly more difficult to judge. Taking 'moral reason' to have the sense of a reason which is different in kind – even *vitally* so – from reasons of other kinds clearly will not do, since one could have a culture which failed to recognise moral reasons, but which did recognise aesthetic reasons and took these to be vitally different from reasons of other kinds – and one should not be forced to think of such a culture as possessing the notion of a moral reason just because of this. There has to be more content to the notion of a moral reason than just that it is vitally different from reasons of other kinds (whatever, indeed, that quite means).[10] Unless we can provide some substantive characterisation of what

---

[7] [933], 6.

[8] So, the Stoics did maintain that there are natural laws – for the importance of this innovation in the theory of natural justice see Striker [66] and Annas [71], 302 f.

[9] This is not intended as a knock-down argument against Miss Anscombe's thesis. For she does not deny that such a claim will seem intelligible, merely that it is indeed so. That it *does* seem so provides strong prima facie evidence that it is – but an inability to characterise, even if not to define, what it is for a reason to be a moral reason would count in her favour here.

[10] Annas in her [71] argues that 'in any intuitive understanding of morality', 'the ancient theories are not theories of some alien mode of thought, but theories of morality, in the same sense that Kant's and Mill's theories are' (p. 452). In her discussion of Williams, she takes the point of distinguishing moral from non-moral

makes a reason a moral reason, Williams' thesis that the ancients lacked the notion of a moral reason will be seen to be too vacuous to be of interest.[11] The problem here is that the more precise the sense one gives to the notion of a moral reason, the more difficulty there will be in finding such reasons recognised in the ancient texts – but, equally, the less plausible it will be to maintain that in failing to recognise reasons so defined, the ancients thereby lacked the concept of a moral reason altogether.

As we have seen, even Williams himself in the passage cited above acknowledges that, despite his denial that the ancients did distinguish moral reasons as a class, he had nevertheless found it convenient to discuss their ethical theories in terms of views about morality. That this was not just a matter of laziness can be seen by considering how naturally the term is employed in that discussion. Thus, earlier in his piece, Williams had contrasted the defence of justice offered by Glaucon and Adeimantus in book II of the *Republic* with that provided by Plato in the rest of the work. According to the former, 'morality is represented as a device for promoting egoistic satisfactions which could in principle occur without it, but which are as a matter of fact unlikely to do so because of everyone's weak position in an amoral state of nature'.[12] On the instrumentalist account, the reason people

reasons to be that the former 'have a special place in our deliberations': 'moral reasons are special just because of this place they have in our deliberations: they override other kinds of reason just because of the kind of reason they are' (p. 121). In this respect, as she points out, reasons of virtue, as understood by ancient writers, are entirely similar to moral reasons – 'all ancient theories think the same way about the fact that the action is cowardly: this is a consideration which is not just weighed up against the profit and time expended, but which sweeps them aside; and to think otherwise is to misconstrue what cowardice is' (pp. 121–2). It is important to note that whilst this is entirely correct – and is indeed sufficient to dispose of Williams' claim that the ancients did not possess the notion of a moral reason because they did not recognise a class of reasons which were vitally different from other kinds – it is not in itself sufficient to show that the ancients did have the notion of a moral reason, precisely because of the inadequacy of Williams' characterisation of a moral reason here. Annas herself provides further reasons for her claim that the ancients are concerned with morality: see [71], 122–31 and ch. 22.

[11] Irwin, who also takes issue with Williams over the attribution of the notion of morality to Aristotle, and so who also has to give some reasonably determinate sense to the claim that the ancients lacked the notion, culls three theses from Williams [979] in an attempt to see what Williams might think to be at stake: that moral obligation is concerned with action that 'must be in the agent's power'; that moral obligations cannot conflict 'ultimately, really or at the end of the line'; and that they are inescapable. As Irwin points out, however, there is a suspicion that Williams identifies that notion of morality too closely with the Kantian version of it: see [505], 117. It would, of course, be less interesting to discover that the ancients did not share Kant's particular conception of a moral reason. I do not take up the question of responsibility here – although see Sauvé Meyer's chapter below.

[12] [70], 245.

have for performing actions which are directly in the interests of other people is that a general practice of so acting will in fact serve the interests of all the participants. Williams quite rightly sees Plato's response to this as one which is concerned to attack the contingency of the link between acting self-interestedly and acting justly. Glaucon and Adeimantus – and, indeed, Thrasymachus in book I – assume that what is in an agent's own interest can, and should, be fully characterised independently of considerations of justice, so that these latter considerations will be in competition with the agent's own interests unless they can be shown to serve those interests. Whilst Thrasymachus denied that they could be shown to do this, and so affirmed what he claimed to be the irrationality of acting justly, Glaucon and Adeimantus allow that, as the world is, people are better off by acting justly, as this will in fact secure their interests better than acting unjustly. Plato, in contrast, seeks to show that being a just person, and thus someone who will perform just actions because they are just, is itself something which it is in one's interests to be – in which case, considerations of justice will no longer even in principle be in competition with reasons of self-interest. An agent who is not disposed to act justly will thereby not be an agent who leads a fully valuable life, and it cannot be properly self-interested to lead a life which is less valuable than it might be.

Williams comments:

> It has been said by Kantian critics that Platonic morality is egoistic, in a sense incompatible with real morality. This misses the point. It is formally egoistic, in the sense that it supposes that it has to show that each man has good reason to act morally, and that the good reason has to appeal to him in terms of something about himself, how and what he will be if he is a man of that sort of character. But it is not egoistic in the sense of trying to show that morality serves some set of individual satisfactions which are well defined antecedently to it. The aim was not, given already an account of the self and its satisfactions, to show how morality (luckily) fitted them; it was to give an account of the self into which morality fitted.[13]

We can leave to one side the question of how accurately Williams here captures the Platonic aim – worries over this would perhaps focus, for instance, on whether it is entirely happy for him to cast it in terms of providing a moralised account of the *self* – what is of present concern is just the propriety of his construing the argument of the *Republic* as being about morality at all. If the terms of Williams' construal of that argument are used merely for the sake of convenience, and so it is at best misleading to describe Plato as having views about morality, then the defence of Plato against the

---

[13] *Ibid.*, p. 246.

Kantian critics will be meretricious: instead of taking Plato to provide an account of the relation between morality and the self which is not in fact vulnerable to the Kantian charge of egoism, one should rather say that since we can find in the *Republic* no attempt to show how moral reasons might rationally motivate an agent, the Kantian charge was simply misdirected. For Williams' defence of Plato to be appropriate, there must be a notion of morality, of what it is for a reason or an action or an agent or a practice or whatever to be a moral reason etc., which is both non-technical and yet sufficiently determinate to be contrasted with other kinds of reason or agent, and which one can employ when reading, for instance, both the argument of the *Republic* and the practical philosophy of Kant.[14] If there is no such notion, then, whatever the convenience of using the term 'moral' when interpreting the writings of the ancients, the distorting effect of doing so will make its use simply improper.

Should Williams, then, have followed his theoretical instincts and rewritten his account of the argument of the *Republic*, removing the now, for him, inconvenient references to morality? The official topic of the dialogue, after all, is that of being *dikaios*, a term which is traditionally translated by 'just' rather than 'moral'.[15] Perhaps we should do best to minimise the risk of distortion, take Plato's concern in the *Republic* simply to be that of warranting being a *dikaios* agent, and forget about trying to match this with whatever concerns others have expressed using the terminology of morality. Here, however, the very naturalness of Williams' construal of the *Republic*'s challenge as being to show how it can be rational to act morally, given that such action is directly motivated by concern for other people's interests and not one's own, should make one hesitate before imposing such interpretative limitations.

That it is natural to construe it in this way does not, of course, follow simply from the contrast between reasons of *dikaiosunē* and reasons of self-interest: reasons cannot be straightforwardly divided into those which derive from self-interest and those which come from considerations of

---

14 It might have been open to Williams to claim that whilst Plato does not have the notion of morality, nevertheless his discussion of justice (*dikaiosunē*) contains the materials which we could use in discussions of the nature of morality: this would not sit happily, however, with his contention that Plato's *aim* is to place morality within his account of the self. It may be, however, that a more carefully framed discussion might have avoided inconsistency here.

15 Although note that a recent translation – Waterfield [324] – does in fact translate it as 'moral' and the cognate noun, *dikaiosunē*, as 'morality'. In a translation, this is over-bold: the reader should be aware that taking Plato's concern to be with the justification of morality is, even if correct, a matter of some interpretation and not just a matter of seeing it on the page.

morality. Thus, a pianist who practises to perfect his technique need not be doing this for either of those kinds of reason, but may simply regard the acquisition of the ability to perform music without technical impediments as a valuable goal in its own right. That the requirements of *dikaiosunē* may conflict with those of self-interest is not in itself sufficient to show that those requirements can properly be taken to be moral requirements. Nevertheless, whilst aesthetic reasons or perfectionist aims could sometimes be taken to conflict with considerations of self-interest (at least given a restricted notion of self-interest of the kind which motivates the puzzlement about the rationality of moral action and which it is part of the point of the *Republic* to challenge), someone who fails to be motivated by such reasons will not thereby be characterisable as selfish or egoistic in the way that someone who fails to recognise or be motivated by moral reasons will be. It is striking in this context that Thrasymachus in *Republic* I should find it natural to characterise justice, *dikaiosunē*, as 'what is in the interests of another' – the characterisation which sets the problem of how just action can be rational which the argument of the *Republic* is intended to solve. Nor is this characterisation simply a tendentious requirement of Thrasymachus' argument that to be just is to be stupid or weak. When Aristotle discusses the different types of *dikaiosunē* in the *Nicomachean Ethics* (*EN*) v.1, he describes the broadest kind as being 'complete excellence, not absolutely, but in relation to others': 'justice, alone of the excellences, is thought to be another's good, because it is related to others; for it does what is advantageous to another, either a ruler or a partner' (1130a2–3). Neither Plato nor Aristotle denies that to act justly is indeed to act in the interests of other people – their aim is rather to show how such action serves the agent's own interests as well.

It is partly in this link between justice – and hence virtue – and altruism that we can find the needed relation between the ethical concerns of the ancients and the interests of later moral philosophers – a relation which will vindicate Williams' discussion of Plato, despite his own theoretical protestations. This link is not sufficient by itself, however, since one cannot simply equate altruistic behaviour with behaviour which is motivated by moral reasons. For one thing, if someone acts against the moral reasons which obtain, then his action is wrong, but one can fail to act altruistically without acting badly. Whenever I can promote someone else's interests, I have reason to do so – and that reason will be an altruistic one – but it need not be wrong for me not to act accordingly. Further, someone can act altruistically without his action's being motivated by a moral reason, and so altruism is not by itself sufficient to capture the notion of a moral reason. Even a simple, and effective, concern for someone else's interests is not in itself sufficient to make an agent a moral agent: there is a space between being an entirely self-interested agent (an agent, that is, whose desires are all for his own well-being) and an agent whose actions are motivated by moral reasons. One can act on desires for the well-being of other people without thereby acting for a moral reason – or a requirement of virtue. Thus, a parent may have the desire that his child should flourish and act on this, by, say, bribing examiners to give the child favourable treatment: his actions would not be self-interested, but neither would they be motivated by a moral reason. This requires not just that one act for the sake of someone else's interests, but that one regard the reason they provide for acting as independent of one's desire to act that way. Someone might have a passing fancy to give money to a tramp in order to help him out, but this would not count as a moral action – an action motivated by moral reasons – if, in the absence of this desire, the agent would see no reason to give the money.

To see what needs to be added to the account, it is helpful to contrast two rather different styles of the assessment of action. One might ask, concerning an action, how successfully that action satisfies the agent's existing desires and goals. Thus, if someone wishes to become wealthy, one might well view his investing in the low-priced shares of a newly privatised industry as an appropriate action. In this mode of practical assessment, the success of an action is determined by considerations which are internal to the agent himself. Alternatively, one might assess an action by reference to criteria whose applicability is not circumscribed by facts about the agent's own motivations. Thus, if one judges an action to be, say, unjust or greedy, then the force of this judgement is not dependent upon whether the agent himself has any desire to act justly or to avoid acting greedily. In this sense, moral reasons are 'categorical': their normative force is not derived from reasons of other kinds, and so, in particular, is not dependent upon the motivational states of the agent to which they apply.[16]

By focusing on these two features – that the agent should be motivated by

---

[16] Note that one can accept this Kantian claim without accepting the stronger claim that it is *distinctive* of moral reasons to be categorical in this way. The force of one's judgement, or complaint, that another's action is inelegant or graceless or impolite is similarly independent of his motivational states. So, one can accept, say, Philippa Foot's arguments in her [944] that there is as much reason for treating the requirements of etiquette as categorical as there is for taking those of morality to be so without thinking, as she does, that this casts doubt on the categorical force of moral reasons (for Mrs Foot's own reconsideration of these issues, see her [946]). There are those, of course, who deny that any reasons are categorical in this way; but we can take this to involve the denial that there are any moral reasons. It is perhaps helpful here to see that taking a reason to be a moral reason is not to be committed to its having overriding normative force. One can plausibly deny, that is, that any reason which is categorical should defeat any reason which is not.

sensitivity to the interests of other people and that the force of the reasons which motivate him is independent of his current desires – we can come up with a core notion of a moral reason, even if this turns out not to provide the conditions for dividing all reasons clearly into the moral and the non-moral.[17] Indeed, it is important when seeking to clarify the notion of a moral reason that one does not assume from the start that conditions of that kind can be found. One can maintain that there are certain reasons which are certainly – paradigmatically – moral without being committed to the claim that all reasons can be determinately divided into the moral and the non-moral. Thus, whilst it is obvious enough that the notion of justice should be classified as a moral one and that of elegance should not be, it is less clear how one should classify, say, the tacky. To say of something that it is tacky is to give a reason for not doing or having it – but is this a moral reason? That one can criticise the way someone dresses as tacky might suggest that the notion of the tacky is an aesthetic, and not a moral, one; but one can also criticise the way someone treats, for instance, his boyfriend as being tacky, where this is not an aesthetic complaint. It may well be that the question whether the reason not to perform tacky actions is a moral one is not capable of a determinate answer. Such indeterminacy should not be found troubling, however. It is not a constraint on any proper characterisation of a moral reason that it should be sharp enough to allow us to decide of any reason for action whether it is to be classed as a moral reason.[18]

If, however, we do take the two central features of moral reasons to be, first, that they arise from considerations to do with the interests of other people than the agent (considerations which could in principle turn out to extend to those of other sentient beings as well) and secondly, that their normative force is not dependent upon the motivational states of the agent, then we indeed have good reason for thinking that the ancients did recognise the distinctive character of such reasons. The *Republic*'s central concern is, as we

---

[17] Someone who sought to maintain that there are moral reasons not to engage in certain types of, say, sexual acts, even though these reasons have nothing to do with altruism, might wish to deny the centrality of the reference to other people's interests and to limit the range of moral reasons by replacing this feature with a condition that moral reasons should be secured in some way or other – for instance to their having the status of divine injunctions. Whilst this would be a possible strategy, however, it is difficult not to feel that those who do claim that there is *moral* reason not to have non-marital sex are using the term 'moral' merely to impart a spurious dignity to superstition.

[18] This will be problematic only if one thinks that moral reasons have their force in virtue of being moral reasons. Such a thought is not a compelling one, however. The notion of a moral reason is a second-order one: something is a moral reason in virtue of being a reason of some other kind. The force of the reason not to be tacky does not depend on whether that reason is a moral one or not.

have seen, with showing how it can be (practically) rational to act justly,
even when to do so is to act in the interests of other people and, at least
directly, against one's own. Again, as the discussion of justice in *EN* v.1
makes clear, whilst Aristotle does not think that the operations of virtue are
restricted to acts in which the agent subordinates his direct interests to those
of other people, virtue nevertheless certainly requires such acts, and indeed
it is the willingness to perform these which Aristotle seems to take to be the
test of an agent's virtue. Justice turns out to be not just one virtue amongst
others; it is 'complete excellence in its fullest sense because it is the actual
exercise of complete excellence. It is complete because he who possesses it
can exercise his excellence towards others too and not merely by himself'
(1129b31–3):

> This is why the saying of Bias is thought to be true, that 'rule will show the
> man'; for a ruler is necessarily in relation to other men and a member of a
> society. For this same reason justice, alone of the excellences, is thought to
> be another's good, because it is related to others; for it does what is advan-
> tageous to another, either a ruler or a partner. Now the worst man is he
> who exercises his wickedness both towards himself and towards his friends,
> and the best man is not he who exercises his excellence towards himself
> but he who exercises it towards another; for this is a difficult task.
> (1130a1–8)

To be truly virtuous, one needs to be sensitive to the interests of other people:
to act virtuously in respect of other people is more difficult than acting virtuously merely in respect of oneself. What Aristotle has in mind in forcing this
distinction here would seem to be something like this: someone may perform
apparently courageous acts in pursuit of his own interests without yet being
disposed to do so to promote the interests of others.[19] Thus, he might be
willing to face greater dangers when fighting to recover some land he has
lost than he would in fighting to recover someone else's land. When fighting
for one's own benefit it is easier to be courageous than it is when fighting for
that of another, presumably because one is likely to be less sensitive to the
importance of other people's interests than to that of one's own.
Nevertheless, it is a mark of genuine virtue that one will be motivated to
perform actions which are virtuous in respect of other people – that is, one
will be motivated to perform actions which are not merely virtuous but actually moral.

Aristotle's distinction between virtuous actions as such and virtuous
actions which are related to other people shows both that the notion of a

---

[19] In which case, he will not in fact be courageous: even when he performs
courageous acts, he will not do so 'as the courageous man does'. See below,
pp. 22 f.

moral reason was recognised in the ancient world and that we cannot identify the demands of virtue with the requirements of morality. For whilst it would be odd to claim that one is morally constrained in how one can act when one's actions will have no relevant effect on other people, it was not taken to be at all odd that one could display virtue and vice in such actions. Nevertheless, the demands of virtue will include those of morality: to be virtuous is to be excellent, and one will not achieve this without being disposed to treat other people as they should be treated – and that will require acting to promote (or not acting to violate) their interests even when doing so will damage one's own. By distinguishing justice from virtue generally, Aristotle – in effect taking up the concerns of the *Republic* – succeeds in distinguishing moral requirements and sets these up as a test of virtue.

What, then, of the other feature of moral reasons – that they have a normative force which is independent of the agent's existing motivational states? As we saw, in his discussion of ancient ethics, Williams asserted baldly that it 'makes no use of a blank categorical moral imperative'.[20] If this claim is to have any force, then, of course, it cannot simply be intended to be accepted in virtue of the claim that the Greeks lacked the notion of a moral requirement, for that would be to beg the question in hand.[21] So, for our current purpose, the relevant question can be taken to be whether the Greeks accepted that the requirements of virtue are categorical. Williams provides no argument to encourage one to believe that they did not, and it is difficult to see why this should be thought to be plausible – certainly given the belief, generally held by ancient writers, that virtue requires knowledge.

It is here that the difference between the Humean conception of practical reason and that which is to be found in the ancient discussions is of great importance. According to the former, an agent's motivational states are distinct from his cognitive states, and the role of practical reason is limited to that of determining how best to achieve the goals set up by one's desires. The ancients certainly recognise this capacity of practical reason, but do not regard it as exhausting its operations. Thus, Aristotle in *EN* vi.12 distinguishes practical wisdom, *phronēsis*, from mere cleverness: to possess the latter is to be 'such as to be able to do the things that tend towards the mark we have set before ourselves, and to hit it' (1144a24–6). Although *phronēsis* requires cleverness, it is a distinct capacity since cleverness places no constraints on what its target is: 'Now if the mark be noble, the cleverness is laudable, but if the mark be bad, the cleverness is mere villainy; hence we

---

[20] Williams [70], 251.

[21] To be fair, the claim that the Greeks made no use of a categorical moral imperative is not presented by Williams as part of an argument for the claim that they lacked the notion of a moral reason: the latter is rather given as a reinforcement of it.

call clever both men of practical wisdom and villains' (1144a26–8). To have practical wisdom is to be able 'to deliberate well about what is good and expedient for himself, not in some particular respect, e.g. about what sorts of thing conduce to health and strength, but about what sorts of thing conduce to the good life in general' (*EN* VI,5.1140a25–8). Deliberating well requires being able to deliberate successfully about achieving *eudaimonia*, the good life, and part of this is determining what things we have reason to do and to achieve. This is not a question which is to be answered in the light of the agent's existing desires, but itself requires that one come to *recognise* what is good or bad: *phronēsis* is 'a true and reasoned state of capacity to act with regard to the things that are good and bad for man' (1140b4–6). In order to have *phronēsis*, one must have *true* beliefs about what is valuable and worth doing – and these are not beliefs which are about or grounded in the motivational states of the agent.[22]

The idea that practical reason requires evaluative knowledge is one which is common amongst the ancients. Thus, Diogenes Laertius reports that whilst Chrysippus 'holds that virtue can be lost, on account of intoxication or depression', Cleanthes 'takes it to be irremovable owing to secure cognitions' (D.L. VII.127 = Long and Sedley [719] (LS) 61I2). According to the Stoics, *phronēsis* is the knowledge (*epistēmē*) 'of what should and should not be done and of neutral actions, or the science of things that are good and bad and neutral as applied to a creature whose nature is social' (Stobaeus, *Eclogae* II.59.4 = LS 61H1). Sextus too reports that they took virtue to be knowledge of what is good, bad and neither of these (*adversus Mathematicos(M)* XI.170). So, to be temperate or just is to have a certain kind of knowledge:

> Temperance is the knowledge of what should be chosen and avoided and neither of these. Justice is the knowledge concerned with distributing individual deserts. Courage is the knowledge of what is fearful and not fearful and neither of these. (Stobaeus, *Ecl.* II.59 = LS 61H2–4)[23]

Both Aristotle and the Stoics take virtue, and virtuous action, to be intrinsically valuable – and the virtuous person, the person with practical wisdom, will know that they are. The virtuous person is someone who has the correct *cognitions* about what reasons he has to act, and these cognitions will themselves be motivating.[24] The normative force of the demands of virtue are something the virtuous person has come to recognise – and about which he

---

[22] For a contemporary exploration of the consequences of adopting a more substantial account of practical rationality than that offered by the Humean, see Lawrence [956].   [23] I have slightly adapted Long and Sedley's translation here.

[24] For an influential contemporary discussion of the virtuous person's distinctive recognition of reasons for action, see McDowell [959].

has knowledge and of which other people can be ignorant. Both the virtuous and the vicious person are judged by the same standards, however. The vicious person does not know how he should act, but that he *should* act as the virtuous person does is not taken to be in doubt. The reason which he has to act virtuously is not in any way derived from his own existing motivations: he suffers from a failure of practical reasoning, but that failure is a failure to recognise the reasons which apply to him and not a failure to see what his existing desires commit him to. The requirements of virtue – the reasons to act virtuously – are thus indeed categorical, and we can accept that the notion of a moral reason is one which is to be found in ancient thought.

If we do not need, then, to see the concerns of ancient ethics as entirely dissociated from those of their modern successors, we must nevertheless be careful not to assimilate those concerns so closely that we end up distorting the style and structure of the ancient theories. One very important difference between the ancient discussions and modern moral theories – and one which has been much emphasised by recent critics – is that whilst the ancient discussions focused on the questions of what sort of character one should have and what makes a life a good life, the major schools of modern moral philosophy (at least those which do not take their lead from Aristotle) have principally been concerned to determine how one should act in particular circumstances. Thus, the utilitarian tells one that in any circumstance one should perform whatever action will maximise general happiness (or is prescribed by whichever rule will maximise happiness when universally followed) and a Kantian requires that one acts in whatever way falls under a maxim which can be taken to be a universal rule (which meets certain constraints). Ancient ethical theories, in contrast, are not centred upon the provision of principles for the determination of action: certainly we do find discussions of whether particular actions, or types of action, are right or wrong, but the ancient theorists do not manifest the ambition to provide the materials necessary for determining how to act in any particular circumstance. Of course, there would be agreement that one should always act virtuously, but this injunction will be of practical benefit only for those who already know what virtue requires in the circumstances in which they have to act.

A second, and related, difference is that the ancient writers are concerned to show that virtue is necessary for – and, according to some, will actually determine – happiness. This is hardly a concern which has generally been shared by modern moral philosophers. The utilitarian, for instance, takes the proper motivation for action to be that of promoting general happiness: there is no claim that in doing that, one must thereby promote one's own.

For the ancients, providing an account of virtue is a part of providing an account of happiness, *eudaimonia*. It was a point of general philosophical agreement that being virtuous is at least a necessary part of a happy life, and the Stoics actually take it to be both necessary and sufficient for happiness. The *Republic*'s challenge is to show that being just benefits the just person, and although Aristotle does not seek to justify being virtuous, he does maintain that whilst virtuous activities are to be chosen for their own sake, they are also chosen for the sake of the agent's own happiness: it is *eudaimonia* which cannot be chosen for the sake of anything else, and not virtue. There is thus at least a suspicion that instead of taking moral reasons to be self-standing, ancient writers subordinate them to reasons of self-interest (and so cannot after all think of them as having categorical force).

These distinctions between ancient ethics and the main traditions of modern moral philosophy are certainly important, and it is true that they make the structure of ancient and modern theories somewhat different, but one still needs to be careful not to be so attentive to the dangers of anachronism in assimilating ancient to modern concerns that one takes ancient ethics to be more alien to us than in fact it is. Clearly, given the range of ancient ethical discussions, it is difficult to make true and helpful general claims about the nature of those discussions – but it will be worth providing a brief, and tentative, consideration of the consequences of these two features of those discussions: that the ancients focus on character rather than action and that they subordinate moral reasons to reasons of prudence.

The latter claim is in fact quite easily dealt with. There is an important difference between claiming that something can be chosen for the sake of something else and claiming that the thing chosen is only instrumentally valuable – worth choosing only because it achieves something else. This is clear from a passage in book 1 of the *Nicomachean Ethics* where Aristotle is talking about the relation between *eudaimonia* and other goods:

> We call complete without qualification that which is always desirable in itself and never for the sake of anything else. Now such a thing happiness, above all else, is thought to be; for this we choose always for itself and never for the sake of something else, but honour, pleasure, reason and every virtue we choose indeed for themselves (for if nothing resulted from them we would still choose each of them), but we choose them also for the sake of happiness, judging that through them we shall be happy.
> (*EN* 1.7.1097a34–b5)

There is a range of things – including virtuous activity – which we have reason to pursue because doing so will contribute to our *eudaimonia*, but this is consistent with its also being the case that we have reason to pursue them which is independent of such considerations. Indeed, the natural way to understand the passage is as saying that one achieves happiness through attaining just those things which are themselves intrinsically valuable.[25]

The Stoics also maintain that *eudaimonia* is the final end: 'being happy is the end, for the sake of which everything is done, but which is not itself done for the sake of anything' (Stobaeus, *Ecl.* II. 77.16–17 = LS 63A1). However, whereas Aristotle thinks that the happy life requires a variety of goods, the Stoics take it to be achieved, and only achieved, by the acquisition of virtue. Stobaeus' report continues: 'This consists in living in accordance with virtue, in living in agreement or, what is the same, in living in accordance with nature.' Virtue can be pursued for happiness, whereas happiness cannot be pursued for anything else – but, again, that is because virtue is itself a good: the Stoics 'regard virtue as choiceworthy for its own sake. For we are ashamed at our bad behaviour as if we knew that rectitude is the only good. And virtue is sufficient for happiness' (D.L. 7.127 = LS 6113). According to Stobaeus, 'all the virtues are both instrumental and final goods – for they both generate happiness and complete it, since they are its parts' (II.72. 4 = LS 60M). The value of having virtuous dispositions is not something which is derived from their determining role in the virtuous person's happiness: it is because they are good in themselves that one can choose to pursue them not only for themselves but also for the sake of happiness.[26] Those ancient writers who think that one can acquire virtuous dispositions and perform virtuous actions in order to be happy do not provide a more egoistic account of the motivation for virtue but rather hold to a more moralised notion of happiness than do their modern counterparts. This constitutes an important difference between ancient and modern moral philosophy (at least modern moral philosophy which, again, does not take its lead from the ancient discussions of these matters), but one which is entirely compatible with taking the value of virtuous action to be autonomous and the reason for such action to be independent of the agent's self-interest.[27]

What, then, of the other putative distinction between ancient ethics and modern philosophy – that the former is focused on questions of character whilst the latter is concerned rather with determining how to act? It is in fact slightly misleading to characterise ancient ethics tout court as interested primarily in questions of good character rather than right action. So, whilst Socrates in the 'Socratic' dialogues of Plato (those in which it is plausible to

---

[25] See the discussion in my own chapter below, pp. 84 f.

[26] See Irwin's chapter below.

[27] This is not to say that all ancient theorists take virtue to contribute to happiness because it is itself intrinsically valuable: Epicurus, for instance, gives it an instrumental role. The point is just that in taking virtue to be choosable for the sake of happiness, ancient writers did not thereby deny its intrinsic value.

think that the views and concerns of Socrates are presented) is indeed concerned to understand the nature of virtue and of particular virtues, at least sometimes he seems to think that such understanding can be gained through knowing what it is for an *action* to be a virtuous action. Thus, in the *Euthyphro*, he challenges Euthyphro to justify his prosecution of his own father for impiety by showing that he actually knows what it is for an action to be pious.[28] Although the dialogue ends without a satisfactory account of piety, it is clear enough that a presumption of the argument is that were a proper account of pious action to be offered, then this would enable one to act piously. Certainly, the idea that the right way to understand what it is to have a particular virtue is to know what sort of actions will count as virtuous actions of the relevant type is one which is frequently expressed by the participants in Plato's dialogues (although there is no example of a proposed definition of this kind being accepted as satisfactory). Laches, for instance, starts out by characterising the courageous person as someone 'who is willing to remain at his post and to defend himself against the enemy' (*Laches* 190e), and Meno begins by defining 'the virtue of a man' as to 'be capable of managing the affairs of his city, and in this management benefiting his friends and harming his enemies, taking care to suffer no such harm himself' (*Meno* 71e).[29]

In all these cases, an attempt is made to understand a particular kind of virtuous action without reference to what sort of character an agent will have who possesses the virtue in question. Now, to be virtuous, or to have some particular virtue, is to have a character of a certain kind – and to provide a definition of virtue, or of a particular virtue, is to say what it is to have a character of that kind. It would seem that one can go about this in two rather different ways (although they are not in principle exclusive and one might perhaps attempt to combine them): one could try to define the character by reference to the kind of action which someone will be disposed to perform in virtue of having the type of character in question, or one could attempt to define what it is to possess the virtue in non-dispositional terms. Thus in the *Laches*, whilst Laches himself attempts, as we have seen, to characterise courage by reference to how the courageous person is disposed to behave, Nicias proposes a definition of the second kind: courage is 'the knowledge of the fearful and the hopeful in war and in every other situation' (194e–195e). Again, whilst Meno starts out by trying to capture what it is to be virtuous by giving an idea of how the virtuous man or

---

[28] Socrates to Euthyphro: 'Bear in mind that I did not bid you tell me one or two of the many pious actions but that form itself that makes all pious actions pious, for you agreed that all impious actions are impious and all pious actions pious through one form' (6d).   [29] See Kahn's chapter below.

woman will behave, he proceeds to respond to Socrates' clarification of what he takes to be required of a definition by essaying a definition of the second kind: 'virtue is the desire for fine things and the ability to attain them', where, as Socrates points out, 'to desire fine things is to desire good things' (77b). Neither Nicias' definition of courage nor Meno's definition of virtue is taken to stand up to Socrates' objections, however, and in fact it is not until the *Republic* that a definition of virtue is accepted in a Platonic dialogue – and this is very much a definition of the second kind rather than the first.

Indeed, one might readily take the argument of the *Republic* as a whole to be at least in part an elaborate demonstration that one cannot satisfactorily understand virtue – or, here, justice – in terms of the kinds of action which the virtuous agent is such as to perform – at least if one tries to classify those actions without reference to the virtue itself. (Thus, whilst presumably it will be the case that courage, say, *is* the disposition to perform courageous actions, it might be thought that that definition will not be helpful in providing an understanding of what it is to be courageous.) As Julia Annas says, in her *Introduction to Plato's Republic*,

> already in Book I, we saw Plato bringing out the deficiencies of people who think that justice is a matter of knowing lists of duties. This approach was seen to be essentially shallow, because it made justice a matter of the performance of acts that were imposed without springing from the agent's deepest concerns. It could provide no answer to genuine questions whose pressure was felt: Why act like this at all? Is acting like this appropriate to the kind of person I admire and would like to be?[30]

On Annas' reading, Plato in the *Republic* is indeed concerned to refocus our attention away from initial questions about the nature of right action to questions about what it is to be a good person: it provides an 'agent-centred' rather than an 'act-centred' account of virtue.

According to Annas, an agent-centred ethical theory 'takes the primary questions to be "What kind of person should I be?" "What is the good life?" "What kind of life is admirable?"':

> We find out what is the right thing to do, by asking what kind of thing the good person would do in these circumstances. The right thing to do is identified as the kind of thing done by the good person. For the agent-centred approach, the primary notions are not duty and obligation, but *goodness* and *virtue*.[31]

---

[30] Annas [325], 158 – but see the following note.
[31] *Ibid.*, 157–8. A more complicated view of the difference between act- and agent-centred theories is to be found in her [71], 124–6 – see n. 38 below.

If, however, we are to determine what the right action is by considering what the good or virtuous person would do in the relevant circumstances, then we need to be able to characterise the virtuous person independently of his or her right actions. It is certainly tempting to think that this is precisely what Plato does in the *Republic*: to be just is to have one's *psuchē* properly ordered, and so, without begging the question, he can identify just acts as those which the just person would do. Thus, by formulating an account of justice which does not make reference to the kinds of action which the just person is disposed to perform, one can use that account to determine which acts are required by justice.

Now, it is certainly true that Plato, Aristotle and the Stoics all take very seriously the question of what sort of person one should be. It is also true that the fact that this was a question which was pressed by ancient authors gives a distinctive flavour to ancient ethical discussions – and if it is a flavour which has begun again to appeal to recent tastes, this is in large part because contemporary moral philosophers have started to take more seriously the models provided by ancient writers, and in particular by Aristotle. It is much less certain, however, that either Plato or Aristotle thought that one could, by answering this question, determine how one should act in particular circumstances – that one could, to use Annas' formulation, 'identify' the right thing to do 'as the kind of thing done by the good person'. Indeed, there is good reason to think that they did not – and that, because of this, it is misleading to characterise either as providing a moral or ethical theory which is agent-*centred*. This would be a happy characterisation of the theories only if they sought to draw conclusions about the nature of virtuous action from the claims which had been established about the nature of what it is to be a virtuous agent; but it is far from obvious that such inferences are attempted by any ancient ethical theorist.

So, whilst all the just person's actions will be regulated by considerations of justice – since he will do nothing which is *un*just – they will not all be just actions, that is, actions which are *required* by justice. There are many circumstances in which considerations of justice simply do not arise: when a guardian talks to one person at a party rather than another because he is more attractive, his action is neither just nor unjust. (It would be at best odd to claim that justice *requires* that, other things being equal, one talk to more attractive rather than less attractive people – even when, in having grasped the Form of beauty, one has clear knowledge of who is beautiful and who is not.) How, then, does one tell – and, further, how does the just agent tell – which of his actions are in fact just?

Here it is important to look at the account of the just agent which is offered in the *Republic*. An agent is just, according to Socrates, if he has an ordered *psuchē* – that is, if each of the three 'parts' of his *psuchē* 'does its own thing'.

What this requires is that the rational part of the *psuchē*, the *logistikon*, has control over the other parts, the 'spirited' part (*to thumoeides*), and the 'appetitive' part (*to orestikon*).[32] The just person, then, will be one who has rational control over his non-rational motivations. That there is a contrast here between reason and desire should not, of course, lead one to think that Plato is operating within a Humean model of these things: the role of the *logistikon* is not simply to work out how best to act in the light of the motivations for action provided by the desires of the appetitive part of the *psuchē*. Two features of the *logistikon* crucially distance it from Humean reason: the first is that it is capable of acquiring knowledge and the second is that it is itself capable of motivating the subject to action.

For the rational part of the *psuchē* to do its own work is not just for it to direct action in the light of the subject's desires – (although this is certainly part of its role) but to provide the subject with the right desires. A properly developed *logistikon* will be one whose subject has undergone the sort of cognitive development which Plato charts in the middle books of the *Republic*: he will have come to grasp the Forms of things and, most particularly, the Form of the good.[33] Once this has been grasped, the subject will know what it is for something to be good, and will be able to identify which things are good and which not, and hence he will know, it seems, which actions are right and which are not. This knowledge will not be motivationally inert: in knowing that a certain action is the right thing to do, the just agent will desire to do it, and, since his actions are directed by his *logistikon*, he will act on that desire. It is true, then, that Plato can explain why the just agent will perform just actions – that is, will do the right thing – by reference to the nature of his psychology.[34] What this does not provide is any attempt to *reduce* the notion of a just action to one that a just agent will characteristically perform, or perform in virtue of his characteristic psychology. Whilst Plato in the *Republic* describes what it is to be a just agent rather than what it is to act justly, this is not a sign of any inclination to give conceptual or even epistemological priority to the former over the latter.[35] The just agent

---

[32] For this division of the *psuchē*, see Christopher Taylor below, pp. 66 f.

[33] For this, see Taylor below, pp. 67 ff, as well as Fine [342].

[34] Which is not to ratify the argument – resting on the analogy between the state and the individual *psuchē* – that gets him there in the first place.

[35] An alternative would be to think that Plato takes a just action to be definable as one which creates and preserves psychic harmony (and its political analogue),as Christopher Taylor indeed suggests below (p. 70). This would allow Plato to give an account of deliberation which avoids the problems which beset the agent-centred reading under consideration and gains support from *Rep.* 443e (if that passage is understood as intended to provide a (re-) definition of just actions), but would do so at the cost of providing a radically innovative account of what it is for an action to be just.

is able to act justly because he has knowledge of what is just. The cost of maintaining that such knowledge is dependent on knowing how the just agent would act is that of requiring an implausible account of the just agent's deliberation. For the just agent would need to determine what *he* would do in the circumstance in which he deliberates: in that case, however, considerations of justice cannot enter into his deliberation – on pain of regress – and so it would turn out that what the just action is in a particular circumstance can be decided without making use of the concept of justice itself.[36]

This consequence is unacceptable for two reasons. The first is that even the just agent would not be able to discriminate those of his actions which are just from those which are not: all he will know in any circumstance is which action he decides to do, but since this is not discriminated *as* the just action, he will not have the conceptual resources to decide which of the actions he is inclined to do are in fact just.[37] The second is that the philosopher's knowledge of what it is for an action to be just no longer plays any role in explaining his ability to act justly – and this goes against Plato's project of showing that it is by a certain kind of cognitive development that one

---

[36] In her [71], 110,n. 211, Annas anticipates the worry that an agent-centred theory will require that when the brave person 'asks "What should I do in this situation?", [she is] really asking "What would a brave person do in this situation?" ', but takes the 'oddity' to be superficial: 'the problem is not peculiar to virtue ethics; a deontologist will ask himself what a dutiful person would do, a consequentialist, what an efficient maximizer would do'. The oddity here is taken to be that of moral deliberation taking 'the form of asking what some ideal version of you would do in this situation'. The problem, though, is rather that of being able to provide a proper account of the deliberation of the virtuous person himself. Whilst the deontologist and the consequentialist might in effect be deciding what the dutiful person and the efficient maximizer would do, their deliberations need, and should, make no reference to these notions (deciding this would be the up-shot and not the content of the deliberation): on an agent-centred understanding of virtue, however, it seems that the virtuous person cannot but deliberate about what he would do, and this is where the problem lies.

[37] This problem would perhaps be averted if justice were taken to be a 'thin' notion, so that to judge an action to be just would simply be to judge that it was the right action given the presence of other 'thick' reasons – the just agent could then have the ability to recognise that such reasons obtained. He would thus know that this is a situation in which an action will be required by justice and hence that the action which seems to him the right one will in fact be the just one. In the *Republic*, however, justice is not plausibly taken to be a thin notion – and even if it were, this would not help with the other virtues, to which the same problems would apply. (For the distinction between 'thick' and 'thin' ethical concepts, see Williams [979], *passim*: for an earlier, but more subtly drawn, distinction along these lines, see Wiggins [977], 95–6, who distinguishes between what he calls 'valuations' and 'directive judgements'.)

becomes a just agent. It is, after all, this which supports his claim that it is philosophers who should rule the state.[38]

That focusing theoretical attention on virtue rather than on action does not lead to a commitment to giving epistemic or conceptual priority to the former over the latter is, if anything, even clearer in Aristotle's ethical theory – where, again, one might be tempted to find an agent-centred account of the sort described. This temptation might find encouragement, for instance, in a well-known passage in *EN* II.4:

> Actions, then, are called just and temperate when they are such as the just or temperate man would do; but it is not the man who does these that is just and temperate, but the man who also does them *as* just or temperate men do them.   (1105b5–9)

At first sight, this might seem precisely to make the notion of a just action conceptually dependent on that of a just person, and similarly the notion of a temperate action dependent on that of a temperate person: something is a just or temperate action just if it is the sort of action a just or temperate person would do in virtue of being a just or temperate person. Virtuous actions are to be defined by reference to the agents who possess the virtue in question.

Again, to read Aristotle in this way would be to fail to give due weight to the role of knowledge in his explanation of virtuous action – especially since the virtuous agent is not alone in having the knowledge in question. Aristotle's concern in II.4 is to defend his thesis that people become virtuous not by engaging in philosophical analysis but through practice and habituation. He continues from the passage just cited: 'It is well said, then, that it is by doing just acts that the just man is produced, and by doing temperate acts, the temperate man; without doing these no one would have even a prospect of becoming good' (1105b9–12). Now this, as Aristotle recognises, raises a prima facie problem: the moral novice is supposed to become, say, just by doing just actions – but if he is already performing just actions, then it might

---

[38] As noted, Annas provides a more nuanced account of the contrast between act- and agent-centred theories in her [71]. There she says (p. 125) that 'no sensible theory could consider merely acts or merely agents' and that the contrast between ancient and modern theories 'must lie . . . in the relative importance that ancient and modern theories give to acts and to agents'. Ancient theories 'take virtue notions as primary': 'they do not derive standards of right conduct from the notion of the virtuous person alone, but the good agent is the focus of the theory because we understand right conduct in terms of having the virtues, not the other way round'. Despite the extra complexity of this account, it still seems to me to require an unsatisfactory understanding of the virtuous person's deliberation. See further n.41 below.

seem as if he does not need to become just, since he will already be just. Aristotle's solution to this is to distinguish between merely performing a just action and doing so justly. He brings this out by drawing a contrast between virtuous actions and actions which are the exercise of skill. Whilst it is sufficient to act skilfully that one produce something good as a result of one's knowledge (a house, say, in virtue of one's knowledge of house-building), this is not sufficient for someone to act virtuously:

> The products of skills have their goodness in themselves, so that it is enough that they should have a certain character, but if the acts which are in accordance with the virtues have themselves a certain character it does not follow that they are done justly or temperately. The agent must also be in a certain condition when he does them; in the first place he must have knowledge, secondly he must choose the acts, and choose them for their own sakes, and thirdly his actions must proceed from a firm and unchangeable character. These are not reckoned in as conditions of the possession of the skills, except the bare knowledge; but as a condition of the possession of the virtues, knowledge has little or no weight, while the other conditions count not for a little but for everything, i.e. the very conditions which result from often doing just and temperate acts.   (1105a27–b5)

For an action to be valuable as an exercise of virtue, more is required of the agent than just that he do it because he knows that it 'has a certain character' – he must also choose to do it because it has that character, valuing it just because of this, and he must have a standing and firm disposition to choose such actions for themselves.

Thus, not only does one not need to be just or temperate in order to perform just or temperate actions, but one does not even need to be so in order to know what the just or temperate action is in a particular circumstance (and so, possession of the knowledge which is required for virtuous action is not a distinctive feature of the virtuous person's character). The temperate person will choose to perform, or refrain from, a certain action because he recognises it to be the temperate thing to do: knowing that this is the temperate thing to do in his present circumstance, he wants to do it and does not want to do anything else (in contrast here to the merely self-controlled person who does it despite the presence of a conflicting desire).[39] His motivation, however, springs from his knowledge and not vice versa. He does not know that this is the temperate thing to do because he is motivated to do it (not least because being temperate he will have *phronēsis*, and, having *phronēsis*, he will have all the virtues: that he is motivated to act in this way here will not single the action out as a temperate as opposed, say,

---

[39] See McDowell's chapter below.

to a courageous one): he is motivated to do it because he recognises it to have the 'certain character' which temperate actions have.

As with Plato's account of justice in the *Republic*, it is because the motivation for virtuous action is provided by knowledge that Aristotle's theory of virtue cannot be interestingly regarded as agent-*centred*. Again, Aristotle certainly shows an interest in delineating the moral character of agents which is not shared by later moral theories whose only concern is to show how one can determine how to act in particular circumstances – but that interest neither excludes concern with that latter question nor makes any attempt to make answering it subordinate to the account of moral character which he offers. What may mislead the critic here is that Aristotle does not seek to answer that latter question in other terms than those provided by the language of virtue itself. Thus, if one expects Aristotle to provide a definition of, say, temperate actions, then it will be tempting to fasten on his remarks in *EN* II.4 and see him as trying to define these by reference to temperate agents – a definition which will then turn out to be defective since one will not be able to characterise what it is to be a temperate agent without reference to temperate actions.

It is crucial to understanding the nature of Aristotle's ethical theory to see that he makes no attempt to define the various kinds of virtuous action – if by 'definition' here one means something which can be used to convey understanding to someone who does not already possess it. Thus, whilst Aristotle says much about the individual virtues, what he has to say is not such – and is not intended to be such – as to allow someone who does not yet know which actions are required by virtue to determine this by referring to the account he offers of them. That account tells us, for instance, that to be courageous is to have a 'mean' disposition in respect to fear and confidence, and to be temperate is to have a 'mean' disposition in respect to pleasure and pain (*EN* II,7.1107b4–6) – where this amounts to the claim that one should feel these (and then, when appropriate, act accordingly) 'at the right times, with reference to the right objects, towards the right people, with the right aim and in the right way' (1106b21–2). This may be helpful in clarifying the nature of virtue, but as a guide to feeling and action, it is useless – and is not intended by Aristotle to be otherwise. Brave or temperate actions are taken by him to have a determinate character, but this is not a character which is to be grasped by theorising: it is rather grasped by exposure to the relevant actions and, in particular, by performing them.

In *Republic* I, Thrasymachus challenges Socrates to tell him what justice is – without saying 'that it's the right, the beneficial, the profitable, the gainful, or the advantageous, but tell me clearly and exactly what you mean' (336c–d). It is highly plausible to see this as a demand for a definition of justice which does not make use of other ethical or normative notions.[40] Unlike Socrates (as portrayed in the 'Socratic' dialogues), neither Plato in the *Republic* nor Aristotle seeks to provide such definitions of virtuous actions. If one still looked for an account of what it is to act justly or temperately from them, however, then it would be tempting to find it given by reference to the relevant states of character. Expecting the theory to provide the materials for deciding how to act, and not finding it directly given, we might think that it is indirectly given – one should act as the just agent or the person with practical wisdom would – and so understand the theories to be agent-centred. As we have seen, however, the theoretical cost of this is too high. The correct theoretical moral to draw is not that neither Plato nor Aristotle seeks to cast light on the nature of just or virtuous action by describing the virtuous agent, but rather that they give up the Socratic requirement on moral knowledge – including knowing why it is good for the agent to be virtuous – that it should be accessible to those who have not yet fully grasped the relevant concepts.

It is here, I think, that the interesting distinction between ancient ethical theories and certain types of 'agent-centred' theory lies. For what the virtuous agent shows is a sensitivity to certain kinds of reason for action. Instead of seeking to apply moral rules (where the rules do not themselves employ moral terminology) or simply to promote some good whose value is intelligible from a non-moral perspective, the virtuous agent recognises, and acts on, reasons whose normative force is not apparent to those who lack the relevant moral understanding.[41] If the *Republic* marks a break with previous ethical theory, it is not because it gives conceptual priority to agents rather than actions, but because it no longer takes it to be a requirement on the possession of moral expertise that one should be able to share that expertise with those who lack it. Neither Plato nor Aristotle provides an account of

---

[40] See Irwin [294], 174–5.
[41] Contrasting modern with ancient theories (see above, n. 38), Annas characterises the former as tending 'to take questions about what one should do to be the primary ones, in that it is only when these are in hand that we can consider the question of what kind of person to be' ([71], 125). In the light of the present discussion, however, one might think that there is no longer a contrast to be drawn here: one will understand what it is to be a virtuous agent (at least in part) by reference to one's disposition to act virtuously. The real contrast lies rather in the fact that the ancient theorists do not accept that one can understand what it is for an action to be right independently of the notions of the various kinds of virtuous actions. This seems to accord with Annas' succeeding claim that ancient theories are agent-centred only in the sense that they 'see no force in the kind of consideration moving Sidgwick, for example, to demand that ethics become "scientific" and explicitly systematise our ways of coming to decisions' (125).

what the just or virtuous person knows – Plato because he is not yet able to define the good (*Rep.* 505–6) and Aristotle because he thinks that one acquires that knowledge through habituation and not through theory. Both think that it is possible to provide an account of what it is to be a virtuous agent without specifying what such an agent knows, but this should not lead us to think that this demonstrates any intention to subordinate the notion of a virtuous action to that of a virtuous agent, since in order to be virtuous, one must have knowledge of what it is for an action to be virtuous.

I have not attempted here to provide an uncontroversial conspectus of ancient ethical theories. As will have been apparent, many of the claims I have made will be contested by other critics, and many of the distinctive and important features of ancient ethical theories have gone unremarked. Certainly, ancient ethical writings are by no means homogeneous. Socrates and Plato, Aristotle, Epicurus and the Stoics differ in their accounts of moral psychology, of moral epistemology and of what constitutes happiness. Some theories are intended to be commonsensical; others turn out to be highly revisionary of ordinary – even ordinary ancient – moral beliefs. All make use of the notions of virtue and happiness, and most emphasise the role of evaluative knowledge in achieving these. This does give a distinctive appearance to ancient ethics, at least when contrasted with later traditions of moral philosophy. As I have suggested here, however, there is need for interpretative care in deciding just where the differences are between the various traditions. I hope that by focusing on the question of how one should understand the theoretical consequences of taking these notions to be central, I have provided a helpful background against which the ancient theories can be viewed. The important work, however, lies not in providing broad generalisations about ancient ethics but in a more detailed understanding of the ethical theories put forward by ancient writers. That is the work of the chapters which follow.[42]

[42] I am grateful to Julia Annas, David Charles, Hugh Johnstone, Joseph Raz and Ian Rumfitt for comments on an earlier draft of this introduction.

2

Pre-Platonic ethics

CHARLES H. KAHN

Although 'ethics' is a term that comes to us from the Greeks, Greek moral philosophy is notably different from typical modern discussions that fall under the same rubric. Some of our key moral concepts are absent or inconspicuous in Greek ethical debate. For example, much of modern ethics gravitates around the concepts of *duty* or *moral obligation* and *rights*, but neither of these concepts has any equivalent or close analogue in Greek speculation about how one ought to live. Similarly, the various oppositions between *egoism* and *altruism* or *benevolence* have no direct parallel in the ancient discussions. Since the Greeks have no counterpart to the Biblical injunction, 'Thou shalt love thy neighbour as thyself', the question of altruism or benevolence is not a central moral issue. The ancient gods made relatively few moral demands upon their worshippers. There is no Greek parallel to the Ten Commandments, or more generally to the Biblical notion of God as moral lawgiver. As a consequence of this fact, there is also no Greek equivalent to the Kantian notion of the 'moral law', as the secular, internalised version of divine command.

So much for the absence in Greek thought of some of the concepts that structure modern discussions in moral philosophy. On the other hand, the Greek moral vocabulary is dominated by three pairs of opposite terms that have no direct equivalent in modern terminology. The basic terms of moral evaluation are good–bad (*agathon–kakon*), admirable–shameful or noble–base (*kalon–aischron*), and just–unjust (*dikaion–adikon*). The last pair is, from our point of view, the most explicitly moral, the closest to the modern distinction between right and wrong. Thus Plato's defence of justice (*dikaiosunē*) in the *Republic* is, in effect, a defence of morality. The opposition *kalon–aischron*, on the other hand, besides having aesthetic overtones ('beautiful'–'ugly'), refers primarily to the realm of honour and respect, social approval and disapproval. The chief term for 'good', *agathon*, has a long and complex history, with a semantic range including noble birth, valour in battle and excellence in any craft or skill. Perhaps the chief difference from our own term 'good' is that *agathon* is weighted semantically in the direction of utility and advantage. Thus if something is *agathon* it is typically good-for-me, or good-for-the-person-in-question. A Platonic argument often aims to show that what is good (advantageous) for me is ultimately good tout court, in other words, that it is in my interest to be virtuous. The complex interaction of the three pairs of evaluative terms is illustrated by the claim of Polus in the *Gorgias* that although to commit injustice (*adikein*) is more shameful (*aischron*) than to suffer injustice, suffering injustice is worse (more *kakon*), that is, more disadvantageous (*Gorgias* 474c).

As a result of these discrepancies, both positive and negative, Greek moral thinking begins from a different place. It will be convenient to organise our exposition around two principal topics: (1) happiness or the good life, the range of issues that find their classical articulation in Aristotle's *Nicomachean Ethics*, and (2) justice and the status of morality, the theme of Plato's *Republic*. What we shall be surveying, then, is the historical background for these two central works of Greek moral philosophy.

1 Happiness or the good life

The Greek term for 'happy', *eudaimōn*, means that someone is favoured by the gods (*daimones*), 'blessed with a good genius' (as the lexicon puts it) and hence 'fortunate'. What underlies the choice of this term for happiness is a view of the gods as dispensers of good and evil for mankind. This is the view expressed by Achilles in the final episode of the *Iliad*, when he shares his grief over Patroclus' death with Priam, who has come to ransom his son's body:

> Such is the destiny which the gods have spun for wretched mortals, to live our lives in sorrow while they are carefree. There are two storage jars standing at Zeus' door; from one he gives gifts of evil, from the other gifts of good things. When Zeus mingles the two for anyone, that person encounters evil sometimes, but sometimes good. But when Zeus gives only misery, that man's life is blighted. (*Iliad* xxiv. 525–31)

The third possibility, that the gods should bestow only good things, is not mentioned. It is excluded not only by the funereal context and the tone of the whole poem but also by the poet's view of the human condition. Only the gods live a life unmarred by sorrow. The best that a mortal can hope for is a mixture in which good fortune is conspicuous.

A similar view is presented in the famous scene in Herodotus in which the wise Solon converses with the fabulously wealthy King Croesus. After displaying his treasures, Croesus asks Solon to name the happiest person he has ever seen. He asked this question, says Herodotus, 'expecting to be himself the happiest of human beings' (Herodotus 1.30.3). Solon, however, names Tellus of Athens, a citizen with fine children and surviving grandchildren, who died a glorious death in battle and received a public burial on the field where he fell. Croesus then asks who is second happiest after Tellus, and Solon recounts the story of two brothers, Cleobis and Biton, who honoured their mother by drawing her wagon to the Argive Heraion to celebrate the festival of Hera. Their mother in gratitude prayed to Hera 'to give them what is best for a human being to receive'. After the sacrifices and the feasting, the two youths lay down in the sanctuary and never rose from their sleep. By this outcome, says Herodotus, 'the god showed that it was better for a human being to be dead rather than to live'. (1.30.3). When Croesus protests that his own great prosperity is despised by such comparisons, Solon replies that human life is too insecure for us to judge anyone happy until we have seen how his life ends. According to Solon, 'human life is one big accident', not to say disaster (*pan anthrōpos sumphorē*, 1.32.4).

What Solon's two examples have in common is the notion that the happiest life is one that ends in honour and glory. But it is also better to lead a full life, and to leave behind a prosperous family stretching into future generations. Cleobis and Biton died too young to be ranked first in happiness. Continuation of the family, above all in the male line, means that when a man's own life comes to an end, his memory and funeral cult will be preserved. This continuation of the name and the cult of the family tombs represent an essential feature of a successful life for ordinary mortals. On the other hand, glory and 'undying fame' (*kleos aphthiton*) provide larger, more heroic consolations of mortality for pre-eminent individuals.[1] When Diotima in Plato's *Symposium* interprets both the urge to procreate and the pursuit of fame as expressions of the human desire for immortality (*Symp.* 206e–208e), she is giving theoretical formulation to two of the most ancient and fundamental themes of the Greek moral tradition. For Solon, Tellus ranks first in happiness because he excels on both counts. Achilles is the prototype of a tragic hero because his fate is a choice between the two: his immortal fame must be purchased by an early death (*Iliad* IX.411–16).

---

[1] Compare Iliad XII.322 ff., Sarpedon to Glaucus:

> Man, supposing you and I, escaping this battle
> would be able to live on forever, ageless, immortal
> so neither would I myself go on fighting in the foremost
> nor would I urge you into the fighting where men win glory.
> But now, seeing that the spirits of death stand close about us
> in their thousands, no man can turn aside nor escape them,
> let us go on and win glory for ourselves, or yield it to others.
> (Lattimore's translation)

One feature of the Herodotean picture is quite unlike the Homeric view: its ultimate pessimism in the conclusion that death is better than life. The Homeric hero has no illusions about a human life without sorrow. But the ghost of Achilles rejects with contempt the consolations which Odysseus brings him to the underworld; he would rather be day-labourer to a poor man on earth than be lord over the dead (*Odyssey* xi.488 ff.). Both these views of death, as a grateful release from human suffering and as the radical curse of the mortal condition, will be re-echoed throughout Greek literature.[2]

On the whole, however, Greek literature and art give us the impression of intense vitality and love of life. What, then, are the good things that make life worth living? The philosophers will later distinguish three classes. These are (1) goods of the soul: the moral and intellectual virtues, (2) goods of the body: health, beauty, strength, tall stature and (3) external goods: wealth, noble birth, honour, political power, family and friends. It will be the task of the philosophers to define and exalt the goods of the psyche. Beauty and other bodily excellences were always admired by the Greeks. But it is perhaps external goods that are most often praised in the archaic texts. As the Croesus story shows, the Greeks are great lovers of worldly possessions. (Croesus was of course Lydian, but envied by the Greeks for his wealth.) It is no accident that the word for 'happy' in the Croesus story (*olbios*) also means 'wealthy'. Croesus' attitude implies that for him these two meanings were one and the same. But for the Homeric hero the foremost good is honour or glory, and wealth is ultimately valued as the source and symbol of honour (*timē*). In the epic the primary basis of honour is military prowess; that is why Achilles is the primary hero. But he is not only the greatest warrior; he is also the hero most sensitive to questions of honour. Achilles quarrels with Agamemnon because he feels dishonoured, and he re-enters the battle because to leave the death of his friend Patroclus unavenged would be a still greater dishonour.

Honour is essentially a competitive good: if you have more of it, someone else must have less. The heroic code is summed up in the advice given to Achilles by his father: 'always be first and best (*aristeuein*) and superior to the others' (*Iliad* xi.784 = vi.208). In Homeric duels, in athletic games, in politics and even in musical and dramatic competitions, the paradigm is the *agōn*, the contest, in which there can be winners only if there are also losers. (It was Jakob Burkhardt, in his *Griechische Kulturgeschichte*, who first emphasised the agonistic element in Greek culture.) There will be competition between cities, of course; but within the city the competitors are individuals.

---

[2] For two of the most celebrated expressions of absolute pessimism see Sophocles, *Oedipus at Colonus* 1223–7, and Plato, *Apology* 40d–e.

And the unrestrained pursuit of individual 'excellence' (*aretē*) conceived as pre-eminence can ultimately tear the city apart. The tragic careers of Themistocles and Alcibiades can be seen in this perspective as a legacy of the heroic moral ideal.

But Homer is not the only Greek moral teacher, and the heroic code is not the only ideal. In Hesiod we have a different conception of *aretē*, more closely tied to hard work on the land, decent respect for property, and justice in the law court. In contrast to the unlimited self-assertion of the Homeric hero, Hesiod provides a warning against arrogance and excess (*Works and Days* 202–18, 286–92, etc.). This alternative ideal of moderation is more fully developed in the poems of Solon and the aphorisms of the Seven Sages, including the proverbial wisdom formulated in the Delphic inscriptions *mēden agan*, 'nothing too much', and *gnōthi seauton*, 'know thyself', that is, know your limitations as a mortal. The archaic fear of divine jealousy, of provoking the animosity of the gods by transgressing human limits, reinforces the morality of measure and moderation ('mortals think mortal thoughts' and the like) that runs like a recurrent theme through Greek tragic choruses and the pages of Herodotus. The Croesus story includes an illustration of this view. Herodotus reports that, shortly after Solon's visit, divine retribution struck Croesus in the person of his son, 'because, as one may conjecture, he thought himself the happiest of all human beings' (1.34.1).

These two ideals, the drive for pre-eminence and the concern for moderation and restraint, offer alternative and potentially conflicting conceptions of the good life. A tension between the two views is characteristic of Greek moral thinking through the centuries. Much the same duality is reflected in Adkins' distinction between the competitive and the cooperative virtues.[3] At the risk of some simplification we can say that the heroic world of the epic is dominated by the competitive, self-assertive conception of *aretē* expressed in the formula 'always be best' (*aei aristeuein*), and reflected in Croesus' ambition to be the happiest of men. The Delphic view, on the other hand, which Herodotus expresses in his judgement on Croesus, invokes divine jealousy to discourage the kind of self-aggrandisement that poses a threat to the civic community. In military terms, the model for the heroic ideal is personal combat between two champions. The model for the ideal of moderation and restraint, on the other hand, is the serried rank of hoplite soldiers, whose security and success depend upon their advancing and withdrawing in unison, since each hoplite covers his neighbour's flank with the left half of his shield. The 'quiet' virtues of justice and temperance (*sōphrosunē*) correspond in the moral domain to the kind of social solidarity and collaboration

---

[3] Adkins [34].

required for the manoeuvre of a hoplite phalanx. Instead of the aristocratic pursuit of individual excellence we have here the more bourgeois virtue of the good citizen, who can be counted on to stand shoulder-to-shoulder with his peers.

Both the competitive and the cooperative virtues are displayed in external action and social behaviour. To construe them as internal goods, as 'goods of the psyche', is a momentous theoretical development that probably reflects the influence of philosophical ideas. The earliest philosophers, the Milesians, were quasi-scientists concerned with the nature and structure of the physical world. The first we know of to apply the new ideas to questions of human life and mortality was Xenophanes, who attacks the social prestige of athletic prowess and victory in the games with the claim that such success contributes little to the prosperity and good government (*eunomiē*) of a city: 'better than the strength of men and horses is wisdom (*sophiē*) such as ours' (Diels–Kranz, *Fragmente der Vorsokratiker* 21B2, 11). Xenophanes' contrast between wisdom and bodily strength can be seen as prefiguring the classical distinction between goods of the soul and goods of the body, but wisdom is not yet securely located in the psyche.

We come a step closer to the classical conception with Heraclitus, the first thinker known to have identified the psyche as the seat of intelligence and moral excellence. For Heraclitus a dry soul is 'wisest and best' (D–K 22B118), whereas a man who has drenched his soul with drink stumbles on the way home, 'not knowing where he steps' (D–K 22B117). This physical conception of the soul recalls Milesian natural philosophy, but Heraclitus has more than psychophysics in mind: 'You will not find out the limits of the soul by going, even if you travel over every way, so deep is its account (*logos*)' (B45). Heraclitus' thought is notoriously dark, but we can probably recognise here his own mysterious reaction to the new Pythagorean view of the deathless psyche that migrates from life to life.[4] Heraclitus' attitude to traditional conceptions is both critical and ambivalent. On the one hand he endorses the heroic pursuit of fame and magnifies the merit of a death in battle (B29, B24; cf. B25). On the other hand he despises cult in general (B5, B14–15) and funeral cult in particular (B96), and he insists that a man's fortune depends upon his character rather than on the gods (B119). He exalts the role of wisdom as excellence in a way that reminds us of Xenophanes; but Heraclitus is more explicit: 'Sound thinking [or moral restraint, *sōphronein*] is the greatest virtue (*aretē*) and the greatest wisdom: to speak truth and act according to nature, knowingly' (B.112). Here the quiet virtue of temperance or self-control

---

[4] Cf. Heraclitus B27: 'What awaits men at death they do not expect or even imagine' and B62: 'immortals are mortal, mortals immortal, living the others' death, dead in the others' life.'

(*sōphrosunē*) has been reconstrued as an intellectual insight that anticipates the Socratic–Platonic connection between virtue and knowledge.

By the middle of the fifth century the Pythagorean–Orphic view of the afterlife and rebirth of the psyche (which is falsely derived from Egypt by Herodotus, II.123) is publicly documented in the poetry of Pindar, Empedocles and Euripides.[5] Except for the general notion of reincarnation, the doctrine seems to vary from text to text, and different seers or sects may have tried to keep the details of their own teaching secret. What we know least imperfectly is the version of Empedocles, who depicts the human condition as the fall of a divine spirit (*daimōn*) into this world of mortal misery from a primeval state of bliss, with the possibility of some kind of release for those who live a life of appropriate purity. It is difficult to tell how far Empedocles' conception of purification (*katharmoi*) was purely ritual and magical, how far the requirements of vegetarianism and avoidance of bloodshed were interpreted in moral terms. This mystical tradition gets its full literary expression only much later, in the judgement myths of Plato. He is the first philosopher to attempt to give a coherent account of the belief that our destiny beyond the tomb is not only meaningful but vastly more important than our experience here and now.

The Pythagorean–Orphic influence may or may not have a part to play in the explanation of a remarkable fact: in the last decades of the fifth century and the beginning of the fourth, authors as different from one another as Antiphon the orator, Gorgias, Lysias and Democritus can take for granted a conception of the psyche as the seat of intelligence and character, roughly the conception of psyche that is presupposed in Plato and Aristotle and prefigured in Heraclitus.[6] While the term *psuchē* in the oldest texts means only

---

[5] Pindar, Ol. II.56–71 with fragments 116 and 127 (Bowra), Empedocles D–K 31B115–29, Euripides fr. 638 Nauck[2]: 'Who knows if living is dying, but dying is considered life in the world below?' (cited by Plato at *Gorgias* 492c10, on which see Dodds' note in [271], *ad loc*).

[6] For the texts, see Claus [46] ch. 4. There are, I think, clear indications in Sophocles (as early as the *Antigone*, 441 B.C.), Euripides and Aristophanes that the *psuchē* as the seat of character and intelligence was becoming a familiar notion in the last half of the fifth century. Claus' treatment of these texts (pp. 78–89) seems to me much too conservative. The classic sense of *psuchē* as the inner life or 'mind' of a person may well have developed directly from the old (Homeric) sense of 'life' via the use of *psuchē* for the person itself (the uses which Claus, pp. 69–72, calls periphrastic). In that case the hypothesis of Pythagorean–Orphic influence on the semantic development of *psuchē*, mentioned in the text, would be superfluous.
　In any case, there is nothing to be said in favour of Burnet's curious thesis that the classic sense of the term *psuchē* was an innovation due to Socrates (see Kahn [95], 311, n. 112). But it may well be that the central importance of the term in Plato and Aristotle – and in psychology ever since – was due in large part to the Socratic insistence on 'care for the *psuchē*'. See below, p. 46.

'life' or 'life-spirit', and hence 'ghost' (the life-spirit after death, in its spectral existence in the underworld), by the time of Democritus we have the classic contrast between body (*sōma*) and soul or mind (*psuchē*): 'It is fitting for human beings to take more account of the soul than of the body. For the perfection of soul corrects the bad condition of the body [literally 'the tent', the habitation of the psyche]. But strength of body without calculation (*logismos*) makes the soul no better' (D–K 68B187). What is taken for granted here in the mind–body contrast is what we might call the pre-Cartesian dualism of common sense. What is characteristic of Democritus is to make the soul causally responsible for the condition of the body. This causal role is underscored in another text, which speaks of a hypothetical lawsuit in which the body takes the soul to court and accuses it of mistreatment, for 'ruining the body with neglect and dissolving it with drunkenness, corrupting and distracting it with sensuality', like the user of a tool who will be held responsible for its misuse (B159). We know of no one before Democritus who so clearly enunciated the conception of the soul as ruling or controlling the body, the conception which Plato can assume without argument (for example at *Phaedo* 94b).[7]

Democritus is also the first philosopher to develop the moral insights of Heraclitus into an articulate theory of happiness in terms of the goods of the soul, that is, in terms of character and intelligence. 'Happiness (*eudaimoniē*) does not dwell in flocks or in gold. The psyche is the dwelling place of the *daimōn*', that is, of the deity who decides one's happiness or misery (D–K 68B171). Democritus is deliberately echoing and extending Heraclitus' aphorism: 'Man's character is his *daimōn*' (*ēthos anthrōpōi daimōn*, D–K 22B119). But unlike Heraclitus, Democritus tells us quite clearly what he means by the psychic source of good and evil.

> Human beings acquire cheerfulness (*euthumiē*) by moderation in enjoyment and measured balance in their life. But deficiencies and excesses tend to change about <into their opposites> and to cause great commotions in the soul. Souls that move over great intervals are neither stable nor cheerful. So one should keep one's mind (*gnōmē*) on what is possible and be satisfied with what is present and available, taking little heed of people who are envied and admired and not fixing one's attention (*dianoia*) upon them, but observe the lives of those who suffer and notice what they endure, so that what you presently have will appear great and enviable and you will

---

[7] There seems to be a direct reminiscence of Democritus B187 in Plato, *Republic* III.403d. And there is a striking parallel at *Apology* 30b, where care for the soul is said to be more important than care for the body or for wealth, since it is 'from the excellence [of soul] that wealth and all other good things come to human beings'. See Kahn [96], 6–10.

no longer suffer evil in your soul by desiring more than you have . . . [One should] compare one's life to those who are less fortunate and count oneself happy by considering what they suffer and how much better your own life is. If you hold fast to this frame of mind (*gnōmē*) you will live more cheerfully and drive not a few plagues (*kēres*) from your life: envy and jealousy and ill-will. (Democritus B191)

What Democritus offers us, then, is an internalised version of the moral ideal of moderation. Like Heraclitus he sings the praises of *sōphrosunē* (B210), but to a more mundane tune. Restraint is desirable because it produces cheerfulness, peace of mind and self-sufficiency (*autarkeiē*, B209; cf. B210, B246), whereas greater appetites (*orexeis*) produce greater needs (B219). Even the primary social norm of justice is to be respected for psychological reasons. 'The man who is borne cheerfully on to just and lawful deeds rejoices waking and sleeping, is strong and carefree. But whoever neglects justice and does not do what is required, for him all such things are unpleasant when he recalls any of them, and he is afraid and full of self-reproach' (B174).[8] Democritus does not tell us what the unjust man will be afraid of, but clearly his conscience is unquiet.[9] So here again the moral incentive is something like peace of mind.

For Democritus, then, moral wisdom is conceived essentially as psychological prudence. He is the first proponent of what is known today as cognitive therapy: getting people to see that they hold the key to their happiness or misery in their own system of belief and valuation. As Epictetus, the greatest ancient master of this kind of therapy, will say some five centuries later: if we are rational, we shall desire only what is in our power, what is up to us.[10] Democritus does not go so far. But this is the line he inaugurates when he emphasises the control of one's thought (*dianoia*, B191), judgement (*gnōmē*, B191, B223) and reasoning (*logismos*, B290. B187) as the most essential factor in a happy life.

If in these respects Democritus anticipates the Hellenistic sage, in other respects he recalls his great contemporary, Socrates. The two have in common not only their emphasis on the goods of the psyche and the essential link between happiness, moral excellence and intellectual insight, but

---

[8] Translation after J. F. Procopé. See Procopé [98], 319 f. with discussion of textual problems in Procopé [99], 33–5.

[9] Compare the juror in Democritus B262 who acquits a guilty man 'for profit or pleasure': 'he acts unjustly, and this will necessarily be on his heart'. (For commentary see Procopé [98], 318.) Democritus was particularly fierce in insisting on punishment for evildoers, including dangerous animals (B257–60).

[10] In this connection Procopé cites Epicurus fr. 135 Usener: 'If you want to make Pythocles wealthy, do not add to his money; subtract from his desires' (Procopé [98], 331).

also their broad construal of the moral virtues. Democritus never sounds more like the Platonic Socrates than when he insists upon the unifying connections between courage, self-control and wisdom.'The brave man is superior not only to his enemies but also to pleasure. Some men are master of cities but slave to women' (B214). 'It is hard to fight against anger. But it is the mark of a reasonable man to prevail' (B236). Virtue must be internalised by rational persuasion rather than by law and compulsion; 'one is brave and right-minded when one acts correctly from understanding (*sunesis*) and knowledge (*epistēmē*)' (B181).

Our evidence is too fragmentary for us to determine how far Democritus has integrated his prudential and therapeutic considerations into a view of justice, moral virtue and social harmony as intrinsic goods, rather than as necessary conditions for cheerfulness and peace of mind. Probably the distinction was not yet clearly drawn. The most original feature of Democritus' moral thought, his reliance on self-shame, seems to be neutral in this regard. 'One must not respect others any more than oneself, and not do evil if no one will know about it any more than if all men will. But respect yourself most of all, and let this be established as a law for your soul, so that you will do nothing unseemly' (B264). Self-respect or shame before oneself (*aideisthai* here, *aischunesthai* in the parallel versions of B244 and B84) is the deepest motive and the strictest test for moral integrity. We may compare the role which *aidōs* ('shame', 'reverence') plays in the myth of Plato's *Protagoras*, where it figures as the basic moral emotion: respect for the social code as the requirement for occupying an honourable position in society. But Democritus has given the traditional concepts of shame and honour a new twist. Nothing could point up more dramatically the implications of this new internalisation of *aretē* than Democritus' insistence that one should feel shame first of all before oneself, not before others. And the notion of establishing a moral law in your own soul suggests an almost Kantian premonition of the concept of autonomy.

The Hellenistic doxography assigns to Democritus a view of cheerfulness (*euthumiē*) as the *telos* or *summum bonum*, the unique end and goal of human life.[11] Now it is true that Democritus regards cheerfulness and peace of mind as conditions of the soul that any human being would want to have. But to describe this attitude in terms of the post-Aristotelian concept of the *telos* is more than anachronistic. Self-sufficiency and self-respect are not instrumentally or hierarchically subordinated to cheerfulness in Democritus' thought. There is nothing in the fragments to suggest that all human

---

[11] D–K 68A1, 45; A166–9;B4. For modern reformulation of this claim see Gosling and Taylor [53], 29–31.

actions aim, or should aim, at a single goal. We can see this notion of the *telos* emerging for the first time in Plato's dialogues, in his discussion of the good as the unique object of desire; and we find the full development of such a notion in Aristotle's theory of happiness. To attribute this concept to a pre-Platonic thinker like Democritus fundamentally misrepresents the stage which ethical reflection had reached in the late fifth century, and makes it impossible to appreciate the pioneering conceptual work that is being carried out by Plato and Aristotle in the fourth century.[12]

The natural point of comparison for Democritus would be his contemporary, Socrates. But before dealing with Socrates we must turn back and begin anew with the second principal topic of our discussion.

2 Justice and the status of morality

In Greek thought questions of morality are primarily associated with the so-called quiet virtues, justice (*dikaiosunē*) and self-restraint (*sōphrosunē*). In the *Protagoras* myth these are the two gifts bestowed by Zeus on human beings so that they can live together in civilised communities. In the myth, as we have seen, *sōphrosunē* is at first introduced as *aidōs*, 'shame' or 'respect' (at *Protagoras* 322c ff.), before being designated by its own name (at 323a2 ff.). Of the two, justice is the more objective principle of social harmony, and indeed of cosmic order. From the Milesians on, the organisation of the natural world is conceived in terms of justice. As Heraclitus puts it, the measures of the sun's path are enforced by 'the Furies, ministers of Dike' (D–K 22B94). And justice is typically a matter of punishment and retaliation. In the one surviving sentence from Anaximander, the elemental opposites 'pay the penalty and make retribution (*didonai dikas kai tisin*) to one another for their injustice', according to the ordinance of Time (D–K 12B1). Heraclitus invokes this notion of cosmic law as the basis and guarantee for human laws: 'The people must fight for their law as for their city wall' (B44). 'Those who speak with understanding must hold fast to what is common to all, as a city holds on to its law and even more firmly. For all human laws are nourished by a divine one. It dominates as much as it wants; it is enough for all and more than enough' (B114). Heraclitus' conception of law (*nomos*) as the foundation of civilised life prepares the way for the Stoic theory of natural law.

In his defence of human *nomoi* Heraclitus seems to be reacting against an early version of cultural relativism, provoked by the extensive Greek contacts with older civilisations that began in the Orientalising period (eight and seventh centuries B.C.). In Heraclitus' own time, c. 500 B.C., Hecataeus of Miletus brought home strange tales of the customs of foreign lands and

---

[12] For a fuller statement of this criticism see Kahn [96], 25–8.

published some of them in his *Travels Around the World*. In the same period Xenophanes knows that Ethiopians make their gods snubnose and black, while Thracians make them blue-eyed and red-haired (D–K 21B16). A generation or two later, in the middle fifth century, such awareness of cultural diversity is reinforced by the philosophical relativism of Protagoras: 'Of all things mankind (*anthrōpos*, a human being) is the measure, of what is that it is, and of what is not that it is not' (D–K 80B1). We have no verbatim quotation to show how Protagoras applied this measure to questions of morality, but we do have Plato's paraphrase: 'Whatever each city judges to be just and honourable really is just and honourable for that city, as long as this remains that city's custom and belief' (*Theaetetus* 172a-b). On this view there can be no standard of right and wrong other than *nomos*, the social norms of a given community. It is just this positive, conservative version of cultural relativism that is endorsed by Protagoras' contemporary, Herodotus, in his quotation of a famous verse from Pindar: '*Nomos* is king over all.' Thus Herodotus can interpret King Cambyses' deliberate violation of the religious customs of the Egyptians as proof that the Persian monarch was mad. 'If one offered all men the chance to select the finest *nomoi* from all that there are, each group would choose its own *nomoi*' (Hdt. III.38).

This conservative relativism of Protagoras and Herodotus reflects the political insight of Heraclitus without its metaphysical foundation: *nomos* and *dikē*, the accepted standards of right and wrong, may vary from place to place; but they make possible a civilised human life in society. (Without reference to relativism, this is essentially the view assigned to Protagoras in Plato's dialogue that bears his name.) But such conservative relativism exists in an unstable equilibrium; it tends to disappear in the so-called Enlightenment of the last three decades of the fifth century. A much more sceptical attitude to Greek moral and religious tradition finds expression in the popular opposition between *nomos* and *phusis*, where *phusis* stands for the hard facts of human nature (such as sensuality, greed and the lust for power) in contrast to the more artificial restraints of *nomos* or convention.

Behind this negative view of *nomos* lies an epistemological tradition going back to Parmenides, according to which the customary views of mortals can represent only falsehoods or at best mere appearance, whereas *phusis* designates true reality, the way things really are. Democritus stands in this Eleatic tradition when he says 'By *nomos* there is sweet, by *nomos* bitter, by *nomos* hot, by *nomos* cold, by *nomos* colour; but in truth there are atoms and the void' (D–K 68B9).[13] The freethinkers of the late fifth century utilised this

---

[13] For the Eleatic background see Kahn [926], 154 f. My discussion of *nomos* and *phusis* here is substantially the same as in my [84].

negative view of *nomos* in their attack on the virtues of restraint (namely temperance and justice) as repressive social restrictions on the freedom and self-interest of the individual. The most important documentation for this radical view is in the fragments of Antiphon the Sophist (possibly identical with the oligarch executed in 411 B.C. and praised by Thucydides). These texts claim that 'the demands of nature (*phusis*) are matters of necessity; those of *nomos* are matters of agreement or convention (*homologēthenta*)'. 'Most of what is just according to *nomos* is hostile to nature.' Life and pleasure are naturally advantageous, but our pursuit of these goals is restricted by law and moral convention. 'What are established by the laws as advantageous are chains upon our nature; but what is established by nature as advantageous is free' (Antiphon in D–K 87B44a, 1–4). The popular impact of such teaching is brilliantly parodied by Aristophanes in the *Clouds*, where a character known as the Unjust Argument comes on stage to represent the New Education in debate with a representative of traditional virtue: 'Think what pleasures morality (*sōphronein*) would deprive you of: boys, women, gambling, delicacies, drinking, fun and games . . . Respect the necessities of nature (for example sex and adultery) . . . Follow me, obey nature, kick up your heels and laugh, hold nothing shameful' (*Clouds* 1071–8).

Plato was to take this challenge more seriously. The anti-moralist's case is formulated repeatedly in his dialogues, first by Polus and Callicles in the *Gorgias*, then by Thrasymachus in *Republic* I, and finally by his own brothers Glaucon and Adeimantus in *Republic* II. The great speech assigned to Callicles makes eloquent use of the ideas attested in the fragments of Antiphon. Some things are 'honourable by *nomos* but not by nature; in most cases nature and convention are opposed to one another', argues Callicles. The weak have made laws in their own interest, and so they have established the principles of fairness and equality as conventional justice. On the contrary, what is just by nature is that the stronger should rule over the weaker and that superior men should have a greater share of wealth and power (*Gorgias* 482e–484c). Plato is clearly not inventing here, but assigning to Callicles ideas that were current in the late fifth century. Thus in the Melian Dialogue Thucydides makes the Athenians say: 'of gods we believe and of men we certainly know that in every case, by a necessity of their nature, they rule wherever they are strong enough to do so' (Thucydides v.105.2; cf. v.89).

Antiphon in speaking of laws based upon agreement and Callicles in speaking of laws established by the weak both allude to some theory of social contract as the origin of law and morality. In *Republic* II Glaucon says explicitly that men created *nomoi* and principles of justice by some sort of compact or covenant (*sunthēkēi*, 359a). We do not know the original form of this theory, but we do have a fifth-century parallel in a fragment of a *Sisyphus* play assigned variously to Euripides and to Critias the tyrant. 'There was a time when the life of mankind was without order and like the life of beasts, subject to the rule of strength, and there was no reward for the good or any punishment for evil men. And then, I think, men set up laws (*nomoi*) for punishment, so that justice would rule and violence (*hubris*) would be her slave' (D–K 88B25). The author goes on to derive belief in the gods from a similar device designed to curb criminal actions and produce decent behaviour out of fear of divine punishment. The same evolutionary scheme – mankind at first living the life of beasts and only later able to co-exist in civilised communities – is presupposed by the tale told by Protagoras in Plato's dialogue.

Like the origins of early social contract theory, with which it is closely connected, the origins of the *nomos–phusis* antithesis in ethical discussion are undocumented and obscure.[14] What is clear in the fully developed anti-morality of figures like Callicles and Thrasymachus is that their ideal of ruthless self-assertion represents the old heroic conception of *aretē* stripped of the restraints of justice and temperance, since these are now thought of as mere human conventions deprived of any basis either in nature or in divine decree. The social and political climate of the late fifth century, with violent class conflicts reinforced by thirty years of nearly continuous warfare, must also have contributed to the decay of traditional morality. Such at least was the judgement of Thucydides. (See Thuc. II.52–3 on the moral effects of the plague in Athens; III.82–3 on status in Corcyra; v.87–105 for the cynicism of the Melian Dialogue.)

The sophists were of course blamed for this moral decline, and with them Socrates as well. We come to Socrates in a moment. But first we may consider how far men like Protagoras and Gorgias could reasonably be held responsible for the intellectual revolt against the traditional virtues of justice and restraint. Protagoras was certainly an outspoken agnostic with regard to the existence of the gods (D–K 80B4), and his Man-the-Measure doctrine rejects any supernatural sanction for right and wrong. But in regard to normative morality he seems to have been a conservative like Herodotus. Plato represents him as offering to make his pupils better men and better citizens (*Protagoras* 318a, 319a). The case is different for Gorgias. According to Plato, Gorgias was careful not to claim to teach virtue; he promised only to make men good public speakers (*Meno* 95c). This indifference to the moral or immoral ends served by powers of persuasion is no doubt one of the reasons why Plato has constructed his *Gorgias* so as to imply that 'Gorgias' teaching is the seed of which the Calliclean way of life is the poisonous fruit' (Dodds [271], 15). And in Gorgias' written work we find that he is willing to play

---

[14] For an attempt to trace the origins of these theories see Kahn [106].

with words and ideas in ways that seem both morally and intellectually irresponsible. His treatise *On Nature or on Not-Being* undertakes to prove (1) that nothing is real or true, (2) that if there is anything, it is unknowable, and (3) that if it is knowable, it is unsayable. This brilliant inversion of Parmenides' argument for Being was no doubt designed to be entertaining rather than seriously nihilistic. And the same can be said for Gorgias' *Defence of Helen*, on the grounds that she was either (a) compelled by the gods or (b) carried off by force or (c) persuaded by the irresistible power of speech (*logos*), and hence is not to be held responsible in any case. Gorgias describes his *Defence of Helen* as a game or plaything (*paignion*) (D–K 82B11.21). But there could hardly be better ammunition for the standard charge against the sophists: they make the weaker argument the stronger, and hence they pervert justice by their powers of persuasion.

Nevertheless the professional sophists were probably too dependent upon public favour to become open enemies of traditional morality. In Plato's dialogue it is the ambitious politician Callicles, not the sophist Gorgias or Polus, who formulates the extreme anti-moralist position. (The corresponding position taken up by Thrasymachus in *Republic* I is not confirmed by any independent evidence concerning this sophist.) If the Antiphon known as 'the sophist' was in fact Antiphon the oligarch of 411, as many scholars now believe, we have the same phenomenon. If the *Sisyphus* fragment was not written by Critias the tyrant, it was written by Euripides – in either case not by a sophist. The anti-moralism of the late fifth century seems to be primarily the work of practical men, willing to act ruthlessly and happy to learn from the New Education that the traditional restraints of *dikē* and *nomos* are only a conventional artifice, the invention of men more timid than themselves.

The sophists, after all, were a diverse group who had in common only the profession of teaching for pay. They taught success in public speaking, but they also taught 'culture' generally, that is, they 'made it their profession to diffuse and popularise ideas'.[15] But with the exception of Protagoras' relativism (and the possible exception of the moral scepticism and anti-morality just discussed), the new ideas were not their own. What they had to teach was essentially the new philosophy and science of Ionia, Magna Graecia and Sicily. As Aristophanes makes clear in the *Clouds*, by giving a rational explanation for natural phenomena like earthquake, lunar eclipse and thunderbolt, the new science inevitably implied an attack on the traditional

---

[15] Nettleship [328], 23. The broadest notion of sophistic culture is represented by Hippias, who seems to have been a master of every art and science and one of the inventors of literary and intellectual history. See Kerferd [86], 46–9; Guthrie [3], 280–5.

notion of the gods and hence on the religious sanctions for traditional morality. One did not need to be a sophist to be influenced by these new ideas. As professional popularisers, the sophists are simply the most conspicuous representatives of the late-fifth-century Enlightenment: the climate of ideas that is common to Thucydides, the late plays of Euripides, and some Hippocratic treatises – the intellectual ferment which Aristophanes is attacking in the Clouds and which Plato reflects in his dialogues.

Democritus is the only moral philosopher from this period (the last third of the fifth century) from whom we have substantial specimens of written work. But from the point of view of the history of ethics, Democritus stands in the shadow of Socrates. Despite the fact that he wrote nothing, Socrates is the founder of classical Greek moral philosophy, the mentor not only of Plato but, indirectly, of Aristotle, the Cynics, the Stoics and the sceptics. Socrates is the greatest name in ancient ethics. But what did he teach?

The only account of Socrates known to have been composed during his lifetime is Aristophanes' *Clouds*, a caricature of sophistic teaching in general which provides no basis for a historical reconstruction of Socrates' own thought. Socrates' extraordinary personality and skill in conversational argument made a profound impact on a wide variety of younger contemporaries, including several important future statesmen, teachers, writers and philosophers. But apparently no one thought to write down his words while he was alive, as Arrian did for Epictetus and so many students have done for their professors since then. But Socrates was of course no professor. And instead of student notebooks we have something more magnificent: the dialogues of Plato.

There were a number of other authors of 'Socratic conversations' (*Sōkratikoi logoi*) besides Plato, but apparently none of comparable philosophical interest.[16] Xenophon is the only other Socratic writer whose works have come down to us, and it was once thought that Xenophon's portrait of Socrates could be used as an historical corrective to Plato's. But that view of Xenophon has now been generally abandoned. Xenophon has no real understanding of philosophical issues and arguments. What little philosophy we can find in him has probably been borrowed from Plato.[17] The only philosopher other than Plato who gives us what might be considered

---

[16] Their fragments are now collected in Giannantoni [112]. We know most about the dialogues of Aeschines and Phaedo, least about those of Antisthenes and Euclides; the work of the latter would be of greater philosophical importance.

[17] I have defended this claim in *Plato and the Socratic Dialogue* (Cambridge, 1996), ch. 3 and appendix. For the philosophical unreliability of Xenophon see Vlastos [120], 99 ff. Xenophon's dependence on Plato has not, to my knowledge, been systematically studied. For some suggestions see Patzer [126], 438–42.

credible information about Socrates' thought is Aristotle. But Aristotle arrived in Athens more than thirty years after Socrates' death, and most of his information about Socrates seems to be derived from Plato's dialogues.

Ultimately, then, the Socratic problem is the question how far – in what works, and to what extent – Plato's portrait of Socrates can be regarded as historical. This problem might well be regarded as insoluble. Plato and Socrates have been described as a double star which the most powerful telescope will never succeed in resolving.[18] But most historians have considered it their duty to draw some kind of line, and many have thought that Aristotle provides us with the needed telescope.

We may begin by excluding two extreme views that probably do not have, and certainly do not deserve, serious defenders today. One is the negative extreme, which regards Socrates as a mythical figure about whom we can have no reliable information. The other is the positive extreme, which ascribes to the historical Socrates *everything* that is asserted by the character of that name in Plato's dialogues, including the doctrine of Forms. (This was the Scotch heresy of John Burnet and A. E. Taylor.) In between these two extremes we can identify a range of reasonable opinions, all to some extent supported but none decisively confirmed by the available evidence. This range can best be characterised by two opposing tendencies: the tendency to recognise either a reasonable minimum or a reasonable maximum of historical features in the Platonic portrayal of Socrates. I first briefly summarise the maximal view, which is the one that has been most influential above all in English-language scholarship. I shall then expound the minimal view, which seems to me to rest on a more solid historical base.

The reasonably maximal view does not identify the historical and Platonic Socrates. It recognises that Socrates in the dialogues, for example in the *Republic*, often serves as Plato's spokesman for doctrines that Socrates himself would never have espoused. But this is where the Aristotelian telescope has its work to do. Aristotle draws a clear distinction between the Socrates of the dialogues of definition, who seeks to formulate universal concepts, and the positing of 'separate Forms' or metaphysical Ideas, which Aristotle ascribes only to Plato and his school. Furthermore, Aristotle attributes to Socrates a view of *akrasia* and an intellectualist conception of virtue that corresponds closely to the picture drawn by Plato in the *Protagoras*. So the first tendency will be, following Aristotle's lead, to

---

[18] Shorey [298], 19: 'Plato and Socrates, says Emerson, are the double star which no telescope will ever completely distinguish. That is not quite true . . . But the ideal Socrates of the Platonic dialogues and the hypothetical "Socrates of history" do constitute a double star which not even the spectrum analysis of the latest philology can ever resolve.'

recognise the historical Socrates in Plato's *Protagoras* and in the dialogues of definition (*Laches*, *Charmides*, *Euthyphro*). This is the view of Socrates represented, for example, in the standard histories of Greek philosophy by Zeller and Guthrie. It is this same tendency which gives rise to the notion of 'Socratic dialogues' for those earlier works in which the doctrine of Forms does not appear. The strongest, most systematic statement of this position is to be found in the recent book on Socrates by Gregory Vlastos. Vlastos argues that the philosophy of Plato in the first ten or twelve of his works, from the *Apology* down to and including the opening section of the *Meno*, is essentially identical with the thought of his master. Despite the fact that, according to Vlastos, Plato always wrote as a philosopher and not as a historian, during this first period of his work 'disciple and teacher had thought as one' (Vlastos [120], 131). Hence for Vlastos the Platonic Socrates of the pre-middle dialogues just *is* the historical Socrates.[19] Most proponents of the maximal view would be less willing than Vlastos to regard all these pre-middle dialogues as equally Socratic. But they would agree in accepting the what-is-X? question, the denial of *akrasia*, and the doctrine of the unity of virtue in knowledge as historically Socratic.

The minimalist tendency, on the other hand, will reject this view of Socrates as relying too heavily on the authority of Aristotle, as yielding to the temptation for lovers of Socrates to want to know more about their hero than our sources permit, and as doing so at the cost of underestimating Plato's creativity as a thinker and writer. On this alternative view, Aristotle's statements on Socrates are to be regarded not as a historical report but as his own interpretation, based upon his reading of the Platonic dialogues and his own theory as to the logical genesis of the doctrine of Forms.[20] Aristotle is simply the first author to attempt to solve the Socratic problem, and he does so with his own axe to grind (sharpening it for work on the theory of Forms) and without the advantages of a modern training in philology and the history of ideas. If we consider the Platonic evidence from the point of view of historical documentation, the crucial distinction is not between Socrates with and without the metaphysical Forms, but between the *Apology* and the dialogues proper. The *Apology* is, of course, not a dialogue. Plato here adopts the form of an established literary genre, the written version of a courtroom speech. The dialogues, on the other hand, belong to an entirely new form, the 'conversations with Socrates' composed by his disciples after his death. Now Gigon and Momigliano have shown that this new, quasi-biographical

---

[19] Vlastos counts several dialogues (*Euthydemus, Lysis, Hippias Major*) as transitional, less Socratic in form but still Socratic in content, until recollection makes its appearance in the *Meno*.   [20] See Patzer [126], 435 f. and my [123].

form blends historical data with free fiction in a way that is quite 'bewildering to the professional historian'.[21] The fictive element is obvious when Plato's dialogues are situated before his birth (*Protagoras, Charmides*) or in his childhood (*Laches*), or when they represent a private conversation that Plato cannot have heard (*Crito, Euthyphro, Meno*). The *Apology*, by contrast, refers to a public occasion, before a large audience, and Plato's presence at the trial is conspicuously mentioned (*Ap.* 34a1, 38b6). Although the text of the *Apology* is certainly not a verbatim record of Socrates' speech in court, it has some claim to be the report of an historical event, composed by an eyewitness. Plato's *Apology* can thus count as documentary evidence for Socrates' position at the trial, much as Thucydides' Funeral Oration can be regarded as evidence for Pericles' position in 430 B.C. – as interpreted, of course, by the author in each case.[22]

To this documentary contrast between the *Apology* and the dialogues corresponds a remarkable difference in the Socratic practice of philosophy depicted in each case. The *Apology* exhibits many of Socrates' characteristic traits: his disavowal of wisdom, his arguing by *epagōgē* from analogies in the arts and crafts (medicine, horsemanship and the like), his practice of asking questions and often pursuing an elenchus in which the interlocutor is led to contradict himself on the basis of premises which he has accepted. (The latter happens in the cross-examination of Meletus, *Ap.* 26c–27e.) There is clear evidence in the *Apology* of Socrates' overriding concern for moral wisdom and excellence, his commitment to what Vlastos has called the sovereignty of virtue, namely his refusal at any cost to act against his own view of what is just and right. There are vivid hints of the famous paradox that no one does wrong voluntarily (*oudeis hekōn adikei*) at 25d–e and 37a5, and the related paradox that the morally good life is also the happy life ('It is not allowed that a better man be harmed by a worse one', *Ap.* 30d1; Cf. 41d2). If we add the *Crito*, we can also recognise as historically Socratic the epoch-making rejection of the principle of retaliation: the refusal of revenge as unjust, and with it the denial of the standard view that it is right to do harm to one's enemies.[23]

What we do not find, however, either in the *Apology* or *Crito* – or in the *Ion* or the *Hippias Minor*, which have a good claim with the *Crito* to be the three earliest dialogues[24] – is any evidence for (1) the unity of the virtues in wisdom, (2) the denial of *akrasia* and (3) the what-is-X? question. The usual

---

[21] Momigliano [58], 46.
[22] I am inclined to count the *Crito* as a kind of postscript to the *Apology*. In form it is, of course, a fictitious dialogue, but what it purports to represent is Socrates' attitude towards a genuine historical situation, the possibility of his escape from prison.   [23] Vlastos [120], ch. 7.   [24] Patzer [126], 442.

attribution of these three items to Socrates depends upon assuming, with Aristotle, that Plato's portrayal in the *Protagoras* and in the dialogues of definition is essentially historical. It is precisely this assumption that distinguishes the reasonable maximum from the reasonable minimum in the reconstruction of Socrates' thought. I believe that the minimal view reflects a sounder critical estimate of the documentary value of the dialogues as a source for the history of philosophy,[25] and that it does greater justice to Plato's originality both as artist and as philosopher.

On this view, there is no reason to suppose that Socrates prepared for Plato's doctrine of Forms by asking systematically 'What is courage?' 'What is piety?',[26] and no reason to suppose that he held the extreme intellectualist doctrine that to know what-courage-is guarantees that one will be courageous. This account of Socrates is an artefact which the modern historical tradition, leaning on Aristotle, has created out of Platonic material. Judging from the *Apology*, from the remains of Aeschines and Antisthenes, and from Plato's dialogues in so far as they do not suggest a more technical level of philosophical conceptualisation, we can see that Socrates was a powerful moral personality who was able to dominate any social encounter by his massive integrity and his unrivalled skill in argument. His persistent questioning of all and sundry on such topics as moral excellence, wisdom and happiness revealed that most people had not given any serious thought to these matters and hence could not formulate a consistent position. Under interrogation by Socrates they would generally be willing to propose and defend a proposition that was in fact incompatible with their own lives and beliefs. To bring his interlocutors 'to care for themselves', to recognise their ignorance and incoherence on matters of the greatest importance and their need, consequently, to devote their attention to 'wisdom and truth and making their souls as good as possible' (*Ap.* 29e) – this was the mission Socrates felt imposed upon him by divine command. He could render no greater service to his fellow-citizens than to arouse them from their complacent slumber, to bring them to reflect on the primary importance of these inner goods and acknowledge that the goods of the soul are more valuable because more 'our own' (*oikeia*) than the traditionally prized external goods of wealth, honour and fame (29d), just as they are more precious than the

---

[25]   In regard to the personality and character of Socrates (in contrast to the conceptual development of his thought) there is so much consistency between the *Apology* on the one hand and later dialogues like the *Symposium* and *Phaedo* on the other that we can scarcely see Socrates at all except through Plato's eyes. This has produced (in Aristotle, and in many authors since) the mirage of the 'Socratic dialogues' as representative of his philosophical thought as well.

[26]   For the examples of such definitional questions in Xenophon, see Patzer's discussion cited above in n. 17.

goods of the body (30a–b). Socrates thus gives new and more explicit content to Xenophanes' claim that his own wisdom was more beneficial to the city than victory at the games.

Furthermore, both by his words and by his actions Socrates made clear that the good of the soul lies in total loyalty to the principle of justice: namely that the only question to be asked concerning any action is 'whether it is acting justly or unjustly, the deed of a good man or a bad one' (*Ap.* 28b8), and that the evil to be avoided is not death or danger but only what is shameful (*aischron*) (28d9). If the *Crito* can be trusted, Socrates compared justice to the health of the soul, injustice to psychic disease (*Crito* 47d–e), thus introducing the analogy which Plato was to develop in the *Gorgias* and defend in the psychological theory of the *Republic*. Whether or not this particular analogy is historically Socratic, however, it is clear that Socrates completed the development we have traced in Xenophanes, Heraclitus and Democritus: he firmly identified *aretē* and the highest human goods with the goods of the soul. Socrates gives, in effect, the classical interpretation of the view formulated by Democritus in B171: 'the soul is the dwelling place of the *daimōn*'. Through the tremendous influence exerted by his followers, above all by Plato, Socrates produced (as Jaeger put it) 'that emphasis on the inner life that characterises the later stages of Greek civilisation'.[27] It is because moral vice and folly are the greatest evils, the degradation of one's own inner being, that anyone who 'cares for himself', that is who cares for his soul, will never knowingly choose to be evil or to act unjustly. Socrates' most famous paradox is thus a deliberately provocative formulation of the thesis sketched in the *Apology* and *Crito*, defended in the *Gorgias* and most fully developed in the *Republic*: it is folly to act unjustly, because it is in our own best interest to be just.

The debate between the minimal and maximal reconstructions of Socrates' thought bears essentially on the question how far Socrates had passed beyond the conceptual level represented in the fragments of Democritus and how far he had anticipated Plato in the systematic pursuit of definitions and in the early formulation of a theory of moral psychology. If we leave these questions aside, Socrates' importance for the history of ethics is indisputable. Socrates succeeded in defining the task of Greek moral theory as the reconciliation, the identification even, of the two themes we have discussed here: the topics of virtue and happiness, morality and the good life. It was really Socrates, not Plato, who did what Aristotle in a poem said of Plato: that 'he alone or first of mortals clearly showed, by his own life and the force of his arguments, that a man becomes good and happy at the

[27] Jaeger [56], 45.

same time' (Aristotle, fr. 673 Rose[3]). We must be struck here by the contrast with Kant, who has to invoke an omnipotent God in order to reconcile virtue with happiness. It is because of his success in uniting these two central themes of the Greek moral tradition that Socrates can properly be regarded as the founder of classical Greek moral theory.

3
Platonic ethics

C. C. W. TAYLOR

The fundamental question of Platonic ethics is 'How should one live?' (*Republic* 1.352d, *Gorgias* 500c). That question is not to be understood as 'What is the morally best way to live?', as is shown by the fact that in *Rep.* 1 an appropriate, though in Plato's view false, answer to it is that given by Thrasymachus, namely that one should live by emancipating oneself to the best of one's ability from the restraints of morality with a view to the furtherance of one's own interest. Rather it is to be understood as 'How may one achieve the life which is, objectively, but from the point of view of one's own interest, the most worth living?' (*Rep.* 1.344e). The Greek term for the achievement of such a life is *eudaimonia* (literally 'having a favourable guardian spirit' (*daimōn*)), conventionally translated 'happiness', but in view of its objective character better rendered 'blessedness' or 'well-being'. According to Aristotle (*Nicomachean Ethics* (*EN*) 1095a18–20) it was universally acknowledged (a) that *eudaimonia* was the supreme good and (b) that the term meant 'living well' and 'doing well'; nothing in the texts of Plato suggests that his use of the term conflicts with these claims. In the same passage Aristotle tells us that there were substantive disputes about what living well amounted to, some holding, for example, that it consists in acquiring wealth, others that it consists in a life of honour or of intellectual achievement; Plato depicts such substantive disputes in Socrates' confrontations with Thrasymachus in *Rep.* 1 and Callicles in the *Gorgias*.

The agreement on 'How is one to live well?' as the basic question of ethics forecloses certain ethical disputes while leaving others open. Most fundamentally, ethical questions are approached from the standpoint of the individual's interest, the promotion of which is assumed to be the primary function of the individual's practical rationality. On that assumption one has adequate reason to undertake any action if and only if so doing will contribute to one's living well, i.e. to one's having an objectively worthwhile life. The conception of an objectively worthwhile life should not be construed in a narrowly egoistic way, since it may be part of an objectively worthwhile life that one cares for the good of others, not merely instrumentally, with a view to the benefits one may expect to gain from such benevolence, but for its own sake. Nevertheless, it is broadly egoistic,[1] in that it is assumed that the value to the carer of that selfless care lies primarily in its contribution to the *life of the carer*, and only secondarily in its contribution to the life of the person cared for. Since this broadly egoistic conception of the role of practical reason is assumed from the outset, there is no room in Platonic thought for theories of a Kantian type, which seek to identify moral principles as imperatives binding unconditionally on any rational agent in total independence of any considerations of the interest of that or any other agent.[2] It is therefore unsurprising that our texts provide no hint that the very conception of that type of theory had so much as occurred to Plato.

The broadly egoistic starting-point of Plato's ethical enquiries is not, then, open to question. By contrast, the status of morality is an eagerly debated question in some of his major dialogues. By morality I understand a socially regulated system of norms imposing restraints on the pursuit of self-interest with the general aim of furthering social co-operation, for which the nearest Greek terms are *to dikaion* and *dikaiosunē*, conventionally 'the just' and 'justice'. The questions 'What is the morally right thing to do?' and 'Which is the morally best way to live?' were certainly not unintelligible to Plato, or to Greeks of his time generally. They were, however, both distinct from and posterior to the fundamental question which we have already identified, 'How should one live?', i.e. 'How should one achieve the best life for oneself?' The former questions were posterior in that, whereas the rationality of the pursuit of the best life for oneself was unquestioned (indeed one could go so far as to say that that pursuit constituted practical rationality for the Greeks), the rationality of the individual's observance of the dictates of morality required to be established by showing that the acceptance was

---

[1] For a useful discussion of these two varieties of egoism, labelled respectively 'moral solipsism' and 'moral egocentrism', see Irwin [293], 255.

[2] This contrast between Platonic and Kantian theory leaves open the question whether, in the former, the agent's interest may itself be seen as consisting in the acquisition of states of the personality (i.e. virtues) which have value independently of their contribution to the agent's *eudaimonia*. There are theoretically at least three possible views on the relationship of virtue to *eudaimonia*: (i) virtue is valuable purely instrumentally, as a means to *eudaimonia*, (ii) virtue is at least partly constitutive of *eudaimonia*, and is intrinsically valuable *qua* constitutive of *eudaimonia*, (iii) virtue is valuable both in its own right and as either a means to or as a constituent of *eudaimonia*. I argue in note 21 below that (ii) is closer than (i) to giving an account of Plato's view in the early dialogues. I know of no evidence to suggest that Plato was aware of (iii) as an alternative to (i) and (ii). (*EN* 1097b2–5 indicates that Aristotle may have been.)

necessary for the achievement of the individual good life. Plato attempts to meet the challenge to provide this justification of morality in the *Gorgias* and, in a much more elaborate and extended form, in the *Republic*.

He accepts, then, that morality requires justification, in the form of a defence of its rationality, that this justification must be in terms of a broad conception of individual interest, and that such a justification can be provided. The requirement of justification seems an inevitable response to the fact that morality is essentially cooperative, requiring sacrifices from the individual for the common good. By Plato's time there had been developed theories of the social nature of morality, which attempted to ground morality in self-interest (in a similar fashion to the theories of Hobbes and Hume[3]) by showing how norms of self-restraint and social co-operation would naturally develop in primitive societies as a device for mutual protection against the onslaughts of wild animals or (more plausibly) of unsocialised individuals.[4] But the success of such theories seems limited. They show convincingly why self-interested individuals have reasons to prefer the existence of such institutions to a Hobbesian war of all against all, 'since we benefit from one another's justice and goodness' (*Protagoras* 327b). But they are unable to show that, given that the institutions exist, each individual benefits more from the sacrifices which he or she is required by the norms of the institution to make than he would do by taking advantage of the sacrifices of others to promote his own interest. The sacrifices might be regarded as one's subscription to the mutual security club, which it is in one's interest to pay, since the other members would not accept that one should enjoy the benefits of membership without paying one's dues. But if one can get away without paying, as one fairly clearly can *now and again* (though not, doubtless, always), why pay *in those circumstances*? Of course, it is unfair not to pay, which is a perfectly good reason for someone who is already committed to being fair, but the theory was supposed to generate a purely self-interested reason for undertaking that commitment, which it clearly fails to do. As Glaucon points out (*Rep.* 362a), the most that the theory can provide is a self-interested reason for making other people believe that one always deals fairly with them, which falls short of a reason for always actually doing so; but the latter, not the former, is what is required for the justification of morality.

These problems reflect a crisis in traditional Greek morality, to which

---

[3] Hobbes, *Leviathan*, chs. 13, 17; Hume, *Treatise* III.ii.1–2.

[4] Plato provides examples in the myth in the *Protagoras* (320c–322d) and in the theory proposed by Glaucon in *Rep.* II (358e–359b); an example independent of Plato is the so-called 'Anonymus Iamblichi', on which see Guthrie [3], 71–4 and 314–15. For a valuable discussion of the historical sources of this tradition see Kahn [106].

Plato's ethics presents a sustained response. Traditional morality recognised certain states of character, principally courage, self-control, justice or fairness and piety, as the principal qualities which made their possessor an outstanding and admirable person.[5] The young were brought up to regard possession of these qualities as fine and admirable (*kalon*) and the lack of them as disgraceful (*aischron*), and their inculcation was the principal aim of education.[6] These were the most important among the excellences (*aretai*), i.e. those qualities stable possession of which, together with such external goods as wealth, position in society and physical health, constituted success in life (*to eu zēn* or *eudaimonia*), which, we have seen, was universally acknowledged as the supreme good. But the arguments which we have just glanced at show that the claims of certain *aretai*, notably justice, to be constitutive of the agent's good are at odds with the other-regarding character of those qualities. A further difficulty arises from the fact that some of these qualities are no less indeterminate in character than *eudaimonia* itself. Thus even if it is granted that success in life requires piety, i.e. a proper attitude to the gods, including respect for those obligations which the gods impose on us, there can be apparently irresoluble disputes about what kind of conduct really is required by the gods, as in the famous example in Herodotus (III.38) of the diverse customs of different nations in the disposal of the dead, a central case of religious obligation. Both difficulties may be seen to have prompted an emphasis on the distinction between the nature or reality of things (*phusis*) and convention (*nomos*).[7] The lack of coincidence between the agent's interest and the demands of morality leads to the claim that while nature prompts us to seek our own interest, the demands of morality spring from nothing but convention (with the implication that the latter, unlike the promptings of nature, lack any authority).[8] The indeterminacy of some of the conventional excellences is similarly attributed to the facts that

---

[5] Pindar, *Isthmian* 8.24–7; Aeschylus, *Seven Against Thebes* 610; Euripides, fr. 282.23–7; Xenophon, *Memorabilia* III.ix.1–5; Plato, *Prot.* 329c, *Meno* 73e–74a, *Rep.* 427e, etc. (See Irwin [293], p. 287, n. 1.)

'Self-control' renders *sōphrosunē*, a term which lacks a precise English equivalent. It connotes primarily a proper sense of oneself and one's limitations in relation to others, and derivatively various applications of that sense, especially control of the bodily appetites. Hence in many contexts, including those provided by Plato's tri-partite psychology, it is appropriately rendered 'self-control'. Where in this chapter I use the terms 'self-control' and 'self-controlled' they correspond to the Greek *sōphrosunē* and its cognate adjective *sōphrōn*, but I have not attempted total uniformity of usage, preferring sometimes to use the Greek term. (In my commentary on the *Protagoras* ([237]), I prefer the rendering 'soundness of mind', for reasons explained there on pp. 122–4.)   [6] *Prot.* 324d–326e.

[7] Principal discussions of the *nomos–phusis* distinction include Heinimann [54]; Guthrie [3], ch. 4; Kerferd [86], ch. 10.   [8] *Rep.* 359c. Cf. *Prot.* 337c–d.

(a) their requirements arise from nothing more than convention, and (b) different societies have different conventions.[9]

These criticisms of conventional morality should not be assimilated to modern attacks on the objectivity of values. Critics who, like Glaucon or the sophist Antiphon,[10] denigrate conventional morality by contrast with the promptings of nature assume that the latter is a locus of objective value. The extreme form of this position is upheld by Callicles, who maintains that unrestrained self-assertion is naturally *right* (*phusei dikaion*), and that the conventional morality (*nomōi dikaion*) which opposes it is, therefore, naturally wrong, i.e. really or objectively *immoral* (*Gorg.* 483c–484c).[11] While Thrasymachus is not prepared to go that far, he asserts that injustice is a form of wisdom and an excellence, in that it gives the agent a worthwhile life, while justice is weakness and folly, in that it harms the agent and promotes the good of others (*Rep.* 343b–344c, 348c–e). We have no reason to interpret these claims otherwise than as statements of fact. It is significant that the earliest application of the nature–convention contrast to morality, attributed to Archelaus, who is said to have been a pupil of Anaxagoras and a teacher of Socrates, states simply that 'the just and the disgraceful are by convention, not by nature' (Diogenes Laertius II.16; D–K 60A1). Here, what is purely a matter of convention is what is morally right and wrong, not what is good or bad; for example there is no suggestion that it is purely (or at all) a matter of convention that health is a good state and illness a bad one. Later, when the sceptics applied their universal strategy of suspension of judgement to the special case of claims about value, they did not confine their critique to moral value, but applied it to value generally;[12] but that seems to have been a post-Platonic development. At *Theaetetus* 172a–b Socrates asserts that 'in matters of what is just and unjust and holy and unholy [people] are willing to maintain that none of these things is so in reality (*phusei*) or has its own nature (*ousian*), but what is agreed on [sc. by each community] is the truth for as long as it is agreed', but contrasts that conventionalism about morals with the position about what is advantageous, where 'no one would dare to say that what a community lays down as advantageous for itself is so in fact'. That assertion is confirmed by our other evidence: both sides of the dispute about nature and convention accepted that genuine values were part of nature, the critics of conventional morality attacking its values as spurious because they are *merely* conventional and therefore not part of nature, its defenders urging that on the contrary moral values are natural and therefore genuine. We have already noticed one

---

[9] Herodotus III.38.
[10] Diels–Kranz 87B44. See Guthrie [3], chs. 4 (a) (ii) and 11 (5); Saunders [107].
[11] I discuss the point more fully in my [68].   [12] See Julia Annas' chapter below.

defensive move, the theory (outlined in Protagoras' myth) that moral conventions are themselves natural, in that they are strategies for cooperation developed by human beings struggling for survival in a hostile environment. But that defence was insufficient, since it failed to show that moral value passed the primary test for being natural, namely that of promoting the individual well-being of the agent. If his defence of traditional morality was to pass that test, Plato had to develop a better theory of the nature of morality and of human nature, in the hope of demonstrating the objective goodness of the traditional virtues via their contribution to the perfection of that nature, and therefore to the objectively worthwhile life for the agent.

In what follows I shall set out what I take to be the main lines of Plato's attempt to develop such a theory. I shall distinguish three stages in this process:

i the theory of the early dialogues[13]
ii the theory of the *Republic*
iii developments subsequent to the *Republic*

i The early dialogues

A central preoccupation of the early dialogues is the search for definitions, whether of individual excellences (courage in *Laches*, *sōphrosunē* in *Charmides*, piety in *Euthyphro*), of excellence in general (*Meno*) or of friendship (*Lysis*), an aspect of life intimately related to excellence and the good. In order to understand the prominence of definition in these dialogues, and its connection with the theory of the nature of the virtues which emerges in them, it is necessary to consider what Plato's Socrates is looking for when he looks for an ethical definition. In outline, the project of the early dialogues is to give accounts of the traditional virtues which will exhibit them as natural goods; to investigate how that project was carried out would require close examination of the relevant texts, for which space is lacking here.[14] I must confine myself in this chapter to a bald statement of the results of that investigation, focusing primarily on the *Meno*, which, though probably one of the latest of the dialogues which I here count as early, and in its introduction of the theory of recollection transitional to the metaphysical dialogues of the middle period, is of all the early dialogues the richest in evidence for the Platonic/Socratic theory and practice of definition.

A Socratic definition is not, in the first instance, a definition of any of the items that might spring to the mind of the modern reader, such as a term,

---

[13] For the purpose of this chapter I count the following as early dialogues: *Apology, Crito, Euthyphro, Charmides, Laches, Lysis, Euthydemus, Protagoras, Meno, Gorgias*.

[14] For fuller discussion see my 'Socratic Ethics' in [130], 137–52.

the meaning of a word, or a concept. Ideally, a Socratic definition answers the question 'What is . . . ?', where the blank is filled in by a word designating some quality or feature of agents, such as courage or excellence. So, literally, what are to be defined are those qualities or features themselves, not anything standing for them, as words or perhaps concepts might be thought to do. But, of course, we cannot in general draw a sharp distinction between specifying what something is and defining or elucidating the concept of that thing. The concept of F (where 'F' is some general term) is what we understand or possess when we use the term 'F' with understanding, and in some cases saying what F is precisely is defining or elucidating the concept of F. Thus if I answer the question 'What is justice?' by saying that justice is giving everyone their due, I have thereby attempted (however inadequately) to elucidate the concept of justice, in that the answer is intended to make explicit what is standardly conveyed by our talk of justice. The ultimate authority for the correctness of that sort of definition is the competent speaker of the language in which the elucidation is expressed, and the ultimate test which that authority applies is conformity with his or her linguistic intuitions. In other cases, however, the question 'What is F?' is aimed to elicit, not an elucidation of the ordinary concept of F, but an account of the phenomenon couched in terms of the best available scientific theory. For example, 'light is a stream of photons' is not an elucidation of the ordinary concept of light, i.e. of what the standard speaker of English understands by the word 'light'. It is an account of what light is, i.e. of what science has discovered light to be, and that account presupposes, but is not exhausted by, the grasp of the concept which is available to the competent but pre-theoretical speaker of the language.[15] Hence the ultimate test of its adequacy is not its fit with that speaker's linguistic intuitions, but its explanatory power, empirical testability, or whatever else constitutes the test of a good scientific theory. The form of words 'What is . . . ?' may express the search for a definition of either kind (and in any case the distinction between the two is less sharp than the foregoing over-simplification has suggested[16]). Precisely what kind of search is afoot has to be determined by the context, which cannot be guaranteed to provide an unambiguous result.

We learn from the *Euthyphro* that a Socratic definition of a given quality should (a) specify what is common to all and only those things to which the name of the quality applies (5d), (b) specify that in virtue of which the name applies to them (i.e. give the nature of the quality, not a mere distinguishing mark of its presence) (6d, 11a), and (c) provide a criterion by reference to

---

[15] In certain cases the scientific account may even demand revision of the pre-existing concept, as in cases where the latter itself carries connotations of a superseded scientific theory, for example hysteria.   [16] See Putnam [964].

which disputed cases may be determined (6e). Requirements (a) and (b) are explicitly endorsed at *Meno* 72c, where Meno is invited to specify 'the single nature they [i.e. the various types of human excellence] all have in virtue of which (*di'ho*) they are excellences', and though the *Meno* has nothing to say about disputed cases of *aretē*, we have no reason to suppose that the third requirement has been abandoned. These three requirements are satisfied alike by conceptual elucidations and by that kind of account which we have contrasted with those, and which we might call, traditionally, 'real definitions' or, perhaps more informatively, 'substantive or scientific accounts'.

In the course of the discussion Socrates gives two model definitions, of shape and colour respectively. The first of these, 'Shape is the limit of a solid' (76a7), is a conceptual elucidation, whereas the second (76d4–5) is a substantive account of colour in terms of a scientific theory, namely the physiology of Empedocles.[17] He says that the latter is inferior to the definition of shape, but he does not say why it is inferior, and it would therefore be rash to conclude that Socrates' preference for the definition of shape indicates a preference for one *type* of definition, conceptual elucidation, over another, a causally explanatory account. Indeed, the text thus far gives no indication that Plato is even aware of the distinction between those types of definition. So if we are to answer the question 'What kind of definition is Socrates looking for in the *Meno*?', we must take into consideration the rest of the dialogue, where, though nothing more is said about the methodology of definition, the question 'What is excellence?' is answered. Excellence is first (87c–89a) argued to be knowledge, then another argument leads to the revision of that account in favour of the answer 'Excellence is true opinion' (99b–c), an outcome which is further qualified by a strong hint at 100a that the former answer gives the true account of genuine excellence, while the latter gives an account of what passes for excellence by ordinary standards.

What these answers share is a conception of excellence as a cognitive state, or more portentously, a grasp of truth. We are not concerned with the details of the distinction between knowledge and true opinion, but its essence is the firmness or reliability of the grasp; knowledge is a reliable (because systematic) grasp of truth, while true opinion is an unreliable (because unsystematic) grasp of truth. What sort of account of *excellence*

---

[17] 'Colour is a flowing out [sc. from the coloured object] of shapes [i.e. physical particles of various shapes] symmetrical to vision [i.e. of such shapes and sizes as enable them to penetrate the channels in the eye] and perceptible' (76d4–5). (The modern analogue would be an account of colour in terms of light waves of different lengths.)

is provided by the conception of it as a cognitive state? Note that Socrates and Meno are not discussing excellence in some theoretical sphere, such as excellence at mathematics; the paradigms of excellence in this final stage of the discussion are individuals such as Pericles who embody the same ideal of success in public and private affairs as Meno had assumed from the outset. That is to say, cognitive states are presented as giving an account of all-embracing social and political merit, of the state of the totally well-rounded, successful and admirable person (= man, by this stage of the discussion). In what sense is that person's admirable state a cognitive one? The sort of excellence in question is above all practical, manifested in action and a whole style of behaviour; it does not seem that specification of a cognitive state could give an account of *the manifestation* of excellence. In other words, 'knowledge or true opinion' does not offer the same kind of account of excellence as 'having a good service, ground strokes and volley' does of excellence at tennis, since the latter account does precisely specify the kind of actions which manifest that excellence, whereas the former does not. Rather, it gives an account of *what is manifested in* excellent performance, as 'co-ordination, stamina, courtcraft, etc.' does of what is manifested in excellent tennis-playing. And as that account expresses not an elucidation of the concept of excellent tennis-playing but an empirical theory of the causes of the type of play which we count as excellent, so that cognitive account of overall human excellence expresses, not an elucidation of that concept, but a causally explanatory theory, what we may call the Cognitive Theory of Excellence. We find, then, that despite Socrates' expressed preference for the conceptual definition of shape over the causally explanatory account of colour, the account of excellence which he endorses in the concluding section of the dialogue is of a type represented, not by the former, but by the latter.

The aim of our enquiry into the nature of definition in the early dialogues was the elucidation of the nature of the theory of virtue to which that practice of definition is preliminary. That aim has now been achieved in part, with the identification of that theory as the Cognitive Theory of Excellence (more familiar as the first of the so-called 'Socratic paradoxes', the thesis that virtue is knowledge). But that elucidation lacks content without further exploration of just what the Cognitive Theory claims. That exploration will also, I hope, indicate the connection between the Cognitive Theory and the second paradox, the thesis that no one does wrong willingly,[18] and also with the much-discussed question of the unity of virtue.

---

[18] On the paradoxes see Santas [161].

The Cognitive Theory is a theory to the effect that overall success in human life is guaranteed by the possession of certain cognitive states.[19] This theory in turn rests on a theory of the explanation of intentional action, which combines to a remarkable degree a staggering audacity and simplicity with a high degree of plausibility. It states that provided that the agent has a conception of what is overall best for the agent, or (equivalently) what is maximally productive of *eudaimonia* (for the agent), that conception is sufficient to motivate action with a view to its own realisation. That is emphatically not to say that motivation does not require desire as well as belief. On the contrary, Socrates makes clear his view (77c1–2, 78b4–6) that everyone desires good things, which in context has to be interpreted as the strong thesis that the desire for good is an invariable motive. That desire is then conceived as a standing motive, which requires to be focused in one direction or another via a conception of the overall good. Given that focus, desire is as it were locked on to the target which is picked out by the conception, without the possibility of interference by conflicting desires. Hence, given the standing desire, all that is required for the correct conduct, i.e. for the manifestations of excellence, is the correct focus. And that focus has to be a correct conception of the good for the agent, i.e. a correct conception of *eudaimonia*.

From this theory it follows immediately, given the conception of excellence accepted in the *Meno* as what is manifested in excellent conduct, that

[19] There has been a lively debate among recent commentators on whether the Socratic claim is the extreme claim that virtue (i.e. knowledge) is sufficient for success in life (i.e. *eudaimonia*) *by itself*, or the less ambitious claim that it is sufficient given a (modest) sufficiency of those goods which it is beyond the power of the agent to procure, for instance good health. The former view is maintained by Irwin [293], 100 and [180], the latter by Vlastos [184], and by Brickhouse and Smith [179]. The issue seems to me not to be addressed very clearly in the dialogues. While the Socratic claim that the good man cannot be harmed (*Apol.* 30c, 41c–d), *if taken literally*, implies the former view, that view is clearly inconsistent with the assertion at *Crito* 47e that it is not worth living with a sickly body, unless we attribute to Socrates the implausible view that virtue guarantees good health. He might indeed have held that virtue will minimise the causes of ill-health by eliminating those which spring from lack of self-control, but it seems very implausible that he should have thought that such factors as climate or accident could have no effect on one's health. As Irwin points out ([180], 92–4), Socrates does argue at *Euthyd.* 279–80 that wisdom always makes those who possess it *eutuchein*, so that the wise do not need good luck, but in the context that seems to amount just to the claim that knowledgeable practitioners of any skill (doctors, etc.) are more successful than the unskilled, and that they do not need to rely on luck, as the unskilled do. In general, Socrates' insistence on the paramount importance of the state of one's soul (assumed to be within one's control) and the comparative worthlessness of other reputed goods (*Apol.* 28b, *Prot.* 313a) has the outcome that the virtuous agent will need very little from fortune to give him or her a totally worthwhile life, but it is pressing the literal reading of the texts too far to take him to claim that he needs literally nothing.

the traditional virtues are in fact one and the same state of the agent. Courage is that stable state which is manifested in the proper handling of fearful situations, justice the stable state which is manifested in one's proper dealings with others, piety the stable state which is manifested in one's proper dealings with the gods. And the stable state in question is the same state in every case, namely the agent's grasp of the correct conception of the good. Indeed, that same state is designated by the non-synonymous names of the traditional virtues, whose distinct connotations pick out the distinct manifestations of that single state: for example the connotation of the name 'justice', i.e. 'what is manifested in one's proper dealings with others', is distinct from the connotation of the name 'piety', i.e. 'what is manifested in one's proper dealings with the gods'. The point of retaining these various names is to do justice to the fact that for the achievement of overall success in life the same cognitive state has to be manifested in various ways, whether in various types of conduct which overlap only partially (for example if all courageous actions are self-controlled but not vice versa) or in different aspects of co-extensive action-types (for example if all and only just actions are pious, their being pious, i.e. appropriate to dealings with the gods, is a specific modification of that attribute of the action-type which is their being just, i.e. appropriate to dealings with others). But the retention of the names of the traditional virtues should not disguise the essence of the theory, that what is manifested in all these different ways is identical, namely the agent's grasp of his overall good. The 'parts' of total excellence are not distinct motive-forces or tendencies to action, as on the traditional conception, which allowed that they might be separable from one another. Nor are they distinct cognitive states, for example kinds of knowledge, as knowledge of history is a distinct type of knowledge from knowledge of geometry; knowledge of how to treat others and knowledge of how to control one's passions are not distinct types of knowledge, but rather different aspects of a comprehensive knowledge of how to live, which is what controls one's activity in all areas. That is precisely the account of the virtues which the cognitive theory of the *Meno* would lead us to expect, and it is the theory which we find explicitly argued for in the *Protagoras* and implicit in the accounts of individual virtues in the *Euthyphro, Laches* and *Charmides*.[20]

The central claim of the Cognitive Theory, as so far elucidated, is not one from which Thrasymachus or Callicles need dissent; that theory claims that a reliable grasp of the good is sufficient for overall success in life, but is of itself neutral between incompatible conceptions of the good. In order to realise

---

[20] I discuss the unity of virtue more fully in my commentary on the *Protagoras* ([237]) and in [219]. Vlastos has vigorously contested this account of the doctrine in his [264]. For a reply to his main points see the revised edition of my commentary.

Socrates' aim of vindicating the traditional conception of virtue it has to be supplemented by an account of the good, which will show either that traditional virtue (or a sufficiently close approximation to it) is instrumentally necessary for success in life, or that it is as least partially constitutive of it.[21] In advance of that account the Cognitive Theory entails the self-interested version of the second Socratic paradox 'No one acts intentionally against his overall interest.' The supplementation of the Cognitive Theory with that account yields the moral version of the paradox 'No one does intentionally what is morally wrong.' But when we look for arguments in favour of that account, the dialogues provide us with very little. *Crito* 47e states, but does not argue for, the analogy between health of the body and justice in the soul, asserting that injustice damages the soul as sickness does the body, and that as it is not worth living with a sickly and diseased body, even less is it worth living with a corrupted soul. On the strength of that analogy it is agreed (48b) that living well (the universally acknowledged good) is the same thing as living creditably (*kalōs*) and justly (i.e. that the good life is identical with the moral life), but Thrasymachus could properly point out that no argument has been given for the crucial claims that injustice harms the soul and that justice benefits it. *Gorg.* 504–5 merely gives a more extended version of the analogy: all types of craftsmen aim to produce a good product, and in

---

[21] Irwin argues in [293] (for example on pp. 84–5) that the craft analogy commits the Socrates of the early (= Socratic) dialogues to an exclusively instrumental view of the relation of virtue to *eudaimonia*, and treats acceptance or rejection of this instrumental view as the criterion for distinguishing between the views of 'Socrates' and those of 'Plato'. But first, not all crafts (*technai*) are exclusively instrumental in character. A *technē* is any skilled activity which can be systematically taught, a description which embraces the performing arts as well as the productive: see, for instance, *Symp.* 187b (music), *Laws* 816a (dancing). The craft analogy itself, therefore, need not prevent Socrates from claiming both that virtue is a *technē* and that it is at least partly constitutive of *eudaimonia*, while *Crito* 47e shows him firmly committed to the latter claim. So unless Irwin is to attribute the view of the *Crito* to 'Plato' rather than to 'Socrates', he must abandon the view that the latter's conception of the relation of virtue to *eudaimonia* is *exclusively* that of an instrumental means. Irwin's view is criticised by Zeyl in [186].

　　The above is not to say that the position of the early dialogues on the relation of virtue to *eudaimonia* is consistent. As pointed out in the text (p. 63 below), in different passages Socrates is represented as maintaining both that virtue is knowledge (sc. *of* the good) and that it is itself the health of the soul, and therefore the good itself. Those theses are inconsistent, since knowledge of the good requires that the content of that knowledge should be independently specifiable, which is impossible if the good of which one has knowledge is the very state of having knowledge of the good. The fault, however, lies not with the craft analogy, which can be stated without inconsistency as the thesis that success in life is a skilled activity analogous to skill in the performing arts, but with the conjunction of the claims that excellence is a state of knowledge of how to achieve a goal and that it is that goal itself.

every case the goodness of the product consists in its order and arrangement. So a well-made boat has all its parts properly fitted together, and in a healthy individual all the bodily constituents are properly ordered. As health is the name for the proper ordering of bodily components, the name for the proper ordering of psychic components is justice and sōphrosunē, which expresses itself in proper conduct towards gods and men (piety and justice) and in the proper control of pleasure and pain (courage) (507a–c). Once again, the crucial identification of the proper order of the soul with conventional justice and sōphrosunē is unargued. It is an appropriate *ad hominem* rejoinder to Callicles that his ideal of the unrestrained satisfaction of the pleasure of the moment does not provide an adequate rule for the long-term planning of one's life, and that without some such rule one's life will collapse into a chaos of conflicting desires.[22] To be satisfying one's life must be coherent, and to be coherent it must contain some discrimination of pleasures into the more and less significant, and some circumscription of the pursuit of the latter with a view to the greater enjoyment of the former. But that element of rational planning and self-control might be exercised in the pursuit of a life of injustice and self-indulgence; Don Juan could satisfy that requirement by making the seduction of as many women as possible his paramount aim, and by refusing to be distracted from it by the momentary attractions of a life of scholarship or of quiet domesticity.

Earlier in the *Gorgias* (473–5) Socrates argues against Polus that injustice is against the agent's interest, and hence (by the second paradox) that no one acts unjustly intentionally (509e). The argument does not contain any positive account of the agent's good, but proceeds directly to the conclusion that injustice is bad for the agent, relying on Polus' admission that injustice, while more advantageous to the agent than justice, is more disgraceful than justice; Socrates gets Polus to agree that if *x* is more disgraceful than *y*, then *x* is either more unpleasant than *y* or worse (i.e. more disadvantageous) than *y*, and then concludes that injustice is worse than justice via the claim (agreed by Polus) that injustice is not more unpleasant than justice. The weakness of the argument is obvious; as Callicles points out (482d–e), a tougher-minded opponent (such as Thrasymachus) would not have made the initial concession that injustice is more disgraceful than justice. Further,

---

[22] Of course, one's only rule for planning one's life might be 'Don't plan; take every pleasure as it comes.' Such a rule is not formally self-contradictory, nor is the description of someone as attempting to live by it. It is, however, practically self-defeating, in the sense that anyone who tried to put it into practice would find that the attempt to adhere to it consistently required him to break it. The reason is that some pleasures, as they come, require that one should plan, for example the pleasure of getting started on a career.

even given that concession, Socrates' argument requires the general principle that if action-type *a* is more disgraceful to the agent than action-type *b*, it must be either more unpleasant *to the agent* or worse *for the agent*, but there is no ground to think that that principle is true; an action-type might be disgraceful to an agent (i.e. such as to bring him into justified disrepute) which was neither unpleasant to that agent nor bad for him, but either unpleasant to or bad for others.

The only other early dialogue which contains any account of the good is the *Protagoras*, where Socrates is represented as arguing for the conclusion that courage is a kind of knowledge from the premise that the good is pleasure. Without renewing the controversy as to whether this premise is (as I believe) presented in the dialogue as Socrates' own view or merely that of the majority of ordinary people,[23] it has once again to be observed that it is (a) not itself supported by any argument and (b) insufficient to provide the desired vindication of conventional morality.

Taken as a whole, then, the early dialogues fail to realise Plato's project of providing that vindication. The theory of motivation which is outlined in

---

[23] Commentators are divided on the question of whether Socrates is represented as seriously espousing hedonism. I append a list of some writings on either side of the dispute.

For the thesis that he is serious see:

> Grote [289], vol. 2, pp. 87–9
> J. and A. M. Adam [236], xxix–xxxiii
> Hackforth [252]
> Vlastos [239], xl (note)
> Dodds [271], 21–2
> Crombie [287], vol. 1, pp. 232–45 (with reservations)
> Irwin [293], ch. 4
> Taylor [237], 208–9
> Gosling and Taylor [53], ch. 3
> Nussbaum [60], ch. 4
> Cronquist [242]

Against:

> Taylor [299], 260–1
> Sullivan [263]
> Raven [291], 44–9
> Gulley [117], 110–18
> Vlastos [164]
> Manuwald [258]
> Kahn [175]
> Dyson [245]
> Duncan [244]
> Zeyl [185]
> Stokes [119], 358–439
> Kahn [233] and [253].

them requires to be complemented by an account of *eudaimonia*, but no such account is provided. Instead, the whole theory rests on the analogy between conventional virtue and bodily health, which begs the crucial question of the value of conventional virtue to its possessor. Moreover, that analogy threatens the cognitive account of virtue itself; by that account virtue is knowledge, i.e. knowledge of how to achieve *eudaimonia*, whereas on the analogy virtue is *eudaimonia* itself. If the theory were to fit the analogy, knowledge of how to achieve *eudaimonia* should be analogous to knowledge of how to achieve health, i.e. to medicine rather than to health itself. But then virtue would be of purely instrumental value, whereas the analogy with health represents it as having intrinsic value. A further difficulty is this, that the cognitive account of virtue depends on the thesis that a cognitive grasp of the good is sufficient to motivate the agent to achieve it, a thesis which, though notoriously beset by the counter-evidence of ordinary experience, is defended by nothing more than a single unsound argument (*Meno* 77–8). When we turn to the *Republic* we find Plato developing a more elaborate psychology which enables him at the least to make a serious effort to remedy these deficiencies, in that it not only provides the material for the necessary account of *eudaimonia* but also allows him to abandon the counter-intuitive claims that virtue is knowledge and that it is impossible to act contrary to one's conception of one's overall good.

ii The *Republic*

Among the many ways in which the *Republic* is innovative is its attempt at a comprehensive integration of individual psychology with political theory. That there was some connection was not, of course, a novel idea; naturalistic theories such as those of the *Protagoras* myth had shown how social institutions including morality would naturally have developed in response to the needs of individuals for protection and cooperation. According to these theories morality was therefore both social, i.e. a set of social norms, and natural, i.e. grounded in individual human needs. We saw, however, that these theories failed to show that the observance of morality by any particular individual is an intrinsic good to that individual. Plato's innovation in the *Republic* may be seen as an attempt to bridge the gap between the individual's good and that of the community by internalising the social nature of morality, in that the individual personality is itself organised on a social model, and its best state, which is the supreme good for the individual, consists in a certain social organisation.

However counter-intuitive, the social conception of individual morality is not an arbitrary construction, designed to fill a gap left by earlier theory, but has a firm theoretical base. This may be set out as follows.

1 Key evaluative predicates such as 'good', 'just', 'courageous' and 'self-controlled' are applicable to communities as well as to individuals (368e–369a).

2 Any predicate which applies both to an individual and to a community applies to the one in virtue of the same feature or features as those in virtue of which it applies to the other (435a–b).

3 Since the perfectly good individual is wise, self-controlled, courageous and just, by 2 the perfectly good community is wise, self-controlled, courageous and just (427e).

4 The perfectly good community is just in virtue of the fact that the members of the three functionally defined classes into which it is divided (rulers, military auxiliaries and economic producers) stick to the social function which defines their respective class, and to which they are fitted by their natural abilities, developed by appropriate education (433a–434c).

5 The psychology of every individual comprises a tri-partite structure of intellect, self-assertive motivation and bodily appetite corresponding to the political structure of the perfectly good community (435e–441c).

6 Therefore, by 2, 4 and 5, the perfectly good individual is just in virtue of a relation between the three elements of his or her personality corresponding to that between the classes in the perfectly good community which constitutes the justice of that community (see 4) (443c–444a).

In this derivation premise 2 has a pivotal role, mediating the inferences from the character of the individual to that of the community (step 3) and conversely (step 6). It is an *a priori* thesis, which applies to the case of the community and the individual[24] the Socratic thesis (see above, p. 55) that all the things to which a single predicate 'F' applies share a single common nature in virtue of which they are all Fs. Unfortunately for Plato the thesis is false; even leaving aside cases of simple equivocation like 'pen' or 'cape', a predicate may apply to things of different kinds, not in virtue of the fact that all the things to which it applies share a common nature, but in virtue of the fact that each kind of application relates differently to a central notion.[25] Ironically, 'just' provides a clear example. A political community is just if

---

[24] The crucial sentence (435a5–7) is 'So, if things larger and smaller are called the same, are they alike in the respect in which they are called the same, or unlike?' It is assumed without argument that the community and the individual are examples of 'things larger and smaller'.

[25] As is well known, Aristotle discovered this kind of application. See *Met.* 1003a33–b12, *EE* 1236a16–23: for discussion see Owen [928].

either it is internally organised according to just principles, or in its relations with other communities it acts according to just principles. An individual, however, is just only in the latter way, not in the former, since the notion of just principles has no application to the psychological organisation of an individual. That is because just principles assign rights and obligations to the individuals composing a community, whereas the elements in an individual's psychological organisation are not themselves individuals, and are therefore not subjects of rights and obligations. Even this very crude sketch shows that the justice of a principle is the primary application of the predicate 'just', and that communities and individuals are derivatively just in virtue of different relations to the primary application. Plato's error is twofold, first in assuming the univocity of the predicate, and secondly in applying to the individual member of a community an internal, structural model of justice appropriate to the complex social entity, not to its individual components.

The identification in step 4 of adherence to one's generic social role as the organisational principle of justice in a community may also seem very contrived, but this too has some theoretical backing. First, it depends on step 3, and therefore on premise 2, on which 3 relies to identify the traditional list of *individual* virtues (see above, p. 52) as the virtues of the perfect community. It therefore succumbs to the refutation of 2 in the preceding paragraph. But waiving that objection for the sake of argument and granting that the excellence of the perfect community consists in wisdom, courage, self-control and justice, what grounds the identification of justice with adherence to one's generic social role? Here Plato appeals to the traditional conception of social justice as each one's having his own and doing his own, i.e. that each individual should be secure in the possession of what he or she is entitled to and should not encroach on the entitlement of another (433e–434a). Traditionally this expresses an individualistic principle of ownership, but Plato transforms it into a collectivist principle of service to the community; what belongs to one is above all the contribution one makes to the common good, and to be treated unjustly is to be deprived of that contribution, and thereby of the good itself, which can be realised (for all) only if each makes (and *a fortiori* is allowed to make) his or her specific contribution to it (434a–c).

Social justice is thus redefined, via the 'doing one's own and having one's own' principle, as adherence to optimum social organisation. I shall here assume the conclusion for which I have argued elsewhere,[26] that the criterion of the optimum social organisation is the maximisation

[26] In my [368].

of *eudaimonia*, understood as the provision for every member of the community of the conditions either for the realisation of *eudaimonia* or for as close an approximation to it as the limitations of the individual's psychological capacities allow. Given that account of social justice, it follows by premise 2 that individual justice is optimal psychological organisation, which is that very state of *eudaimonia* which it is the function of social organisation to make as widely available as possible. But the claim that the good for the individual, which it is the aim of social organisation to realise, is optimum psychological organisation advances us little beyond the truism that the good is living well and doing well. It makes some advance, locating doing well in the possession of a certain psychological state, rather than in the possession of external goods, but Heraclitus (D–K 22B119) and Democritus (D–K 68B170–1) had already said as much. If the theory is to say more, and in particular if it is to provide the vindication of morality which eluded the early dialogues, it must (a) give an account of optimum psychological organisation which is both informative and acceptable and (b) justify the claim that that account is an account of individual *justice*.

Since space is lacking for even the most summary account of the psychology of the *Republic*,[27] I must be content with dogmatic statement. There are three principal[28] elements in the personality, the intellect, the bodily appetites, above all those for food, drink and sex, and a loosely defined cluster of motivations which Plato calls 'spirit' (*thumos* or *to thumoeides*), including anger, shame, ambition and a sense of honour or self-respect, all of which may be understood as aspects of a fundamental impulse of self-regard and self-assertiveness.[29] The intellect is not a purely ratiocinative faculty, but has its own motivations; hence the tri-partition is at least in part a distinction between three kinds of motivation, towards intellectual activity, self-realisation and bodily satisfaction respectively. But in addition to providing its own specific motivations the intellect has the function of directing and co-ordinating the activity of all three kinds of motivation with a view to the realisation of the agent's overall good, since only the intellect is capable of the grasp of the good presupposed by that direction and co-ordination. There are therefore two ways in which the intellect is supreme in the state of optimal psychological organisation. First, all the agent's specific desires are directed by the intellect with a view to the agent's overall good, and secondly, that good consists in a life in which the satisfaction of the specific desires of the intellect (i.e. desires for

---

[27] See, for instance, Woods [353].
[28] *Rep.* 443d7 explicitly leaves open the possibility that there may be others.
[29] See Gosling [288], ch. 3. Cf. Rawls [966].

intellectual activity) takes priority over the satisfaction of the other kinds of desire. The satisfaction of intellectual desire should be understood as neither purely theoretical nor (because purely theoretical) exclusively egoistic; according to the metaphysical system of the *Republic*, the supreme object of understanding is the Form of the good, and someone who grasps what goodness itself is is thereby motivated to realise it not merely in his own life but (by the theory of love of the *Symposium* and *Phaedrus*) in the lives of those he loves and in the community of which he is a member.

A central feature of this psychology is Plato's abandonment of the theory of uniform motivation which was presupposed in the early dialogues, and with it the Cognitive Theory of Excellence and the strong version of the unity of virtue which that theory implied. Plato no longer accepts either the strong thesis that every intentional action is aimed at the realisation of the agent's conception of his or her overall good nor the weaker thesis that whenever that conception is present it motivates, since the bodily and 'spirited' appetites motivate independently of, and even in opposition to, the conception of the overall good. Hence what makes the difference between the virtuous and the non-virtuous agent is not simply the possession by the former of a cognitive state which the latter lacks, but the possession by the former of a psychological structure lacking in the latter, in which the specific desires are appropriately responsive to the direction of the intellect. And that responsiveness is not guaranteed by the content of the intellect's direction, but requires that the specific desires should have been conditioned by the process of education described in books II–III to respond instinctively to the guidance of the intellect by loving what the intellect reveals as good and hating what it reveals as bad. Since what is manifested in the various types of virtuous conduct is no longer a single cognitive state, the former version of the unity thesis has to go. But since by the new theory it is the same psychological structure which is manifested in those types of conduct, it might seem that the strong theory could survive the shift from cognitive state to total structure, with 'courage', 'wisdom', etc. functioning as non-synonymous names of that total structure.

In fact the shift is more substantial, for two reasons. First, it seems that those names apply, not to the same total structure under different aspects, but to different aspects of the structure; thus self-control is 'a certain ordering and mastery of pleasures and appetites' (430e) while justice is the state in which each element plays its proper part in the optimal structure, wisdom is the care of the intellect for the whole (441d–e), and courage is the retention by the spirit, despite pleasures and pains, of the instructions of the intellect about what is to be feared and what is not (442c). While justice and self-control are hard to distinguish on this account (except that the terms are non-synonymous), courage and wisdom are not the total structure itself but aspects of it, ascribed in the first instance to particular elements of that structure. Secondly, the possibility of disorderly appetite indicates that while self-control and justice are not only mutually necessitating but severally impossible without wisdom, the possession of wisdom does not guarantee self-control. It appears, then, that the psychology of the *Republic* requires the abandonment of the unity of virtue doctrine, in that even the weakest form of that doctrine, the thesis that anyone who possesses any of the virtues necessarily possesses them all, has to be replaced by a still weaker thesis, namely that courage, self-control and justice all require wisdom (and perhaps require one another also), but wisdom does not guarantee the presence of the other virtues.

Does Plato give us adequate reason to accept that this psychological organisation is in fact optimal? To do so he has to show that each of the elements in the psychological structure functions at its best when co-ordinated by the intellect so as to make the appropriate contribution to a life where the highest priority is given to the pursuit of intellectual satisfactions. We may accept on the basis of the argument against Callicles (see above) that a satisfactory life is possible for the individual only if his or her potentially conflicting motivations are intentionally co-ordinated, which is a rational process requiring the identification of priorities and long-term goals. But we need further argument to show that the supreme long-term goal of the optimal life must be the theoretical understanding of reality (of which the primary object of understanding is goodness), and the realisation of that understanding in practical, including political, life. Plato attempts to meet this challenge by arguing in book ix that the life devoted to those goals is the pleasantest life possible, but his arguments are unsatisfactory. He gives two main arguments: the first (famously recalled by Mill in *Utilitarianism*) is that the devotee of intellectual pleasures is the appropriate judge of which life is the pleasantest, since he has experience of the pleasures of appetite and ambition (the dominant goals of the rival lives), whereas the adherents of those pleasures lack experience of intellectual pleasures. This argument fails because experience of the pleasures of a life requires commitment to the activities and the values constituting that life, but the intellectual is as remote from immersion in the rival lives as the rivals are from the intellectual life. The second argument depends on the conception of pleasure as the making good of a deficiency in the organism (for example hunger is a state of bodily depletion and ignorance a state of intellectual depletion, and the pleasures of satisfying hunger and of discovery are the processes of making good the respective depletions). Plato uses this model to make two basic points, whose relation to one another is obscure; the first is that since the state of bodily depletion is painful, what we think of as bodily pleasures are in fact mostly episodes of getting rid of pain, not genuine pleasure. The second is that whereas bodily deficiencies cannot be properly or genuinely made good, intellectual deficiencies can be. Leaving aside the question of the adequacy of the depletion model in general, its application in this argument is highly obscure, since it is unclear whether the inferiority of bodily pleasures is supposed to lie in the fact that they require to be repeated (since, for instance, one gets hungry again a few hours after having eaten) or in the alleged insatiability of the desires which they presuppose (so that one can never get enough food) or simply in the alleged confusion between bodily pleasure and the getting rid of bodily distress. If the point is the latter, Plato's diagnosis of the alleged confusion is itself confused, since the depletion model yields the result that the process of making good the depletion is pleasant, irrespective of whether the depletion is painful. Hence whenever the depletion *is* painful, getting rid of that painful lack will be genuinely pleasant, and there will be no confusion of genuine pleasure with something else, namely the getting rid of pain. If, on the other hand, the target is the insatiability of bodily desires, the alleged fact should be denied; normal bodily desires are not insatiable, unless 'insatiable' is reinterpreted as 'recurrent', in which case the point is after all the first, i.e. that bodily desires are recurrent whereas intellectual desires are not. But with respect to that point it is not clear that the need for recurrent satisfaction differentiates a life devoted to bodily satisfactions from one devoted to intellectual; no doubt a truth once discovered does not have to be rediscovered, but a meal once eaten does not have to be eaten over again, and an intellectual *life* will require repeated acts of thought (whether new discoveries or the recapitulation of truths already known) no less than a life of bodily satisfactions will require repeated episodes of bodily pleasure. (The point also applies to the pleasures of the life of ambition, which is for the purposes of the argument required to share the defects of the life of bodily pleasure, but which is in fact barely mentioned.)[30]

Plato does not, then, succeed in establishing the optimality of his preferred psychological structure. Does he fare any better in showing that that structure captures the nature of justice as a virtue of the agent? Since his account of justice is avowedly revisionary, he cannot be held to the requirement to show that the presence of that structure in an agent is necessary and sufficient for that person's being just by ordinary standards.

---

[30] For fuller discussion of the arguments of *Rep.* IX see Annas [325], ch. 12; Gosling and Taylor [53], chs. 6 and 17.2; Stokes [119].

Someone who conforms consistently to ordinary morality as it is depicted by Glaucon[31] is just by ordinary standards but not by Plato's, since his commitment to justice is conditioned, not by acceptance of the value of justice for itself, but by the belief that he could not succeed in doing what he would really like to do, viz. to promote his own interests at the expense of others. The most that can be required is that Plato should show that the presence of the structure is sufficient for the performance of a sufficient range of central cases of just dealing and the corresponding avoidance of unjust dealing. At 442e–443a Socrates asserts that the Platonically just agent will never commit any major crime such as theft, sacrilege, treason or adultery, and while he gives no argument we may concede that the control of appetite which characterises such an agent will make him proof against the standard temptations to such wickedness. Moreover, as we saw, his love for the good will make him concerned for the good of others and for that of the community. How, then, could he fail to be just by conventional standards?[32]

The flaw in the theory is that the structure itself defines the good for the agent; hence concern for the good of others and for that of the community is concern to maintain that structure in others and the corresponding structure in the community. Consequently just actions are redefined as whatever actions serve to create and preserve that structure, and unjust as whatever destroy it (443e). That redefinition clearly licenses substantial interference with the autonomy of others, with a view to the promotion of their own good (as redefined) or the good of the community; indeed, if the setting up of the ideal Platonic state required extermination and enslavement of whole populations, by this account such acts would be just (not merely permitted, but required). This is explicitly acknowledged in the text: at 540e–541a Socrates recommends the foundation of the ideal state by the process of expelling the whole population of an existing city over the age of ten, taking the children from their parents and bringing them up in the educational system which he has just described. Plainly the forced evacuation of an entire city and the enforced separation of a complete generation are acts of extreme violence, which could not in practice be perpetrated without considerable loss of life. As regards loss of autonomy, the subjection of the lowest class in the ideal state is complete enough for their state to be

---

[31] This assumes that ordinary morality is not so confused as to make consistent adherence to it impossible. It is not clear that Plato would accept that charitable assumption; the arguments against the accounts of justice proposed in *Republic* I by Cephalus and Polemarchus suggest that he thinks that ordinary moral beliefs are thoroughly confused.

[32] See Sachs [363]; Demos [357]; Vlastos [365]; Irwin [293], ch. 7, secs. 10–11 and 19.

described as one of slavery (590c–d); it is, of course, paternalistic slavery, since it is better for the lower classes to be enslaved to those who have their good at heart and who know what that good is than to be enslaved to their own lower nature and to mistaken conceptions of what is good for them. Yet it is slavery none the less, since in the last resort the direction of their lives rests not with their own intellect and will, but with those of the rulers. The Platonically just agent will not, therefore, be unjust from the vulgar motives of private gain or personal lust, but he will not be just for all that. The form of injustice to which he will be prone is something much more terrible, the enforcement of an ideology which, in virtue of its comprehensiveness and its redefinition of benevolence, admits no limitation in the name of individual liberty, and is therefore liable to press its claims to the extremes of tyranny.[33]

iii Developments subsequent to the *Republic*

The ethical theory of the *Republic* represents Plato's most sustained attempt to vindicate the claims of morality. Subsequent developments in his ethical thought narrowly conceived (i.e. as distinct from political theory, which requires separate treatment) amount to modifications of detail, not to any radical shift of view. They may therefore be dealt with briefly.

The second of the two stages which we have distinguished in the development of Plato's ethical thought was marked off from the earlier by the abandonment of the 'Socratic' theory of uniform motivation and hence by the rejection of the Cognitive Theory of Excellence and the thesis of the unity of virtue. In the dialogues subsequent to the *Republic* the non-uniform character of motivation is even more strongly emphasised, while in the *Statesman* he insists on the *dis*unity of virtue (see below, p. 74). These developments may be attributed in part to an increasing sense of the dichotomy, already present but not dominant in the *Republic* (611a–d), between the rational element in the personality, motivated by the good and only contingently and temporarily embodied, and the

---

[33] Plato is quite explicit in drawing the implication at *Statesman* 293c–d:

> [T]he only constitution worthy of the name . . . must be the one in which the rulers are . . . men really possessed of the scientific understanding of the art of government. Then we must not take into consideration whether their rule be by laws or without them over willing or unwilling subjects or whether they themselves be rich or poor men.
>
> No.
>
> They may purge the city for its better health by putting some of the citizens to death or banishing others. (tr. Skemp from [385])

A similar view is expressed at *Laws* 735b–736c.

non-rational spirit and appetites, which spring from the body and are motivated independently of the good.[34] To the extent that the reason is identified with the real self, spirit and appetite come to be seen rather as alien forces requiring to be kept in subjection by reason than as manifestations of a uniformly rational agency. This allows Plato, despite having abandoned the thesis that knowledge of what is best is sufficient for doing what is best, to continue to maintain the second of the Socratic paradoxes, that no one voluntarily acts wrongly. Contrary to the Socratic position, action against one's better judgement is possible; but such action is not voluntary, since the agent (= the rational self) is overwhelmed by external forces, i.e. the non-rational passions (*Timaeus* 86e, *Laws* 734b, 860–3). On the Socratic model, all purported cases of action against one's better judgement had to be explained as cases of intellectual error; Plato now recognises that some cases have to be explained by a mismatch between intellectual judgement and passion, but saves the doctrine by counting such mismatches as sources of involuntary action.[35] That saving move has its cost, in that it breaks up the unity of the agent, but Plato's dichotomy of rational and non-rational elements in the personality, itself a reflection of the more fundamental dichotomy of rationally apprehended reality and the imperfectly rational material world, already encourages that split. The split is, however, fatal to the project of vindicating morality by showing it to be constitutive of the best life for the agent. For morality concerns the embodied agent, whereas the best life for the agent is the discarnate life of pure thought (*Tim.* 90). The most that Plato could hope to provide by way of vindication of morality would therefore be the claim that immorality as ordinarily conceived hinders the achievement of that life (*Tim.* 90).

This fundamental dichotomy tends to drive Plato further from the doctrine of the unity of virtue: if wisdom is in the last analysis the activity of the immortal 'real self' and courage, self-control and justice different

---

[34] In the *Phaedo* the appetitive and spirited motivations are attributed to the body (66b–c, 68b–c), which is sharply distinguished from the (rational) soul, whose task is to master and control the body (80a). The rational soul is implicitly identified with the self: the survival of the self is the survival of the soul, and the task of the philosopher is to prepare for what is ordinarily thought of as death, but which is in fact the fullness of life, free from the distractions of the body (64c–69e). While it might seem obvious that on this model also the motivations of the body are independent of the good, it is not clear that that is so, since the body is also described as a source of illusions, i.e. false beliefs (81b, 83d). Hence the spurious morality of the non-philosopher, guided by a calculation of bodily pleasures (68b–69c), is, although undoubtedly a state of enslavement of the soul to the body, nevertheless not incompatible with the Socratic theory of motivation.

[35] R. M. Hare makes the same move in [948], ch. 5 (modified in [949], 23–4, 58–60).

aspects of the subjection of the mortal and non-rational by that self, then the connection between the virtues has been loosened to the extent that, so far from being in any sense the same virtue, they are no longer even virtues of literally the same subject. Rather, the perfection of the real self requires, contingently and temporarily, the co-operation of the mortal self. This co-operation consists in the exercise of the four cardinal virtues, wisdom, *sōphrosunē*, justice and courage (*Laws* 631c), as is brought out in a later passage (653a–c) describing the general aim of education. This is essentially that of the primary education of the *Republic*, so to train the motivational impulses by means of the basic stimuli of pleasure and pain that the child comes to like what reason dictates and to hate what reason forbids. The affective responses are formed before the rational judgements, but when the child is mature enough to form those judgements they agree with the content of the affective responses 'and this agreement as a whole is *aretē*' (653b6). This formula may plausibly suggest an account of what courage, *sōphrosunē* and justice have in common; each is an agreement between a specific motivational impulse and a rational judgement,[36] or (perhaps closer to the theory of the *Republic*) each is an aspect of a state of agreement between the agent's motivations taken globally and the deliverances of his or her reason. There is, however, still the problem of what wisdom itself has in common with those virtues whose essence consists in agreement between the non-rational and wisdom. It may be a sense of this difficulty which prompts Plato to say at the end of the work (963) that while it is not hard to see how the virtues differ from one another, it is a real problem to explain how states as different as courage and wisdom are one, i.e. to determine what they have in common; this problem he leaves unanswered.

I suggest that this problem reflects Plato's difficulties in fitting his account of virtue to his sense of the dichotomy between the mortal and immortal elements in the soul. That same difficulty is also, I think, reflected in another feature of the treatment of the virtues in the later dialogues, namely that Plato sometimes reverts to the earlier 'Presocratic' tradition of treating them as separable components of excellence, as when he asserts that the state in which justice, wisdom (*phronēsis*) and *sōphrosunē* are 'unified together with courage' is better than courage alone (630a–b), citing as an example of the latter, as Protagoras had done in opposition to Socrates (*Prot.* 349d), the

---

[36] Compare Aristotle's account of the conditions of correct choice in *EN* 1139a22–6: 'since excellence of character is a disposition concerned with choice, and choice is deliberative desire, for this reason the judgement (*logos*) must be true and the desire right, if the choice is to be good, and the one must say the same thing as the other pursues'.

courage of wicked and licentious soldiers (cf. 696b–e). The conception of courage as a non-rational impulse combating fear, to be found even in animals (cf. *Lach.* 197a–b), recurs at *Laws* 963e and at *Statesman* 306. In the latter passage the Eleatic Stranger goes out of his way to emphasise the *unho-mogeneity* of the specific virtues, by first stating the conventional view of courage and *sōphrosunē* as parts of total excellence, and then urging the 'unfamiliar' thesis (306b13) that they are hostile and opposed to each other, in the sense that courage, understood as an aggressive impulse, is opposed to *sōphrosunē*, understood as an impulse to quiet and unassertive behaviour. It is the task of the statesman to devise forms of education and political institutions which will harmonise these opposed impulses for the benefit of the individual and the community. Here once again we see Plato apparently reverting to conceptions of the specific virtues which were rejected in the early dialogues, courage as aggressiveness in *Laches* (197a–b), *sōphrosunē* as quietness in *Charmides* (159b–160b).[37] In so doing he ignores the crucial distinction between motivational drives and the proper organisation of those in the integrated personality which was one of the main achievements of his mature theory, and thereby generates a spurious paradox. Aggressiveness may indeed be opposed to quietness, but courage is not opposed to *sōphro-sunē*, since both are aspects of a structure of motivations organised under the direction of the intellect.

[37] There is even a trace of these conceptions in *Meno* 88a–c, where Socrates, arguing that knowledge is the only unconditional good, includes the virtues of *sōphrosunē*, courage and justice (as well as learning, good memory, personal splendour 'and everything of that kind') among the things which are good only on condition that they are directed by knowledge (i.e. directed aright), but which are harmful if misdirected. But in fact this passage seems to draw the very distinction between motivational drive and virtue proper which is blurred in the later dialogues. For Socrates asks Meno whether, if it is not the case that the virtues are sometimes beneficial and sometimes harmful, they can be anything other than knowledge. For instance, if courage is not intelligence (*phronēsis*) but a sort of boldness, is it not the case that when someone is bold without thought (*nous*) he is harmed, but when he is bold with thought he is benefited? After citing the examples of *sōphrosunē* and learning Socrates concludes as follows (c1–5):

> So to sum up, all the undertakings and endurances of the soul result in *eudaimonia* if they are directed by intelligence, but in the opposite if they are directed by folly.
> So it seems.
> If excellence, then, is one of the things in the soul and it is necessary that it should be beneficial, it must be intelligence . . .

'Undertakings and endurances of the soul', i.e. the acts which one is prompted to by motivational drives, are clearly distinguished from excellence, which is identified as knowledge. It follows that courage, for example, which is acknowledged to be a part of excellence (see above), is not itself a motivational drive such as boldness, but is itself knowledge.

I confess to being puzzled as to why Plato should have blurred this distinction (which is central to Aristotle's theory of virtue as well as to Plato's own) in his later writings; all that I can suggest is that his sense of the discontinuity between the rational and immortal elements in the personality on the one hand and the non-rational and mortal on the other may have made him uncomfortable with accounts of the specific virtues as modifications of the latter by the directive activity of the former. According to the theory of the *Republic*, the specific virtues, while no longer a single virtue as in the early dialogues, are still virtues of a single subject; yet the argument of *Rep.* x.611b–d that since the soul is immortal and what is immortal cannot be composite the tri-partite soul is not the true soul leads to the conclusion that the tri-partite soul is not a genuine unity, but rather an adventitious agglomerate of disparate elements, like the sea-god Glaucus overgrown with shells and weed. If Plato takes that conclusion seriously, then there is no single subject for all the specific virtues; wisdom is an attribute of the immortal soul, and the other virtues attributes of the mortal elements, which may have made it easier to revert sometimes to the traditional view of them as non-rational impulses, requiring the direction of reason to attain the status of true virtues. Of course, one *need* not conceive of them in that way, since the dualistic conception of the soul still allows the alternative (closer to the Aristotelian view) that, for example, 'courage' is not the name of a non-rational impulse requiring to be modified by reason, but the name of the state of having that impulse properly modified by reason, which seems to be the view which predominates in the *Laws*. There seems, then, to be evidence of some vacillation in the conception of the virtues in the later dialogues, which may perhaps be explained by the increased influence in this period of the dichotomy between the rational and non-rational in Plato's view of the soul.

The above account of the 'moral' virtues as consisting in agreement between affective responses and rational judgement, produced by the pre-rational training of the non-rational elements in the personality, has close and obvious affinities with Aristotle's theory, on which it was doubtless an influence. Another similarity between Plato's later theory and Aristotle's is found in the section of the *Laws* (660e–663d) where the Athenian Stranger discusses the requirement in an adequate code of legislation to show that the good man will be *eudaimōn* and the wicked wretched. Since the point of this provision in a code of legislation is to motivate people to obey the law, it is assumed, in line with the generally hedonistic account of motivation which is taken for granted in the *Laws* (see, for example, 636d–e) that the appropriate way to show that the good agent will be *eudaimōn* is to show that his or her life will be pleasant, and the rival lives unpleasant. The strategy is that of

Rep. ix, but the arguments have none of the metaphysical elaboration of those employed there. Instead, the Stranger argues simply that everyone sees his or her own preferred life as pleasantest from its own perspective, and that the correct perspective from which the assessment should be made is that of the virtuous agent (663b–d). No attempt is made to support this principle; Plato does not, for instance, employ the analogy, to which Aristotle sometimes appeals (see, for instance, *EN* 1173b22–5, 1176a8–22), with the perception of the healthy as the criterion of correctness in judgements of sensible qualities such as colour or taste.

The central theme of this chapter has been Plato's attempt to anchor morality on the 'natural' side of the nature–convention dichotomy by grounding it in an adequate theory of human nature. That theory develops from the optimistic over-simplification of the early dialogues to the more complex psychology of the middle and later periods, leading to a picture of the virtuous agent as one who achieves through intellectual and emotional training the right fit between intellectual judgement and affective response. That picture of the ideally developed agent was perhaps Plato's most important legacy to his successors, from Aristotle through the Stoics to Christian theorists and their post-Christian followers. But the theory underlying the picture faced the problems (a) of giving an account of the element of intellectual judgement which would justify its claim to truth and (b) of defending the integrity of the personality against the threat of dualism, in which the intellect arrogates value to itself, and the affective elements in the personality are correspondingly devalued along with the body. Plato himself solved neither problem: both are visible in Aristotle, Stoicism and Christianity, while at least the former remains to trouble their 'realist' successors.[38]

---

[38] The final version of this chapter was submitted to the editor in December 1990.

4
Aristotle on nature and value

STEPHEN EVERSON

In the last twenty years or so, the account of happiness given in the *Nicomachean Ethics* (*EN*) must have received as much scholarly attention as has ever been given to any philosophical treatment of anything.[1] Not all commentators, however, are agreed that what Aristotle has to say there about happiness is sufficiently interesting to merit intense critical scrutiny. So, Sir Anthony Kenny, who has himself written quite extensively on the topic, concludes that

> Aristotle's belief that the pursuit of happiness must be the pursuit of a single dominant aim, and his account of the nature of philosophy, seem to be both so seriously mistaken as to make unprofitable a discussion of his arguments that happiness consists in *theoria*.[2]

On Kenny's reading of the *EN*, Aristotle begins by assuming that the good life will be one in which the agent centres his life on a particular good and finishes by identifying that good as the activity of *theōria*, intellectual activity.[3] Understandably, Kenny finds this view of happiness far from compelling.

---

[1] The literature is now indeed so vast that it would be foolhardy to attempt to signal all disagreements, and the reasons for them, with even just the most important work, and I have duly tried to limit my dealings with that literature to those items which will cast some illumination on the issues. That a discussion is not referred to here should not be taken as any sign at all of how important it is.

[2] Kenny [521], 58.

[3] To avoid too much transliteration, I shall generally translate Aristotle's term *eudaimonia* rather than just transliterate it. I shall use the terms 'happiness', 'the good life' and 'living well' indiscriminately. The danger of using the term 'happiness' in this context will be minimal so long as one does not think of it as denoting merely contentment – indeed, the use of 'happiness' as a translation of *eudaimonia* may help to rescue the English term from the assumption that it must denote a state whose conditions of ascription vary depending on the vagaries of an individual's desires.

In reading Aristotle in this way, Kenny stands on one side of a long-running debate about what conception of happiness underlies the argument of the *EN*. In contrast to Kenny, many scholars have maintained that the conception of happiness in place until book x is rather an 'inclusive' one – i.e. one which would allow many goods to be included within happiness as its constituents. On this view, the good life would not consist implausibly in the pursuit of just one activity, but would rather involve many different sorts of valuable activity.[4] The problem with this is that, whilst it certainly offers Aristotle a more plausible view of happiness, it apparently does so at the cost of forcing a rift between the doctrine of *EN* x and that of the earlier books. This creates a dilemma which is fastened on by Kenny when, in his more recent *Aristotle on the Perfect Life*, he issues what is in effect a challenge to any sympathetic interpreter of the *EN*: 'No explanation [of Aristotle's argument] succeeds in the three goals which most commentators have set themselves: (1) to give an interpretation of book I and book 10 which does justice to the texts severally; (2) to make the two books consistent with each other; (3) to make the resulting interpretation one which can be found morally acceptable by contemporary philosophers.'[5] Given Aristotle's apparent rejection of an inclusive account of happiness in *EN* x, the interpretative options are to convict him either of inconsistency (by adopting an 'inclusive' interpretation of the earlier books) or of consistent implausibility. Either way, the *EN*, taken as a whole, does not provide an account of happiness which can be taken seriously.

In this chapter, I shall try to meet Kenny's challenge and to show that it is possible, even without violating the texts, to provide a reading of Aristotle's claims about happiness in the *EN* according to which he does hold a consistent view of what constitutes the good life for man – and one which, in its principles at least, is worthy of continued philosophical attention. My reading of Aristotle's argument will diverge from what I take to be interpretative orthodoxy in two main respects. I shall deny that in x.7 Aristotle does in fact recommend the life which is devoted to intellectual activity as the good for man – thus allowing *EN* x to be consistent with an inclusive reading of book I. I shall also call into question the claim that Aristotle thinks that one can discover what it is to be happy by determining what it is to be human. The account of happiness in the *EN* is, I shall argue, neither an intellectualist nor a naturalistic one.

In its concentration on the argument of the *Nicomachean Ethics*, this discussion will seem a overly traditional one. Thanks in particular to Kenny's work on the *Eudemian Ethics* (*EE*), scholars have been made more aware of

---

[4] See Ackrill [508]. For a helpful overview, see Crisp [511].   [5] Kenny [457], 93.

the fact that students of Aristotle's ethical theory need to look more widely than simply at the *EN*. Four ethical treatises have come down to us under the name of Aristotle: the *EN*, the *EE*, the *Magna Moralia* (*MM*) and *On Virtues and Vices*. Of these, the last is universally accepted as spurious, and the *MM* is generally regarded as merely Aristotelian rather than by Aristotle himself.[6] Of the other two treatises, the *EN* has generally been considered the more important and the *EE* treated 'either as spurious or as an earlier, and inferior, attempt to produce an ethical theory'.[7] Determining the relationship between the two works is complicated, however, by the fact that books v–vii of the *EN* also appear in the manuscripts as books iv–vi of the *EE*. Although these common books have been almost universally taken to belong to the *EN*, Kenny's *The Aristotelian Ethics*, published in 1978, presented a serious challenge to this orthodoxy, arguing that these books should properly form part of the *EE* rather than the *EN* and that, with these included, the *EE* has 'as serious claim as the [*EN*] to be considered Aristotle's final and considered system of ethics'.[8] Although I shall indeed concentrate on the *EN* here, this should not be taken to prejudge the issue of which work is the more important or the more considered. Since the account of happiness in the *EE* is certainly an inclusive one – he there talks quite explicitly of happiness as having parts (1.5. 1216a37–b2)[9] – it is the *EN* which provides evidence for attributing to Aristotle the commitment to a dominant and intellectualist conception of *eudaimonia*, and thus it is this work which requires the more careful handling if such a reading of Aristotle is to be rejected. It will, of course, be a further advantage of the interpretation offered here that it allows the position of the *EN* to be not only internally consistent but also broadly consistent with Aristotle's other ethical and political writings.

1 The final end

> Verbally there is very general agreement; for both the general run of people and those of superior refinement say that [the highest of all goods achievable by action] is happiness, and identify living well and faring well with being happy; but with regard to what happiness is they differ, and the many do not give the same account as the wise.   (EN 1.4.1095a17–22)[10]

---

[6] For discussions of the provenance of the *MM*, see Cooper [445] and Kenny [438], 217 ff.   [7] Kenny [438], 1.

[8] Kenny [457], appendix 1, p. 113. For criticisms of Kenny's argument, see the reviews by Irwin [442] and Cooper [441]. Kenny provides rejoinders to these in appendix 1 of his [457].

[9] See also the end of 1.2, where Aristotle complains that a common mistake is to take the necessary conditions for happiness to be its parts.

[10] Translations are from Barnes [401], but I have felt free to make changes.

Happiness is agreed by all to be the highest good: where people disagree is over what they take happiness, or living well, to consist in. Determining where the truth lies on this question is what will occupy Aristotle for the rest of book I and in book X. His first move, however, is formally to identify happiness with what he has established in I.1–2 to be the object of political science: the final end of action – that which is desired for its own sake and for which everything else is desired.

Aristotle moves into his discussion of what the good life consists in by reflecting on the nature of action. Starting from the fact that every action has a goal – is performed for the sake of some good (*EN* I,I.1094a1–2) – he proceeds to note first that the ends of actions can form a hierarchy[11] and then to claim that there is a final end of action. The last step is crucial to the argument of the *EN*, but it is hardly a step which seems immediately secure. It is one thing to claim that every action is goal-directed and quite another to claim that all actions aim at the same goal.

Right at the start of I.1, however, Aristotle seems to conflate these two claims.[12] He states that 'the good has rightly been declared to be that at which all things aim' on the grounds that 'every action and choice (and art and inquiry) is thought to aim at some good' (1094a1–3).[13] Aristotle's switch here between claiming that each action aims at some good to his talk of *the* good as that at which everything aims seems either to ignore the distinction between the two claims or, fallaciously, to assume that the second follows from the first. Both these problems can be avoided, however, if we take 'the good' here not as a name of the final good but rather as a term referring to goods in general.[14] Aristotle would then not already be endorsing the claim that there is some one thing at which all actions aim, but rather making the point that whatever is a good is something which is (such as) to be aimed at in action.

Unfortunately, this seems only to postpone the problem – for at the beginning of I.2, he does present an argument for the existence of a final end, and here the apparent fallacy is less easily managed.

---

[11] 'The end of the medical art is health, that of shipbuilding a vessel, that of strategy victory, that of economics wealth. But where such arts fall under a single capacity . . . the ends of the master arts are to be preferred to all the subordinate ends; for it is for the sake of the former that the latter are pursued' (I.1.1094a8–10; 14–16).

[12] So, Anscombe, in [932], 34, claims that 'there appears to be an illicit transition in Aristotle, from 'all chains must stop somewhere' to 'there is somewhere where all chains stop'.   [13] See also *MM* I.1.

[14] For the ambiguity enjoyed by terms formed by coupling the definite article with a neuter adjective, see, for instance, Bostock [918], 104. Bostock calls the two different usages 'naming' and 'generalising'.

If, then, there is some end of the things we do, which we desire for its own sake (everything else being desired for the sake of this), and if we do not choose everything for the sake of something other than itself (for at that rate the process would go on to infinity, so that our desire would be empty and vain), clearly this must be the good, that is the chief good.
(*EN* 1,2.1094a18–22)

As it stands, of course, the claim is merely a conditional one: *if* there is something which is desired for itself and for which everything else is also desired, *then* this is the chief good. It is clear enough, however, that Aristotle takes himself to have shown that there is a chief good, as he proceeds immediately to affirm that his project is to determine what that chief good is:

Will not the knowledge of it, then, have a great influence on life? Shall we not, like archers, who have a mark to aim at, be more likely to hit upon what we should? If so, we must try, in outline at least, to determine what it is, and of which of the sciences or capacities it is the object.
(*EN* 1,2.1094a22–6)

Since a principal task of the *EN* is precisely to elucidate the nature of this chief good, there can be little doubt that Aristotle accepts both that there is such a thing and that he has just been talking about it.[15] Given this, we need to see the middle of the opening sentence of 1.2 as providing an argument for the truth of the antecedent of the conditional, and thus also for its consequent.

The argument works as a *reductio*. It cannot be the case that everything is desired only for the sake of something else, since if this were the case, desire itself would be 'empty and vain' – which it manifestly is not.[16] Since, therefore, it is not the case that everything is only desired as a means to something other than itself, there is a chief good. It is this last step which appears to reimport the fallacy which was just avoided at the start of 1.1. All the argument will give Aristotle is the conclusion that there is *at least* one thing which is desired for itself. It does not give him the claim that there is *only* one thing which is desired for itself – and this is what he needs if he is to show that there is some good for which everything else is desired.

We cannot assume, of course, that Aristotle was incapable of fallacious

---

[15] He proceeds to identify the final end as the object of political science, which is 'the most authoritative art and most truly the master art' (1094a26–8).

[16] The point is not just that if everything were only desired as a means to something else, one would never be able to satisfy one's desires but also that nothing would be truly desired. If something is merely instrumentally valuable, then its value is parasitic on the value of something else: if everything is only instrumentally valuable, then there is nothing to put value into the system.

reasoning but it must be noted that the fallacy here is one which is particularly gross – not least because it is so obvious. It is as if, having shown that everyone has a father, Aristotle were to take this to entail that there is one father who is the father of everyone. When Aristotle says in 1.3 that it is 'the mark of an educated person to look for precision in each class of things just so far as the nature of the subject admits', thereby warning that 'in speaking of [ethical] subjects, we must be content to indicate the truth roughly and in outline', he is certainly not intending to license this sort of logical blunder. If there is a way to read this passage which will absolve Aristotle of this fallacy, there will be strong reason to accept it.

One way out would be to take the claim that not everything is chosen for something else as a consequence of, rather than a reason for, the claim that there is a final end, for which everything else is pursued.[17] This is not an attractive option, since it makes Aristotle support a reasonably uncontroversial claim (which is anyway supported by the *reductio*) with a highly controversial claim – and this would hardly be good argumentative practice. In contrast, if we take the filling of the sentence to provide an argument for the antecedent of the first conditional, then Aristotle can be seen quite rightly to be attempting to secure a controversial thesis (but one to which he is committed and on which his project depends) on claims which cannot reasonably be disputed.

We seem, then, to be presented with an uncomfortable interpretative choice: either Aristotle assumes without argument the apparently implausible claim that there is a final end for which everything is done or he does provide an argument for that claim – but an argument which is obviously fallacious.[18] The way to escape this unpleasant dilemma is to recognise that Aristotle's move from the claim that there is at least one thing which is desired for itself to the claim that there is some one thing for which everything else is desired is fallacious only if one thinks that the final good must be the same sort of thing as other goods. If, however, we accept that Aristotle takes happiness to be something which *includes* those things which are desirable in themselves, then the apparent fallacy in his argument disappears. For if the final end were, for instance, the set of things which are themselves

---

[17] This is advocated, for instance, by B. Williams in his [503], 292.

[18] Williams [503] supports his reading of the passage by claiming that it would be uncharitable to take Aristotle as arguing here for the existence of a final good. The present considerations show that neither option can be recommended by charity. He also (p. 295) claims that the *ergon* argument of 1.7 provides an independent argument for the claim that there is a final end. I attempt to show that this is false in the next section. Even on the orthodox understanding of that argument, however, it is difficult to see how it is supposed to support the claim that there is some one end for which all actions are performed.

intrinsically valuable, it would follow from the fact that there is at least one thing which is intrinsically valuable that there is such a set – even if, for all that has been said, it has only one member. Thus, even at the beginning of the *EN*, before Aristotle has said anything substantive at all about the content of the good life, he must be seen as operating with an inclusive notion of happiness.[19]

The difference between happiness and other goods is highlighted by a passage from 1.7, where Aristotle lays out as requirements for the highest good that it be 'self-sufficient' (*autarkes*) and 'most final' (*teleiotaton*).

> The self-sufficient we now define as that which all by itself makes life desirable and lacking in nothing; and such we think happiness to be; and further we think it most desirable of all things, without being counted as one good thing among others – if it were so counted it would clearly be made more desirable by the addition of even the least of goods; for that which is added becomes an extra good, and of goods the greater is always more desirable.
>
> (*EN* 1.7.1097b14–20)

To attain happiness is to lack nothing which would make one's life better, and so happiness is not to be counted as one good amongst many, otherwise one could add a further good to it and the resulting combination would be preferable to happiness taken by itself. The best way to make sense of the claim that happiness is not to be counted as a good in the way that other goods are is to take it to have an inclusive nature – so that, in so far as something is desirable, it thereby becomes a part of happiness, is included within it. In this way one could not add a good to happiness, since, if it is a good, it is thereby a constituent of happiness. Were it not contained within happiness, then happiness would lack something, and this by definition it does not.[20]

This requirement of completeness is imposed by the role of happiness as the final end. The ends of action, on Aristotle's view, have degrees of finality:

> Since there are evidently more than one end, and we choose some of these for the sake of something else, clearly not all ends are final ends; but the chief good is evidently something final ... Now, we call that which is in itself

---

[19] Ackrill [508], 25–6, sees that the beginning of 1.2 is evidence for Aristotle's accepting an inclusive notion of happiness, but takes this to 'explain and excuse' the fallacy rather than to remove it.

[20] It should be noted that this construal of 1097b14 f. is a contested one: for the ambiguity of the passage and a different reading, see Kenny [457], 24 f. It is worth noting that *MM* 1.3 provides some support for the reading given: 'For happiness is composed of certain goods. But to raise the question whether a given thing is better than its own components is absurd. For happiness is not something else apart from these, but just these' (1184a26–9).

> worthy of pursuit more final than that which is worthy of pursuit for the
> sake of something else, and that which is never desirable for the sake of
> something else more final than the things that are desirable both in them-
> selves and for the sake of that other thing, and therefore we call final
> without qualification that which is always desirable in itself and never for
> the sake of something else.   (*EN* I.7.1097a25–8; 30–4)

When I perform an action, it will always make sense to ask why I am doing
it (since every action is done for the sake of some goal): when I specify the
goal of the action, it will often make sense to ask further *why* I want to
achieve that goal. In the case of the final end, however, to ask why an agent
wants to achieve that is to ask a question which can receive no answer, since,
whilst one can perform actions for the sake of happiness, and pursue goals
because they will help to attain happiness, one does not – and cannot – want
happiness for the sake of anything else. 'But why do you want to be happy?'
is simply not an intelligible question.[21]

What is important here is that there are some things which are desired
both for their own sakes *and* for the sake of happiness:

> Now such a thing [i.e. final without qualification] happiness, above all else,
> is held to be, for this we choose always for itself and never for the sake of
> something else, but honour, pleasure, reason, and every excellence we
> choose indeed for themselves (for if nothing resulted from them we should
> still choose each of them), but we choose them also for the sake of happi-
> ness, judging that through them we shall be happy. (*EN* I.7.1097a34–b5)

If one follows through an agent's reasons for performing a particular action,
one will come, either immediately or eventually, to a goal which is desirable
in itself – for instance that the action was virtuous or pleasurable or would
elicit honour. It is *through* achieving such things as virtue and pleasure,
however, that one achieves happiness. Although nothing more is needed to
make an action intelligible than to claim that it was virtuous or pleasurable,
it still makes sense to add that one was also acting for the sake of happiness.
The assertion that it is believed to be through such things as these that we
are happy suggests that Aristotle's criterion for inclusion within the
constituents of happiness is that one would choose that good even if nothing
further came of it. Thus, anything which is intrinsically valuable will be a
part of happiness, and happiness must include every type of thing which is
intrinsically valuable. The point is that the constituents of happiness do not
derive their value from the role they play in the achievement of happiness;

---

[21] Of course, if we have antecedently identified happiness with some putative good,
such as contentment, then the question may be intelligible. It is not when
happiness is taken to have the formal properties Aristotle assigns to *eudaimonia*.

rather, they are able to play that role just because they are worth pursuing for themselves. There is reason to act virtuously even if, for some reason or other, this will not in fact play a part in making the agent happy.[22] Happiness, in contrast, could not be the only good – for there would be nothing to give it content. Its value is parasitic on the value of its constituents, despite the fact that it is the final end of action. How this is so will be clearer once we have considered Aristotle's claims about the value of intellectual activity and of external goods.

2 Human nature

If the argument of the previous section is correct, then Aristotle's claims about what is valuable and worth pursuing are secured upon considerations of what we do choose and pursue; and hence what we find intelligible to choose and pursue. What makes virtue a constituent of the good life is that we desire it for its own sake – and, since the good life cannot lack anything, if virtue is a constituent of happiness, it is a necessary constituent. It needs to be noted, however, that taking this to be Aristotle's method for deciding on what is involved in living well runs against the traditional reading of Aristotle, according to which his substantive account of *eudaimonia* is determined by his claims about what it is to be human. So Thomas Nagel, who thinks that the *EN* 'exhibits indecision between two accounts of *eudaimonia* – a comprehensive and an intellectualist account', sees this indecision as resulting from a prior indecision over human nature: 'it is because he is not sure who we are that Aristotle finds it difficult to say unequivocally in what our *eudaimonia* consists.'[23] On this sort of reading, Aristotle accepts that not only will the nature of the final end be affected by the nature of what it is to be human, but it will be determined by it.

In fact, Aristotle does not talk explicitly of human nature (*phusis*) in 1.7, but rather of the human *ergon*, which he introduces once he has established that *eudaimonia* meets the requirements of unqualified finality and self-sufficiency demanded of the supreme good:

> Presumably, however, to say that *eudaimonia* is the chief good seems a platitude, and a clearer account of what it is is still desired. This might perhaps be given, if we could first ascertain the *ergon* of man.
> (*EN* 1.7.1097b22–5)

---

[22] If, for instance, like Priam in 1.10 the agent has suffered and lost so much that he is no longer capable of being happy. I examine the role of external goods in happiness in section 3 below.

[23] Nagel [528], 7–8. In fact, of course, on Nagel's view, it is not that Aristotle does not state unequivocally what happiness is – rather he does state this quite clearly but incompatibly in different places.

What, then, is the human *ergon*? Once it was standard to translate '*ergon*' as 'function', but this has quite properly fallen out of favour amongst Aristotle's critics.[24] As Kenny says, 'it is tendentious to translate "*ergon*" as *function*: we need not credit Aristotle with believing that men serve a purpose'.[25] Kenny suggests that we think of the human *ergon* rather as the 'characteristic activity' of humans, which gives as 'the burden of the passage', 'where an *F* has a characteristic activity, ϕ-ing, then a good *F* is an *F* which ϕs well'. This fits well with what follows in 1.7:

> For just as for a flute-player, a sculptor, or any artist, and, in general, for all things that have an *ergon* or activity, the good and the 'well' is thought to reside in the *ergon*, so it would seem to be for man . . . What then can [the *ergon*] be? Life seems to be common even to plants, but we are seeking what is peculiar to man. Let us exclude, then, the life of nutrition and growth. Next there would be a life of perception, but it also seems to be common even to the horse, the ox, and every animal. There remains, then, some sort of practical life of that which has reason.
>
> (1097b25–8; 1097b33–1098a4)

Humans possess all the various capacities of the *psuchē*, including nutrition and perception.[26] Neither of these can count as the human *ergon*, however, since these are not distinctively human: if we restrict our attention to what is *idion* to humans, then we are left with 'some sort of practical life of what has reason', where this might be understood either as a life of practical – as opposed to theoretical – reason or as a life of activity of theoretical reason. (I shall return to this later on.)

Once Aristotle has determined the human *ergon*, he is able to use this to ethical purpose:

> Now, if the *ergon* of man is activity of the *psuchē* in accordance with, or not without, rational principle and if we say that a so-and-so and a good so-and-so have an *ergon* which is the same in kind, e.g. a lyre-player and a good lyre-player, and so without qualification in all cases, eminence in respect of excellence being added to the *ergon* (for the *ergon* of a lyre-player is to play the lyre and that of a good lyre-player is to do so well): if this is the case . . . the human good (*to anthrōpinon agathon*) turns out to be activity of the

---

[24] So, the Oxford translation employs 'function', as, for instance, does Williams in his [503], 295 – so, in fact, do Whiting in her [552] and Kraut in his [458]. Perhaps 'function' has acquired a technical sense as part of a dialect used by Aristotle's readers and so ceased to carry its usual natural-language sense.

[25] Kenny [521], 27.

[26] *Psuchē* is another key term which is not readily translated. The standard translation is still 'soul' – but this has unwanted religious and Cartesian connotations. The *psuchē* is that in virtue of which a living substance is alive and has the life-capacities it does. For an outline of Aristotle's psychology, see my [921].

psuchē in accordance with excellence, and if there are more than one excellence, in accordance with the best and most complete.

(*EN* 1,7.1098a6–12; 16–18)

It is here that commentators have found what has come to be called the '*ergon* argument': an argument which is supposed to begin with a premise about human nature and end with a conclusion specifying the content of the good life. If what it is to be human is to engage in rational activity, then happiness – *to anthrōpinon agathon* – will be to engage excellently in rational activity.[27]

One obvious worry with this argument as it stands is that it seems to commit Aristotle to the claim that if some activity is distinctively human – that is, if only humans are capable of that activity – then performing that activity well will be a part of human happiness. Since such activities as prostitution and queer-bashing are distinctively human in this sense, the human good, it seems, should involve excellence in respect of these (where, presumably, excellence would not amount merely to abstention).[28] One way to avoid this problem would be to deny that what it is for a capacity or activity to be *idion* to a species is for it to be peculiar to members of that species. This is suggested, for instance, by Jennifer Whiting, who appeals to the discussion in *Topics* 1.4 of what is *idion* in an attempt to show that the notion of what is *idion* should rather be seen as related to the essence of a species than to what is peculiar to it. There Aristotle acknowledges that *idion* can be used to refer to the essence of something (101b19–20). Taking *idion* to refer to 'the human essence as a whole' would, she claims, have the twin advantages of providing a motivated reason to disbar such activities as prostitution and queer-bashing from inclusion within the human *ergon*, whilst allowing Aristotle to include *theōria* within it, despite the fact that we share the capacity for *theōria* with the gods but do not share that for prostitution with any other creatures. A property can be an essential property of one species even though it is possessed by members of a different species.

The trouble with this is that whilst Aristotle does start out in *Top.* 1.4 by saying that the term '*idion*' is applied both to the essence of a thing and to

---

[27] Aristotle emphasises in 1.8 that it is the *activity* of the capacity which plays a role in happiness and not its mere possession – 'for the disposition may exist without producing any good result, as in a man who is asleep or in some other way quite inactive, but the activity cannot' (1098b33–1099a2).

[28] Actually, this last point is far from obvious: adultery is a peculiarly human activity, but Aristotle is clear that excellence in respect of this requires abstention. However, although this move would block any commitment to making adultery (or prostitution or queer-bashing) a part of happiness, it would still allow that the activities themselves are part of the human *ergon*, and that, of course, cannot be right.

what is not essential, he then proceeds precisely to disambiguate the usage, introducing the term 'horos' for the specification of something's essence and restricting 'idion' to what 'does not reveal the essence of something but which belongs only to that thing and is predicated convertibly of it' (1.5.102a18). Thus, a capacity C will be idion to a species S, if and only if $\delta \forall x$ (x has $C \leftrightarrow x$ is a member of S). The example which Aristotle gives is that of being human and having the capacity to become literate (*grammatikos*): it is not part of what it is to be human that one has this capacity, but if something is human it will have that capacity, and anything which has that capacity is human.[29]

Top. 1.4 does not, then, provide external reason for taking idion in *EN* 1.7 to refer to the human essence, and, taken together with *Top.* 1.5, it actually provides some reason not to do so. What it does, at most, is to allow that one *could* take idion in *EN* 1.7 in this way, if the argument there demanded it, since Aristotle acknowledges this usage of the term – but, as we have seen, Aristotle rejects the possibility that nutrition and perception are part of the human *ergon* on the grounds that these are common to other sorts of living thing, whereas what is being sought is something idion. If one takes 'idion' to refer not to what is peculiar to a species but to what is essential to it, then one will not be able to make sense of this contrast between what is idion to a species and what is common to it and other species – something emphasised by the fact that one of the supposed advantages of this interpretation is to allow *theōria* into the human *ergon* despite the fact that it is shared with the gods.[30]

The details of the argument for the conclusion that the human *ergon* is some kind of rational activity do not, then, fit with the claim that 'idion' refers to essential properties rather than ones which are peculiar to humans. However, if we reject this suggestion, we are still left with the apparent problems which motivated it in the first place. How can Aristotle deny that excellence in respect of undesirable or indifferent but distinctively human

---

[29] That becoming *grammatikos* means becoming literate and not acquiring the knowledge of grammar is clear from *Top.* VIII,5.142b31. I owe this reference to Hugh Johnstone.

[30] Also, there is the further problem that once one allows activities which are not peculiar to the species into the *ergon* of the species, it is difficult to see how Aristotle can deny that nutrition and perception are part of the human *ergon*. Whiting anticipates this objection and seeks to meet it by making use of the Aristotelian distinction between essential properties and properties which are necessary but non-essential: Aristotle could 'then argue that our nutritive and reproductive capacities are necessary but non-essential properties of us, while our capacities for moral virtue and contemplation are components of our essence' ([552], 47, n. 18). He *could* but, as far as I can see, he does not – and, in any case, this would not meet the problem that these lower activities are rejected on the grounds that they are common to other species as well.

activities is not a necessary part of human happiness and how can he include intellectual excellence within it if it is not peculiar to humans and hence not something *idion* to us? I shall try to answer this second question by the end of this chapter, since a central claim which I intend to establish will be that Aristotle does not think that the content of *eudaimonia* is exhaustively determined by considering what our *ergon* is. If that is right, then it does not follow from the indisputable fact that Aristotle takes the activity of *theōria* to be a major component of the human good that he thinks that it is also part of the human *ergon*.

What, though, of prostitution and morris-dancing? Such activities as these present a more immediate difficulty, since I do not challenge the claim that if an activity is (perhaps a part of) the human *ergon*, then this is a sufficient condition for excellence in respect of that activity to be a component of human well-being. If the condition for an activity's being part of a species' *ergon* is that it is *idion* to that species, and if any activity is *idion* to a species when the capacity for it is not shared by the members of any other species, then any activity of which only humans are capable will be part of the human *ergon* – and so, its excellent performance will be required for happiness. This is too quick, however. An activity will be peculiar to a species just if only members of that species have the capacity for that activity, but this is not quite the condition given in *Top.* 1.5 for something to be *idion*. There the condition was that the *idion* should be 'convertibly predicable' with what possesses it. Thus, it is not sufficient that a capacity should be possessed only by humans for it to be *idion* to humans: it must also be the case that anything which is human has that capacity. This will knock out prostitution, queer-bashing and quite possibly morris-dancing as well. Let us assume that, on Aristotle's view, prostitution and queer-bashing, like adultery, are vicious – but, in that case, virtuous people will not possess the capacity for these activities.[31] The point to draw here, I think, is just that in order for a capacity to be *idion* in the way specified in the *Topics* that capacity will need to be specified at a fairly general level, which would help to explain why in *EN* 1.7 itself, Aristotle restricts his attention to the capacities of nutrition, perception and thought, the capacities which are the basic psychological capacities of the *de Anima*.

Further, although it is a condition of the human *ergon* that it should be *idion* to humans, Aristotle does not say that this is the only condition. It need not be the case that any capacity or activity which is *idion* to humans will be part of the *ergon*. This would allow us to accept Whiting's proposal in a

---

[31] As to morris-dancing, presumably it is not vicious, but it is perhaps unlikely that someone with excellent, or at least fastidious, aesthetic sensibilities would be able to go in for it.

modified form. Rather than taking what is *idion* to be the essential properties of a thing, and its *ergon* to be whatever is *idion* to it, we could take the *ergon* to be whatever essential capacities are *idion*. This does not have the disadvantage of having to restrict a living thing's essential capacities in an arbitrary way whilst it still secures the thought that discovering what the *ergon* of a species is tells one something important about what it is to be that kind of thing.[32] Although part of what it is to be human, for instance, will be to have the capacity to perceive, this will not be the human *ergon* since it is not specific to us. One can pursue excellence in perception (for instance, perhaps, in training oneself to make careful observations), but this will not be to make oneself excellent in a distinctively human way.[33]

On the traditional understanding of the *ergon* argument in *EN* I.7, achieving happiness involves just that – engaging in activities which constitute being an excellent human. Later, I shall challenge the claim that Aristotle does commit himself to this claim. First I shall consider whether that claim is consistent with what he has to say elsewhere about the nature of human *eudaimonia*.

3 The external goods

One sure sign that Aristotle does not accept that the content of happiness can be determined simply by reflecting upon the human *ergon* would be if he were to accept that what he calls 'external goods' are needed for happiness because they are intrinsically valuable. External goods are precisely contrasted with the goods of the *psuchē* (*EN* I,8.1098b12–14),[34] and so

---

[32] In *Parts of Animals* I.5, Aristotle says that since 'each of the parts of the body is for the sake of something, that is for the sake of some activity, it is obvious that the body as a whole is composed for the sake of some complex activity' (645b16–17). This suggests strongly that the essence of an animal species is the complex of the capacities which define its organic parts and, in the case of humans, these would include the capacities of nutrition and perception.

[33] Note that in *Generation of Animals* I.23, Aristotle says that the *ergon* of plants is 'nothing other than the creation of the seed' (731a25). Since this is not the only activity of which plants are capable (they can also take nourishment and grow), this would confirm that not all something's essential properties are part of its *ergon*. Slightly later, he says that animals differ from those things which are merely alive (i.e. which have only the nutritive capacity) in virtue of having the capacity for perception, but since an animal is necessarily alive, 'when the time comes for it to accomplish the *ergon* of what is alive, it copulates and unites and becomes as it were a plant' (731b4 f.). Members of one species can (essentially) possess the capacity for an activity which is the *ergon* of another species without its being part of their *ergon*.

[34] Indeed, they are contrasted with both the goods of the *psuchē* and those of the body. The important contrast, however, is with psychic goods – so good looks are, for instance, treated as an external good at 1099b3.

if any are included within the constituents of happiness, this cannot be because their value is derived from the value of being excellently human. Although some commentators have attempted to interpret Aristotle so that he claims that external goods are valuable only as the necessary conditions for virtuous actions, such an interpretation will not, I think, fit with what he actually says about them without attributing to him quite bizarre evaluative claims.

So, whilst he affirms that the goods of the *psuchē* are 'most properly and truly goods (*kuriōtata kai malista agatha*)' (1098b14–15), he does not contest the idea that there are external goods as well:

> Yet evidently, as we said, *eudaimonia* needs the external goods as well; for it is impossible to do noble acts without the proper equipment. In many actions we use friends and riches and political power as instruments. (1099a31–b2)

Some external things, that is, are *instrumentally* valuable – they are goods in so far as they enable one to engage in excellent activity. These, however, do not exhaust the class of external goods. He continues:

> But some things when lacked disfigure the good life (*to makarion*), such as good birth, good children, good looks – for the man who is ugly or ill-born or solitary and childless is scarcely happy (*ou panu gar eudaimonikos*), and perhaps a man would be still less so if he had thoroughly bad children or friends or had lost good children or friends by death. (1099b2–7)

Aristotle does not say that these goods are good in virtue of being instrumental in any way – rather, it seems, one's happiness will be marred just by lacking them.[35] The doctrine is a hard one here: if one is childless or solitary or ugly and low-born, one will not be happy.[36]

Although this reading is surely what the text requires – otherwise one cannot account for the contrast drawn between the two different sorts of external good – it is not quite uncontroversial. Thus, John Cooper argues that whilst 'one might conjecture that the disfigurement of one's blessedness in all these cases might be a matter of simply lacking or being deprived of something one very much prized and wanted to have',[37] this is not in fact what Aristotle intends. Cooper points to a sentence in *EN* VII.13, where

---

[35] Note that the distinction is between different ways in which external goods can be valuable and not between different external goods: friends are cited in both halves of the passage.

[36] Although the doctrine is palliated by Aristotle's claim in *Rhetoric* I.5 that good-looks are relative to age.

[37] Cooper [567]; citation from p. 180. Note that Cooper here does not include the possibility that the lack of these mars one's happiness just because they are (objectively) valuable.

Aristotle, having said that pleasure is unimpeded activity, claims that 'this is why the *eudaimon* needs the goods of the body and the external goods, i.e. those of fortune, so that he will not be impeded in these ways' (1153b17–19). According to Cooper, since Aristotle makes no explicit distinction here between different kinds of external good, he must have in mind all of them, including good looks, etc. On this basis, Cooper argues that the second group of external goods in 1.8 – those the lack of which mars happiness – must also be valuable not in themselves but for their contribution to a life of excellent activity:

> Aristotle's thought, I believe, is this. Some external conditions (being good-looking, having good children, coming from a good family), while not used by the virtuous person as a means to achieving his purposes (as e.g. his money or his personal influence might be), put him in the position where the options for action that are presented to him by his circumstances allow him to exercise his virtues fully and in ways one might describe as normal for the virtues.[38]

So, the ugly person will not be given the opportunity to exercise temperance as consistently as will the good-looking person, since fewer people will provide him with the choice of going to bed with them – and, perhaps, those who do will not offer much in the way of temptation. This sort of thing will apparently happen 'across the board': 'people', expands Cooper, 'will tend to avoid you, so that you will not be able to enter into the normally wide range of relationships that pose for the virtuous person the particular challenges that his virtue responds to with its correct assessments and right decisions'.[39]

Now, it may well be an unfortunate fact of human life that the ugly and vulgar are shunned – but there is no sign at all that it is this which Aristotle has in mind in *EN* 1.8. The most natural reading of this passage is precisely that good looks, etc. are things which one would find desirable to possess and that one would regret it if one did not have them. The idea that, for instance, beauty is valuable only in so far as it enables one to decline other people's advances is, I think, a perverse one, and fortunately not one which we have any reason to think occurred to Aristotle.

Indeed, if one looks at the other items on the list and tries to apply Cooper's account to them, the results move from the mildly perverse to the quite grotesque. Friends and children, apparently, are valuable just because they afford one the opportunity for virtuous activity. Thus, when someone close to one dies, what one mourns is the loss of opportunities for one's own virtue rather than feeling the loss as something which is bad in itself. Presumably

---

[38] *Ibid.*, p. 182.   [39] *Ibid.*, p. 182.

if one had sufficiently many children, one could bear the loss of any particular child with something close to equanimity. No doubt friends and children do provide opportunities for the exercise of virtue, but Aristotle shows no indication of holding the view that it is only or even principally in this that their value resides. (Certainly, if this were what is valuable in such relationships, it would be puzzling that, as Aristotle says, parents tend to value good children more highly than bad – since the latter clearly afford greater opportunities for virtue than the former.) There is something chilling about the idea that parents value their children, or friends value each other, merely as 'particular challenges' to which their virtue has been able to respond 'with its correct assessments and right decisions'.[40]

This would be a very odd view indeed for someone who is committed to adhering as far as possible to common opinions, and the evidence provided by the single sentence in *EN* vii is simply not strong enough to support it: all this claims is that external goods are needed if one's activities are not to be impeded. Aristotle does not claim that this is the *only* reason why external goods are valuable. Moreover, that Aristotle takes at least one external good to be intrinsically valuable is clearly evidenced in the list given at 1,7.1097b1–5 of things through which we think we shall be happy. Alongside pleasure and intellect, Aristotle cites honour, which, according to *EN* iv,3.1123b20–1, is 'the greatest of the external goods'. Honour is thus something we would choose even if nothing further came of it – that is, something which is intrinsically valuable. Given this, Aristotle cannot think that one can determine whether something has intrinsic value (or even intrinsic value for humans) only by considering what it is to be human. If the '*ergon*' argument' is to play the role traditionally ascribed to it, then, it will have to be the case that Aristotle thinks that by appealing to the human *ergon*, one can distinguish between those intrinsic goods which play a role in happiness from those which do not. Given that Aristotle describes honour as something through which one expects to achieve happiness, we should already be suspicious of such a claim – and that suspicion will be confirmed by considering Aristotle's discussion of the relative merits of *theōria* and *phronēsis*, practical wisdom.

4 Nature and value

A principal objection which Nagel raises against the *ergon* argument, as he construes it, is that Aristotle commits himself to identifying an activity (or activities) which is (or are) peculiar to humans: a commitment which is impossible for him to meet. No activities, it seems, are peculiarly

---

[40] Similar reactions are expressed by Annas [71], 378 f.

human: all of the capacities of the *psuchē*, except *nous*, are shared with other animals, and *nous*, the theoretical intellect, is shared with the gods. What is peculiarly human is the *combination* of capacities – other animals do not have *nous* and the gods do not perceive or grow. Identifying the human *ergon* with this combination, however, would have led to absurdity, as there would then have been no principled reason for excluding the lower psychic capacities, such as nutrition, and this would have the effect of including 'all the lower life functions in the measure of human excellence'.[41]

It is not true, however, that there is no capacity which is distinctively human. In *EN* 1.7, once Aristotle has dismissed the life of perception and growth because these are shared with animals and plants, he concludes, 'there remains then the practical (*praktikē*) life of what has reason'. Commentators have generally understood this to involve a reference to *nous* and so understand it to mean, as the Oxford translation has it, 'an active life of the element that has a rational principle'. This, however, is strained: *praktikē* does not signify the activity of rather than the mere possession of a capacity but practical rather than theoretical activity.[42] It *is* distinctive of humans that they have practical reason: neither the gods nor animals share this capacity.

That Aristotle identifies the human *ergon* with practical reason is confirmed by *Politics* 1.2, in which we find a much less schematic *ergon* argument as part of the argument for the conclusion that man is a political animal – that is, he cannot be happy unless he is a citizen of a state. 'It is evident that the state is a creation of nature, and that man is by nature a political animal – and he who by nature and not by mere accident is without a state, is either a bad man or above humanity' (1253a3–5). To justify this assertion about human nature, Aristotle appeals, as a reader of the *Ethics* should expect, to the peculiar characteristics of man. I give his argument in full:

> Now, that man is more of a political animal than bees or any other gregarious animals is evident. Nature, as we often say, makes nothing in vain, and man is the only animal who has speech (*logos*). And whereas mere voice is but an indication of pleasure or pain, and is therefore found in other animals (for their nature attains to the perception of pleasure and pain and the intimation of them to one another, and no further), speech is to set forth the expedient and the inexpedient, and likewise the just and the unjust. And it is a characteristic of man that he alone has any sense of good and evil, of just and unjust, and the like, and the association of living beings who have this sense makes a family and a state. (1253a7–18)

---

[41] Nagel [528], 10.   [42] This is recognised by Broadie in her [451], 36.

This *ergon* argument is much more substantive than that given in *EN* I.7. Whereas in the *EN* Aristotle merely specified distinctively human activity as that which 'is in accordance with, or not without, reason', here he provides a somewhat more sophisticated account of the cognitive difference between humans and animals, and does this by focusing on what is indeed the most noticeable difference between them – that is, that humans have the capacity for language. Whereas animals can only respond to the immediate stimuli of pleasure and pain when they make noises, humans are able to say things about the world.

What is striking here is that Aristotle associates the capacity for language not with theoretical but with *practical* reason. The purpose of speech is to 'set forth the expedient and the inexpedient, and likewise the just and the unjust'. This should not surprise us. Aristotle, after all, maintains a psychologistic theory of language, according to which the meaning of words is to be explained by reference to the content of thoughts rather than vice versa.[43] On Aristotle's view, we do not need language in order to think – and so one can see why he would take its function to be a communicative and hence a social one. The gods have thoughts, but they do not have language – just as they do not have dealings with each other. Only humans have language, just as only they have practical reason. Since the purpose of the first is to express the latter, the activity which is peculiarly human is that of practical reasoning, and Aristotle duly identifies it as the human *ergon*. This will only be unnerving if one thinks that Aristotle's recommendation of *theōria* in *EN* x.7 must rest on the view that by engaging in theoretical reasoning we are thereby expressing our human nature. In fact, however, Aristotle's arguments for the supreme value of *theōria* have nothing to do with the human *ergon* nor do they need to.

Aristotle begins his treatment of the life of the intellect in x.7 with the claim that 'if happiness is activity in accordance with excellence, it is reasonable that it should be in accordance with the highest excellence; and this will be that of the best thing in us' (1177a12–13) – and that is the excellence of *sophia*, theoretical understanding. Aristotle then presents a series of arguments to show that *theōria* is our highest activity, and hence that *sophia* is our highest excellence. Thus, 'not only is *nous* the best thing in us, but the objects of intellect are the best of knowable objects' (1177a20–1). It is also 'the most continuous, since we can engage in thought more continuously than we can do any action' (1177a21–2). Again, it is the most self-sufficient activity:

> And the self-sufficiency that is spoken of must belong most to the theoretical activity. For while a wise man, as well as a just man and the rest, needs

---

[43] See *de Interpretatione* 16a3–8.

> the necessaries of life, when they are sufficiently equipped with things of that sort, the just man needs people towards whom and with whom he shall act justly . . . but the wise man, even when by himself, can engage in *theōria*, and the better the wiser he is; he can perhaps do better if he has fellow-workers, but still he is the most self-sufficient.   (1177a27–b1)

Thus, in x.7 Aristotle does exactly what Kenny described him as doing – he runs through the properties which he has identified as those which distinguish happiness and demonstrates that the life of intellectual activity perfectly manifests them. He duly concludes:

> If . . . the activity of intellect which is theoretical seems both to be superior in worth and to aim at no end beyond itself, and to have its pleasure proper to itself (and this augments the activity), and the self-sufficiency, leisureliness, unweariedness (so far as this is possible for man), and all the other attributes ascribed to the blessed man are evidently those connected with this activity, it follows that this will be the complete *eudaimonia* of man, if it be allowed a complete term of life.   (1177b19–25)

Surely, then, in the light of this there can be no doubt that in book x Aristotle recommends the intellectual life as the life of perfect *eudaimonia* and so, contrary to the claims of the earlier sections, is operating with a conception of *eudaimonia* according to which it can be identified with a single good rather than one which is such as to include various goods.

In fact, however, Aristotle does not *recommend* the life of the intellect – for the simple reason that there is no point in doing so. Immediately after concluding that a life of *theōria* would constitute complete *eudaimonia*, he says

> But such a life would be too high for man; for it is not in so far as he is human that he will live so, but in so far as something divine is present in him; and by so much as this is superior to our composite nature is its activity superior to that which is the exercise of the other kind of excellence.
> (1177b26–9)

Far from its being the case that Aristotle's claims about the perfection of the intellectual life are secured upon an intellectualist view of human nature, it turns out to be human nature which *prevents* our achieving such a life.

The principal difference between humans and gods is that humans, unlike gods, have a composite nature. Whereas both are capable of *theōria*, for which there is no associated organ since it does not involve bodily change, humans, because they are living *bodies*, have other psychological capacities as well – the activities of which supervene on bodily changes.[44] The result of

---

[44] See *de Anima* (*DA*) i.1 for the bodily nature of the 'affections of the *psuchē*' and iii.4 for the incorporeality of *nous*. The relation between bodily changes and psychological activities is discussed in my [922], ch. 6.

this, of course, is that there is a range of dispositions and activities for which humans are assessable and gods are not.[45] To be an excellent person requires a wider range of excellences than is required to be an excellent god. Someone whose only activity was *theōria* would not be able to develop the peculiarly human excellences. Since he would not have lost the capacities which are well-conditioned in the virtuous person, he would have them in a defective condition and so be vicious. This is why Aristotle claims in *Politics* I.2 that 'he who by nature and not by mere accident is without a state, is either a bad man or above humanity' (1253a4–5). To be naturally 'without a state' is to be able to fulfil one's natural capacities living by oneself, and only the gods can achieve a solitary *eudaimonia*.[46] Unless someone is a citizen of a state, he will be able neither to acquire nor to exercise the excellences of character – and, since he must have a character of some sort, he will be a defective member of his species if that character is not an excellent one.[47]

That human nature is such that people are blocked from the perfect *eudaimonia* described in x.7 is reinforced in x.8, where Aristotle discusses 'secondary' *eudaimonia*:

> The life according to the other excellence is *eudaimōn* to a secondary degree, because (*gar*) its activities are human.   (1178a9–10)

This, as we should now expect, is precisely because the life of practical virtue is that of creatures whose nature is composite:

> Practical wisdom (*phronēsis*), too, is linked to excellence of character, and this to practical wisdom, since the principles of practical wisdom are in accordance with the moral excellences and correctness in the excellences of character is in accordance with practical wisdom. Being connected with the passions also, the excellences of character must belong to our composite nature; and the excellences of our composite nature are human; so, therefore, are the life and the *eudaimonia* which correspond to these.
> (1178a16–22)

Human happiness consists in the life of moral excellence, since this is the excellence which is peculiarly human.

If what it is for an individual to be happy were simply determined by his *ergon* as a human, then, living well would not involve the exercise of *theōria*, the highest activity of which we are capable. Fortunately, Aristotle is not

---

[45] See *EN* x,8.1178b8–15.

[46] For the inability of other animals to achieve *eudaimonia*, see *EN* x,8.1178b24–8.

[47] There is a genuine question as to why Aristotle thought that his arguments established that man is a *political* rather than merely a *social* animal. I shall not attempt an answer to this here and am assuming that, given his account of *eudaimonia*, he does show the former, but the problem should at least be noted.

committed to the antecedent of that conditional – and indeed he actually attacks the claim that we should restrict ourselves in this way:

> If intellect is divine, then, in comparison with man, the life according to it is divine in comparison with human life. But we must not follow those who advise us, being men, to think of human things, and, being mortal, of mortal things, but must, so far as we can, make ourselves immortal, and strain every nerve to live in accordance with the best thing in us; for even if it be small in bulk, much more does it in power and worth surpass everything. (*EN* x,7.1177b30–1178a2)

Those who are attacked by Aristotle here are putting forward just the argument which is so often attributed to Aristotle himself by his commentators – that one can determine what is worth while for humans to pursue simply by reflecting on what is characteristically human activity.[48] What makes *theōria* valuable is not that it is a human activity – and certainly not that it is an activity which is peculiar to humans – but precisely that it is the best activity: it is characteristic of the highest beings, has the highest objects, and allows the greatest self-sufficiency.

5 The good life for man

I hope that these considerations are such as to show that if we do accept a reading of 1.7 in which he presents 'the *ergon* argument' – an argument according to which human *eudaimonia* will consist of the excellent performance of whatever activity is distinctively human – then we also have to accept that this will make the doctrine of that chapter inconsistent not only with the *Politics* and the *Eudemian Ethics* but also with the rest of the *Nicomachean Ethics* itself. Outside that chapter, there is no sign of any

---

[48] It may seem strange that Aristotle can maintain both that all humans have the capacity for *theōria* and that this is nevertheless not part of what it is to be human – or, at least, that it is not part of the human *ergon*. The initial oddity of this will only be reinforced by Aristotle's claim that *nous* 'would seem to be each man himself, since it is the authoritative and better part of him. It would be strange, then, if he were to choose not the life of himself but that of something else' (x,7.1178a2–4). It seems, then, that Aristotle is prepared to claim both that every person is his intellect and that the intellect is not a human capacity. The oddity here can be diminished first by noting that the second conjunct is just the claim that the intellect is not a peculiarly human capacity and then by remembering that in the *DA*, Aristotle takes individual psychic capacities to be conceptually prior both to the *psuchē* taken generally and to the species which have those capacities (see my [922], 2–4). He is thus able to identify *nous* as a divine capacity, since it is the only capacity possessed by the gods, and *phronēsis* as the human capacity, since it is distinctive of humans, whilst allowing both that humans possess both capacities and that any individual human is to be identified with his intellect.

commitment to the claim that the content of *eudaimonia* can be determined simply by appeal to deciding what is distinctively human activity, and there are many signs that Aristotle would reject that claim. On any reading, it is not consistent with allowing that at least some external goods have a necessary role in *eudaimonia* because they are intrinsically valuable and, if excellence in respect of the human *ergon* is indeed the possession of *phronēsis* and practical virtue, then it is also inconsistent with the inclusion of intellectual activity within the good life. As we have seen, precisely this seems to be noticed, and rejected, in x.7 when he tells us that we should not be put off the pursuit of intellectual activity by those who tell us to restrict our attention to human things.

We have good reason, then, to consider whether Aristotle does in fact say in 1.7 what he has so often been taken to say. Certainly, he introduces the search for the human *ergon* as something which will clarify the nature of *eudaimonia* and not as something which will determine it. It comes as something of a surprise, then, when, having decided that there is a human *ergon*, he appears to conclude from this that human *eudaimonia* consists in performing that *ergon* well. It will be seen immediately that if this is Aristotle's argument, then it is fallacious, as his putative parallel with the lyre-player makes all too obvious. What one gets when a lyre-player performs his *ergon* well – that is, is good at playing the lyre – is an excellent lyre-player and *not* a happy one.[49] Similarly, if humans have an *ergon*, then someone who performs the relevant activity well will be an excellent human but (for all that has been said) not a happy one. If Aristotle thinks that an excellent human is thereby a happy one, he needs to put up an argument for this – and he does not. Aristotle's argument at best shows (in a very schematic way) what it is to be a good man: it does not show what the good *for* man is.[50]

For those who are impressed by these considerations and who wish to save Aristotle from endorsing the argument he has been traditionally offered, there are two different strategies available. One would be to claim that that argument is not to be found in 1.7 itself, whilst the other would be to deny that its presence in 1.7 is sufficient to warrant the attribution. Someone attracted by the possibility of pursuing the first course might well focus on an ambiguity in the argument's conclusion – that 'the human good' (*to anthrōpinon agathon*) is activity of the soul in accordance with virtue. This could mean that what is good for humans is such activity, but it need not do so. One might equally take it to mean that what it is to be a

---

[49] Even if he were happy, of course, this would not be in respect of his being a *musician* – which shows the unsuitability of the analogy as traditionally taken.

[50] The potential fallacy here is noted in Glassen [546]. See also Wilkes [553].

good human – the good in respect of being human – is activity in accordance with virtue.[51] This is very tempting since, if one did take it in this way, the analogy with the musician would stand: when a lyre-player plays the lyre well, he is an excellent lyre player and when a human performs his characteristic activity well, he is an excellent human. Knowing what is required for someone to be an excellent human will help to bring substance to our understanding of *eudaimonia*, since being an excellent human is something which is desirable in itself and so will be required if one is to be happy.

Unfortunately, reading Aristotle's conclusion in this way will not square with other passages in the *EN*. So, at the start of 1.13, we find Aristotle claiming that *happiness* is an activity of the *psuchē* in accordance with virtue and there is nothing between 1.7 and 1.13 which would bridge the gap between this claim and the claim that what it is to be a good human is to engage in activity of the *psuchē* in accordance with virtue. In the light of this, we have to accept that the conclusion of the argument is indeed a direct claim about the nature of *eudaimonia* and not one about human excellence which has consequences for the understanding of *eudaimonia*.

A different way to weaken the conclusion would be to emphasise that Aristotle does not say that happiness consists in virtuous activity, but only that it consists in activity which is in accordance with virtue. This would provide an affirmation of the claim that one needs to be excellent if one is to be happy, and so will not do anything which is against the requirements of excellence, but will not restrict what is worth pursuing to the exercise of distinctively human excellence. As we have seen, Aristotle's intellectualism, such as it is, requires that he should not make this restriction. However, whilst this may be correct, it will not do all the work of squaring the conclusion of the *ergon* argument with Aristotle's general account of *eudaimonia*.[52] For if the constituents of *eudaimonia* were restricted to activities, this would exclude all external goods – something which, as we have seen, Aristotle properly resists.

We cannot, then, read the conclusion of the *ergon* argument so that it can

---

[51] The term *to anthrōpinon agathon* occurs only three times in the corpus: here, in *EN* 1.2 (1094b6–7), where it is clearly used to refer to the final end, and in *EE* 1.7 (1217a22), where Aristotle talks of *eudaimonia* as the best of the human goods (*anthrōpina agatha*) – where this qualification is to allow for a possible contrast with the goods available to a higher being. However, although these passages provide some reason for taking *to anthrōpinon agathon* to refer to happiness, they are not sufficient to fix a technical meaning for the term.

[52] That it is correct is urged by Irwin in his [459]. The problem it faces is that whilst it makes good sense when the virtue in question is that of *phronēsis*, it is more difficult to make sense of when the virtue is that of *sophia*, as it is at the start of x.7.

be reconciled with what Aristotle has to say elsewhere about the good life. In fact, this is as we should expect, since to try to do so is to misconstrue the place of 1.7 within the argument of the *EN*. For once he has drawn his conclusion – and added the qualification that the activity must be over a whole lifetime – he immediately notes that what has been given is an outline of *eudaimonia*, something which is to be filled in by further enquiry (1098a20–5). That the account of happiness offered in 1.7 is provisional is then confirmed by the argument of the chapters which follow. So, he begins 1.8 by saying that one must further consider what is said about *eudaimonia*: 'we must consider it in the light not only of our conclusion and our premises, but also of what is commonly said about it'. Aristotle proceeds to show that the definition accords with the beliefs that it is the goods of the *psuchē* (as opposed to the goods of the body and external goods) which are most strictly goods and that the end is certain activities and actions. Now, so far this would seem to endorse the conclusion of the *ergon* argument fairly straightforwardly. Aristotle's next confirming move is less obvious, however. He notes that some people take happiness to be virtue, and some take it to be practical wisdom, whilst to others it seems to be wisdom (*sophia*); further, some combine one or more of these with pleasure and others combine them with external prosperity. None of these is written off: 'some of these views have been held by many men and men of old, others by a few persons; and it is not probable that either of these should be entirely mistaken, but rather that they should be right in at least some one respect or even most respects' (1098b27–9). He proceeds to show that the definition offered in 1.7 is consistent both with the claim that happiness is virtue and that it is pleasurable, and then, as we have seen, moves to consider the role of the external goods and concludes that these are indeed necessary for happiness (and not merely as instruments to virtuous activity). Once he has considered the role of external goods and of fortune in happiness, he is able to move to a less provisional conclusion: 'Why then should we not say that he is happy who engages in activity in accordance with complete virtue and is sufficiently equipped with external goods, not for some chance period but throughout a complete life?' (1.10.1101a14–16). It is *this* definition, and not that offered in 1.7, which is given as the official definition in book 1, and it duly fills in the outline account of the earlier chapter.[53]

---

[53] This way of placing 1.7 within the overall argument of the work helps further to block a potential objection to the earlier claim that the highest virtue in 1.7 is that of *phronēsis* rather than *sophia*. One might try to resist this by comparing Aristotle's claim in 1.7 that *to anthrōpinon agathon* will be activity of the *psuchē* in accordance with virtue 'and if there are more than one excellence, in accordance with the best and most complete' (1098a16–18) with the opening of x.7: 'If happiness is activity

Thus, the appeal to the *ergon* of man in *EN* 1.7 is not intended by Aristotle to do all the work required to determine the content of *eudaimonia*. It certainly does what Aristotle claims of it, which is to make clearer what the good life consists in, but it in no way commits Aristotle to restricting what is needed for *eudaimonia* to the expression of peculiarly human capacities. If it did, then, as we have seen, it would in fact rule out what Aristotle takes to be the most valuable activity of all – that of the theoretical intellect. To see the conclusion of Aristotle's argument as a specification of happiness requires taking him to be committed to the following principle: that if it is the human *ergon* to ϕ, then to be happy will be to engage in ϕ-ing and all actions, if they are to contribute to happiness, will be done for the sake of ϕ-ing. There is no explicit commitment to this principle in 1.7, and the claim that knowledge of the *ergon* will help to elucidate what is involved in achieving happiness will be true either if what it is to be happy is to be an excellent human or if excellent human activity is simply a requirement for happiness – is a component of the good life. That consideration of the *endoxa* leads Aristotle to introduce reference to external goods into his final definition shows that it is the latter alternative that he accepts. Aristotle takes it for granted that people have reason to become excellent humans but does not maintain the implausible thesis that this is all that they have reason to do – or even all they have reason to do in order to be happy.[54]

in accordance with excellence, it is reasonable that it should be in accordance with the highest excellence; and this will be that of the best thing in us' (1177a12–13). Since the latter serves as part of an argument for taking the happy life to be one of theoretical activity, it will seem reasonable to take the best virtue in 1.7 also to be *sophia*. This is not forced on us, however. For, on the present construal of Aristotle's argument, the conclusions of 1.7 are provisional, and restricted to those activities which fall within the *ergon* – which *theōria* does not. In 1.7, then, the highest virtue will be *phronēsis*. In x.7, when Aristotle's attention is no longer restricted to the human *ergon*, the same general principle will lead him to focus on *sophia* rather than *phronēsis*.

54   Whiting, in her treatment of the *ergon* argument, begins by defending the claims that 'Aristotle suggests *a* connection between something's membership in a natural kind (or its essential properties) and what is unconditionally or categorically good for that thing' ([552], 36, my italics) and that 'Aristotle thinks that a man's rationality (*at least partly*) determines what is beneficial for him' ([552], 41, my italics), but ends up maintaining that 'these things which are objectively good for a person, whatever his actual beliefs and desires, are the categorical goods which Aristotle thinks will benefit him simply in so far as he is essentially human. What these things are will depend on what the human essence is' (p. 45). As far as I can see, however, no work is done to bridge the gap between the claim that it is valuable, and part of human happiness, to act excellently in respect of one's *ergon* and the claim that *eudaimonia* just is such activity. This problem is the more acute, of course, if one accepts (as Whiting does not) that whilst the capacity for *theoria* may be part of the human essence, it is not part of the human *ergon*.

What is important here is that Aristotle's readiness to include external goods within the constituents of *eudaimonia*, and indeed his willingness to test the conclusion of 1.7 against our beliefs about what is valuable, shows that he does not subscribe to a style of ethical theory which has often been attributed to him – a theory according to which things are valuable just in so far as they contribute to *eudaimonia* and the nature of *eudaimonia* is determined by the nature of man. This can now be seen to get things the wrong way round: it is not that something is valuable because it contributes to happiness, rather, something will be a constituent of happiness because it is intrinsically valuable. Aristotle's appeal to the human *ergon* gives him an initial characterisation of happiness – an outline characterisation which is to be tested against, and if confirmed, supplemented by what is said and thought about happiness. The point is that Aristotle does not offer a *theory* of the good, an account which will show of any good why it is good.

That Aristotle should resist any such theory is, of course, just what we should expect given his complaints in *EN* 1.6 against Plato's claim that all goods are called 'good' by reference to a single Form or Idea:

> What sort of goods would one call good in themselves? Is it those that are pursued even when isolated from others, such as wisdom, sight and certain pleasures and honours? For even if we pursue these for the sake of something else, nevertheless one would class them as goods in themselves. Or is nothing other than the idea good in itself? In that case, the form will be empty. But if these things are good in themselves, the account of the good will have to appear as identical in them all, as that of whiteness is identical in snow and white lead. But of honour, wisdom, and pleasure, just in respect of their goodness, the accounts are distinct and diverse. The good, therefore, is not something common answering to one idea.
> (1096b16–26)

Aristotle's complaint against Plato is precisely that one *cannot* give a general account of why those things which are good are good. This is the case even if one restricts the class of goods to those which are attainable by humans, for whilst every science aims at some good, each leaves 'on one side the knowledge of *the* good' :

> Yet that all the exponents of the arts should be ignorant of, and not even seek, so great an aid is not probable. It is hard, too, to see how a weaver or a carpenter will be benefited in regard to his own craft by knowing this 'good itself', or how the man who has viewed the Idea itself will be a better doctor or general thereby. (1097a6–11)

The practitioners of the individual arts do not need to know what the good is in order to know that particular things are good, and this will be because, as

Aristotle has just said, the good is not something common answering to one idea. *A fortiori*, not everything will be good, or even good for man, because it is somehow related to the human *ergon*. Just as honour, wisdom and pleasure are different kinds of thing, they are good in different ways, even though all are attainable human goods. If Aristotle had thought that one could show that all human goods are good because they are in some way related to the human *ergon*, his criticisms of Plato in 1.6 would ring rather hollow.

Moreover, just as Aristotle does not provide a theory which will determine what things are good for humans, and hence constituents of the good human life, nor does he provide, or allow for, a theory or set of rules to determine how one should integrate the pursuit of the various values within a happy life. This has worried even some of those who have accepted that happiness is constituted by the many valuable things which are humanly attainable. Thus, John Ackrill is concerned that Aristotle provides – and can provide – no 'rule for combining *theōria* with virtuous action in the best life':

> It may seem that one could say: maximise *theōria*, and for the rest act well; and Aristotle's own famous injunction 'to make ourselves immortal as far as we can' might be understood in this way.[55]

Ackrill, however, finds this to be much less innocuous than it seems:

> Such a rule, giving absolute priority to *theōria*, would certainly avoid conflicting claims: it will only be if and when *theōria* cannot be engaged in and nothing can be done to promote *theōria* in any way that the other value will enter into consideration . . . [Its implication is] that one should do anything however seemingly monstrous if doing it has the slightest tendency to promote *theōria* – and such an act would on this view actually be good and virtuous.[56]

This misses the point, however. The practically virtuous agent will have become habituated so that, to use McDowell's metaphor, the considerations of virtue 'silence' all others.[57] He is simply not capable of monstrous actions and he values virtuous actions not because they promote anything but just because they are virtuous.[58]

Whilst Aristotle does think that the more time one spends in *theōria* the

[55] Ackrill [508], 32.   [56] *Ibid.*, p. 32.

[57] See McDowell [959] and also his chapter below.

[58] Ackrill [508] 30 f., worries that, although Aristotle does not answer the question 'what makes virtuous actions virtuous' by maintaining that an action is virtuous only in so far as it promotes *theōria*, 'no alternative answer . . . seems to present itself' (p. 31). Aristotle, however, does say a great deal about what makes brave actions brave and just actions just – what he does not do is to provide an answer to the question 'what makes virtuous actions *valuable*?' – but Aristotle would have taken it to be a sign of a deficient character even to ask *that* question.

more value one's life will have, it does not commit him to the view that it would be proper or even properly self-interested to do vicious things in order to spend time in speculation. For it is a necessary condition of a happy life that one be excellent – and since our nature is compound (and so we have bodily as well as intellectual capacities), we shall be excellent only if those capacities are themselves excellently disposed. A man who had *sophia* without the excellences of character would not be happy because he would indeed lack something of value; excellence in a part of his nature. *Theōria* may be the most valuable activity, but it is not the final good. *Theōria* is a constituent of happiness because it is worth choosing for itself – but it is not worth choosing at the expense of happiness.

Aristotle offers no rule for determining how to integrate the pursuit of different values – nor should he. Just as a misplaced desire for theory where one should rather look for judgement leads to defective accounts of practical reasoning (and now of literature), so it has led to a misunderstanding of Aristotle. What has encouraged Aristotle's commentators to find in his remarks on the human *ergon* a criterion for determining what counts as happiness is an expectation that Aristotle will provide a *theory* of what is valuable in human life – or, if not actually a theory, at least some principle for deciding either what has value or what has sufficient value to be required for the good life. This expectation is not a sensible one. When Aristotle says in 1.8 that we should not call someone happy if he were lonely and childless, this does not require any theoretical apparatus to convert it into the claim that children and friends are required for happiness. What secures that claim is just the recognition that certain personal relationships have sufficient value for a life which lacks them to be so etiolated that it will not count as a happy one. We do not need a theory to tell us this, but rather experience and proper judgement.

What is needed, of course, is *phronēsis*, practical wisdom. It is this which has the supreme good as its object and whose possession enables one to deliberate correctly about the ends of action: 'it is thought to be a mark of a man of practical wisdom to be able to deliberate well about what is good and expedient for himself, not in some particular respect, e.g. about what sorts of thing are conducive to health or to strength, but about what sorts of thing are conducive to the good life in general' (*EN* VI,5.1140a25–8).[59] Thus, it

---

[59] Note that in *EN* VI.8 Aristotle tells us that 'political wisdom and practical wisdom are the same disposition, but what it is to be each is not the same' (1141b23–4). The point seems to be that there is a single ability, which is the ability to deliberate well about the ends of action, and this ability can be exercised either in respect of the agent's own well-being (in which case it is practical wisdom) or in respect of the well-being of the state as a whole (in which case it is political wisdom). What unifies these capacities is the ability to make correct judgements about *eudaimonia*, and thus about what is valuable.

turns out after all that someone who has achieved excellence in respect of the human *ergon* will indeed be happy, for such a person will, as we have seen, be someone who possesses *phronēsis*. What makes him happy, however, is not that he has achieved excellence in respect of his *ergon*, but that, in possessing *phronēsis*, he is able to make correct judgements about what is valuable and what is not – and the correctness of these judgements is independent of considerations to do with human nature and functioning. The person of practical wisdom does not need to have a correct theory of the human *ergon* in order to be able to deliberate successfully about how to act, even if, in doing so, he is indeed manifesting excellence in respect of his *ergon*.

What enables the practically wise person to deliberate well in this way is not theoretical expertise but experience and the possession of a virtuous character:

> And this eye of the *psuchē* acquires its formed state not without the aid of excellence as has been said and is plain; for inferences which deal with acts to be done are things which involve a starting-point, viz. 'since the end, i.e. what is best, is of such and such a nature', whatever it may be (let it for the sake of argument be what we please); and this is not evident except to the good man.
>
> (*EN* VI,12.1144a29–34)

To the practically wise person, the starting-points of action are *evident*: they are not achieved through theory. If someone cannot see why friendship or virtue are valuable or why a life without either is not a happy life, Aristotle has no proof to offer him – and there is none to be given. This is not a subject which is amenable to the methods of the theoretician. As Aristotle almost says, to expect proofs and rules where there are none to be had is itself a mark of barbarism.[60]

[60] Earlier versions of this chapter were given in two graduate classes in Oxford, the first given by Jonathan Barnes and Robin Lane-Fox on ancient political philosophy and the second presented by David Charles and myself on Aristotle's ethics. Much useful criticism was given on both occasions. I received further helpful comments, especially from David Velleman, when I presented an early version at the University of Michigan. Conversations with Dominic Scott further refined the argument. As always, Hugh Johnstone saved me from mistakes of various kinds. I have been spinning my line on the *EN* in tutorials for some time now, and my sense of the text has gained immeasurably from having to defend it against informed undergraduate scepticism. I completed the final version of this chapter whilst at Trinity College, Cambridge. I am grateful to the members of Trinity, in particular Nick Denyer, and to the philosophical community in Cambridge for helping to make my stay there such a happy one.

5

Some issues in Aristotle's moral psychology[1]

JOHN MCDOWELL

1. Action that displays the ethical character of its agent does so by virtue of the purposiveness that is operative in it. (See *Nicomachean Ethics* (*EN*) 1111b5–6.) The category of purposive behaviour, behaviour that can be explained by giving its end, extends to brutes as well as human beings. But human beings are special among animals in having a capacity for articulable thought. Purposive behaviour in brutes is an immediate response to an opportunity for gratification of non-rational motivational impulses: its explanation draws only on those impulses and unconceptualised perception. The peculiarly human capacity for thought allows for purposiveness without that immediacy; thought can mediate gaps between project and execution. Thought that bridges such gaps is what Aristotle calls '*bouleusis*' ('deliberation'): see *EN* III.3.

Deliberation as Aristotle discusses it seems to be a process of thinking engaged in before acting. But we can sometimes make sense of human behaviour in an importantly similar way, even though the agent did not actually deliberate. The form of deliberation is a form into which we can cast an explanation by reasons, and such an explanation can be appropriate for actions that did not issue from prior deliberation. And it is the nature of an agent's reasons, whether explicitly thought through or not, that reveals his ethical character. It seems best to give Aristotle a pinch of salt on this: to take it, for instance, that when he suggests that choice (*prohairesis*) is the upshot of prior deliberation (*EN* 1112a15), his point is really that the conceptual structure that is characteristic of deliberation figures in the proper explanation of the relevant actions, whether or not prior deliberation takes place.[2]

[1] This chapter is a descendant of a talk I gave to a National Endowment for the Humanities summer school on Aristotle in 1988; I am grateful to participants for helpful responses. Some of the material appears, in a slightly different form, in McDowell [683].
    [2] See Cooper [453], 5–10.

2. The most straightforwardly intelligible application for the idea of a gap between end and behaviour, to be bridged by deliberative thought, is to cases in which the end sought is *instrumentally* remote from the agent's immediate behavioural possibilities. In such a case, there is no problem about what it would be for the end to have been achieved (for instance for the agent to possess a winter covering). But the end as posited does not select from among the things that the agent can do here and now, so the motivating power of the end gets no grip, so far, on the agent's behavioural predicament. Deliberation overcomes this kind of remoteness of the end from the predicament by finding a *means*, which it is within the agent's present power to realise; perhaps step-wise, by finding intermediate means so as to bring the project successively closer to something the agent can set about doing.

If behaviour-directed thought is to be recognisable as thought at all, an exercise of the intellect, there must be room for the notion of getting things right. With instrumental deliberation, this requirement is comparatively easy to satisfy. This kind of deliberation is not called on to establish that the posited end is worthy of pursuit; we can take that as given from outside the deliberation itself. (See *EN* 1112b11–16.) Assuming the end, we can satisfyingly base the notion of deliberative correctness on the notion of reliable efficacy.[3] (Not 'reduce to', because there are other desiderata that bear on the decision what to do: see *EN* 1112b16–17. But efficacy must be central.) This does not require us to countenance an excellence in thought that is in any real sense distinctively practical: the ideal for this kind of deliberation is to apply, in the pursuit of given ends, knowledge that is in itself theoretical, about what can be relied on to bring about what.

3. But this is only part of the story about how behaviour can manifest the distinctively human kind of purposiveness.

When behaviour is intelligible in terms of an instrumentally deliberative structure, the end in view is external to what is done: it will be brought about by what is done, if all goes well. But one of Aristotle's conditions for action to manifest ethical character (virtue in particular, if the character is as it should be) is that the action undertaken be chosen for its own sake (see *EN* 1105a31–2 for the case of virtue). If choice here retains its usual link with deliberation, there must be a non-instrumental kind of deliberative structure.

It can seem difficult to fit this requirement into Aristotle's scheme. He says of choice (*prohairesis*), as of deliberation, that it fixes on means to ends (as

---

[3] Notice that the fact that the goal is achieved does not suffice for deliberation to have been well done; success may be due to luck. It has to be that the achievement of the goal could reasonably be expected.

the most familiar translation has it): *EN* 1111b26–7, 1112b11–12. How can something chosen as a means be chosen for its own sake?[4]

But this difficulty is a mere creature of the translation. Aristotle's Greek distinguishes ends from 'things towards' ends; and 'towards' ('*pros*') expresses just what is expressed elsewhere by 'for the sake of' or 'with a view to' ('*hina*' or '*heneka*'). Now in the very first chapter of *EN* (1094a3–5), Aristotle has equipped himself with the point that that for the sake of which some activity is undertaken can be either something separate from the activity, a product, or the activity itself.[5] Some commentators have made heavy weather of the idea of an activity as its own end, but the basic point is straightforward. Answering the question 'For the sake of what?' makes sense of behaviour by revealing how it strikes the agent as worth undertaking; and an intrinsic characterisation of an activity, not in terms of an external product, can reveal the worthwhileness that the agent sees in it.

The choices that display character are choices for the sake of doing well (*eu prattein*, which according to *EN* 1095a18–20 is platitudinously equivalent to *eudaimonein*: that is the verb corresponding to the noun '*eudaimonia*', standardly translated 'happiness'). These choices reveal character because they display in practice the agent's conception of how a human being should conduct his life. The fact that these choices are for the sake of doing well ensures that they conform to the general claim about choice, that what is chosen is chosen 'towards' an end. But in these cases an agent's choosing his action for the sake of doing well is his choosing it as a case of doing well. If he is right, what he does (say, facing the enemy at just this juncture of the battle) is what doing well, here and now, is; doing well is not something external to what he does, to be brought about by it.[6] And this secures conformity to the other claim, that actions that reveal character are chosen for their own sake: they are chosen under intrinsic specifications that reveal them as worth engaging in, in the specific way signalled by 'doing well'.

4. This brings into view a different application for the idea of a gap between end and action which thought can bridge. It is no longer the case

---

[4] 'Means' is the translation in Ross [426].
[5] This distinction is related to the distinction between production (*poiēsis*) and action (in a strict sense: *praxis*), for which see *EN* 1140b6–7, 1139b1–4. But the distinctions do not seem to be exactly the same: it seems plausible that an activity can be undertaken for its own sake (for example, for the fun of it) without being undertaken for the sake of doing well (*eupraxia*), which seems to be the mark of *praxis*. 'For the sake of doing well' restricts us to reasons for acting that draw on a conception of human excellence; this is the point of the 'function' argument in *EN* 1.7. (See McDowell [525]; for a contrasting view, see Engberg-Pedersen [454].)
[6] Or 'promoted' by it; Irwin's substitute for the Ross rendering, in Irwin [425], does not fit the bill. See McDowell [683], 90–1.

that it is clear what it would be for the end to have been attained, and deliberation is required to select a means of bringing that about. The initial remoteness of end from action is now, as we can put it, *specificatory*: to say that the end is doing well singles out nothing the agent can here and now undertake, because the question is what doing well here and now would be.

What shape does thought directed at this sort of question take? And what is the content, in this case, of the idea of getting things right?

Many commentators respond to such questions by equipping Aristotle with a kind of practical thinking that applies rules to cases.[7] The idea is that a conception of doing well (the virtuous person's correct conception among others) can be spelled out as a set of rules of conduct, presumably in some such form as this: 'In such-and-such conditions, one should do such-and-such (doing such-and-such is what doing well is).' The answer to our first question is: applying such rules when one recognises that the specified conditions obtain.

If we had a set of rules of this kind, there would be no problem about what it would be to apply them correctly, as it were by their own lights; that would be a matter of deduction. So if there is anything interesting about the second question, it directs us to the question what it is for the rules to be the right ones; and this picture encourages the idea, to which we shall return, that the practical intellect must determine the content of the correct conception of living well.[8]

5. There are two connected difficulties about this 'rule'/'case' picture, as an account of the non-instrumental kind of deliberative structure that Aristotle must have in mind.

First, to have the required deductive powers, the rules would need to be formulable in universal terms, with all conditions made explicit. But Aristotle repeatedly insists, surely with great plausibility, that we should not look for this kind of universal truth in ethics. (See, for instance, *EN* 1094b11–27, 1109b12–23; there are many similar passages.)[9]

---

[7] The *locus classicus* for this idea is probably Allan [664]. I am anyway committed, by the remarks at the end of section 3, to an application of the notion of a case or instance: the virtuous person chooses an action as a case of doing well. But the idea of 'rule'/'case' practical thinking goes beyond that: it is meant to yield an answer to the question *how* the choice locates its object.   [8] See Allan [623].

[9] Aristotle does seem (reasonably enough) to envisage universal prohibitions on, for instance, adultery or murder (see *EN* 1107a9–12). The point is, as he makes clear, that badness is part of the very idea of such actions. If we formulated universal rules in such terms, the sort of specificatory problem that 'rule'/'case' thinking is supposed to address would show up, on occasion, in the form of questions about the applicability of the key terms in the rules. In any case, it is hardly plausible that a conception of how a human being should live could be fully captured in terms of these universal prohibitions.

Secondly, this reading cannot make sense of Aristotle's claim that practical wisdom (*phronēsis*), the intellectual excellence operative in behaviour that manifests good character, is a perceptual capacity. (See *EN* 1142a23–30, 1143a5–b5.) In the 'rule'/'case' picture, the most obvious role for perception is to contribute awareness that certain conditions, which are in fact the conditions specified in a rule, are satisfied.[10] That is a kind of awareness that is presumably available to anyone. It is hard to see why this kind of perception should seem distinctive of someone whose practical intellect is as it should be. On this picture, the proper state of the practical intellect should consist rather in having the right universal principles.[11]

We need a non-instrumental kind of deliberative structure in order to make sense of action that puts into practice an agent's conception of doing well, which is correct if his character is virtuous. Aristotle's scepticism about universal ethical truth implies that the content of the conception acted out by a virtuous person cannot be formulated in such a way that its application can be expressed in the 'rule'/'case' form.[12] Now the appeal to a notion of perception makes perfect sense as, precisely, a response to that. The picture we need (applied to the case of virtue in particular) is on these lines.[13] Having the right conception of the end is, at least, a state of one's motivational propensities. It involves having a number of concerns: that is, motivational susceptibilities, for instance to opportunities to help others. Now it may be that more than one such concern is potentially appealed to by features of a situation one finds oneself in. One response to this is to credit Aristotle with 'ordering

[10] This is the role credited to perception on Aristotle's behalf by Irwin [680]; see especially 65.

[11] Cooper [453], 39–45, offers a different reading of Aristotle's appeal to perception, which seems unsatisfactory in a similar way. Cooper suggests that Aristotle is alluding (in 1143a5–b5) to the capacity to recognise kinds of object (and so forth) that is necessary if one is to be able to put into practice a course of action hit on by prior deliberation, and (in 1142a23–30) to the capacity to tell that deliberation has been taken as far as it needs to be, that is, to an action-specification that the agent can immediately put into practice. That the action-specification arrived at specifies the right action, from among those that are feasible here and now, is taken care of by the deliberation's being done correctly, which is conceived as a separate matter. But my sense of *EN* 1142a23–30 is that affirming the perceptual character of the capacity in question is a way of claiming that it yields right answers (cf. 1109b23), not just that it recognises when a procedure that is anyway such as to yield right answers has been taken far enough.

[12] Of course Aristotle undertakes to formulate, in a sense, the content of the conception of doing well that he himself endorses, when he gives his character sketches of the possessors of the various virtues in books III–V of the *EN*. But one could not extract rules, such as the 'rule'/'case' picture requires, from those passages.

[13] What follows is, in its essentials, the account offered by Wiggins [663].

principles', whose effect is to rank the concerns in urgency, perhaps relatively to features of situations.[14] But this is just a version of the 'rule'/'case' picture; it flies in the face of Aristotle's scepticism about the codifiability of virtuous action. Aristotle's picture is rather this: a correct conception of how one should live does not yield a method of determining which concern one should act on; but one rather than another of the potentially practically relevant features of the situation would strike a virtuous person, and rightly so, as salient, as what matters about the situation. If there were 'ordering principles', they would yield an argument that what appeals to one rather than another of the concerns is what matters about the situation. In the absence of such an argument, it comes naturally to say 'You have to see it', with the perceptual concept marking a point at which discursive justifications have run out (cf. *EN* 1143b1).

We can set out this picture in terms of the 'practical syllogism'.[15] What the perceptual capacity that Aristotle appeals to yields is not awareness of the truth of the minor premise (which is presumably afforded by ordinary cognitive capacities), but its selection from among other features of the situation *as* minor premise: as what matters about the situation. The *de Motu Animalium* (701a9 ff.) distinguishes premises of the good and premises of the possible. In those terms, the premise of the good in the cases we are considering is the content of the correct conception of doing well (cf. *EN* 1144a31–3). If someone gets things right in the kind of practical thought we are considering, what happens is that one feature of the situation rather than another (say, that a friend is in trouble rather than that one has a professional obligation to be elsewhere) comes to serve as premise of the possible, that is, as pointing to something that can be done to gratify the orectic or desiderative state whose content is the premise of the good.[16] We have here a recognisable version of the structure indicated by the terms 'premise of the good' and 'premise of the possible': we can make sense of a piece of behaviour, in this case in a way that involves understanding the fact that the agent identifies behaving in that way as what doing well amounts to in the circumstances in which he finds himself, in terms of the interaction between an orectic state and a doxastic state that registers the feasibility of a specific gratification of it.

---

[14] See, for instance, Cooper [453], 97.

[15] I use this phrase as orthodox commentators do, to label a structure, parallel in some respects to the structure of a certain sort of theoretical argument, that can be used to characterise cases of deliberation or practical reasoning, or the deliberative shape in which an agent's reasons for action can be organised even if no deliberative process entered into the generation of his action. For an unorthodox account of the notion, see Cooper [453], 24–46.

[16] I presuppose the reading of the *de Motu Animalium* passage given by Wiggins [663].

6. We can see the orectic state and the doxastic state as interlocking elements in a mechanism, like the ball and socket of a joint. But the capacity that determines which of the potentially motivating features of the situation is to serve as premise of the possible cannot be separated from the orectic state whose content constitutes the premise of the good. Having the right end is not a mere aggregate of concerns; it requires the capacity to know which should be acted on when. If that capacity does not consist in acceptance of a set of rules, then there is really nothing for it to be except the capacity to get things right occasion by occasion: that is, the perceptual capacity that determines which feature of the situation should engage a standing concern. The premise of the good, and the selection of the right feature of the situation to serve as premise of the possible, correspond to a single fact about the agent, which we can view indifferently as an orectic state or as a cognitive capacity. This explains how Aristotle can equate practical wisdom both with the perceptual capacity (*EN* 1142a23–30) and with a true conception of the end (*EN* 1142b33). It is not just that he credits each of these to the practically wise person, as if they might be independent attributes of him; he says of each that it is what practical wisdom is.

This double aspect of practical wisdom, as correctness of motivational orientation and as cognitive capacity, is something that Aristotle risks obscuring in passages like *EN* 1144a7–9, where he says that 'virtue makes the goal right, practical wisdom the things with a view to the goal'. (There are similar remarks at 1144a20–2 and 1145a3–6.) This claim might seem to represent having the right goal, which is, presumably, having one's desiderative element (one's *orektikon*) as it should be, as one thing, and practical wisdom as quite another; as if practical wisdom, the intellectual excellence operative in virtuous behaviour, serves merely as handmaiden to a separate motivational propensity, which exerts its influence from outside the intellect.

There is an exegetical tradition, not nowadays widely in favour, that reads these passages on such lines. On this interpretation, Aristotle's view is quasi-Humean: intellectual excellence is the slave, not indeed of the passions, but at any rate of a non-intellectual motivational directedness. On the usual reading, *EN* 1142b33 says that practical wisdom is a true conception of the end; that would be inconsistent with representing the proper motivational orientation as simply separate from anything intellectual. The quasi-Humean interpretation requires a different reading of that passage, giving the relative pronoun a different antecedent; the upshot is to make the passage identify practical wisdom with a true conception not of the end but of what is conducive towards it.[17]

---

[17] This quasi-Humean interpretation traces back to Walter [69].

Much modern discussion has been shaped by a recoil from this reading. The recoil is surely right, but we need to be careful where it takes us. One common result is taking Aristotle to hold that it must be the intellect that determines the content of the virtuous person's correct conception of the end. This requires an embarrassed discounting of passages like *EN* 1144a7–9, or a more or less strained reading of them that softens their apparent contrast between the roles of practical wisdom and virtue.[18]

But we can avoid the quasi-Humean reading while taking passages like *EN* 1144a7–9 fully at their word. The point of such passages is this: what determines the content of a virtuous person's correct conception of the end is not an exercise of the practical intellect, but rather the moulding of his motivational propensities in upbringing, which is described in book II of the *EN* as instilling virtue of character. This is not a quasi-Humean thought, because there is no reason why a state whose content is so determined cannot *be* an intellectual excellence. The claim is that it is not practical wisdom that *makes it the case* that the goal is the right one. This leaves intact the thesis that *having* the right goal, being, as it is, inseparable from the ability to know what is to be done occasion by occasion, is what practical wisdom is. (Recall the double aspect of practical wisdom.) Having the right motivational orientation can be something other than a product of argument (or intellectual intuition), without any implication that is extra-intellectual, something that directs the practical application of the intellect from outside.

7. Commentators sometimes suggest that if we take passages like *EN* 1144a7–9 at face value, we restrict the practical intellect to a merely instrumental role. But this is simply wrong. The claim is that the content of a virtuous person's correct conception of the end is determined by upbringing, not by an exercise of the intellect; this makes no difference to the fact that a virtuous person confronts practical questions of the form 'What does doing well here and now amount to?' The deliberation that such a question calls for is precisely not instrumental deliberation: instrumental deliberation looks for how to bring about an end where what counts as its having been brought about is not part of the problem.

We should distinguish two possible kinds of practical thought, both of which can be seen as responding to questions of that specificatory type. One kind would confer determinate general content on an end hitherto adopted only under a quite indeterminate specification like 'doing well'; this kind of deliberation would work towards a blueprint for the sort of life a human

---

[18] See, for example, Irwin [483], 268. He suggests that 'virtue's grasp of the goal' is itself dictated by a prior exercise of practical wisdom. This ignores the clear implication, from the contrastive structure of 1144a7–9, that what makes the goal the right one is virtue *as opposed to* practical wisdom.

being should lead, perhaps by reflectively identifying components of a good life and working out principles for their combination. The other would be aimed not at forming a general conception of the end, but at putting one into practice in specific circumstances. If the content of a general conception of the end cannot be formulated in rules, applying it to particular predicaments is not a straightforward matter. No doubt we cannot always sharply distinguish between determining part of the general content of a conception of the end and discerning what an already held conception of the end requires of one in a given predicament. But that is not to say that we should always gravitate to the former description.

The second of these conceptions of specificatory practical thought is enough to make room for a non-instrumental kind of practical thinking. Commentators have almost universally found in Aristotle a concern with the first; but I do not believe this has any textual basis, and I think it reflects saddling Aristotle with alien, and dubious, philosophical aspirations.[19]

We should discount the possibly confusing effects of using the expression 'determinate end' for the kind of end whose pursuit calls for instrumental deliberation.[20] The point of the expression is that instrumental deliberation does not have to address the question what it would be for the end to have been achieved. That contrasts with deliberation needed to determine what it would be to achieve the end. Now this description fits occasions for the second kind of specificatory deliberation distinguished above, no less than occasions for the first. But the corresponding label, 'indeterminate end', tends to restrict attention to the first: to cases where what still needs to be determined is the general content of the end, so that deliberation is towards a general blueprint for a life rather than towards a specification of what to do here and now.

8. There is a philosophical motivation for a reading of Aristotle in which what determines the content of a virtuous person's conception of the end is an exercise of the intellect.

The thought is this. If the shape of one's conception of the end is the upshot of upbringing, as opposed to an exercise of one's intellectual powers, then one's having one rather than another conception of the end is (merely)

---

[19] This is why, in discussing the two sorts of application for phrases like 'for the sake of', I did not follow the usual practice (derived from Greenwood [432], 46–7) of distinguishing instrumental from constituent means. That terminology does not discriminate between thought which concludes, say, that satisfactory social relations are a component of the good life and thought which concludes, say, that facing the enemy is what doing well is here and now. It is the latter, not the former, that exemplifies the 'for the sake of' relation that I believe we need to consider: constituents of doing well, in the relevant sense, are not components in a general blueprint for a life but particular actions.

[20] I believe this use derives from Irwin [293].

a non-rationally moulded state of one's desiderative make-up. One such state is rationally speaking on a level with another. So this way we lose what Aristotle obviously wants to have, the idea that just one conception of the end is the correct one. That requires, according to this line of thought, that the correctness of the conception can be established by argument. And, on pain of falling back into reliance on a mere non-rationally moulded motivational and valuational propensity, the argument's persuasiveness would have to be independent of the specific propensities to value this and despise that which are inculcated in a proper upbringing (by Aristotle's lights). The validating argument would have to be, in an obvious sense, from outside the initially merely inherited ethical outlook that it would validate.[21]

I suggested that commentators who accept the 'rule'/'case' picture do not take Aristotle's scepticism about universal truth in ethics with sufficient seriousness. This line of thought may underlie the tendency to miss the full force of that scepticism. If there were to be an external certification that a given conception of the end is the right one, we would need to be able to formulate the content of the conception in such a way that the certification could get a grip on it. The content of the conception would need to be capable of figuring as the conclusion of a discursive argument, whose cogency would have to be clear in abstraction from any particular series of practical predicaments. Only a set of rules, with all relativity to situations made explicit in universal terms, could serve the purpose.[22]

---

[21] Irwin [293] (see, for example, 9, 159, 175) attributes the idea of an external standard for the rationality of virtue exclusively to Socrates, whom he takes (wrongly in my view, but that is another story) to have represented virtuous actions as instrumental means to an end that everyone pursues. For Irwin's Plato, the standard by which virtue is revealed to be rational is not (as for Irwin's Socrates) external to the distinctive valuations of a virtuous person; being persuaded into acceptance of the standard is the same thing as being persuaded into virtue. And Irwin's account of Aristotle's view on this matter is similar. This is certainly an important distinction: for Irwin's Socrates, the rationality of virtue is reducible to something extra-ethical, and for Irwin's Plato and Aristotle this is not so. The fact remains, however, that Irwin conceives persuasion into accepting the standard (certainly for Plato; see 167–72) as proceeding stepwise in such a way that each step is revealed as rationally required according to standards of rationality already endorsed before the step is taken. This is precisely a picture of validation from outside; that it is non-reductive makes no difference to that.

[22] Even commentators who appreciate Aristotle's hostility to the idea that the truth about how to live can be captured once and for all in a set of rules tend to suggest that we can meet Aristotle's point by thinking in terms of 'broad principles', to be applied with discretion. (See, for example, Cooper [453], 134–5.) The idea here is that discretion mediates between something general, suitable to be validated from outside, and the detail of real life. I believe this underplays the importance for Aristotle of situation-specific discernment, in the interest of keeping in the picture a suitable conclusion for the supposed external validation.

9. An external validation of the correctness of a specific ethic would be of enormous significance. If Aristotle really thought he could give such a thing, one would expect him to highlight it. In fact one looks for it in vain. At *EN* 1095b4–6 he implies that he is not even going to address questions of validation. And wherever someone who believes in this kind of external validation might expect Aristotle to use it, in saying what determines the rightness of right action, or the propriety of proper deliberation, or whatever, he disappoints such expectations; rather than giving a criterion that works from outside the ethic that he takes for granted, he says that such things are as the virtuous person determines them. (See, for example, *EN* 1107a1–2, 1139a29–31, 1144a34).

To many commentators the argument from the 'function' (*ergon*) of a human being in *EN* I.7, reprised in II.6, suggests that Aristotle envisages an external validation for his ethic, starting from the facts about human nature. But proponents of all sorts of non-Aristotelian conceptions of doing well could accept the conceptual connections which that argument exploits, between 'function', excellence and doing well. Such people would dispute a view of the human 'function', and hence of human nature, that made Aristotle's own list of virtues come out correct, and they would not thereby be disputing anything in the 'function' argument.[23]

In fact there are only two substantive points on which Aristotle suggests that facts about human nature constrain the truth about a good human life, in a way that might be supposed to be independent of inculcated propensities to value this and despise that. First, a good human life must be an active life of that which has *logos* (*EN* 1098a3–4): this excludes, for instance, the ideal of uncontrolled gratification of appetite with which Socrates saddles Callicles, in Plato's *Gorgias*. Secondly, human beings are naturally social (*EN* 1097b11, 1169b18–19): this excludes a solitary life. Obviously these two points fall a long way short of purporting to afford a validation of Aristotle's ethic in full; but it is that for which he wants to claim objective correctness.

10. The reading I am considering is shaped by the thought that, as far as objective correctness goes, one non-rationally moulded state of one's desiderative make-up (one's *orektikon*) is on a par with another, unless the conception of the good embodied in one of them can be certified as true from outside. But why should we suppose that Aristotle would accept that? It is common ground that, in his view, at most one of two different conceptions of the end could involve the desiderative element's being as it should be. Suppose he were pressed about the valuation implicit in that 'should'. Why should he not say something like this: only by living in accordance with the

²³ See McDowell [525].

correct conception of the end can we fill our lives with actions that are noble (*kalon*)? That would exactly not be offering to ground his valuational scheme from outside; it would be appealing to the habits of valuation that are inculcated in the kind of upbringing that he is confident his audience has had (*EN* 1095b4–6).

This may make it seem that the background of Aristotle's moral psychology is an unreflective contentment with the mores of his audience. Such an accusation would probably not be completely unfair. There are, however, passages that do not fit this picture, but place Aristotle rather in a line of descent from Socrates' commendation of the examined life (for instance the distinction between having 'the that', which is where properly brought up people begin, and having 'the because', at *EN* 1095b6–7).[24] But the reflection involved in working towards a comprehending acceptance of a scheme of values (having 'the because' as well as 'the that') need not be conceived as stepping outside the standpoint constituted by an inherited mode of thought, so as to supply it (if all goes well) with an external validation. There is an alternative, which seems fully in keeping with Aristotle's conception of philosophical method: a conception of reflection for which the appropriate image (at least for us: see below) is Neurath's, of the mariner repairing his ship while afloat.

There is a temptation to think that Neurathian, or internal, reflection could only be second best. This belongs with the tendency to be disappointed when Aristotle rests within the circle of his own ethic, letting the virtuous person be the measure of (say) how one should act. Here the philosophical basis for the kind of reading of Aristotle that I am deploring comes to the surface; and we can begin to see, at least in outline, how it falsifies him. Neurathian reflection on an inherited scheme of values takes place at a standpoint within that scheme; the scheme can be altered piecemeal, but not suspended in its entirety, with a view to rebuilding from the ground up. The disappointment results from the idea that one could not achieve a justified conviction of objective correctness, in thought about anything, from within something as historically contingent as a conceptual scheme; what is required is to break out of a specific cultural inheritance into undistorted contact with the real. Now this idea is distinctively modern. I do not mean that it has happened to occur to people only in modern times, but that it is not really even intelligible except as a response to modern currents of thought. Loss of confidence in internal reflection just as such requires an awareness, not shared by all ages, of the historical contingency of actual modes of thought;[25] and the consoling counterpart idea, that of a mode of

---

[24]   See Burnyeat [569].

[25]   Ancient ethical scepticism, vividly represented in, for example, Plato's *Gorgias*, was not like this.

contact with the real in which we transcend our historicity, can seem to be available only by way of a philosophical misconception of the achievements of modern science, something that is itself in turn partly motivated by that loss of confidence.[26]

It is not that we can patronise Aristotle for insensitivity to a good question about ethical objectivity, which we have learned since his time to ask. The question looks like a good one only in that modern philosophical framework, and we ought to be suspicious of our tendency to hanker after something more than Neurathian reflection. One of the benefits of studying a great philosopher from an alien age is that it can help us to see that we do not have to swim with the currents of our own time.

It would be anachronistic to suggest that the Neurathian image might fit Aristotle's own conception of the reflection that the transition to having 'the because' would require. The image is apt for expressing explicit rejection of the hankering for an external standpoint; it has its resonance only in the context of felt pressures towards losing confidence in internal reflection as such. My claim is that Aristotle is healthily innocent of all that. The point of the image for us is to express a philosophically knowing stance that is as close as we, with our irrevocably lost innocence, can come to Aristotle's outlook.[27]

11. Aristotle organises his discussion of the human virtues by distinguishing virtues of character (courage, temperance, and so forth) from intellectual virtues (see *EN* 1103a3–18). The intellectual virtues include excellences in behaviour-directed thought, notably practical wisdom, and this sets up a link between the sorts of virtue: practical wisdom is an intellectual excellence displayed in those actions that manifest virtues of character strictly so called (see *EN* 1144b1–17).

I have been discussing a reading of Aristotle that recoils as far as possible

---

[26] Insisting that scientific modes of thought are products of history too is often represented as disparaging them. But it looks like that only in the context of a conception of what it would be to give science its due that is shaped by the questionable philosophy I am describing.

[27] Contrast Irwin [411], who represents Aristotle as a 'metaphysical' (as opposed to 'internal') realist. I think this is damagingly anachronistic. Wanting one's realism 'metaphysical' as opposed to 'internal' is a confused response to distinctively modern intellectual pressures. There is anachronism in reading Aristotle as an 'internal' (or Neurathian) realist, but it is not symmetrical, because the point of labelling one's realism 'internal' is to reject a modern philosophical confusion: 'internal' realism is the nearest we can get to an outlook which (to its advantage) would not so much as understand the temptation towards 'metaphysical' realism. (These remarks exemplify how issues in the history of philosophy are inextricably bound up with issues in philosophy; the history looks different to Irwin and to me because the philosophy does.)

from the quasi-Humean reading. In the quasi-Humean reading, the intellectual excellence exercised in actions that display virtue of character is subservient to an extra-intellectual motivational orientation. In the polar opposite, there is still a relation of subservience, but in an opposite direction. It is an exercise of the intellect that determines a fully virtuous person's motivational orientation. The virtues of character whose origin in upbringing is described in *EN* book II (which turn out, on this view, not to be virtues of character in the strict sense) are non-intellectual motivational propensities, moulded by habituation, whose ultimate role in the psychological organisation of a fully virtuous agent is to make him receptive to the independent dictates of the practical intellect. A virtue of character strictly so called is a harmonious composite of intellectual and non-intellectual elements; the non-intellectual element ensures the agent's obedience to requirements set by pursuit of an end whose content is autonomously fixed by the intellectual element.[28]

I have urged that we need not opt for one of these polar opposites. We need not read Aristotle as attributing dominance in the genesis of virtuous behaviour either to the practical intellect, conceived as operating autonomously, or to a wholly non-intellectual desiderative state. In fact the wholly extra-intellectual motivational propensity which both these extreme readings find in the initial discussion of virtue of character is an abstraction; it fits nothing with which Aristotle seems to be concerned. Correspondingly, there is no reason to credit him with a picture of the practical intellect as operating independently of moulded motivational propensities.

Already in book II of *EN*, in which the stress is on states that result from upbringing, he insists that the actions that manifest virtue of character must be chosen (1105a31–2). By way of the link with deliberation, this imports the specially human capacity for discursive thought; it is already implicit that virtue of character requires an intellectual excellence. We travesty Aristotle's picture of habituation into virtue of character if we take the products of habituation to be motivational propensities that are independent of conceptual thought, like a trained animal's behavioural dispositions. On the contrary, the topic is clearly initiation, by way of being taught to admire and delight in actions in the right way, into a conceptual space. The space is the one that we move in as we read the subsequent character sketches of possessors of the particular virtues; it is organised by the concepts of the noble and the disgraceful (see, for instance, *EN* 1120a23–4).[29] Possessing 'the that', those who have undergone this initiation are already beyond uncomprehending habit; they are already some distance into the

---

[28] For an especially clear exposition of an account on these lines, see Cooper [677].
[29] See Burnyeat [569].

realm of the relevant intellectual excellence. They have a conceptual attainment which, just as such, primes them for the reflection that would be required for the transition to 'the because'. And that transition need not involve the injection of new conceptual substance from outside. Reflection towards 'the because' can be Neurathian; it needs no material besides the substance of the conceptual space already inhabited, in a partially comprehending way, in consequence of upbringing.

On this reading, practical wisdom does not issue orders, whose content it determines by its own independent operations, to motivational propensities that have been separately moulded to obedience. The harmony of intellect and motivation in a virtue of character, strictly so called, is more intimate than that. Practical wisdom *is* the properly moulded state of the motivational propensities, in a reflectively adjusted form; the sense in which it is a state of the intellect does not interfere with its also being a state of the desiderative element.[30]

12. Aristotle frames his treatment of the virtues within a discussion of 'the good and the chief good' (*EN* 1094a22). He appeals to common consent in favour of identifying the good with 'happiness' (*eudaimonia*), which in turn is equated with living well and doing well (1095a14–20). The first part of EN 1.7 spells out the content and basis of this common consent: the identification of the good with *eudaimonia* is justified on the ground that *eudaimonia* meets some quasi-formal requirements involved in the idea of the good (1097a25–b21), and the argument from the 'function' of man confirms the equation of *eudaimonia* with acting well, with 'well' spelled out as 'in accordance with virtue' (1097b22–1098a20).

This connection between virtue and *eudaimonia* is often thought to mark the point at which the supposed external validation of Aristotle's ethic gets its grip. The concept of *eudaimonia* is supposed to locate a kind of reflection whose upshot would be a blueprint for a life, capable of being recognised as determining what it is rational to do even from a standpoint outside the valuations that result from being brought up into a particular ethical outlook. The connection of virtue with *eudaimonia* would then serve to

---

[30] Cooper [677] deliberately refrains from offering a justification from the texts for his different reading of Aristotle. The case would have to rest largely on *EN* 1.13. I think we should be careful not to over-read that passage; its purpose is to introduce an architectonic structure for expository purposes, and the subsequent development itself shows that we should not take the structure too rigidly. Cooper's main justification comes from a view about how Aristotle fits into the evolution of Greek moral psychology, from Socrates to the Stoics. Obviously I cannot discuss the whole sweep of Greek ethics in this chapter. I can only say, dogmatically, that I think Cooper's account is badly mistaken; and I suspect the main culprit is a misreading of Stoicism, reflected back into the earlier thinkers.

establish, from outside those valuations, that Aristotle's own list of virtues is correct, in the sense that a life of activity in accordance with them will meet independent standards for being worth going in for.

This view of the role of *eudaimonia* in Aristotle's thinking reflects the philosophical expectations whose alienness to Aristotle I have been urging. Unsurprisingly, I think it distorts his intentions. In any case, it should be of interest to consider an alternative reading, whose possibility is obscured by the assumption that Aristotle aims at an external validation.

According to the alternative, the point of the concept of *eudaimonia* is not to suggest a general determination of what can be practically rational, on the basis of some idea like that of an optimal combination of items that can be seen to be elements in a good human life anyway, independently of any particular ethic. We need not credit Aristotle with such a monolithic, if comprehensive, conception of reasons for acting in general; and in any case reasons for acting in general need be no concern of his when he discusses *eudaimonia*. The concept of *eudaimonia* marks out, rather, just one dimension of practical worthwhileness. Practical worthwhileness in general is multidimensional, and the considerations that occupy different dimensions are not necessarily commensurable with one another.[31] The significance of the fact that it is *the* good with which *eudaimonia* is equated is not that all possible reasons for acting (all goods, in one obvious sense: see *EN* 1094a1–3) are embraced under *eudaimonia*, but that worthwhileness along this dimension is worthwhileness *par excellence*. The dimension in question is that of reasons for acting that depend on a conception of human virtue; this is the point of the 'function' argument. If one's conception of human virtue is the right one (by Aristotle's lights), that will show in one's valuing the right actions as noble; and the value of nobility will be what organises one's conception of the eudaimonic dimension of practical worthwhileness. It is not that nobility as Aristotle understands it is certified as an authentic value on the basis that a life of noble actions can be seen to meet independent standards for being worth going in for; it is rather that someone who has learned to delight in noble actions has thereby come to see those actions as pre-eminently worth going in for, just because they are noble.[32]

I think the main obstacle to a reading on these lines is the philosophical disappointment that I have already discussed; but I shall mention some texts that may seem to raise problems for it.

EN 1097b6–20 says that *eudaimonia* is self-sufficient, that is, 'on its own makes life pursuit-worthy and lacking in nothing'; this is one of those quasi-formal requirements for being the good. The passage goes on to say that *eudai-*

---

[31] See Burnyeat [569], 86–7, and 91, n. 29.   [32] See McDowell [525].

monia is 'most pursuit-worthy not counted in with others; if it were so counted, clearly it would be more pursuit-worthy with the addition of the smallest of goods'. This can seem to represent *eudaimonia* as embracing anything whose presence would in any way make a life more desirable. But such a reading will in any case not cohere with the fact that Aristotle is unwilling to count gifts of chance, which surely do make a life more desirable, as contributing to *eudaimonia* (see *Politics* 1323b24–9; cf. *Eudemian Ethics* 1215a12–19, *EN* 1099b18–25).³³ So the passage anyway requires a restricted dimension of desirability, with other dimensions irrelevant to the claim that *eudaimonia* leaves nothing to be desired on the dimension that is relevant. The dimension I have extracted from the 'function' argument, that of considerations whose appeal depends on a conception of virtue, will suit.³⁴ As for the rejection of 'counting in with others', I take it that the point is the one I have tried to capture in terms of worthwhileness *par excellence*. The dimension of worthwhileness in question is such that, if a consideration belonging to it bears on one's practical situation, anyone who has learned to appreciate such considerations will see that nothing else matters for the question what shape one's life should take here and now, even if the upshot is a life that is less desirable along other dimensions. If the upshot is a life that is more desirable along other dimensions, that is irrelevant to the self-sufficiency of *eudaimonia*.³⁵

EN 1102a2–3 says 'it is for the sake of this [*eudaimonia*] that we all do everything else that we do'. But Aristotle does not think all purposive behaviour, even of the distinctively intellect-involving human kind, is aimed at *eudaimonia*; this is clear from the case of the calculating incontinent person, who uses his intelligence in purposive behaviour that precisely flies in the face of his conception of *eudaimonia*. (See *EN* 1142b18–20, 1146b22–4.) We had better read 1102a2–3 so as not to contradict that; one way to do so is by finding in it a special, quasi-technical concept of 'doing' (*praxis, prattein*), to be understood precisely in terms of a conceptual link to *eudaimonia*.³⁶ So

---

³³ These citations are from Cooper [453], 123–4; see his discussion there.

³⁴ On this view, the nature of the restriction becomes clear only after this passage, with the 'function' argument itself. This is unsurprising in view of the way Aristotle approaches his favoured framework through dialectical exploitation of common and philosophical ideas: we may need the whole development for a full comprehension of what a claimed correspondence with common sense means in Aristotle's own framework.

³⁵ It will be clear that I am not reading Aristotle's conception of the end as inclusive, in the sense of Hardie [517]. (But I do not think I am reading it as dominant – Hardie's alternative – either.)

³⁶ Equivalently (on the strength of *EN* 1095a19–20), *eupraxia* (the word is an abstract noun corresponding to the verb phrase 'doing well'): for *eupraxia* as the end of *praxis*, see *EN* 1139b1–4, 1140b6–7. There is more discussion of this in McDowell [525].

read, the passage does not represent *eudaimonia* as embracing reasons for acting quite generally.

EN 1098a18–20 makes it clear that Aristotle conceives *eudaimonia* as, primarily, an attribute of a whole life. This can encourage the idea that the point an agent sees in an action undertaken for the sake of *eudaimonia* must be derivative from the independent attractiveness of a life lived according to a certain blueprint.[37] But this idea is anyway hard to make cohere with the thesis that character-revealing action (which reveals character precisely by revealing, because undertaken so as to act out, its agent's conception of doing well) is undertaken for its own sake; that seems to rule out taking the point of such action for the agent to lie outside itself, in the independent attractiveness of a life into which, if all goes well, it will fit. (Suppose all does not go well, and one's life does not achieve the projected shape: does that mean that this particular action, say one of standing one's ground in battle, did not after all have the point it seemed to have?[38] Surely not. Of course it would be another matter to deny that if one's life as a whole goes badly enough one can lose one's grip on the distinctive point that virtuous behaviour has: see, perhaps, *EN* 1099b2–6.)

There is a different way to take the idea that seeing a particular action as doing well is seeing it under the aspect of a whole human life, which is suggested by the links exploited in the 'function' argument. The point is that doing well is acting in accordance with virtue, and the proper location for the question what the human virtues are is reflection on what shape a human life should take. If such reflection is Neurathian, the 'should' here need not take us outside the ethical. And this allows us to respect Aristotle's claim that the concept of doing well is in the first instance the concept of a way of life, while holding that when one sees an action as a case of doing well, the point one sees in it need not be independent of the delight one's upbringing has taught one to take in noble actions just as such.[39]

---

[37] This may account for Irwin's use of 'promote'; see n. 6 above. The primacy of the whole life can render invisible the possibility that when one acts on a particular occasion for the sake of doing well, what one does can be (not promote) that for the sake of which one does it.

[38] Irwin [293], 262, responds to this sort of problem by simply separating 'for its own sake' from 'for the sake of happiness': 'Aristotle's virtuous man . . . recognises that part of the life which secures happiness will be virtuous action for its own sake, without caring about happiness'. But for Aristotle virtuous action, undertaken for its own sake, is what 'happiness' is; he would surely find this separation of concerns ('without caring about happiness') unintelligible. (The translation 'happiness' seems seriously damaging here.)

[39] Cooper [453], 124–5, sees that *eudaimonia* must *be* (a life of) virtuous action for its own sake, not something 'secured by' such action (if all goes well). He keeps a role for the idea of an orderly combination of elements independently recognisable to

13. We can take the central books of the *EN* to spell out a conception of doing well as living in accordance with virtue, comprehensively understood. Book x introduces a conception of the highest *eudaimonia* as living in accordance with the highest virtue, the virtue of what is best in human beings (1177a12–13): this is a contemplative life. Such a life engages that in us in respect of which we come closest to the divine. From this point of view, the life of ordinary virtue of character which has seemed to be Aristotle's main topic so far, although it is distinctively human in so far as it involves the intellectual excellence of practical wisdom, can be depreciated as *merely* human; and we have it in us to be more than merely human. With hindsight, we can perhaps find this 'intellectualistic' conception of the highest *eudaimonia* alluded to already in the conclusion of the 'function' argument, which, having identified *eudaimonia* with activity in accordance with virtue, goes on to say 'and if there are several virtues, in accordance with the best and most perfect' (*EN* 1098a17–18).

If we suppose that a conception of *eudaimonia* is meant to embrace all potential reasons for acting, and yield a procedure for resolving conflicts between them, this singling out of contemplation is extraordinarily difficult to swallow. We have to take it that all other activity is to be evaluated in terms of conduciveness to contemplation, which makes the picture of book x contradict the earlier suggestion that the actions required by the ordinary virtues of character are worth going in for in their own right; alternatively we have to suppose that book x presents not just a novel conception of *eudaimonia*, but a novel concept of it.[40] But if we exorcise the idea that a conception of *eudaimonia* is a general conception of practical rationality, we can

be worth pursuing, not, as in Irwin, as what *eudaimonia* is, but as serving in a confirmation that what Aristotle takes to be virtues are indeed states worth cultivating: virtuous activity for its own sake is what *eudaimonia* is, and it is worth becoming the kind of person who lives like that because such a life is likeliest to be satisfactory by independent standards. This is a great improvement on Irwin's picture, but the supposed external validation still strikes me as foreign to Aristotle. And the position seems vulnerable to a version of a standard problem for any indirect consequentialism. Suppose one knows the story about why the virtues are worth cultivating, and knows that the independently recognisable satisfactoriness of life that figures in that story will probably not be achieved by a virtuous action that one has in prospect (say because the action in question is facing the enemy in battle, and one will probably be killed or maimed). How can this not tend to undermine one's virtuous motivation? We have no such problems if we simply stop looking for external authentication for virtuous motivation. The only relevant satisfaction is that which one has learned to take in noble actions as such.

40 There is no sign anywhere in Aristotle of the idea that conduciveness to contemplation is supposed to yield a criterion for the worthwhileness of other activity. On *EE* 1249a21–b23, which comes closer to this than anything else, see Cooper [453], 135–43.

take the introduction of the contemplative life in our stride. We can see how Aristotle might want to single out, as the highest worthwhileness of the distinctively eudaimonic sort (that is, worthwhileness depending on a conception of virtue), the worthwhileness of exercises of our highest excellence. This selection does in a way disparage the worthwhileness of acts of ordinary civic ('merely human') virtue; but there is no tension with the thesis that that worthwhileness, although second-grade, is genuine, and intrinsic, not derivative from a higher end to which such acts are conducive. Without needing to explain away the treatment of *eudaimonia* in book x, as an expression of an inconsistent alternative view, we can avoid letting it disrupt our appreciation of the main body of *EN*, which we naturally find more congenial.

14. No discussion of Aristotle's moral psychology could be complete without mentioning his interest in 'incontinence' (*akrasia*). There is no space for a proper treatment here, but the general outlines of an interpretation are implicit in what I have already said.

Practical wisdom is a capacity to discern which of the potentially action-inviting features of a situation is the one that should be allowed to engage with one of the standing concerns of a virtuous person so as to induce an action. Consider a situation which calls for the most striking sort of exercise of temperance, namely abstaining from an available but excessive bodily pleasure. That the pleasure is available is a fact about the situation, at the disposal of a temperate person no less than anyone else. Such facts can engage a motivational susceptibility which is one of the standing concerns of a virtuous person. (Too little interest in the pleasures of appetite is a defect of character: see *EN* III.11.) But on this occasion what matters about the situation, as the practically wise person correctly sees it, is not the opportunity for pleasure but, say, the fact that this would be his fifth doughnut at one sitting. The practically wise person registers, but counts as irrelevant to the question what to do, an instance of a kind of consideration (that pleasure is available) which does bear on that question in other circumstances; and his counting it as irrelevant shows in his being unmoved by it, by contrast with the merely continent person (the *enkratēs*), who has to overcome temptation in order to get himself to do the right thing (see *EN* 1151b34–1152a3).

This makes it obvious why Aristotle should have a problem over the possibility of incontinence (at any rate the variety distinguished at *EN* 1150b19–22 as weakness). The intuitive picture of a weak person is of someone whose practical thinking matches that of a practically wise person (he knows what he should do), but who succumbs to temptation and acts differently. But a practically wise person sees the potential temptations in temperance-requiring predicaments as practically irrelevant, and this conception of their status prevents them from actually tempting him (which would make his best prospect be continence). There cannot be both a perfect match with the practical thinking of a fully virtuous person and a felt temptation to do otherwise. (It does not matter whether the felt temptation is acted on or not; continence poses the same conceptual difficulty.)

If we discount the possibility of simply denying the existence of weakness, the shape of a resolution for this difficulty is virtually dictated by the shape of the difficulty: the match with the practical thinking of a practically wise person has to be imperfect. In the operation of full-fledged practical wisdom, the agent singles out just the right one of the potentially action-inviting features of a predicament, in such a way that all his motivational energy is concentrated into the concern to which that feature appeals; he has no errant impulses that threaten to lead him astray, so that he would be at best continent even if he managed not to be sidetracked. The closest we can get to this, while allowing errant impulses to arise, is a flawed approximation to the special perceptual capacity that is practical wisdom: something capable of yielding a similar selection of what matters about the situation, but without the singleness of motivational focus on that feature of the situation that practical wisdom would achieve. I believe we can find such an idea in *EN* VII.3.

It is important to realise that Aristotle's problem about incontinence is a problem about acting otherwise than, as one (in a way) realises, doing well requires. *Eudaimonia* is just one dimension of practical worthwhileness, although those who appreciate it take it, rightly, to be pre-eminent over others; it is not a balance in which all potential reasons for acting are somehow combined. This means that Aristotle's difficulty over incontinence does not reflect an unwarranted expectation that practical exercises of intelligence *in general* should progress inexorably into action, so that there would be no room for breakdowns and no need for executive virtues to ensure that one sticks to one's decisions. (Such a general expectation is often attributed to Socrates, wrongly in my view.) Aristotle has specific reasons for supposing that a properly focused application to a situation of a correct conception of doing well, in particular, must issue in action; that idea, which dictates his attitude to incontinence, reflects no general dogma of the efficacy of the intellect.[41]

---

[41] These remarks are directed against the way Wiggins [691] deplores what Aristotle says about incontinence as excessively 'Socratic'. Wiggins' account of what Aristotle should have said instead relates to the progression of thought into action in general; as far as I can see, nothing in Aristotle stops him taking Wiggins' view of that topic, consistently with being as 'Socratic' as he is about the efficacy of practical wisdom in particular. (Wiggins also suggests that the view I am urging

In full-fledged practical wisdom the correct conception of doing well, with the understanding that the worthwhileness that it embraces is pre-eminent, is so ingrained into one's motivational make-up that when an action is singled out as doing well, any attractions that alternatives might have are seen as having no bearing on the question what to do. An incontinent or continent person has a flawed approximation to practical wisdom. He has, in a way, a correct conception of doing well, and applies that conception to particular predicaments; but he reveals that his resemblance to a possessor of full-fledged practical wisdom is only partial by the fact that he is swayed by the attractions of alternatives to what he (in a way) knows to be doing well. It helps to make this idea of a flawed approximation to practical wisdom intelligible if we take continence and incontinence to characterise people who are on their way to acquiring virtue. There are genuine attractions in some courses of action that virtue requires us to renounce, and the renunciation is not compensated in kind by the course of virtue;[42] so it is only to be expected that there should be stages of moral development at which an appreciation, of sorts, of virtue's requirements, and even of their status as pre-eminent, does not yet have its full motivational realisation, the capacity to be unmoved by competing attractions. Apart from the intrinsic interest of the conceptual puzzle about its possibility, then, we can attribute to incontinence a more systematic significance in Aristotle's exposition of his moral psychology: reflection on the nature of the flaw in incontinence (or continence) can help us to understand what these states fall short of, the intimate integration of conceptual thought and moulded inclination that makes up Aristotle's picture of full-fledged virtue of character.[43]

requires a cognitive or perceptual difference between a continent person and an incontinent person; but that is a misunderstanding. The perceptual difference that is needed is between a virtuous person on the one side and, indifferently, a continent or incontinent person on the other; this leaves it open what determines whether someone who is tempted astray, thereby showing that he does not fully share a virtuous person's view of his situation, acts on the temptation or not.)

[42] See Wiggins [691].   [43] See Burnyeat [569].

6

The inferential foundations of Epicurean ethics

DAVID SEDLEY

I An outline of Epicurean ethics[1]

Pleasure, according to Epicurus, is the single positive value, or 'end', towards whose attainment and maximisation all human and animal life is geared. An ideal Epicurean life gains its distinctive flavour from an orchestrated set of calculations aimed at that result, balancing in particular the relative contributions of bodily and mental pleasures, and, within those categories, of two distinct types, 'kinetic' and 'katastematic' pleasures. Bodily feeling is in a way focal, since mental pleasure and pain consist ultimately in satisfaction and dissatisfaction respectively about bodily feeling. For instance, the greatest mental pain, fear, is primarily the expectation of future bodily pain (which is the main ground, and a mistaken one, for the fear of death). And the greatest mental pleasure lies in confidence that bodily pain can continue indefinitely to be avoided or overcome. But although mental feelings ultimately depend on bodily ones, and not vice versa, mental feelings are a more powerful factor in the overall quality of a life. Someone in bodily pain – which may be unavoidable – can outweigh it by the mental act of reliving past pleasures and anticipating future ones. It is this ability to range over past and future that gives mental feeling its greater power. But misused, especially when people fear everlasting torture after death, it can equally well become a greater evil than its bodily counterpart.

Katastematic pleasure is the absence of pain. The bodily version of it is called 'painlessness' (*aponia*), the mental version 'tranquillity' (*ataraxia*, literally 'non-disturbance'). Tranquillity depends above all on an understanding of the universe, which will show that contrary to the beliefs of

---

[1] This chapter is largely identical to one with the same title printed in G. Giannantoni and M. Gigante (edd.), *Epicureismo greco e romano* (Naples, 1996), apart from the addition of the introductory section. In this section I shall not (with one exception) quote chapter and verse. The primary sources can be found in Long and Sedley [719], §§21–5.

the ignorant it is unthreatening; and this is, strictly speaking, the sole justification for studying physics. Kinetic pleasure is the process of stimulation by which you either arrive at static pleasure, such as by drinking when thirsty, or 'vary' it, such as by drinking when not thirsty. There are mental as well as bodily kinetic pleasures, which may include the 'joy' of resolving a philosophical doubt or holding a fruitful discussion with friends. Kinetic pleasures have no incremental value: they are said not to increase pleasure beyond the painless state, but only to vary it. Nevertheless, Epicurus does apparently consider them a vital part of the good life. This is particularly because the mental pleasure which serves to outweigh present pain will inevitably consist in reliving past *kinetic* pleasures and anticipating future ones: they alone have the variety that makes this possible. So a successful Epicurean life cannot be monotonous, but must be textured by regular kinetic pleasures. In the letter written on his deathbed, Epicurus claimed that despite the intense bodily pains this was the happiest day of his life, because of all the past joys of philosophical discussion that he could relive.

At the same time, these kinetic pleasures must be carefully managed. Some desires are natural, others empty. The latter, for example thirst for honours, should not be indulged, because their satisfaction will bring either no pleasure or at all events a preponderance of pain over pleasure. Even of the natural ones, some are non-necessary. For instance, the desire for food is necessary, but the desire for luxurious food is not. In order to be maximally independent of fortune, it is important to stick primarily to the satisfaction of natural and necessary desires. But occasional indulgence in those kinetic pleasures which are natural but non-necessary has a part to play, so long as you do not become dependent on them. True to this principle, Epicurean communities lived on simple fare, and even trained themselves in asceticism, but held occasional banquets.

But how was communal living itself justified? As readers of Plato and Aristotle know well, ancient ethics does not problematise altruism as such, but does seek the moral foundations of two specific forms of altruism: justice, i.e. respecting the interests of your fellow-citizens, and friendship. Given that Epicurean hedonism is egoistic – that all your choices as an agent aim at your own pleasure – is it possible to put someone else's pleasure before your own?

Epicurus analyses justice not as an absolute value but as a contractual relation between fellow-citizens, its precise character engendered by current social circumstances. Sometimes it proves mutually advantageous to abstain from forms of behaviour which harm others, in return for a like undertaking from them. So long as such a contract proves socially advantageous, it is correctly called 'justice'. It imposes no moral obligation as such, and the ground for respecting it is egoistic – that even if you commit an injustice with impunity, the lingering fear of being found out will disrupt your tranquillity. With regard to his own philosophical community, Epicurus attached positive value to justice and to the specific laws which enforced it, not because philosophers need any restraint from wrongdoing but because they need protection from the harm that others might inflict. 'Do not take part in politics' was a celebrated Epicurean injunction: political ambition was seen as a misguided and self-defeating quest for personal security. But the school nevertheless upheld the need for legal and political institutions, and sought to work within their framework.

Where the political life fails to deliver personal security, friendship can succeed. The very foundation of the Epicurean philosophical community was friendship. And the mutual dealings of Epicurus and his contemporaries within the school were held up as an ideal model of friendship by their successors. Unlike justice, friendship is held to have intrinsic value – meaning not that it is valuable independently of pleasure, but that it is intrinsically pleasant, not merely instrumentally pleasant like justice. Moreover, the pleasure lies in altruistic acts of friendship, not merely in the benefits received by way of reciprocation.

Later Epicureans were pressed by their critics for a more precise reconciliation of friendship with egoism, and developed the position as follows.[2] According to one group, it is indeed for our own pleasure that we form friendships, and it is as a means to this, not ultimately for our friends' sake, that we share their pleasure and place it on a par with our own. A second group veered away from egoism: although friendship starts out as described by the first group, the outcome is something irreducibly altruistic, whereby we come to desire our friends' pleasure purely for their own sakes. A third group sought to rehabilitate egoism: the second group is right, but with the addition that friendship is a symmetrical contract, analogous to justice: *each* friend is committed to loving the other for the other's own sake. This third version can claim to be the most successful in harmonising Epicureanism's two defining ethical concerns: egoistic hedonism, and the cult of friendship.

That, viewed panoramically, is Epicurean ethics, a practical and theoretical approach to human life and conduct which won itself innumerable adherents over many centuries. But in the tradition founded by Plato and Aristotle ethical systems were not simply unveiled as pre-constructed wholes: they were dialectically worked out and defended. Does Epicurean ethics fall outside that tradition? Such a conclusion would be surprising, in view of the rigorous argumentation which underlies the school's work in its

---

[2] Cicero, *de Finibus* (*Fin.*) 1.66–70.

other main areas, physics and epistemology. In what follows, I shall seek to reconstruct the inferential framework on which Epicurean ethics was constructed.

2 The physics–ethics analogy

Thanks to the survival of Epicurus' *Letter to Herodotus*, and to Lucretius' expansion and supplementation of its arguments, it is possible to discern a clear argumentative structure in Epicurean physics, especially in its first, foundational moves.[3] My thesis will be that the foundations of Epicurean ethics had a closely analogous structure.

After stating his principles about criteria, Epicurus' physical exposé argues that whatever the universe consists of must exist for all time. The argument is scrupulously worded so as not to presuppose any answer to the next question, what it is that the universe does consist of.[4] This strictly linear development, whereby nothing must be presupposed before it has been formally established, is a guiding principle of Epicurus' entire enterprise. It is strongly present in Epicurus' own text, although unfortunately it is often neglected by Lucretius, whose more rhetorical exposition leads him to smuggle in advance references to the atomic structure of matter almost from the outset.[5] The principle carries with it a further requirement. The opening statement of what the universe consists of must confine itself to what is self-evident, i.e. underivatively known and, it is hoped, unchallengeable. What Epicurus does at this stage is to map out the universe into two items which he hopes indubitably both have independent (or *per se*) existence. These are, in fact, bodies and space. They are deliberately introduced as quite unrefined notions.[6]

---

[3] The main texts are Epicurus, *Letter to Herodotus* 38–41 and Lucretius 1.149–634. Cf. also Long and Sedley [719], §§4–8.

[4] This point is very well made by Brunschwig [920], who observes that the argument that there can be no addition to or subtraction from the sum total (*Letter to Herodotus* 39), since there is nothing outside it, carefully avoids specifying this as body or space, whereas on later occasions (see Lucretius II.303–7, III.806–18), when body and space have been introduced, the same argument is permitted to specify them.

[5] Lucretius' arguments against absolute generation and destruction (1.149–264) contain numerous advance references to the atomic structure of matter. Epicurus (*Letter to Herodotus* 38) had said that if there were absolute generation 'nothing would need a seed', referring to biological seeds. Lucretius repeats this remark (1.160), but as his arguments continue the 'seeds' required gradually take on the profile of atoms (see, for example, 167–71, 176–7, 185, 188–91, 221).

[6] There was no safe generic word for 'space' in ordinary usage, and Epicurus had to coin his own technical term 'intangible nature' (*anaphēs phusis*), whose specific guises are 'place' when occupied, 'void' when unoccupied, and 'space' (*chōra*) when bodies pass through it. At *Letter to Herodotus* 39, when first introducing space, he calls it 'place, which we name "void" and "room" and "intangible

What we shall see in the ensuing moves is a gradual sharpening up of both, so that in the end we can be certain just how it is that they jointly constitute the universe. What makes bodies and space the natural choice, I think, is that bodies are the things which have obviously *independent* existence; and, since that independence is most evident in their ability to move in space, the bits of space which they vacate as they move must exist independently of *them.*

Space at this stage, then, is simply what the bodies are in, and what they move through. The technical notion of pure void or vacuum begins to emerge with a series of arguments which almost certainly followed, although Lucretius for his own purposes takes them earlier.[7] In these arguments it is shown that such phenomena as motion and permeation depend on the existence of unoccupied portions of space. As for body, it remains for now largely unanalysed, beyond a set of arguments to show that it must exist microscopically as well as macroscopically: its underlying atomic structure cannot be demonstrated until it has been shown that body and space are the sole constituents of the universe. And the next move is to show just that. First, body and space are analysed as contradictory opposites: this is the positive proof that they are not only irreducibly distinct but also jointly exhaustive. There then follows a supplementary argument, in which all other contenders for *per se* existence – including properties, events and time – are written off as secondary attributes, parasitic on body and/or space. Only now that it is fully established can the body–space dualism be deployed to show that at the lowest level of analysis there will be not only portions of empty space uninterrupted by body but also portions of body uninterrupted by empty space – and therefore, since there is no third thing,

---

nature"', thus leading with the most familiar term, and equating it with the others without at this stage also differentiating their functions. For the reading of the text, and the interpretation of Epicurus' terms for space, see Sedley [929] or Long and Sedley [719] §5.

7 Lucretius I.265–417. Following his disproofs of absolute generation and destruction (1.149–264), Lucretius omits Epicurus' arguments for the impossibility of subtraction from or addition to the universe, which he no doubt found far too abstruse for his purposes because of their refusal to name body and space (see note 4 above). He moves directly to the arguments for the existence of microscopic body and those for vacuum (1.265–417), the former serving the useful protreptic role of introducing to Memmius the idea of the non-evident (1.267–70). This need was no doubt more urgent in a Roman context than for Epicurus' more physically attuned readership, so it would not be surprising to find Lucretius bringing it forward in the order of exposition. And his text at the end of this section suggests that he did. He shows some awareness that he has lost the proper sequence: he announces that there are lots more arguments available for the existence of void (1.398–417), then introduces the basic bodies–space dualism as a return to where he left off ('sed nunc ut repetam coeptum pertexere dictis', 1.418).

totally uninterrupted. Being perfectly solid, these are 'atoms'. Now and only now can the detailed work of investigating the universe's underlying causal processes begin.

Can it be shown that there was a similar methodology for ethics? If we rely on the *Letter to Menoeceus*, Epicurus' sole surviving treatise on ethics, the answer will be negative. This text is an eloquent celebration of Epicurean morality. It presents the main Epicurean articles of faith non-inferentially, in the canonical sequence sanctioned by the school's 'fourfold remedy' (*tetrapharmakos*) and the first group of Epicurus' 'Key Doctrines' (*Kuriai Doxai*). It gives away nothing about their argumentative foundations. But there is a much more promising candidate: book I of Cicero's *de Finibus*. Using this as a guide, I believe I can show that Epicurus' ethics had an argumentative structure similar to that of his physics – so similar, in fact, that it cannot have been unconscious or accidental.[8]

Now it has to be conceded that the exposé of Epicurean ethics in *On Ends* I is not directly drawn from Epicurus. The spokesman Torquatus claims to be reporting Epicurus' views, but since he at least twice incorporates divergent views of different factions within the Epicurean school,[9] we can hardly suppose that Cicero is relying on an unmediated text of Epicurus. My aim here will not be to do anything like justice to Cicero's own rather elegant composition, but to see through it back to Epicurus' original text. My contention will be that the passage's structure is strong evidence of Epicurus' original methodology, even if (and this is what convinces me that it has not been imposed on the material by Cicero's immediate source)[10] that methodology is itself not often directly asserted.

I say 'not often', because Epicurus' methodology clearly is asserted in the initial move. Torquatus' opening is as follows (*Fin.* I.29):

---

[8] One might try comparing Democritus' system. Scholars have had little success in establishing a close theoretical dependence of his ethics on his atomic physics, and it has been argued (esp. by Taylor [100]) that the furthest one should venture in seeking a connection between the two is in their use of analogous conceptual frameworks. Although my claims about Epicurus will have little if any detailed resemblance to this conclusion about Democritus, a similar lesson will nevertheless emerge. Epicurus' account of pleasure owes little directly to his atomism (apart from the dependence of *ataraxia* on the conclusions of physics about god and death). There is no analysis of pleasure in terms of atoms and void, and his metaphysical outlook should never have led us to expect one (as I argue in Sedley [930]). Despite this, his ethics and his physics are structurally analogous.

[9] Cicero, *Fin.* I.31 (discussed below), 66–70. Cf. also 39 on Chrysippus' statue.

[10] When at I.6 Cicero speaks of 'my order of writing' (nostrum scribendi ordinem'), this need not imply that he has imposed his own ordering on the material within each book. The words are adequately understood as a reference to his own ordering of the five books themselves.

I shall start, then, in the way in which the founder of this school holds one should. I shall establish what the thing into which we are inquiring is and what it is like[11] – not because I think you don't know, but so that the disquisition can proceed methodically. Our question then is, what is the final and ultimate good, which all philosophers hold must be such that all things are to be traced back to it, while it itself is to be traced back no further? Epicurus located this in pleasure. He wants pleasure to be the chief good, pain the chief bad. And he set about teaching it in the following way.

Torquatus' explicit testimony that Epicurus taught this to be the proper way to open an ethical discourse confirms that the *Letter to Menoeceus*, which only gets to the topic of pleasure nearly half way through, cannot be held up as a specimen of ethical methodology.

3 The basic division

Epicurus' first move, then, was to place the *summum bonum* in pleasure, the *summum malum* in pain.[12] We are clearly at a point analogous to that in the physical exposition at which the whole universe is analysed as self-evidently consisting of two *per se* existents, bodies and space.[13] Here likewise Epicurus will proclaim the analysis of values into the two *per se* values of pleasure and pain as self-evident fact. There he was mapping out the extended universe, here he is drawing up the scale of value, but the procedure is the same. The two items are initially sketched in with broad brushstrokes: only later, when their status has been confirmed and clarified, will the fine detail be added. Pleasure and pain are, at this initial stage, as unrefined notions as bodies and space were at the comparable stage of the physics. Already to identify the good with specific kinds of pleasure would be fatal to the claim of self-evident truth from which Epicurus starts out, just as in the physics to proclaim from the start that the bodies are, or consist of,

---

[11] 'What, and of what kind, it is' ('quid et quale sit') will be a demand for an 'outline account' ('hupographē'), not a definition (cf. *Fin.* II.4–6). On this point of Epicurean method, see Asmis [757], 39–47. But it is left unclear whether the reference is to establishing (a) what is *meant* by 'the final and ultimate good', or (b) what it consists in, namely pleasure, or whether (c) *quid* refers to the first of these and *quale* to the second, or (d) whether *quid* is answered by 'pleasure' (29–36), *quale* by the analysis of pleasure-types (37 ff.). But at any rate at 37, and again at II.6, the *quid et quale* question is clearly a single one, so (a) and (b) are likelier than (c) or (d). On (a), the answer to the question would have to be located in the relative clause 'which all philosophers hold . . . ', and that is stylistically odd. Thus (b) emerges as the best reading.   [12] On the use of *summum bonum* here, see §6 below.

[13] I take it that the very first steps of the physical discourse, in which the laws of conservation are established, have no analogue in the ethics. In view of our world's ephemeral existence, there would be little point or plausibility in trying to show that whatever values there are now must hold good for all time.

atoms would have sabotaged any pretence of starting from incontrovertible fact.

That it is self-evident that pleasure is the chief good, pain the chief bad, is maintained by means of the celebrated Cradle Argument (1.30):

> Every animal, as soon as it is born, seeks pleasure and enjoys it as the chief good, while shunning pain as the chief bad and averting it so far as it can. And this it does before it can be perverted, with nature herself the uncorrupted and honest judge. Epicurus therefore denies that there is any need for reasoning or argument as to why pleasure should be chosen and pain avoided. He thinks that this is felt, in the way in which it is felt that fire is hot, snow white, and honey sweet. None of these needs to be proved by elaborate reasoning: it is enough to draw attention to them.

This passage has been minutely studied by Jacques Brunschwig in his seminal article, 'The Cradle Argument in Epicureanism and Stoicism'.[14] He notes that it consists of a factual statement, that all animals naturally seek pleasure and avoid pain, followed by a normative statement, that there is no need for argument to establish that pleasure *should* be chosen and pain avoided. He maintains that the normative statement cannot be an inference from the factual statement, or Epicurus would not be able simultaneously to assert that the normative statement needs no arguing. Brunschwig suggests instead that the normative statement appeals directly to the intuition of rational adult humans that pleasure is to be chosen, pain avoided; the preceding factual statement, he concludes, has just the subsidiary supporting role of showing that that intuition need not be distrusted as a corrupted one, since all animals manifest a similar intuition, even at too early a stage for them yet to have been corrupted.

I retain doubts about this analysis. Even if Brunschwig were right to assign some such supporting role to the factual statement, it would be, in Epicurean terms, an appeal to *ouk antimarturēsis*, absence of counterevidence – that is, an appeal to *consistency* with the rest of our experience. And that in such contexts is a, if not the, regular Epicurean form of proof.

It turns out, paradoxically, that the better way to make the normative statement an unargued one is to give its introductory 'therefore' (*itaque*) its face value and to let it follow directly from the factual statement. It is the fact that all animals already pursue pleasure as the good that makes the choiceworthiness of pleasure too obvious and uncontroversial to need arguing.

---

[14] Brunschwig [44].

Presumably for animals to pursue pleasure as the good just *is* for them to treat it as the thing to be chosen. Nothing in the argument or its context appears to turn on any distinction between the good and the choiceworthy.[15] It is true, as Gosling and Taylor have urged,[16] that there is an apparent conflict with *Letter to Menoeceus* 129–30, where the notions of goodness and choiceworthiness come apart: 'although every pleasure is good . . . not every pleasure is choiceworthy'. But the point there is that some *individual* pleasure, while good in itself, may be the wrong thing to choose *in the circumstances*, if it actually militates against the achievement of final pleasure. In the Cradle Argument, by contrast, Epicurus is talking not about individual pleasures but about pleasure as an end, which animals' behaviour shows them to be pursuing in *all* circumstances. Hence the very same behaviour betrays their evaluation of pleasure as both unconditionally good and unconditionally choiceworthy.

Epicurus' contention can therefore be paraphrased as follows. The feeling that pleasure is the thing to pursue is manifest in the behaviour of all animals from birth; therefore, since the choiceworthiness of pleasure is as immediately self-evident to all living beings as the coldness of snow, it needs no arguing. As Torquatus goes on immediately to observe, merely to draw attention to something is not in itself to argue. And all he has done, as he sees it, is to draw our attention to our existing consensus that pleasure is the good.

Not only is this simpler reading more successful at saving Epicurus from arguing for what in the same breath he says does not need arguing, but it also fits better what I have suggested ought to be his strategy. It is to be expected that pleasure and pain should at this stage be maximally unrefined notions. The concern is to come up with an initial assignment of value which it can be claimed is universally obvious, just as at the equivalent stage of the physics the existence of bodies was said to be 'universally witnessed by perception'. The unchallengeable look of that assertion would have been lost if Epicurus had confined himself to the sense-perceptions of adult humans. Likewise we should not try to narrow down to the class of adult humans the witnesses to whom Epicurus

---

[15] Cf. *Fin.* II.5, where Cicero supposes that if Torquatus had defined 'good' it might have been as 'what was by nature choiceworthy' ('quod esset natura appetendum').

[16] Gosling and Taylor [53], ch. 20. They themselves interpret pleasure's goodness and its choiceworthiness as two radically different properties, misleadingly lumped together by Cicero. But that is based on their guess – an unfounded one in my opinion – that for Epicurus pleasure is awareness of one's own proper functioning, so that pleasure's goodness consists in its appropriateness to proper functioning.

appeals for the desirability of pleasure.[17] Universality, not precision, is his present concern.

Besides, Epicurus' subsequent discussion will make it quite clear that adult humans are the worst possible witnesses on this matter, since their hedonistic intuition will often be obscured by an artificially imposed value system. That *even* rational adults, deep down, agree with the primary hedonistic intuition is something which, as we shall see, he has to argue at length.

The same point about the need at this stage for absolute generality applies to another issue mischievously raised by Cicero in his reply to Torquatus. Invoking a familiar Epicurean distinction, Cicero asks whether the pleasure sought by infants is kinetic or katastematic pleasure (*Fin.* II.31–2). Cicero makes it tolerably clear[18] that Epicurus did not specify, but that his followers, when pressed, replied that it is kinetic pleasure. Cicero proceeds to use this concession as a stick with which to beat them, by observing that, since the Epicurean supreme moral goal is not kinetic but katastematic pleasure, the goal sought by infants turns out not to be the *summum bonum* after all. Now on the analysis I am offering, Epicurus' own silence on the point was not simply a ruse for avoiding the trap into which his less canny followers were later to walk. It was methodologically correct for him to preserve the absolute generality of his account, by specifying nothing at all about how individual creatures conduct their pursuit of pleasure. To have specified the goal of infants as kinetic pleasure, or as any other kind or kinds of pleasure (katastematic, bodily, short-term, etc.), would have been analogous to opening the physical analysis of the universe not by naming *bodies* and space, but by cataloguing the specific kinds of body which sense-perception attests, for example earth, air, fire and

---

[17]   This insistence on the universality of the hedonistic intuition is, it seems to me, equally manifest in Epicurus, *Letter to Menoeceus* 128–9: 'This is why we say that pleasure is the beginning and end of the blessed life. *For it is pleasure which we recognised as our first and congenital good* (ἀγαθὸν πρῶτον καὶ συγγενικὸν ἔγνωμεν); it is from pleasure that we initiate every choice and avoidance; and it is to pleasure that we have recourse when we use feeling as our criterion for all good.' There is a deliberate tone of temporal universality here in the three limbs: pleasure is (1) our congenital good; (2) the aim from which we always start; and (3) that by which *post eventum* we measure our success. In this context, it seems over-cautious for Brunschwig [44] to doubt that Epicurus has the Cradle Argument at least partly in mind in the first limb, when he calls pleasure the thing which 'we recognise*d* as our first and *congenital* good'. The past tense (ἔγνωμεν) contrasts significantly with the present tenses (καταρχόμεθα, καταντῶμεν) in the second and third limbs. Another upshot of my argument is that, contrary to Brunschwig's contention, the reports of the Cradle Argument at Sextus Empiricus *PH* III.194 and *M* XI.96 and at Diogenes Laertius X.137 are broadly correct: the argument does directly establish that pleasure is 'by nature choiceworthy' (cf. below).

[18]   See the careful arguments of Brunschwig [44], 126–8.

water, or animals, plants, rocks, etc. To do so would have seriously preju-
diced the ensuing enquiry, and invited the objection that atoms are not
even included among the bodies which self-evidently exist. It would also
have weakened the claim of an absolutely indisputable starting-point. The
object at this stage is simply to get body, generically, on to the list of things
that exist independently. In what forms body exists is a question which
cannot even be asked until later, when we know what else is on the list.
Likewise, at the opening of the ethical enquiry the aim is to get pleasure
and pain, generically, on to the scale of values. The detailed structure of
that scale cannot be established until it has been proved, *inter alia*, that
pleasure and pain are its *sole* occupants.

4 The division defended

At 31, Torquatus goes on to outline a dispute within the Epicurean
school.

> There are, however, some in our school who want to impart these points in
> a more subtle way, and who deny that it is enough to make feeling[19] the
> judge of what is good or what is bad, but hold that it can also be understood
> by the mind and by reason both that pleasure is *per se* to be chosen and that
> pain is *per se* to be avoided. So they say that this is as it were a natural
> conception and one rooted in our minds, that we should feel that the one is
> to be sought, the other shunned.
>
> Others, however (with whom I agree), hold that because numerous
> philosophers have a great deal to say about why pleasure should not be
> counted among the goods, or pain among the bads, we should not be too
> confident of our case. They think that on the subject of pleasure and pain
> we should use arguments and precise discourses, and should fight our
> cause with careful reasoning.

This is regularly read as indicating a split between Epicurus and two groups
of his followers: he had said that the foundational premise of his hedonism
needed no arguing; they replied by offering two competing reasons why it did
need arguing. This seems to me a misreading. For one thing, it would be
unheard of, and a breach of the elementary code of ancient school loyalty,
for Epicureans to express overt disagreement with their founder.[20] For
another, the interpretation fails to connect the passage with what immediately follows at 32. (The paragraph division imposed by the editors at the end
of 31 has helped to disguise this important connection.) At 32, Torquatus
develops the line taken by the second faction, that the hedonist premise

---

[19] Or 'perception'? Cicero's use of *sensus* spans both 'feeling' (*pathos*) and 'perception'
(*aisthēsis*).   [20] I argue this in Sedley [64].

needs arguing in order to resist rival philosophical theories, and he does so by quoting arguments *from Epicurus himself*:

> But in order to make clear to you how the entire mistake of those who denounce pleasure and extol pain arose, I shall explain the whole matter to you, and unfold the actual words of that discoverer of the truth and, as it were, architect of the blessed life.

Clearly Torquatus, at least, presents his own faction's view as one endorsed by Epicurus himself. And that is, of course, the standard way in which these factional disputes were conducted, both parties claiming to be the authentic interpreters of the master's *ipsissima verba*.[21] We may take it, then, that Epicurus, having said in the initial stage that the hedonist premise needed no argument, did nevertheless subsequently offer these arguments for it, and that the school was split as to his justification for doing so. The first faction said that it was in order to unpack and clarify our intuitive conception of pleasure as the thing to pursue. The second, supported by Torquatus, said that it was in order to resist those moral philosophers who had set out to subvert the intuition and to replace pleasure with some other primary value. Which (if either) party is right? We must look at the arguments.

They can be summarised as follows (32–3). All those painful actions which appear to us to be properly chosen prove on inspection to be so only for the sake of the greater ensuing pleasure. And pleasant actions are irreproachable if they do not lead to pain; to opt for pleasures, or the avoidance of pain, is reprehensible only in those cases in which the immediate attraction blinds us to the longer-term painful consequences of our choice. Therefore in absolute terms pleasure is always the proper aim, and pain is only preferable instrumentally, for the sake of pleasure.

This line of argument is familiar enough to us through a hedonist tradition stemming from Plato's *Protagoras*. Consequently it can easily be accommodated to the first faction's interpretation. Like Socrates at *Protagoras* 353–4, Epicurus can be seen clarifying ordinary people's intuitions about pleasure, in order to show that, *whether or not they realise it*, their principles of conduct are hedonistic. They may deny that they always pursue pleasure, but when they re-examine their motivations for painful choices, for example for accepting surgery or for avoiding self-indulgence, they will appreciate that they do in fact treat pleasure as the only good.

On the other hand, the passage can equally comfortably be accommodated to the second faction's interpretation. Epicurus may be arguing that

---

[21] Sedley [64], esp. pp. 105–17.

the kinds of values which anti-hedonist *philosophers* stress, such as temperance, are at root pleasure-driven. Torquatus, as a supporter of this second faction, does in fact use Epicurus' argument for that end, but that is not until rather later (36), at the conclusion of his ensuing moral diatribe about his own family's history (34–6) – which shows that it represents his own input, not Epicurus'. What he does there is to invoke Epicurus' hedonistic analysis as quite adequate to account for the motivation of heroic acts, and to use this explicitly as a reply to the Academics for citing heroic exempla in dialectical defence of virtue–ethics.

Which faction is right? My hunch is that both are half-right, but that both are being too exclusive. The point can be made by comparing the analogous section of the physical exposé. Having set up the primary body–space dichotomy as empirically self-evident, Epicurus, to judge from Lucretius' fuller presentation (1.265–427),[22] went on to offer a variety of arguments which defended this dualistic ontology downwards below the threshold of direct experience. First he demonstrated the existence of microscopic as well as macroscopic body, arguing that it was required in order to make sense of the powers of wind, odour, etc. Then he extended his notion of space in the same downwards direction, arguing that there must be hidden pockets of *empty* space – pure vacuum. Some of these arguments read as if they corresponded to the first faction's interpretation of the arguments for hedonism, and are aimed quite generally at *anyone* who tries to leave microscopic body and void off the world map: for example the argument that the similarity of wind's behaviour to that of water shows it too to consist of bodies, and the argument that the phenomena of relative weight and the permeation of rocks by water cannot be envisaged without the supposition of void gaps. In effect, we are being assured that microscopic body and void are already implicitly built into our world-view, whether or not we yet realise it. Other arguments correspond more closely to the thesis of the second faction, especially the argument which seeks to confute those philosophers who explain motion as the redistribution of matter within a plenum, like a fish swimming through water (Lucretius 1.370–83). Another in this category is his description of an experiment for the artificial creation of a momentary void (Lucretius 1.385–97), which we may take to be a confutation of those thinkers (Eleatics and others) who maintained that void is a conceptually incoherent notion. In these Epicurus no doubt saw himself as resisting any philosophers who sought to overrule people's correct intuitions about space. But the two kinds of argument are presented side by side, and are hard to disentangle.

---

[22] See n. 7 above for the likely position of these arguments in Epicurus' original discourse.

Rather than go all the way with either faction, it is better to say the following. Both in the physics and in the ethics, the first substantive stage consists of the crude mapping out of the territory, sticking to what is empirically or intuitively obvious to the untutored mind. The second stage, which we have now reached, is to amplify that first sketch by a closer conceptual analysis, showing how it accords with our other experiences and intuitions, and, as part of this project, forestalling any doctrinally motivated attempts, actual or imaginary, to turn those experiences and intuitions against it.

5 The division's exhaustiveness

We now come to the third and most controversial stage of the ethical exposition (37–8). The removal of pain is itself already a pleasure. Therefore the transition from pain to pleasure does not involve passing through some intermediate state. Therefore there are just the two states, pleasure and pain, each being identical with the absence of the other.

In seeking to make sense of this doctrine, the obvious strategy is to investigate its relation to Epicurus' general ethical outlook. As a matter of fact, that is how Torquatus himself introduces it, first describing the Epicurean ideal of ascetic pleasure, then saying that this is the reason why Epicurus denied an intermediate state between pain and pleasure. It is hard to know how far the first of these parts reflects Epicurus' own original exposition at the corresponding point. On my account of his general methodology, he might have been expected not to have presupposed the character of the ideal Epicurean life at so early a stage, but, as we shall see later, it remains quite likely that he did. At all events, we need to consider the two parts together (37–8):

> I shall now explain what pleasure itself is and what it is like, in order to dispel all the incomprehension of the ignorant, so that it may be understood how serious, restrained and sober is that doctrine which is considered self-indulgent, luxurious and soft. For we [Epicureans] do not pursue only that pleasure which moves our very nature with a kind of smoothness and which the senses perceive in a rather agreeable way [i.e. kinetic pleasure], but we hold that to be the greatest pleasure which is perceived once all pain has been removed [i.e. katastematic pleasure]. For since, when our pain is removed, we rejoice in the actual freedom from and absence of all pain, and since everything we rejoice in is a pleasure, just as everything we are upset by is a pain, the removal of all pain is rightly called pleasure. For just as, when hunger and thirst are dispelled by food and drink, the very elimination of the discomfort brings pleasure as its result, so too in everything the removal of pain generates pleasure in its wake.
>
> For this reason Epicurus did not believe that there was anything intermediate between pain and pleasure. For the very thing which some people

considered intermediate, when all pain is lacking, he considered to be not just pleasure, but even the highest pleasure. For whoever feels how he has been affected must be in a state either of pleasure or of pain. But Epicurus thinks that the highest pleasure finds its limit in the absence of all pain, so that thereafter it can be varied and differentiated, but not increased and expanded.

What is the connection being described here between Epicurean asceticism and the denial of the neutral state? Dodging a number of interpretative controversies, I shall sketch the following brief answer. Both doctrines emerged against a background of protracted debate on the nature and value of pleasure, above all in Plato and Aristotle, as expertly traced by Gosling and Taylor in their book *The Greeks on Pleasure*.[23] But principally it was seen, and can still be seen, as a response to Epicurus' contemporaries the Cyrenaics.

In Cyrenaic hedonism, pleasures are smooth *kinēseis* (movements or processes of change) – the temporary states of stimulation or excitement which are the equivalent of Epicurus' kinetic pleasures. Likewise all pains are *kinēseis*, namely rough ones, and the unstimulated state is neither pleasant nor painful, but neutral. Since these kinetic pleasures are generally short-lived, the pursuit of pleasure requires their constant renewal.

Epicurus' response is that this kind of pursuit is unrewarding. People who naively expect otherwise set out to cram their lives with luxuries and indulgences, only to find that life becomes no pleasanter thereby. On the contrary, their dependence on luxury makes them needlessly vulnerable to the whims of fortune, and therefore more liable to the pain of deprivation. He concludes that the luxurious life, although undeniably different from the simple life, is not thereby any pleasanter at all. Or, as he puts it in the more doctrinal terms echoed by Torquatus, once all pain has been removed the further positive stimuli of luxurious living to not increase one's pleasure – they only vary it. Given this defence of moderate asceticism, Epicurus has no choice but to hold that once all pain has been removed one has already achieved a pleasant state, since he believes it to be in fact the pleasantest possible state. Therefore painlessness is pleasure – katastematic pleasure, as he calls it, to contrast it with kinetic pleasure.

---

[23] Gosling and Taylor [53]. However, I dissent from much of their account of Epicurean pleasure, especially their erasure of the normal distinction between kinetic and katastematic pleasure. For instance the objection (pp. 370, 374–5, 392–3, etc.) that there are *no* 'static' pleasures because all pleasures are atomic motions relies on the unfounded attribution of atomist reductionism to Epicurus (see Sedley [930]). Above all, I hope that my present argument will help to vindicate (against Gosling and Taylor's objections, esp. pp. 382 ff.) the reliability of Cicero's evidence, including *Fin.* 1.37–8, which makes clear use of the distinction.

His critics, including Cicero in *On Ends* book II, demanded to know why the same word 'pleasure' should be used for two such very different kinds of experience as these.[24] But Epicurus' chosen usage in fact makes excellent sense in its context. According to him, eating sweets when not hungry is, though different, no more pleasant than the satisfied state of simply not being hungry. If we grant him this, it follows that either both conditions – indulgent eating and stable satisfaction – are pleasures, or neither is. To opt for making them both pleasures, as he does, is hardly more counter-intuitive than the alternative of saying that neither is.

So much for Epicurus' ethical motivation and formal justification in excluding the middle state between pleasure and pain. But I now want to suggest a quite different perspective on his motivation. For this, I must go back to his physics.

Atomism had always made a virtue of its metaphysical economy. For Democritus, body and void are defined as 'being and not-being', or 'the full and the empty'. Body and void are thus each defined as the other's formal contradictory. If a thing is not being, it can only be not-being. If it is not full, it must be empty. This simple dyadic scheme has the merit of guaranteeing that body and void are the *sole* contents of the universe. In mapping out the universe, we have only to say of each part of it whether it is full or empty, assured that there is no further possibility. The dyadic scheme, yielding as it were a monochrome map of the universe, may not be the only way of achieving this result, but it is unbeatably economical.

Epicurus' basic ontology is in some ways very different. Void for him is not equated with portions of emptiness, as I believe it was for Democritus, but with space in its (to us) familiar Euclidean sense.[25] That is why I have been describing his ontology throughout as one of body and space, rather than body and void. Epicurean body and space do not combine to produce a monochrome map of the universe, like black and white pixels on a screen. Space is co-extensive with the entire universe, and some parts of space are (temporarily) co-extensive with portions of body, although other parts, called 'void' in the specific sense, are not. Nevertheless, Epicurus follows Democritus' lead in defining body and space as formal contradictories. Anything that has *per se* existence must have some volume. If in addition it has the power of resistance, that makes it a body. If it lacks all power of resistance, so that bodies can pass straight through it, it can only be space. Since everything with volume must be either resistant or non-resistant, it is thus

---

[24] Cicero *Fin.* II.6 ff., cf. Gosling and Taylor [53], 370.
[25] I argue for this contrast in Sedley [929].

formally established that everything with *per se* existence is either body or space.[26] Atomism quickly follows, because since there is now known to be nothing other than empty space that could punctuate a portion of body, a body with no empty space within it must be perfectly solid.

Given its honourable history and foundational role in atomism, the dyadic ontology must have been highly prized by Epicurus. What could be less surprising, then, than to find him at the corresponding point in his ethics, when drawing up the scale of value, attracted by a dyadic scheme analogous to the one which had borne such fruit when mapping out three-dimensional existence? By eliminating the neutral state, he relates pleasure to pain as body to space, that is, as formal contradictories,[27] thus ensuring a value system in which no further *per se* value can have been overlooked. The full version of the formal argument is, I take it, that all the intrinsic values, positive or negative, of a sentient being lie in how it feels about things, and that any feeling that is not painful is *ipso facto* pleasant, and vice versa. Therefore all *per se* values are, generically, either pleasure or pain.

What if Epicurus *had* allowed a neutral state of feeling between pleasure and pain? Obviously the scheme could no longer be dyadic, but could it not have been successfully triadic? Couldn't the definitions have been framed so as at least to guarantee that any *per se* value belongs to one of the *three* generic categories, pleasant, painful and neutral? In the physics, if there were *per se* existing things which were neither body nor space, there would seem to be no restriction on what they might be, and metaphysical anarchy would break out. But it is hard to envisage a similar danger on the scale of value. Epicurus need hardly fear that to allow an intermediate class of feeling which is neither pleasant nor painful would be to risk the intrusion of a mysterious third value. The third value need only be a neutral hedonic state which is better than pain but worse than pleasure, one that could in principle be accommodated to the hedonistic calculus. In short, it is not clear that a dyadic scheme, for all its conceptual elegance, could ever prove as indispensable to ethics as it was to physics. (Incidentally, this disparity is a ground for assuming, as I have been assuming throughout, that the methodology was evolved originally for physics, for which it is tailor-made, and only thereafter transferred to ethics.)

---

[26] Lucretius 1.433–9, retaining the MSS order for 434–5.

[27] Body and space, although contradictories, are frequently co-extensive. But this need not constitute a disanalogy with pleasure and pain. For example the kinetic pleasure of drinking may coexist with the pain of incompletely quenched thirst. The height of pleasure is reached when all the remaining pain has gone – just, one might speculate, as pure space, i.e. void, is achieved only when all body has left it.

Despite any such reservations, the ranking of pleasure and pain as formal contradictories was an almost inevitable outcome for Epicurus. His systematic reapplication to ethics of the physical methodology, in which the dyadic analysis had proved so useful, must from the start have inclined him towards the reclassification of the neutral state as pleasure. And the very same move turned out to give him just the realignment of values he needed to work out his disagreement with the Cyrenaics. When both factors are brought together, it seems almost a foregone conclusion that he would opt for the dyadic scheme.

6 The Epicurean good life

We have now seen the parallelism of physical and ethical exposition run through three crucial stages. First a basic dualistic scheme is sketched as self-evident. Secondly it is confirmed, amplified and defended by conceptual analysis. Thirdly it is shown to be an exhaustive dichotomy by defining the two terms as a pair of contradictories.

What follows next, at 40–1, is at first sight rather disconcerting for my analysis. Torquatus switches to a direct argument for pleasure as the *summum bonum*, pain as the *summum malum*. And to a large extent it is conducted by describing the ideally good Epicurean life, and contrasting this with the supremely un-Epicurean life. The good life includes fearlessness based directly on two Epicurean tenets, that death is nothing more than the loss of all sensation, and that intense pain is short-lived, mild pain bearable; and it has other unmistakably Epicurean features. Is he really entitled at this stage to presuppose the Epicurean good life, when so much groundwork still has to be covered?

Now as far as the actual expression *summum bonum* is concerned, there is nothing new or surprising about finding it here. Pleasure was introduced at the outset, back in the Cradle Argument, as the *summum bonum*, and pain as the *summum malum*. The phrase *summum bonum* occurs literally hundreds of times in Cicero's philosophical writings, yet it is by no means clear to me what Greek term it could represent. Expressions like 'the ultimate good' (*to eschaton tōn agathōn*) and 'the primary good' (*to prōton agathon*) are far too rare in Hellenistic philosophy to account for such frequent occurrence. My own guess is that *summum bonum* is in most cases simply Cicero's rendition of 'the good' (*to agathon*). When one looks through the contexts in which it occurs, the overwhelming majority are ones in which the mere word *bonum* would, in the absence of a Latin definite article, have been ambiguous between 'the good' and 'a good'. For instance in the Cradle Argument, where all animals rejoice in pleasure 'as in the highest good' (*ut summo bono*), a mere 'as in the good' (*ut bono*) would have been indistinguishable from 'as in a good'.[28] The addition of *summum* before *bonum* neatly removes the ambiguity.

Let us take it, then, that *summum bonum* in *Fin.* 1.40–1 just represents 'the good'. For an Epicurean, to call pleasure 'the good' is to label it, if not strictly as the only good thing, at least as the only underivatively good thing, that by courtesy of which other things are good – in other words, the ethical 'end' (*telos*). But the present passage goes further than that. The thing labelled the *summum bonum* (and also, more elaborately, 'the highest (*summum*) or ultimate (*ultimum*) or extreme (*extremum*) of goods, which the Greeks call *telos*') is not pleasure tout court, but the pleasant life (*iucunde vivere*, or *cum voluptate vivere*), the very life amply filled out with a portrayal of the ideal Epicurean. To see what has happened, we need here a distinction between a primitive and a substantive account of the good or the *telos*. In Aristotle, for instance, the primitive account is simply *eudaimonia*, or perhaps 'activity of the soul in accordance with virtue', while the substantive account would be a detailed analysis of this as acted out in the civic life, the contemplative life, or both. What has happened in the course of Torquatus' speech is not a shift in the meaning of *summum bonum*, but a shift from the primitive to the substantive specification of what it consists in. Is this legitimate? How can Torquatus assert that the Epicurean life is the best possible life, when he has not yet even dealt with the question whether virtue has a place in it; or with the relation of mental to bodily pleasure; or with the lessons of physics for dealing with fear of death and god; or with the function of friendship?

Certainly the Epicurean life-style has been looming ever larger in 37–42, and it looks as if it was considered admissible as empirical evidence regarding the correct quantification of pleasure. Thus back at 37 one important source of evidence that pleasure is maximised by the removal of all pain seems to have been the empirical results of the Epicurean life-style. But why choose the present point in the discourse to move on from the primitive characterisation of the good as pleasure to the substantive specification of the ideally good life? The answer, I think, is supplied by what it leads up to – the next long section, 42–54, in which the role of virtue is finally tackled.

In brief, the argument of 42–54 is the familiar Epicurean one that the value possessed by the virtues is not intrinsic but purely instrumental, as a means to pleasure. Wisdom, for example, is of value as the intelligent management of fears and desires, indispensable for securing the most pleasant

---

[28] The only clear exceptions I have found are a handful of cases where *summum bonum* has to mean 'the greatest good [among others]': Cic. *de Legibus* I.55, *de Officiis* III.11, 35; and in a couple of speeches close in date to *de Officiis*: *Pro Marcello* 19.9, and *Pro Rege Deiotaro* 37.

possible life. And similar instrumental accounts are offered of the other virtues. The point is, I think, that this instrumental analysis of conventional morality would lack all plausibility if pleasure had still been left as an unrefined notion. To say that wisdom is valuable because it enables us to cram more pleasure into our lives is to invite the standard slurs against Epicurean morality as crude sensualism. To carry the day, Epicurus must say something far more substantive – that wisdom is valuable as a means to the supreme pleasure of a rationally balanced life, one based on a correct understanding of the limits of desire and the nature of the universe and of man. Only by offering the practical model of enlightened hedonism could he hope to achieve this. And that, I think, is quite enough to account for the early appearance in Torquatus' discourse of the ideal Epicurean life.

7 The instrumentality of virtue

Our final task is to examine the instrumental account of virtue in its own right. Here I want to bring in a puzzle about the passage which has been well raised by Phillip Mitsis in his outstanding book *Epicurus' Ethical Theory*.[29] Mitsis writes as follows:

> First of all, the virtues singled out for discussion by Cicero seem to correspond narrowly, and somewhat suspiciously, to a standard Stoic list. Similarly, instead of articulating a positive theory of his own, the Epicurean Torquatus seems at times somewhat too eager to redescribe this standard list in Epicurean terms, as if he were trying to convince a Roman audience that Epicurus' theory really can accommodate commonly recognised features of morality. Perhaps an even greater obstacle in the way of recovering Epicurus' doctrine arises from the potential distortions of Cicero's political and moral vocabulary. For instance, Torquatus rather casually lists *iniustitia* (injustice) with such strong terms of moral disapproval as *improbitas* (depravity), *libido* (violent desire), and *ignavia* (cowardice) (*Fin.* 1.50). Many have argued, though, that this kind of moral censoriousness is uncharacteristic of the Epicurean contract . . . Moreover, Cicero's moral vocabulary is heavily weighted toward societal attitudes and obligations in a way foreign to Epicurus. Torquatus' arguments are generously sprinkled with such common terms of Roman public approval as *liberalitas* (liberality), *caritas* (esteem), and *benevolentia* (kindness) (*Fin.* 1.52). He thereby injects into his account of Epicurean justice strong overtones of social class and social obligation that are absent from Epicurus' own account.

This seems to me to put its finger on a serious problem about the passage. It is only Mitsis' solution that I shall quarrel with. He suggests that

[29] Mitsis [760], 69–70.

Torquatus' account has become contaminated with (a) the Stoic four cardinal virtues, and (b) the value system of Roman society. Before acquiescing in this, we must ask about the passage's methodological function. At the equivalent point in the physical discourse Epicurus (*Letter to Herodotus* 40, expanded at Lucretius 1.449–82), having shown that all independently or *per se* existing things must be body or space, set out to disqualify all further items that might appear entitled to inclusion in the list. Plato had defended the independent existence of properties like justice and beauty; and anyone, philosophical or not, who accepted Epicurus' contention that space had independent existence was likely to ask why the same should not be true of time. Epicurus' reply was to show systematically how all such items are parasitic on bodies and/or space for their existence, and must therefore be relegated to the status of dependent properties (*sumbebēkota*)[30] of things which themselves do exist *per se* (*kath' hauta*).

In ethics the equivalent stage is clearly as follows. Having shown that *per se* values divide up exhaustively into pleasure and pain, Epicurus must once again set out to disqualify all further items that might appear entitled to inclusion in the list. All the additional positive values that might be proposed must be shown to be valuable not intrinsically, but parasitically on the pleasure they are supposed to generate. And this means not so much working through the items in his own preferred value system, as dealing one by one with the values which others, philosophers and non-philosophers alike, would be likely to put forward for inclusion.

This is all we need to explain the curious character of the passage. Of course it deals with the conventional values of the Platonist ethical tradition and of political society: not because they are privileged within an Epicurean moral framework, but because they are the most prominent explananda, the items of value which most pressingly need to be reduced to the status of derivative rather than intrinsic goods.

Epicurean ethical doctrine can be expected to surface, as indeed it does, only when the actual reductions are being performed. Temperance and courage, for example, are not prominent Epicurean virtues, and are initially described in purely conventional terms (47–9). But then, in accommodating them to a hedonistic framework, Torquatus does press home the relevant Epicurean tenets. Temperance is a route to the maximisation of pleasure, the calculation of which pleasures to forgo for the sake of other, greater pleasures. Courage is achieved by the resolution of anxieties about pain and death, through correct Epicurean understanding of their true nature. He

---

[30] This is the genus of which 'permanent properties' and 'accidents' (*sumptōmata*) are the two species: see Sedley [930], 304–9.

does not, of course, mean that everyone who tries to be brave is already, consciously or unconsciously, aiming to be an Epicurean philosopher; just that the aim which characterises courage is, as a matter of fact, achievable only through Epicurean enlightenment.

In short, we must agree with Mitsis that much non-Epicurean morality is included in the passage. But, paradoxically, we need not agree with him that any of it does not stem ultimately from the pen of Epicurus.[31]

8 Epilogue

By now I have traced the parallelism of ethical and physical methodology through four distinct stages: (1) a primitive dyadic sketching-in of the territory; (2) conceptual amplification and defence of the sketch; (3) formal proof of its exhaustiveness; (4) elimination of further claimants to inclusion. Thereafter the parallelism can be followed, if at all, only in rather looser terms. In physics, body will now be refined into atomic chunks, followed *inter alia* by a detailed discussion of their range of shapes and sizes, and of their behaviour in compounds. In ethics, the next step will be the loosely analogous one of classifying individual pleasures and pains into the bodily and the mental, and examining their respective contributions as components in a good life.

I doubt if it would serve any purpose to press the details of this parallelism. My real concern has been limited to structural analogies in the foundational moves of ethics and physics. It will probably be wiser to rest my case there.[32]

[31] Annas [764] and [71], esp. pp. 339 ff., discusses the split in Epicurus' writings between passages which emphasise this tough instrumentalist approach to virtue and others which minimise it, and makes the challenging suggestion that the former are designed to shock, the latter closer to Epicurus' true beliefs. But if I am right about the Cicero text, the instrumentalist analysis is absolutely foundational to Epicurus' moral thought, and should not be argued away. Many texts assert, and none actually denies, that virtue's own value is purely instrumental. What some texts emphasise but others disregard is pleasure's intimate causal dependence on virtue. Torquatus eloquently conveys both aspects – virtue's instrumental role (esp. 42, 54), and its indispensability for pleasure (50).

[32] I am grateful for comments received from audiences at Princeton, Cambridge and Naples, and for further written comments from Julia Annas, Phillip Mitsis, Julius Rocca, Voula Tsouna-McKirahan and Stephen Everson.

7
Socratic paradox and Stoic theory[1]

T. H. IRWIN

1 Reactions to Stoic ethics

Stoic ethical doctrines provoke severe criticism from both ancient and modern readers. The criticism, however, expresses two sharply opposed views of the character and implications of Stoicism. These opposed views appear already in Cicero's comments on Stoicism, and they have affected interpretation and criticism of the Stoic position ever since.

Some critics attack the apparently extravagant, indeed outrageous, character of the Stoic conclusions. In the view of these critics, someone who actually accepted and practised Stoic doctrines would be so alien to us that he would be inhuman. Critics normally rest the charge of inhumanity on two features of Stoicism: (1) Since all reputed goods and evils except virtue and vice are indifferents, the sage sees no reason to be strongly concerned about anything other than virtue and vice.[2] (2) The sage is free of all

---

[1] I originally submitted this chapter in (as far as I remember) 1990. The delay in publication has allowed me to cite a few of the many important contributions to the subject that have appeared in the last few years, but I have not tried to discuss the issues that have arisen. Readers will especially benefit from the contrasting general treatments of Stoic ethics by Striker [865] and by Annas [71]. (I have discussed Annas in [72].) Engstrom and Whiting [16] contains chapters (esp. those by Annas, Cooper and Irwin) discussing Stoicism.

I cite passages from the original sources, in cases where these are readily accessible. In other cases I add or substitute a reference to von Arnim [791], cited as SVF, or to Long and Sedley [719], cited as LS.

[2] This view of Stoic ethics is expressed by Sorabji, in his discussion of whether Stoics believe in human rights: 'The just Stoic employer aims at doing everything in his power to give the workers the just wage. But, to use an English expression, "the game's the thing", not whether he scores; not in other words whether the money actually reaches them. Money is described as a part of the subject matter of virtuous action; it is not the goal. I doubt whether a believer in human rights would take this attitude. If a living wage is a human right, its delivery will be a goal, not merely the subject matter in pursuit of some other goal, one's own virtue. Indeed, treating delivery as a mere subject matter may seem to us a rather

emotions, and so has no non-rational motive for being strongly concerned about anything.

When Cicero defends Lucius Murena in court, he seeks to undermine the effects of Cato's damaging and credible testimony against Murena, by ridiculing Cato's well-known Stoicism:

> For there was a man of outstanding intellect, Zeno, the followers of whose doctrines are called Stoics. His opinions and precepts are of the following sort. The sage is never moved by favour; he never forgives anyone's offence; no one except a foolish and trivial person is merciful; a real man is never moved or mollified by pleas; only sages are wise; only they are handsome, however disfigured; only they are rich, however sunk in beggary; only they are kings, however sunk in slavery. We, on the other hand, who are not sages are, in their view, fugitives, exiles, enemies, indeed madmen. All errors are equal; every offence is a shocking crime, and needlessly suffocating a cock is no lighter an offence than suffocating one's father. The sage has no opinions, regrets nothing, makes a mistake in nothing, never changes his mind.   (*Pro Murena* 61)

These absurd (in Cicero's view) Stoic claims about the sage are the result of single-minded obsession with moral virtue. Cicero contrasts the comically inhuman rigour of the Stoics with the warmer and more sympathetic attitude of the Peripatetics (63).

While Cicero's attack is the work of a defence counsel trying to undermine a prosecution witness, and certainly not a sober assessment of Stoicism, the picture it presents reflects a seriously held and deep-seated reaction to

repulsive attitude' ([65], 140.) Sorabji goes on to qualify, but not to reject, this initial reaction to the Stoic position.

A similar view is expressed in several places by Nussbaum, in [731]. She recognises that preferred indifferents are sometimes said to have some worth 'even if only a derivative or second-grade worth' (p. 360). But still she takes it to be a consequence of the theory of indifferents that the Stoics 'are committed to denying the intrinsic worth of external worldly actions and even, as they explicitly assert, the intrinsic worth of life itself (DL VII.102). Not only traditional "external goods" . . . not only "relational goods" . . . but also individual forms of virtuous activity . . . are held to be, strictly speaking, worthless' (p. 362). When we appreciate this, we begin 'to get a picture of the radical detachment of the Stoic sage' (p. 363).

Nussbaum comes back to this question about the worth of indifferents when she considers whether Stoics will regard as important the sorts of things that other people get angry about. Commenting on the Stoic belief in the value of indifferents, she says: 'It is difficult to believe that this account of devotion to friend, family, and country would . . . justify (without elaborate circumnavigation via Stoic teleology) the sort of risk taking in defence of others that he needs to endorse' (pp. 416 f.). Nussbaum seems to assume that if we regard something as an indifferent, even a preferred indifferent, then we cannot suppose that it warrants us in facing danger or taking risks to secure it.

Stoicism.[3] The same charge of inhumanity is urged by Lactantius, who particularly attacks the Stoic view that the virtuous person is free of passions:

> In this area there are no precepts of philosophers. For they were deceived by a false appearance of virtue and removed kindness[4] from human beings. In trying to cure vices they increased them.[5] And while these same people often agree that participation in human society is to be continued, they altogether separate themselves from society by the rigour of their inhuman virtue.   *(Divinae Institutiones* (= CSEL 19) VI.10.11 = SVF III.450)

> The Stoics, therefore, are mad; they do not moderate [passions], but cut them off, and in a way want to castrate a human being of things that are implanted by nature.   *(Div. Inst.* VI.15.2)[6]

Lactantius accuses the Stoics of leaving no room for sympathy with others (*humanitas*).

A sharply opposed reaction to the Stoics appears in the critics who claim that the apparent paradoxes of Stoic ethics are just misleading formulations of views that really do not disagree with Aristotle on any substantive issues. Cicero suggests that when we see the Stoic 'paradoxes' from close range, they no longer seem so paradoxical (*de Finibus* IV.74). A more acute critic than Cicero, the Academic Carneades, actually claims that the Stoics' disagreements with Aristotle are merely verbal:

> Carneades never ceased to contend that in all of this enquiry under the head of goods and evils, the Stoics' dispute with the Peripatetics was about names, not about facts.   *(Fin.* III.41)[7]

If this reaction is correct, then, even if the Stoics intend their doctrines to be as inhuman as Cicero and Lactantius take them to be, they cannot have succeeded.

This is the conclusion drawn by Augustine, who argues that neither the

---

[3] A suitable comment on Cicero's speech is attributed to Cato by Plutarch, *Cato Minor* 21. Other satirical comments on Stoicism appear in Horace, *Epistles* I.1.106–8; *Satires* I.3.76–142; II.3.40–6.   [4] Or perhaps 'pity' (*pietas*).

[5] 'Dum volunt sanare vitia, auxerunt.' The older mss. read 'Dum volunt sanare, vitiaverunt.'

[6] I am not sure that Von Arnim was right to regard the first of these passages as a remark about the Stoics. The context is Lactantius' criticism of the Epicurean attempt to base justice in reciprocal advantage. But in the second passage, and generally in VI.14–15, Lactantius expresses the same general view about Stoic inhumanity.

[7] For other remarks about the purely verbal character of Stoic disagreements with Aristotle see *Fin.* IV.20, 72, V.22, 74, 88–9; *Tusculan Disputations* V.32, 120; *de Legibus* I.38.

Stoics' doctrine of indifferents nor their doctrine of the passions really separates them from ordinary human attitudes and responses to external circumstances.

> For what difference does it make whether they are more appropriately called goods or advantages (*commoda*), as long as the Stoic shudders and goes pale, no less than the Peripatetic, lest he be deprived of them, not describing them in the same way, but valuing them in the same way?
> (*de Civitate Dei* ix.4)

Augustine believes, in sharp contrast to Lactantius, that, whatever the Stoics say, their attitudes are the practical equivalent of having emotions and recognising goods other than virtue.

It is perhaps difficult to say whether the charge of inhumanity or the charge of triviality is more unflattering to the Stoics. We must try to see how Stoic ethics could provoke both reactions, and whether a more favourable reaction can be defended.

2 Stoic ethics and Socrates

The Stoics themselves recognise that many of their leading ethical views are controversial, even paradoxical. Cicero comments:

> Since these [Stoic views] are amazing, and contrary to the opinions of everyone (and the Stoics themselves call them *paradoxa*), I wanted to try to see whether they could be brought into the light . . . And I wrote all the more readily in so far as these views that they call *paradoxa* seem to me to be Socratic to the highest degree and by a long way the truest.[8]
> (*Paradoxa Stoicorum* 4)

Cicero suggests that Stoic views are paradoxical because they are fundamentally Socratic.

Two Socratic paradoxes that have struck both ancient and modern readers of the relevant Platonic dialogues are his claims that (1) virtue is sufficient for happiness, and (2) knowledge is sufficient for virtue. The paradoxical character of these claims is certified not only by Socrates' interlocutors, but by Aristotle. The first claim, Aristotle says, is so implausible that no one would maintain it except as a philosophical exercise (*Nicomachean Ethics* (*EN*) 1095b30–1096a2; cf. 1153b14–25). The second claim 'conflicts with things that appear evidently' (*EN* 1145b27–8), and therefore, in Aristotle's view, cannot be accepted as it stands.

---

[8] For the paradoxical character of Stoic views cf. Cic. *Fin.* iii.45, iv.74; *Laelius* 45; *Parad.* 35; Plutarch, *Cat. Min.* 21; Origen, *Commentaria in Evangelistum Joannis* ii.10 = SVF iii.544; Proclus, *in Eucl.* 35.27 (Friedlein) = SVF iii.547. On their Socratic character see Cic. *Parad.* 23; *Academicae Quaestiones* ii.136; *Tusc.* iii.10; Long [127], Striker [830].

According to the first Socratic paradox, the good person cannot be harmed (Plato, *Apology* 41c–d), because being virtuous is sufficient for being happy (Plato, *Gorgias* 470e9–11). To explain the sort of sufficiency he has in mind, Socrates maintains that virtue is a purely instrumental means to happiness (as taking medicine is a purely instrumental means to health; cf. Plato, *Republic* 357c5–d1), neither identical to happiness nor a part of happiness. Hence he thinks it is sufficient for happiness by being an infallible instrumental means to happiness.

Plato and Aristotle argue, against Socrates, that virtue is to be valued both for its own sake and for the sake of happiness; they infer that it must be a component of happiness, not just a purely instrumental means to it. They could still agree with Socrates that virtue is sufficient for happiness, if they claimed that virtue is the only component of happiness. But they reject this claim; for they regard external, non-moral goods (health, physical safety, freedom from pain, etc.) as components of happiness that are not infallibly secured by virtue. Hence Plato and Aristotle deny that virtue is sufficient for happiness.[9]

The Stoics accept Plato's and Aristotle's criticism of Socrates, in so far as they agree that virtue is not simply a purely instrumental means to happiness. But, unlike Plato and Aristotle, they still agree with Socrates' belief that virtue is sufficient for happiness. And so they argue that virtue is the only genuine good, and is therefore identical to happiness. In their view, all the recognised non-moral, external goods and evils are really neither good nor bad, but simply indifferent, since they neither promote nor impede happiness. On this point the Stoics agree with Socrates and the Cynics.[10]

It the Stoics defend the Socratic paradox this far, they must face the objection raised by Plato and Aristotle, that happiness clearly includes external goods for which virtue is insufficient. In reply, the Stoics stick to their claim that all external 'goods' are really indifferent, but they insist on a division among indifferents. Though health, in their view, is not good and illness is not bad, we have good reason to try to be healthy rather than ill. The Stoics recognise this reason by claiming that some indifferents are 'preferred' and others 'non-preferred'.

According to the second Socratic paradox, knowledge is all we need for

---

[9] My summary of Socrates', Plato's and Aristotle's views is controversial. Some issues are explored by Vlastos [120], ch. 8 (discussed in Irwin [122], 251–64, with some reference to Stoicism); Irwin [294], chs. 5, 12; Irwin [568]; Cooper [567].

[10] The Cynics are one source of Zeno's moral views. See LS 1, p. 3, 435. Zeno was a pupil of Crates the Cynic: Diogenes Laertius (D.L.) VI.91, VII.2–5. Ariston of Chios goes furthest in a Cynic direction: LS 58F. Plato is alleged (and at least it is a good story) to have described Diogenes the Cynic as 'Socrates gone mad', D.L. VI.54.

virtue. An obvious objection appeals to the apparent facts of incontinence (choosing one option even though we believe another option to be better). Socrates answers by denying the possibility of incontinence. His denial does not convince Plato (in *Republic* IV) and Aristotle, who argue that non-rational desires, including those responsible for incontinent action, belong to a distinct non-rational part of the soul. The Stoics counter on Socrates' side by arguing that the supposedly non-rational 'passions' or 'affections' (*pathē*) do not belong to a distinct non-rational part of the soul. Fear, anger, sexual desire and other emotions are really false judgements about what is good for us. Since they are false judgements, Plato and Aristotle are mistaken in supposing that a virtuous person will have well-trained passions; on the contrary, virtue requires the elimination of all passions. Still, the virtuous person has 'good affective states' (*eupatheiai*), which have some of the features of passions, and so it is unfair to accuse sages of the unfeeling attitude that would justify the charge of inhumanity.

We can now see some connection between the Stoic treatment of the Socratic paradoxes and the charges of inhumanity and triviality. In affirming their versions of the Socratic positions, the Stoics invite the charge of inhumanity; in defending these versions, they invite the charge of triviality.

3 Stoic strategies

The Stoics might reasonably try to defend the Socratic paradoxes by arguing in either of two ways: (1) They might support the paradoxes, by trying to show that, no matter how paradoxical these doctrines may appear, we must none the less accept them, because of overwhelming arguments. (2) They might defuse the paradoxes, by trying to show that if we understand these doctrines better, they turn out not to be as paradoxical as they first seemed.

In general, these two lines of defence might be expected to help each other; finding more arguments to support a claim will often lead us to be less surprised by it. But they need not always go together; however strongly we may be convinced by quantum physics or Trinitarian theology, we may still find them sharply at odds with our intuitive beliefs, and perhaps we would be wrong if we did not react to them in this way. By contrast, the view that free will is compatible with determinism turns out (according to compatibilists) not to be so surprising once we understand what it says and what our intuitive beliefs really assert and presuppose.

The Stoics use both lines of defence to support their versions of the Socratic paradoxes, and their different lines of defence. The first line of defence, 'supporting' the paradoxes, provokes the charge of inhumanity, and the second line of defence, 'defusing' the paradoxes, leads to triviality.

We can perhaps connect these two lines of defence with a more general issue about the Stoics' method of ethical argument. Once again, we can see two lines of argument apparently leading in two different directions. For convenience, and without intending to beg any questions by using the terms, I shall call the two lines of argument 'dialectical' and 'systematic'.

In speaking of dialectical argument I have in mind the Stoic arguments about ethics that appeal especially to ethical 'preconceptions' (*prolēpseis*; cf. Plutarch, *de Stoicorum Repugnantiis* (*SR*) 1041e) – beliefs that are basic in our ethical thinking because they constitute the principles in the light of which we assess our other ethical beliefs.[11] The apparent paradoxes of Stoic ethics are the result of adherence to preconceptions. Though the Stoics seem to violate common sense, and though the contrary view may seem persuasive (Epictetus 1.27.6; 28.28), they reply that in fact they keep closer to common sense, properly understood, than rival theories do. If some other beliefs conflict with preconceptions, we ought, in the Stoic view, to give up the other beliefs rather than the preconceptions.

Epictetus describes the proper use of preconceptions as follows:

> Preconceptions are common to all human beings; and preconception does not conflict with preconception. For which of us does not assume that the good is beneficial and choiceworthy, and that we must seek and pursue it in every circumstance? Which of us does not assume that the just is fine (*kalon*) and fitting? Whence then comes the conflict? In the application of preconceptions to particular realities[12] when one says 'He has done finely, he is brave', while another says 'not at all; he's crazy'. Hence people's conflict with one another arises. (1.22.1–4)

> What then is it to be educated? It consists in learning to apply the natural preconceptions to the particular beings conformably to nature. (1.22.9)

Though Epictetus admits that different people's assent to the same preconceptions does not prevent disagreement, he argues that careful attention to these agreed preconceptions will remove disagreement.

Epictetus thinks it is reasonable to assume that the preconceptions are consistent; for since all of them are basic principles for assessing our other ethical beliefs, the belief that they are inconsistent would implicitly challenge all our ethical beliefs.[13] Before we concede that our ethical beliefs are subject to this radical objection, it is reasonable for us to see whether we

---

[11] The *prolēpsis* of a craft or a profession is its fundamental assumption or conception; see Epictetus IV.8.6, 10.

[12] *Ousiai*; i.e. the particular cases that Epictetus goes on to mention.

[13] An example of this sort of challenge would be the one that Sidgwick considers in the concluding chapter of [970].

can reasonably reject the apparent evidence of inconsistency in our preconceptions. In Epictetus' view, we falsely suppose that our preconceptions conflict because we confuse the real content of a preconception with the hasty conventional assumptions that we rely on in applying preconceptions to particular situations. If, however, we are careful not to follow hasty conventional assumptions, and if instead we apply preconceptions systematically, then we find (in Epictetus' view) that their application to specific types of situations undermines our unreflective conventional judgements about these situations. It may seem plausible to suppose that someone who is suddenly impoverished has suffered some genuine loss of welfare; but the Stoics argue that we shall no longer suppose this, once we try to apply all our preconceptions to the situation, and once we interpret each of them so that it is consistent with all the others.

This doctrine of preconceptions suggests the standards that the Stoics take to be relevant for evaluating ethical arguments. In their view, acceptance of a rival theory requires the violation of principles that we can recognise as basic in our ethical thinking; and if the Stoic view is the only way to avoid conflict with these principles, it must be accepted, however paradoxical it may initially seem. If we want to evaluate Stoic arguments, we ought to see what they take the relevant preconceptions to be, how they try to reconcile them, and whether other theories fail to reconcile them.

A different line of argument proceeds from the rest of the Stoic system to draw ethical conclusions. For this purpose, the most important parts of the system are the closely connected doctrines of cosmic teleology and natural theology. According to the Stoics, the world as a whole is a single goal-directed system, the produce of intelligent design and cosmic reason. It is designed for the good of the whole, and rational agents have the capacity to take a conscious part in the fulfilment of the design of cosmic reason. This participation of our individual reasons in cosmic reason presents us with ethical aims and aspirations to guide our lives.[14]

It would be a mistake to suppose that the 'dialectical' and 'systematic' arguments are completely separate. Dialectical argument about ethics reasonably refers to the coherence of ethical beliefs with the rest of one's philosophical outlook; moreover, preconceptions themselves, according to the Stoics, lead us towards the acceptance of cosmic teleology and theology. Still, it remains true that different strategies of argument from different starting-points and with different aims are open to the Stoics; an ethical conclusion that might seem ungrounded from a dialectical point of view may turn

---

[14] The relation between dialectical and systematic argument in Stoic ethics is discussed by Striker [865], 8–10; Annas [71], ch. 5; Long [833]; Brunschwig [873]; Cooper [831].

out to be an appropriate conclusion from a cogent argument whose premises are drawn from other parts of the Stoic system.

We cannot simply take it for granted that 'systematic' argument will lead to 'inhuman' conclusions, and that 'dialectical' arguments will lead to 'trivial' conclusions. Socrates certainly believes that dialectical argument supports his surprising ethical claims. Even if we begin from preconceptions, as opposed to what an interlocutor happens to find initially plausible, we may find that our preconceptions force us into conclusions that, even when we understand them, seem strange. But it is reasonable in general to suppose that dialectical argument will reduce our surprise at Stoic conclusions; for if we proceed from our preconceptions and articulate them as we go, we are likely to find that our intuitive beliefs, as clarified in our articulated preconceptions, are closer than we supposed they were to the Stoic conclusions. If we argue systematically, from premises established elsewhere in the Stoic system, we do not have the same reason to expect that our surprise at the Stoic conclusions, compared with our intuitive beliefs, will be reduced.

I do not propose to examine Stoic ethics from both the dialectical and the systematic point of view. I shall take the dialectical point of view, to see whether the Stoic conclusions avoid inhumanity, and, if so, whether they fall into triviality. I shall focus on one central issue on which the Stoics reject Carneades' criticism of their position for triviality. Cicero presents Cato, the Stoic spokesman, as affirming the crucial differences between the Stoic and the Peripatetic views. The first, and most important, point of genuine disagreement that Cato mentions is this:

> The Peripatetics say that all the things they call goods contribute to living happily, whereas our school do not think the happy life is constituted by everything that deserves some value.   (Fin. III.41)

The Stoic doctrine of goods and happiness is supposed to vindicate the first Socratic paradox, showing why virtue is sufficient for happiness. It also contributes to the vindication of the second Socratic paradox, since it helps us to see why knowledge is sufficient for virtue, and why the sage lacks passions.[15]

One way to consider the dialectical strength of the Stoic position is to raise a still narrower issue: how well do the Stoics meet Aristotle on his own ground? Since some ancient critics suppose that it is useful to compare the Stoic with the Peripatetic position, it is worth seeing how well the Stoics can

---

[15] I have not discussed questions about the development of Stoic views. I do not believe that in fact these questions matter much for the features of Stoic doctrine that I discuss; but this view is itself open to dispute (see, for example, Long [839]; LS I.407–10).

argue for their side, if they rely on arguments that Aristotelians accept.[16] I shall pursue these questions in a deliberately one-sided way, by trying to make the strongest prima facie case for the Stoics; I shall not consider all the replies that might be open to Aristotle.

4 The natural origins

The Stoics argue that the pursuit of natural advantages[17] (health, physical security, social relations, family life, and so on) is a reasonable result of our natural development. On the other hand, this same natural development also shows us why these objectives[18] are not genuine goods, and why virtue is really the only good. This argument from natural development relies on the Stoic account of 'conciliation' (*oikeiōsis*; D.L. VII.85, Cic. *Fin.* III.16–20).[19]

The Stoics begin with a creature's initial impulse towards its own preservation and its own good. The creature is conciliated to its environment, because it can detect there the things that are good for it. As soon as it is born 'it is conciliated to itself and commended towards conserving itself and towards loving its state and those things that conserve its state' (Cic. *Fin.* III.16). These systematically goal-directed activities manifest self-love:

> It is not surprising that they are born with that without which they would be born pointlessly. This is the first piece of equipment that nature placed in them for their preservation – their conciliation and attachment to themselves. They could not have been preserved unless they wanted it. (Seneca, *Epistulae* 121.24)

To explain why some goal-directed behaviour implies self-love, the Stoics appeal to system and co-ordination. An animal's behaviour is not a series of

---

[16] In focusing on Aristotle, I do not mean to assume anything about whether the early Stoics did or did not know of, or intentionally respond to, the main works of Aristotle (i.e. the contents of the surviving Aristotelian treatises, in contrast to Aristotle's dialogues). An able defence of hyperbolic doubt about Stoic knowledge of Aristotle is presented in Sandbach [829], 24–30. In ethics the situation is complicated by the fact that many 'Aristotelian' positions can also be found in Plato, whose ethical views (in contrast to Socrates') the Stoics criticised; see, for instance, Plutarch *SR* 1038e, 1039e, 1040a–e; *de Communibus Notitiis contra Stoicos* (*CN*) 1070e–f; Irwin [294], §140. (On the reference to Aristotle at 1040e see Sandbach [829], 14; but cf. perhaps *EN* 1174b4–8.)

[17] I translate *ta prōta kata phusin* (lit. the 'primary things in accordance with nature') by 'natural advantages'. They correspond to Aristotle's 'external goods'; but for reasons to be explained later (see section 8) the Stoics do not regard them as goods.

[18] 'Objective' is the Stoic term; see section 5 below.

[19] For discussion of conciliation see White [868]; Striker [861]; Engberg-Pedersen [856]. The translations 'appropriation', 'endearment' and 'adaptation' are also defensible. An interesting fragment of Hierocles is discussed by Inwood [876]. The text appears, with discussion by Long, in [49], 268–451.

random movements. Nor does it simply display local adaptation of means to ends; its apparently goal-directed actions are not rare episodes in largely random or apparently self-defeating movements. The agent displays some broad overall system and consistency in attitudes to the environment.

> There must be something to which other things are to be referred. I seek pleasure. For whom? For myself. So I take care of myself. I avoid pain. On whose behalf? On my own. Hence I take care for myself. If I do everything because of my care for myself, my care for myself comes before everything. (Seneca, *Ep.* 121.17).

The Stoics assume that an agent's overall system of attitudes must focus on what benefits the agent. Self-love need not regulate every single desire or attitude, but it regulates a creature's desires as a whole, making them broadly systematic and co-ordinated.

While some sort of conciliation and self-love are characteristic of all animals, a distinctive feature of rational agents is the growth of preconceptions (Epictetus II.17.5). These are beliefs – at first rough and implicit, but gradually clearer and more explicit – about the sorts of things that are good for us. These preconceptions are formed by a reliable process; for they express the assumptions and actions that have been found to promote our good, and the better we articulate the preconceptions, the more effectively they promote our good. The Stoics argue:

> Since reason has been given to rational creatures as a more complete form of leadership, living in accordance with reason correctly turns out to be in accordance with nature for them; for reason is added later [to the initial impulses] as a craftsman of impulse.   (D.L. VII.86)[20]

We articulate and modify our initial assumptions in so far as we learn to apply preconceptions correctly to particular cases, and to adjust them to each other so that they no longer seem to conflict.

In applying reason to our preconceptions and actions, we achieve a more consistent and coherent life. The sort of consistency and coherence (*homologia*) that concerns the Stoics, however, is not mere internal consistency.[21] If they follow their rule about the preconceptions, the appropriate form of consistency must be the consistent following of all the preconceptions that

---

[20] On the translation see LS II.344. I follow Striker [861], 155, n. 12, in taking 'correctly' with 'turns out' rather than with 'in accordance with reason'. The argument suggests a contrast between 'living in accordance with impulse' and 'living in accordance with reason'.

[21] For different Stoic formulae explaining the kind of 'agreement' or 'consistency' that is intended see Stobaeus, *Eclogae* II.76.19–21 (Wachsmuth) = SVF III.3; II.75.11–76.15 (cf. SVF III.12); D.L. VII.85–9.

affect our good. If, for instance, I decide to pursue health as my only objective, my plan is (we may assume) internally consistent, but it is not consistent with the preconceptions, since I have a preconception that other things besides health are worth pursuing. Hence this one-sided plan fails the Stoic demand for consistency.

A life that is guided by explicit and articulate preconceptions is guided by self-love, and in particular by an expanded conception of the self:

> The most important difference between human beings and beasts is this: Beasts, in so far as they are moved by sense, conciliate themselves only to what is at hand and present, since they are aware of very little of the past and future. A human being, on the other hand, shares in reason, through which he traces consequences, sees the causes of things, notices the mutual relations of effects and causes, compares similarities, and combines and connects future with present things; and so he easily sees the course of his whole life, and prepares the things necessary for living that life. (Cicero, *de Officiis* I.11)[22]

Seneca (*Ep.* 12.6) compares a total human life to a series of concentric circles – the largest extending from birth to death and smaller ones covering youth and childhood. This picture suggests that the conception including the later stages must also include the earlier. With maturity we come to conceive of our lives as having a wider extent, and we include in them the earlier stages that had a narrower horizon. Two stages belong to the same person in so far as at least one of them has a conception of a life that includes the conception of the other stage as a part of it.[23]

Practical reason produces a similarly comprehensive view, when it is applied not only to different times in my life but also to different aspects of myself. A rational agent with articulated preconceptions has a conception of herself in so far as she thinks of different concerns as belonging to a circle that includes all of them in a systematic connection to each other.

5 The primacy of reason

The Stoics claim that when we become aware of rational order in our choices and desires, we prefer it over the objects that we initially aimed at. Cicero (*Fin.* III.23) offers a suggestive analogy with being introduced to a new friend, whom you then come to value more than the person who introduced you. Natural impulses introduce us and 'commend' us to reason; but once we have recognised it, we value it more than we value the natural

---

[22] This passage is appositely quoted by Reid in his discussion 'of our regard to our good on the whole' [967], II.2, p. 206.

[23] For further development of this appeal to concentric circles see Hierocles = LS 59G. Cf. Cicero, *Off.* I.12.

advantages. The Stoics suppose that once I form the habit of using practical reason instrumentally, I discover that the value I attach to it is not purely instrumental. How can I discover this?[24]

In general I can discover that even though I value x as a means to y, I also value x for itself; I discover this by discovering that I prefer x and y together over y without x. If I attached only instrumental value to x as a means to y, then I would be perfectly satisfied to get y by some other (equally efficient) instrumental means than x. But clearly we do not look at all instrumental means as purely instrumental. If I walk in order to get to work (not simply for the sake of walking), I still might not be equally pleased if I could get to work in some other equally efficient way. If I would not prefer this equally efficient alternative, I show that I attach some intrinsic value to walking.

The Stoics suggest that something analogous is true about practical reason. The analogy with walking is not complete. For while we might go for a walk with no further purpose, practical reason seems to depend on our having some further purpose that we want to achieve; as the Stoics say, practical reason needs some material to work on. Still, even if practical reasoning must always be partly instrumental, it does not follow that its value is always purely instrumental. Here the analogy with walking is useful. For I prefer to achieve my objectives by rational planning, rather than to achieve them by some other equally efficient means; hence I do not value practical reason simply as an instrumental means; hence I attach intrinsic value to it.

Self-love is present from the start, but I discover only gradually what the self I love really is. After the piecemeal exercise of practical reason, I remember how my past plans succeeded and failed, and I plan for the future. I become aware of myself as something more than a collection of impulses; I regard myself as a temporarily extended rational planner. When I notice this I come to value my preservation as a rational planner more than I value the satisfaction of the particular impulses (*Fin.* III.21–3).

Once we have discovered practical reason, we discover that the value we attach to it is not purely instrumental. For suppose – even counterfactually[25] – that some method other than practical reason is equally efficient in securing our other objectives. We might imagine, for instance, that natural instinct does just as well as practical reasoning would, or that a fairy god-mother is willing to save us the effort of practical reasoning. This does not

---

[24] This passage is discussed by Striker [865], 8–10 (who believes that the argument needs supplementation from Stoic theology); Annas [41]; Irwin [55].

[25] Kant argues that reason is less efficient than other means for achieving satisfaction of our other desires would be. See [953], 394. Hence he thinks the supposition I have mentioned is not merely counterfactual. His main argument is not weakened, however, if the supposition is false, as long as the counterfactual claim is true.

show that we ought to give up practical reasoning in these circumstances; for we have seen that we take our practical reasoning to be essential to ourselves.

If this is our view, then we would not be ready to give up the exercise of practical reasoning for the sake of achieving our other objectives, if our (supposed) fairy godmother offered us this Mephistophelean bargain. It would in fact be irrational for me to give up the exercise of reason for the sake of some specific objective. For the value of the objective is its value for me, and as I become self-conscious I become aware of myself as an essentially rational agent. Rational agency is not wholly separate from the other objectives and purposes I attribute to myself, since it plans for their achievement; but it also specifies the conditions under which they are valuable for me. If I ceased to be a rational agent, I would cease to exist, and any objective I would have gained by doing so would no longer be valuable for me, but only for the non-rational agent who would replace me. In offering this argument, the Stoics explicate Aristotle's own claim that external goods are goods for me only when I use them correctly, in accordance with virtue (cf. *EN* 1129b1–6).

To show how the intrinsic value of practical reason is connected with the virtues, the Stoics appeal to preconceptions about the intrinsic value of actions that are taken to be virtuous. Human beings and animals alike will sacrifice themselves even at enormous cost to themselves; and we admire these actions as virtuous and fine.[26] These preconceptions are reasonable if the virtues that are normally valued for themselves are just manifestations of practical reason; and the Stoic doctrine of the virtues tries to show this.

6 Ends and objectives

These parts of the Stoic argument might seem attractive to a Platonist or an Aristotelian.[27] They might persuade us that virtue is an intrinsic good and a necessary condition for happiness, and that it is not to be sacrificed for any other component of happiness. But the Stoics seem to go further; for they believe that arguments from conciliation, if we interpret them correctly, prove that virtue is the only good, the only thing worth choosing (*haireton, expetendum*, Cicero, *Fin.* III.21) for its own sake, and that the other supposed goods – the natural advantages – are really indifferent.[28] They still agree, however, that the natural advantages are to be 'selected' (*eklekton, seligendum, Fin.* III.22).

---

[26] See D.L. VII.127; Cicero, *Leg.* I.37–42; *Fin.* III.37–8. Some feeble sceptical criticisms are reported by Sextus, *adversus Mathematicos* (*M*) XI.99–109.

[27] On non-Stoic appeals to conciliation see Annas [826].

[28] See Stob. *Ecl.* II.46.5–10 = SVF III.2; II.77.16–19 = SVF III.16.

The Stoics recognise that in saying this they might seem to be putting forward two ultimate ends – virtue and the natural advantages. They deny that they are doing this, however (III.22). To clarify their position, the Stoics introduce the important distinction between the end (*telos, finis*) and the objective (*prokeimenon, propositum*) of an action; and we must see how they use this distinction.

People's welfare appears to be promoted or damaged by the presence or absence of the natural advantages that are our primary objects of pursuit. If this belief in the goodness of some natural advantages is a firm pre-conception, the Stoics violate their own method. They argue, however, that the preconceptions really support their apparently counter-intuitive claim. They rely on the preconception that (i) happiness is the ultimate end; then they argue that (ii) natural advantages are not part of the ultimate end, and so they infer that (iii) natural advantages cannot be part of the happiness.

The controversial step in this argument is the second one. The Stoics admit that we pursue some natural advantages for their own sakes, and they recognise that this pursuit is the natural and reasonable result of conciliation; how, then, can these natural advantages not be part of our end? In reply the Stoics argue that only happiness is the end of our action, and that the natural advantages are not the end, but only the objective.

To explain this distinction between the end and the objective, the Stoics refer to the defining features of a 'stochastic' (*stochastikē*, i.e. 'aiming') and a non-stochastic craft. In a non-stochastic craft, such as arithmetic, the achievement of the end of the craft, which is the faultless exercise of the craft, is sufficient for achieving the objective; if, then, we are adding and subtracting and get the wrong answer, we must have made a mistake in the exercise of the craft and failed to achieve its end. The parallel claim, however, does not hold for archery. Archers have achieved the objective of archery, for instance, when they have hit the target; but they have achieved the end of the craft if they fully exercise their craft in shooting at the target. This craft is stochastic because achieving the end does not imply achieving the objective. Even if our exercise of the craft is faultless, we may still miss the target (if, for instance, the wind blew it over or someone moved it) (Cic. *Fin.* III.22).[29]

---

[29] For further discussion of ends and objectives see Striker [871]; Irwin [832], 228–34; Taylor [732], 237–9; Inwood [838], 550–2 (which seems to me to distinguish insufficiently the contrast between *telos* and *prokeimenon* from the contrast between *telos* and *skopos*; see Irwin [832], 228n.25). Annas [71], 400–5, is sceptical about the extent to which the Stoics use the comparison with a stochastic craft.

This is not meant to be an eccentric Stoic view about a craft, or a view that will appeal to us only if we already accept Stoic ethics. It is meant to be a recognisably plausible account of some crafts. Alexander accepts the division between stochastic and non-stochastic crafts.[30] The same division is implicitly marked by Aristotle. He agrees with the Stoics that external success should not be the aim of someone practising the stochastic crafts of rhetoric, dialectic and medicine (*Rhet.* 1355b10–14, *Top.* 101b5–10). It is not the doctor's task to think about everything that might go wrong between his competent treatment and the external success; the patient might simply be unreceptive to treatment, or he might be hit by a falling tree on the way home from the hospital. Similarly, the dialectician should not waste time thinking about how to persuade someone who will not listen to rational argument, or who has, say, been bribed to maintain the opposing position no matter what arguments are offered. If craftsmen tried to adapt their practice to fit all possible external hazards, they would guess wrongly and come out worse than they would have if they had just aimed at the appropriate exercise of skill in the craft.

If this division between end and objective is correct, the medical practitioner, as such, has no choice about whether to be guided by the end or by the objective. If she is practising a systematic craft directed at the objective of medicine, she must be guided by the end; for otherwise she would not be practising medicine. We have a choice, however, about whether in a particular case we shall consider the end or the objective; if I am an orator, but I choose to answer bribery with bribery, I desert the rhetorical craft for some other way of trying to achieve my objective.

The division between stochastic and non-stochastic crafts seems to apply quite well to virtue, in some respects. According to the Stoics, a virtue is similar to a stochastic craft, in so far as it has an objective (achieving the natural advantages) and an end (doing all we can to achieve the natural advantages), and achieving the end is not sufficient for achieving the objective. Virtuous action, therefore, is not sufficient for achieving the life according to nature, which includes the natural advantages.

The Stoics are quite right to compare virtue with a stochastic craft to this extent. We believe, for instance, that justice in a state requires laws that protect people against arbitrary arrest; to explain this, we must

---

[30] See Alexander, *in Topicorum Libros Octo Commentaria* 32.20–34.5; *Quaestiones* II.16, p. 61.1–28 = SVF III.19. Alexander's examples of non-stochastic crafts (*in Top.* 33.10) – building and weaving – do not in fact seem entirely non-stochastic. He prefers to use 'function', *ergon*, where the Stoics use 'end', and to use 'end' where the Stoics use 'objective'. Here he follows Aristotle's usage in the *Topics* and *Rhetoric*.

claim that freedom from arbitrary arrest is valuable for agents with the aims and natural limitations of human beings. In the normal case[31] we do not undertake a craft unless we value the product; and the features of the product determine what counts as skill in the craft. Carneades notices that our conception of the craft must be guided in this way by our conception of the product (Cicero, *Fin.* v.16), and we have no good reason to believe he is telling the Stoics something they do not recognise already.[32]

The Stoics, however, resist a further apparent consequence of the comparison with stochastic crafts. In many stochastic crafts the end is not valued for its own sake; though we can distinguish the end of medicine from the objective, we have no reason to care about the proper exercise of the craft except in so far as we take it to be the best prospect for securing the objective of curing people. In the case of virtue, on the contrary, the Stoics insist that the end has non-instrumental value. If we value the exercise of practical reason for its own sake (as we learn to do in the course of conciliation and rational development), we admit that the end of virtuous action is not to be valued purely for the sake of the

---

[31] I say 'in the normal case' to allow for cases where the point of the productive process is not the existence of the product but the mere display of skill. (Perhaps, for example, a skilful cook might cook an absurdly elaborate and inedible dish simply to display culinary skill.) Something similar is true in games, where the usual distinction between the objective and the end can be drawn, but where the objective is not important in its own right (setting prizes, for instance, to one side), and the point is to devise a game that requires the display of certain kinds of skill (for example by making it artificially difficult to do some things). There is no reason to suppose that (in this sense) the Stoics regard life as a game. (For the use of a comparison with games see Cic. *Off.* III.42.) It would be a mistake to suppose that a comparison with games captures Stoic views about ends and objectives. Adam Smith's use of the comparison with a game seems to make this mistake about the Stoic position; see the passage quoted below. The comparison with games is explored further by Striker [871].

[32] This passage does not suggest that Carneades intends the point as a criticism of the Stoics. If he really thought the Stoics were overlooking his point about crafts, his objection would apparently conflict with his claim that the Stoic position differs only verbally from the Peripatetic position (*Fin.* III.41, discussed in section 1 above); for neglect of his point about crafts would involve the Stoics in more than terminological eccentricity. Contrast LS 1, 409. The view that Carneades intended his point as a criticism of the Stoics, and that the Stoics tried to answer Carneades, is founded on Plutarch, *CN* 1072d–f. Plutarch considers the formula that identifies the good with *eulogistein para tas eklogas tōn axian echontōn* (and he falsely adds the claim that in the Stoic view things have *axia* only *pros to eulogistein*). He comments that some people say the objections to this formula apply to Antipater; 'ekeinon gar hupo Karneadou piezomenon eis tautas kataduesthai tas heurēsilogias'. Plutarch is not necessarily reporting a claim based on historical evidence; it may simply reflect someone's incorrect supposition that Antipater would never have said this had he not needed to say it for controversial purposes.

objective, but is also to be valued for itself, because it exercises practical reason (Cic. *Fin.* III.24).

On this point the Stoics agree with Aristotle. For he also believes that virtuous action is to be chosen for its own sake. He recognises that acting well (*eupraxia*) is the end; the wise person sees that the value of the activity does not depend on any end beyond the activity itself (*EN* 1140b6). The Stoics, then, can claim Aristotelian support for their view that virtue is something more than a stochastic craft – that virtuous action has some value in itself apart from its instrumental value. Virtuous action is the realisation of practical reason, and it also consists in doing what we reasonably can to secure the natural advantages. Aristotle agrees that virtue has these two features.

On a further point, however, Aristotle believes, and the Stoics deny, that virtue is parallel to a stochastic craft. Alexander uses the parallel to argue that virtue is not sufficient for happiness:

> But in the case of stochastic crafts, it is no longer true that the end is up to the craftsman, just as neither is being happy up to virtuous people, if it is not true that only the fine is good.[33]   (*in Top.* 34.3–5)

Alexander assumes, quite reasonably, that virtuous action is the end,[34] and that happiness is the objective. The Stoics disagree, claiming that happiness is the end, not the objective, of virtue. In saying that happiness is the end of virtue, they agree verbally with Aristotle; but once they distinguish the end from the objective, they are not entitled to assume without argument that Aristotle treats happiness as the (internal) end rather than the (external) objective of virtue.[35]

Are the Stoics simply trading on a verbal similarity between the Aristotelian position and their own, in order to conceal the controversial character of their claim that happiness is the end, and not the objective, of virtue? Or can they fairly claim that Aristotle, despite what he sometimes says, really ought to agree with them? This is not simply a question about Aristotle; his attitude seems to express a reasonable view of the relation of virtue to happiness, and if the Stoics cannot show why he ought to abandon his apparently reasonable view in favour of their view, they leave a large gap in their argument.

---

[33] I translate *to kalon agathon* following Striker in [871].

[34] I am expressing Alexander's distinction in Stoic terms; see n. 30 above.

[35] For present purposes I am speaking interchangeably of virtue and of virtuous action. The Stoics do not disagree with Aristotle's view that virtue ought to be realised in virtuous action (though they disagree about what this realisation consists in).

7 Aristotle on happiness

To see why the Stoic view about happiness might be reasonable, it is useful to notice that Aristotle looks at happiness in two ways. First of all, happiness is something that we aim at, and indeed part of the point of thinking about it is to change our aims. Aristotle believes that the discovery of what the good is should have a significant influence on our way of life, so that 'like archers with a target to aim at we are more likely to hit the right mark' (*EN* 1094b22). He implies that if we have an explicit and correct conception of happiness, that will improve our practical reasoning. Hence he thinks practical reasoning begins with a first principle: 'Since this is the end and the best thing' (1144a32). Happiness is the ultimate object of wish that provides the starting-point for deliberation (1111b28). Practical reasoning begins from a desire for doing well, and doing well is the end (1139b3–4); hence wisdom is the correct apprehension of this end (1142b32). Aristotle clearly believes that happiness is an end that we can explicitly conceive, and that our explicit conception of it guides our deliberation and decision.

Aristotle also looks at happiness in a second way, treating it as a measure of success. Our conception of happiness shows us whether someone has had the sort of life that it is reasonable to hope for. This second way of looking at happiness is most obvious in Aristotle's remarks on the relation of good fortune to happiness. One's initial circumstances constrain the possible results of rational deliberation, and further external circumstances affect the actual results of our particular deliberation. (If I do not inherit wealth, for instance, I cannot deliberate about how I am to use my inherited wealth wisely; and if I invest money wisely to raise further funds for famine relief, but the stock market unexpectedly crashes, my wise project fails.) Aristotle does not think happiness is determined by external goods independently of an agent's deliberation, but he insists that it is not wholly determined by what one chooses to do. We consider someone's life not with reference to the agent's aims, but with reference to what has actually happened and to the sort of life someone has had. This second view of happiness is retrospective, concerned with the actual results of someone's deliberations and actions, whereas the first view is prospective, concerned with the basis of someone's deliberations.

Aristotle denies that virtuous action is sufficient for happiness, on the ground that it is insufficient for achieving the valuable external results that are sought in virtuous action. It seems obvious that he must mean that happiness is, in Stoic terms, the objective, not the end, of virtue; and so he seems to use 'end' in the cases where the Stoics use 'objective'. He believes that virtue and virtuous action are to be chosen for their own sakes, and therefore (since happiness includes all intrinsic goods) are parts of happiness.[36] His argument would have no force if he were identifying happiness with the (internal) end, which would consist of doing all we can to secure these valuable results. He does not think happiness is entirely external to virtuous action, since virtuous action is a component of happiness; but since he thinks happiness is not exhausted by virtuous action, he appears to regard happiness as (in Stoic terms) the objective rather than as the end.[37]

From the Stoic point of view, Aristotle's two ways of conceiving happiness reflect some confusion. For he also recognises the legitimacy of marking the Stoic division between end and objective. We saw that he recognises it in the case of crafts. He does not mention an analogous division in the case of virtue and happiness, but he relies implicitly on such a division when he considers the relation of virtue to its external results. For he often claims that virtuous people act 'because an action is fine', or 'for the sake of the fine',[38] while at the same time they act for the sake of their happiness. Reflection about happiness tells us that the good of others plays an essential role in it, and that therefore we have sufficient reason to act for the benefit of others (if they are suitably related to us) without any further thought about our own good. Brave or just people, for instance, do not stop to think about whether facing this danger now or keeping this promise now is part of their happiness. Indeed, it would be a bad thing – just as it is in the stochastic crafts – if they did stop to think about this.

This relation of virtuous action to happiness suggests that Aristotle implicitly recognises the Stoic distinction between end and objective. He sees that an objective (the virtuous person's conception of happiness, as Aristotle understands happiness) regulates our aims, but is not itself an aim in particular actions. Our conception of the external advantages achieved by bravery helps to explain why we regard bravery, rather than cowardice, as a

---

[36] For some evidence see Irwin [411], §§240–1. Here I accept a 'comprehensive' interpretation of Aristotle's account of happiness, in contrast to the narrower view that identifies happiness strictly with virtuous activity (see Kraut [458], 198–200, 264–6; Heinaman [519], 48–50; Irwin [459], 390). The comprehensive view makes Aristotle's position more different from the Stoic position than it would be if the narrower view were correct; in assuming the comprehensive view, then, I am making the Stoics' task more difficult. If their argument works against the comprehensive view, it should work against the narrower view.

[37] For different interpretations of Aristotle's views see Cooper [567] and Irwin [568]. Alexander takes Aristotle to believe that 'virtue is not sufficient for happiness', and defends him against the Stoics in his short work with this title (de Anima Liber (de An.) II.16, p. 159.15 ff.; see, for example, SVF III.63–6 for some extracts).

[38] See, for instance, EN 1115b12–13, 1116a11, 1120a4–8, 1122b6–7. For discussion of Aristotle's views on the fine see Irwin [411], §§237–41, and [505].

virtue to be chosen for its own sake; but we do not focus on these external advantages in deciding to act bravely. The Stoics can use this point to support their view of happiness. For the sort of life that Aristotle regards as happy is subject to misfortunes of certain sorts; and so when we deliberate about what to do, we ought not to be thinking about the ways in which things might go wrong – for we may not be able to take any systematic or beneficial account of these factors anyhow. It is better to follow the conception of the practical aim – virtuous action – that has been formed in the light of the various things that belong to the preferable way of life (which Aristotle identifies with happiness), and in the light of a reasonable strategy for getting them. Aristotle seems to admit that the conception of the end that actually guides virtuous people is their conception of fine action; and since our conception of happiness is our conception of the end that guides our action, he ought to identify happiness with fine action. Aristotle, therefore, ought to conclude that virtuous action is the ultimate end, and is thus to be identified with happiness.

The Stoics might fairly support this argument by appealing to Aristotle's claim that our conception of the end is the proximate efficient cause of our action.[39] The Stoics call this sort of cause the 'perfect' or 'principal' or 'containing' cause;[40] it is the one that explains the action, given the external conditions and antecedent events. Now it is reasonable to claim that what explains my action directly is my conception of the internal end.[41] My conception of the external objective partly explains why my end has the specific character it has (just as the archer's end is explained by reference to what is required for hitting the target); and so my conception of the objective is (in Stoic terms) an antecedent cause, not the principal cause, of my action.

---

[39] At *EN* 1139a31–3 Aristotle says decision (*prohairesis*) is the efficient cause of action; but he makes it clear that decision plays this role in so far as it includes a conception of the end (which it receives from the 'reasoning for the sake of something' which is the efficient cause of decision).

[40] The main sources are Clement, *Stromatae* VIII.9 = LS 55.I; Cicero, *de Fato* 41. See Frede [923], Irwin [832], 229. The introduction of causal distinctions into ethical doctrines is not un-Stoic. A possible parallel is suggested by Kidd [870]. Kidd takes the emphasis on causation to be characteristic of Poseidonius; but see the discussion of his paper in the same volume, pp. 22–4.

[41] Admittedly, it is difficult to say how in general we should distinguish what 'directly' explains an action from other causally relevant factors. But Aristotle cannot afford to do without this distinction. He seems to need it if he is to defend his claim that our actions are up to us because the origin of them is 'in us'; for by this claim he does not mean that (in Stoic terms) our actions have no antecedent causes external to us. See Meyer [642], ch. 6, and ch. 9 of this volume.

The Stoic conception of action and explanation clarifies Aristotle's claims about the end of action; and clarification seems to show that his position is inconsistent. For since he believes that (i) our conception of the end of an action is its proximate efficient cause, (ii) happiness is the end of action, and (iii) the proximate efficient cause of virtuous people's actions is their conception of fine and virtuous action, he should infer that (iv) happiness is fine and virtuous action. But he rejects (iv), since he maintains that happiness includes external goods. The Stoics argue that this conception of happiness conflicts with the role that Aristotle assigns to happiness as an end.

If this is the right way to connect Aristotelian with Stoic views, then the Stoics are justified in claiming that Aristotle ought to endorse their distinction between end and objective, and that he ought to agree that the virtuous person's end is the fine. It is a further question whether happiness ought to be counted as the end or as the objective. The Stoics can give an Aristotelian quite a good reason for deciding to reform Aristotle's own usage, and to confine the use of 'happiness' to the end. Aristotle agrees that an explicit conception of happiness should be the starting-point for our deliberation and choice; to assign this role to happiness is to treat it as the internal end, rather than the external objective. But Aristotle also seems to admit that the conception of the end that actually guides virtuous people is their conception of fine action; and so he ought to identify happiness with fine action. Aristotle, therefore, ought to conclude that virtuous action is identical to happiness.

In setting out the Stoic and the Aristotelian positions, it is difficult to avoid giving the impression that virtuous action for the sake of the fine is different from virtuous action for the sake of external advantages (when one has a correct conception of them). This impression is in a way correct, but in a way misleading. For the Stoics argue that in taking virtue as my end, I am not neglecting external advantages; my end is doing all I reasonably can to secure the external advantages. Virtuous people do not, in the Stoic view, give up some reasonable opportunity that Aristotle advises them to take for pursuing external advantages. To see why the Stoics can fairly claim that they take external advantages as seriously as Aristotle does, we must consider the account of external advantages in the Stoic doctrine of indifferents.

8 Indifferents

The Stoics assume (with Aristotle) that every good must contribute to happiness, and hence that every good in itself must be a part of happiness; and since virtue is identical to happiness, only virtue is a good. Since other valuable things turn out not to be goods, the Stoics call them 'indifferents'. On the other hand, the Stoics say that virtue is the craft of rightly choosing the natural advantages; how can they say this if the virtuous person regards them as indifferent and so presumably does not care about them at all? And how can they claim that these goods really make no difference to happiness? Would we not be foolish to choose fewer of them, other things being equal, if we could have had more (cf. Alexander, *in Top.* 211.9 = SVF III.62)?

If we notice that the Stoics speak of external advantages as indifferents, and we do not consider their explanation of 'indifferent', we may readily form the impression that they think external advantages are unimportant, not worth much effort or serious concern in themselves. Adam Smith makes this mistake:

> Human life the Stoics appear to have considered as a game of great skill; in which, however, there was a mixture of chance, or of what is vulgarly considered to be chance.[42] In such games the stake is commonly a trifle, and the whole pleasure of the game arises from playing well, from playing fairly, and playing skillfully. If notwithstanding all his skill, however, the good player should, by the influence of chance, happen to lose, the loss ought to be a matter, rather of merriment, than of serious sorrow . . . Human life, with all the advantages which can possibly attend it, ought, according to the Stoics, to be regarded but as a mere two-penny stake; a matter by far too insignificant to merit any anxious concern. Our only anxious concern ought to be, not about the stake, but about the proper method of playing. (Smith [971], pp. 278 f.)

Part of Smith's account of the Stoics rests on his (partly mistaken) assumptions about their doctrine of passions, which we must consider later. But his main point rests on the assumption that when the Stoics describe everything else besides virtue as indifferent, they imply that it is also unimportant.

The Stoics argue that their conception of an indifferent does not lead to the sorts of consequences alleged by Smith, and that the criticisms rest on a misunderstanding of their doctrine. Once ends are distinguished from objectives, the claim that nothing except virtue is a good does not imply that nothing except virtue is important or deserves rational concern; for rational concern for ends does not exclude rational concern for objectives. The Stoics try to show how their account of happiness allows, and indeed requires, rational concern for other things. Their position will sound odd if we accept the eudaemonist claim (accepted by Socrates, Plato and Aristotle) that all objects of rational concern must be included in happiness. But the Stoics have no reason to accept this particular eudaemonist claim, once they have distinguished ends from objectives. While they accept some eudaemonist claims (in taking happiness to be the ultimate end, and in taking it to include

---

[42] Smith alludes to the Stoic doctrine of providence.

all goods), their interpretation of these claims requires them to advocate rational concern for indifferents.

They insist, therefore, that there are different sorts of indifferents (Cic. *Fin.* III.50; D.L. VII.104–6),[43] and that not all indifferents are indifferent from all points of view. Pure indifferents give us no reason from any point of view to prefer them. The natural advantages that are the initial objects of a creature's desire are not pure indifferents. They are only (let us say) limited indifferents. They are indifferent towards happiness, since they are neither parts of happiness nor instrumental means to it.[44] These limited indifferents are not all equally indifferent, since we have reason to prefer some and reject others. The Stoics do not agree that indifferents are 'chosen' (*haireta*); for choiceworthiness is confined to goods, and hence confined to virtue and what promotes it.[45] But they allow that some indifferents are 'preferred' (or 'promoted', *proēgmena*), and others non-preferred (Cicero, *Fin.* III.51–2). The Stoics seek to distinguish concern directed to happiness from concern directed to an objective distinct from happiness. Once they are allowed this distinction, they have no difficulty in showing that some indifferents are to be preferred over others.[46]

An essential part of Stoic ethics, then, must be concerned with the proper treatment of indifferents by the virtuous person. Once again the Stoics work out the consequences of their distinction between ends and objectives. Their definitions of an 'appropriate action' (*kathēkon*) and a 'successful action' (*katorthōma*) make their view clear.[47]

An appropriate action is an action of which a reasonable defence can be given (Stobaeus, *Ecl.* II.85.13–15; cf. D.L. VII.107, Cicero, *Fin.* III.58). If appropriate action had to succeed in getting a preferred indifferent (its objective), it would not be a wise person's end; for we cannot expect that our efforts to gain preferred indifferents will always succeed, and we ought not (for the reasons previously given in distinguishing ends from objectives) to think directly about external success when we make our choices. But in referring to a 'reasonable defence' the Stoics make it clear why we can reasonably aim at appropriate action (i.e. take it as our end). For we can give a reasonable defence of an action

---

[43] I do not discuss Ariston's views on indifferents (see Cic. *Fin.* III.50; D.L. VII.160; n. 10 above).

[44] Chrysippus believes that this essential point underlying the claim about indifferents can be conveyed even if we follow common usage and call preferred indifferents goods; see Plutarch, *SR* 1048a.

[45] On choiceworthiness and other types of value see Stob. *Ecl.* II.83.10–84.3 = SVF III.124; D.L. VII.105 = SVF III.126.

[46] Different views of the value of indifferents are taken by LS I, 357–9 and Lesses [845], 110–17. I agree with the view of LS that the Stoics attribute non-instrumental value to some indifferents.

[47] For further discussion of appropriate actions and successful actions see White [823] and Irwin [844].

even if it turns out to have bad results, as long as we can show that we could not reasonably have been expected to foresee them, and that the action was reasonable in the light of what we could reasonably have been expected to foresee. This definition of appropriate action makes it clear that in so far as the virtuous person is expected to do appropriate actions, she is not expected to succeed in reaching the external result that she reasonably hopes for.

Appropriateness is not enough for a successful action, which is characteristic of the virtuous person. A successful action is a 'complete' appropriate action (Stob. *Ecl.* II.93.14–16; cf. 85.19). It differs from an incomplete appropriate action in being performed in the right way, so that, for instance, if returning a deposit is an appropriate action, returning it justly is a successful action (Cic. *Fin.* III.59). The relevant success is not success in reaching the preferred external results (Sextus, *M* XI.200; Stobaeus, *Florilegium* 103.22 = SVF III.510). The virtuous person's doing the appropriate actions for the right reason, because of their appropriateness, constitutes the distinguishing feature of virtue, and therefore constitutes the success proper to successful action. Hence happiness and virtue are constituted by 'acting reasonably (*eulogistein*) in the selection of things according to nature' and by 'living completing (*epitelounta*) all the appropriate actions' (D.L. VII.88).

If this is the right account of the Stoics' doctrine of virtuous action and the indifferents, then they cannot fairly be accused of failure to take indifferents seriously. Since the Stoic account of conciliation gives us reason to pursue the natural advantages, and since virtue itself consists in exercising reason in doing all we can to secure them, Stoic sages will do the best they can in pursuit of the natural advantages.

Admittedly, the Stoics do not take preferred indifferents so seriously that they pursue them in all circumstances, even when they conflict with the demands of virtue; when they claim to do everything possible, 'possible' must be understood to refer to the limits imposed by the virtues on the pursuit of any given preferred indifferent on any particular occasion. But these limits on the pursuit of indifferents do not distinguish the Stoic from the Aristotelian position, and so they do not give us a reason for claiming that the Stoics do not take indifferents seriously.

The Stoics' attitude is made clear in Seneca's defence of their view of preferred indifferents. According to Seneca, some external goods provide a wide field for several virtues, whereas poverty leaves room only for endurance; others add enjoyment to life.[48] The sage will prefer both sorts of advantages, and attributes value to them in themselves:

---

[48] Seneca marks Aristotle's division between external goods that provide resources (*chorēgia*) for virtuous actions and those that 'adorn' (*sunepikosmein*) a virtuous life (*EN* 1099a31–3, 1100b8–11, 26–8).

> Indeed, which of our sages – I mean, of our school, for whom the only good
> is virtue – will deny that these things we call indifferents also have some
> value in themselves (*aliquid in se pretii*) and that some are preferable to
> others?
> (Seneca, *de Brevitate Vitae* 22.4)

When he is asked whether he will seek (*petere*) preferred indifferents when
they do not hinder virtue, Seneca answers that he will seek them because
they are in accordance with nature, not because they are good.

> 'Won't you seek them?' Of course I'll seek them. Not because they are good,
> but because they are in accordance with nature, and because they will be
> taken by me with good judgement. 'Then what will be good in them?' Only
> this, that they are chosen well.
> (Seneca, *Ep.* 92.11 = LS 64J)

The only thing that is good in the pursuit of preferred indifferents is the exercise of good judgement in selecting them, but Seneca avoids saying that this
is the only reason for seeking them.

For these reasons, the fact that Stoic sages regard external goods and evils
as indifferent does not mean that they regard them as unimportant. Their
doctrine of suicide illustrates their general view. The Stoics believe that
external conditions can deteriorate far enough to justify a sage in commit-
ting suicide:

> A sage will make his own reasonable departure from life, for the sake of his
> country or his friends, or if he falls into excessively severe pain or suffers
> mutilation or contracts an incurable disease.
> (D.L. VII.130)

Since sages remain virtuous, they remain happy, and so they do not commit
suicide because their happiness has been threatened. They are influenced,
however, by the actual or threatened loss of preferred indifferents for themselves or for people they care about. This doctrine that happy people will
commit suicide because of external conditions that present no threat to their
happiness strikes opponents of Stoicism as bizarre (Plutarch, *SR* 1042de =
SVF III.759; Alexander, *de An.* II.16, p. 168.1–20 = SVF III.764). But once we
understand the status that the Stoics assign to indifferents, we need not find
their doctrine so bizarre. On the appropriate occasions, the sage treats preferred indifferents with the appropriate seriousness.[49]

If the Stoic doctrine of indifferents does not imply that the preferred
indifferents are unimportant, what is its point? Are the Stoics just being perverse in claiming that a virtuous action is a successful action, no matter how
unsuccessful it may be in acquiring the preferred indifferents?

In their defence they can fairly appeal again to Aristotle. For he claims that
the virtuous person will characteristically be 'practically without regret' (*EN*

---

[49] On suicide see Annas [71], 408 f.; Cooper [47].

1166a29), whereas the vicious person is full of regret. Aristotle evidently does not mean that virtuous people can be sure of always being lucky. The regret they avoid is the regret of doing something that they later come to believe they ought not to have done, given what they knew at the time. Virtuous people avoid this sort of regret, because they reliably do what is most reasonable in the light of their information at the time; and, being virtuous, they attach supreme value to action in accordance with right reason. But this is to say that virtuous people succeed in doing what they value most.

This is precisely the Stoics' reason for claiming that virtuous people's action is always successful action. Their conception of the end is formed in the light of reasonable views about how to acquire the preferred indifferents; but they aim at actions that are reasonable in the light of these reasonable views. Since virtuous people actually achieve this sort of action, they achieve their end, and have no reason to blame themselves or to wish that (given what they knew) they had done something else. On this point the Stoics and Aristotle agree. If virtuous people truly believe that they always succeed in these respects, they can still recognise that they fail in other respects. It is still open to them to regret what happened, in so far as they recognise that it would be preferable, for themselves or for others, if something else had happened; recognising this, they can see that (for instance) it would be appropriate to do something to relieve that victim of their action.

This defence of the Stoics may seem to miss the most serious objection to their position. Even if we do not wish we had done something else, and we do not blame ourselves for having done what we did, perhaps we ought to be sorry that our actions turned out badly, if they failed to reach their objective. Simply recognising that success would have been preferable does not seem an adequate response.

This objection turns our attention from the first to the second of the Socratic paradoxes that the Stoics defend. They support Socrates' claim that knowledge is sufficient for virtue by arguing that the virtuous person has no passions at all. The Stoics deny that sorrow is a proper response to non-preferred results, since sorrow is a passion and the sage is free of passions. Does this Stoic doctrine commit Stoic agents to an inhuman attitude?

9 Reason and passion[50]

Plato's and Aristotle's view that the passions belong to a distinct non-rational part of the soul may well seem plausible; for we assume, as

---

[50] Discussions of the Stoic doctrine of passions include Frede [848]; Striker [865]; Annas [917], ch. 5; Nussbaum [731], chs. 10–11.

Plato and Aristotle do, that we have non-rational desires that can arise and persist in us and move us to action contrary to our beliefs about what is best to do. Facts about weakness of will have often seemed to constitute a decisive objection to the Stoics' rationalist view. Aristotle remarks that the Socratic view conflicts with apparently evident facts about incontinence, and we may be inclined to say the same about the Stoic defence of Socrates.[51]

The Stoics, however, believe that their view rests on firm preconceptions that are violated by other accounts of the passions. They rely especially on two claims:

1. Passions characteristically depend on constituent evaluative beliefs. If, for instance, you resent what I have done to you, then you believe that I have inflicted some harm on you that I could reasonably have been expected to avoid. If you lacked these beliefs, you might well have some adverse reaction to what happened, but you would not hold it against me in exactly the same way. If, for instance, you discover that the harm I did to you was a complete accident that I could not have been expected to avoid or foresee, then the feeling you have towards me could not be resentment.

2. We can be praised and blamed for having particular passions and for acting on them (Cicero, *Tusc.* IV.31). But we could not fairly be praised and blamed if our passions were outside our rational control, and so not determined by our rational assent (which the Stoics take to be crucial for control and responsibility).[52] But if we accept a non-Stoic view of the passions, we must (in the Stoic view) regard passions as compulsive states; and then we cannot explain why they are not outside the area of responsible action (as bodily diseases often are).

Even if these are good reasons for taking the Platonic and Aristotelian view to be inadequate, they do not vindicate the Stoic view. The Stoics need to give an account of the passions that explains why they influence in the ways they do. We tend to assume that the influence of the passions is incompatible with their simply resting on beliefs about the good. The Stoics seek to show that we are wrong to assume this.

Socrates regards passions as simply beliefs about what is best all things considered, so that fears, for instance, are common to vicious and virtuous people. The Stoics disagree; they regard passions as products of a certain kind of mistaken judgement and false belief (D.L. VII.110–12;

---

[51] Galen conducts a long polemic (partly derived from Poseidonius) against the Stoics along these lines, in *de Placitis Hippocratis et Platonis* (*PHP*). For a translation see De Lacy [794], and for discussion see Edelstein and Kidd [793].

[52] See Cic. *Tusc.* IV.14: passions come about 'iudicio et opinione' and are 'in nostra potestate'. Cf. Epictetus I.11.33.

Cicero, *Tusc.* IV.10–15; *Acad.* I.38–90. A passion is (i) an 'immediate' or 'fresh' assent that consists in (ii) yielding to (iii) an appearance that (iv) something that is (in fact) a preferred (or non-preferred) indifferent is good (or evil).[53] Each of these elements in the Stoic account helps to answer a possible objection.

In part (i) the Stoics identify a passion with mistaken assent (*sunkatathesis*) (Stob. *Ecl.* II.88.1–12). An assent is a rational judgement about the character of an appearance (*phantasia*), and so it has to be distinguished from simply having an appearance. Some people confronted with a stick in water that looks bent assent to its being bent, whereas others (after experience of sticks in water that look bent, and after seeing that this stick was straight before it was put into the water) assent to its being straight (cf. Cicero, *Acad.* I.40; D.L. VII.177). In the Stoics' view, simply having an appearance is not enough for a passion, since it does not explain the fact that passions move us to action. They emphasise the role of assent in passions so strongly that they actually deny passions to animals and to young children.[54] By insisting that passion involves assent, the Stoics reject the view that we sometimes act against our beliefs[55] and on our emotions. They must argue that these are cases in which we have wavering or oscillating beliefs. For the same reasons, they deny that passions persist without corresponding beliefs about good and bad.[56]

In speaking of immediate assent, however, the Stoics recognise that not every mistaken belief about good and evil can be identified with a passion. We seem to be able to acquire a false belief about good and evil without acquiring a passion. If we reflect on the dispute between the Stoics and the Peripatetics and become rationally (though mistakenly, in the Stoic view) persuaded that health is a good and it would be bad to fall ill, we have not necessarily acquired a passion. Similarly, a false belief may persist even though the passion goes away; we may still believe, for instance, that all snakes are dangerous even if we have ceased to be afraid of them.[57] Recognising this, the Stoics insist that a passion is not simply an assent, but an immediate assent. In immediate assents we yield to our first appearances of how things are. Sometimes we yield immediately because the appearance comes on us suddenly and without preparation.[58] At other times, however, we may yield immediately not because the appearance comes suddenly, but

---

[53] See LS 65C–D.
[54] See Cic. *Tusc.* IV.31; Origen, *Comm. in Matt.* XII.16 = SVF III.477.
[55] I use 'belief' broadly, to cover both true and false assents (and so more broadly than the Stoics use '*doxa*').   [56] Cf. Epictetus I.28.6 (on Medea), II.26.4.
[57] See Galen, *PHP* 284.18 (De Lacy [794]).
[58] Hence Poseidonius advises preparation (Galen, *PHP* 282.5 ff.; we should imagine the situations in advance (*proanaplattein, protupoun*)).

because we have not questioned the truth of the suggestion made by the appearance.[59]

In part (ii) of their account, the Stoics seek to capture the common assumption that there is something passive about the passions – that they are ways of being affected rather than ways of acting. They cannot accept this assumption completely, since they identify passions with assents, which are active. Still, they argue that when we act on passion we fail to interfere with or to question the suggestion that the appearance makes. Hence part (iii) has to be understood as the claim that the appearance relevant to a passion makes a strong suggestion that something is good or evil. If we flee from danger out of fear, that is not to be explained simply by our assenting wrongly in the light of a 'neutral' appearance that could equally easily precede the facing of danger. In speaking of 'yielding', the Stoics imply that the appearance itself suggests strongly that we ought to flee and makes it much easier to flee; if we are to face the danger we must inhibit the tendency that comes from the appearance. When we do not inhibit this tendency, but accept the suggestion made by the appearance without question, our assent is 'immediate'.

The first three features of a passion do not explain why all passions are to be avoided. Part (iv) explains this, since it identifies every passion with a false assent, involving the sort of false belief that sages avoid, since they are fully

---

[59] At Galen, *PHP* 284.13 (De Lacy [794]), an immediate opinion seems to be formed as a result of some immediate stimulus or occasion. This seems to be what Poseidonius assumes when he asks Chrysippus to explain why the temporal closeness of the occasion for the belief should matter (Galen, *PHP* 282.5). Cicero, however, argues effectively that mere lapse of time ought not to make a difference; if the passion goes away, that is the result of continued thought about it (*Tusc.* III.74: 'hanc vim non esse in die positam, sed in cogitatione diuturna . . . Cogitatio igitur diuturna nihil esse in re mali dolori medetur, non ipsa diuturnitas'). If we do not think properly about it, we shall be like Artemisia, whose grief did not lessen with the passing of time. Cicero suggests, therefore, that when the Stoics speak of immediacy, they are not really speaking of temporal closeness, but of a certain sort of force that they may keep a belief immediate even after some lapse of time (*Tusc.* III.75: 'ut non tantum illud recens esse velint quod paulo ante acciderit, sed, quam diu in illo opinato malo vis quaedam inest ut vigeat et habeat quandam viriditatem, tam diu appelletur recens'). This is not very satisfactory as it stands. Cicero seems to come close to saying that immediacy is whatever it is that makes a belief constitute a passion, whether it is recent or long-standing. But perhaps we can see what the Stoics mean if we attend to his remarks on the effects of thought about the passion. If we simply retain, as Artemisia presumably did, the impressions, thoughts and attitudes that led to the passion, the relevant belief remains immediate; to make it less immediate, we have to go beyond the impressions that gave us the passion. Even if we retain the false belief that something bad has happened to us, it will no longer be a passion; for we shall not simply have yielded to how things initially appeared to us, but we shall have decided that, everything considered, what happened to us was bad.

convinced that virtue is the only good. To see what the Stoics mean, let us consider someone who administers just punishment because of the belief that it is just, and let us contrast someone else who is moved both by the belief that the punishment is just and by anger against the wrongdoer. In being moved by anger we form some tendency to go beyond the reasonable limit in inflicting punishment. Practical reason tells us to limit punishment, reminding us that failure to limit it will interfere with other preferred indifferents. But if our inflicting punishment were really a good or evil, it would mean that our happiness depended on it, and so it would justifiably be ranked ahead of the various things that would be threatened by continued punishment. The tendency of passions to insist on their current concerns in the face of other rational considerations is intelligible if they regard their current concerns as matters of good and evil.[60]

A passion, then, is uncompromising to an extent that (according to the Stoics) is intelligible only if it presents its present concern as genuinely good, and not simply something to be compared with other things that deserve consideration. Hence fear, for instance, involves the belief that some situation is intolerable, not simply that there is something to be said against it.[61] For the Stoics, this uncompromising attachment is the mark of believing that something is good. The Stoic is attached in this way to virtue, and so is not willing to listen to arguments that invite trading virtue for something else. The same uncompromising attitude is characteristic of the passions, except that in the passions it rests on immediate assent.

The Stoics can fairly claim to capture an intuitive feature of passions and to explain it within their general position. For we are likely to agree that passions refuse compromise on the basis of rational comparative considerations. When anger prompts a particular reaction, we may be unmoved by the thought that this is an unwise reaction in the light of other things we care about. The Stoics infer that anger is a mistaken belief in the goodness – the overriding choiceworthiness – of a particular course of action. The uncompromising attitude that results from such a belief is the rationally justified attitude to virtue; such an attitude directed to the wrong things is a passion, when it is formed by immediate assent to a suggestive appearance.

In the light of this account, the Stoics can explain the sense in which they recognise that passions sometimes conflict with reason even though they depend essentially on false evaluative (and therefore, in one sense, rational) beliefs (Cic. *Off.* I.136; *Tusc.* IV.31; Galen, *PHP* IV.2 = SVF III.462). We may

---

[60] Perhaps this point is suggested in Posidonius frr. 33, 166 (LS 65I).

[61] See the definitions of different passions in Cic. *Tusc.* IV.14 (including, for example, 'rectum', 'tolerabile'). The uncompromising aspect of passions is discussed by Nussbaum [731], 377 f.

form a belief irrationally, on insufficient evidence, or without adding up the evidence correctly. And once we have formed it, we may stick to it irrationally, because we are wrongly unimpressed by counter-evidence. But the fact that a passion is unreasonable in this way does not mean that the underlying belief is wholly non-rational or immune to rational persuasion. For we may still change it when we come to realise that our reason for holding it is less good than our reason for accepting the counter-evidence; and we realise this, in the Stoic view, when we recognise that the natural advantages are really preferred indifferents and not goods.

This account of the passions helps to explain why we falsely suppose that they are non-rational in the sense that the Stoics deny. We think we follow our passions against our rational assent, because we do not realise that our belief that (say) we ought always to avenge insults is very tenacious. It is so tenacious that even when we think we have persuaded ourselves out of it, we are not really persuaded, but still revert to our old view if we are insulted. Where common sense thinks it sees a conflict between rational assent and passion, the Stoics see wavering and vacillation between two conflicting rational assents resting on conflicting beliefs about what is best. Though the Stoics' view may be surprising, they argue that it is the only one that does justice to the relevant preconceptions about the relation of passions to evaluative beliefs and to responsibility.

The Stoics' view of the passions suggests a reply to alleged counter-examples. Aristotle seems to suggest that I may reach the view that it would be, all things considered, better to refrain from satisfying my appetite or anger, but my appetite or anger may none the less be so strong that I act on it; this is how incontinence happens. The Stoics cannot accept this description of an incontinent action. In their view, the allegedly incontinent action in these cases is action on assent, since it is a voluntary action; and if it is an action on assent, then the agent must judge that the action is best, all things considered. Hence we should suppose that the agent's rational assent wavers and vacillates, not that it is overcome by non-rational desires.

It is not clear that Aristotle can reply convincingly to this Stoic argument. Though he describes incontinence as failure to follow my rational judgement of what is better on the whole, his own account shows that he does not think it is possible to know that x is rationally preferable to y and, at the same time as one knows this, to choose and do y rather than x. Incontinent people, in his view, lose their grasp of the true principles whenever they act incontinently, so that in some way ignorance is the explanation of incontinence (*EN* 1149b9–17). It is difficult to say exactly how far Aristotle goes towards a Socratic and Stoic account that explains incontinence by appeal to ignorance; but it is at least not clear that he has a defensible alternative.[62] Indeed it might be difficult for Aristotle to explain how incontinence is voluntary and blameworthy if he were to take the strongly anti-Stoic view that incontinence is possible even without ignorance of what is best. In admitting that ignorance must be part of any explanation of incontinence, Aristotle seems to concede the vital point to the Stoics.

We might still find the Stoic position incredible, because it seems to make passions more readily corrigible than most people find them to be. If the passions rest on false beliefs about goods and evils, ought they not to be easier to eliminate than they actually seem to be? The Stoics can answer this objection by referring to their account of the content of the passions. The false beliefs underlying the passions are beliefs that natural advantages are good and natural disadvantages are evil. These are beliefs that we all acquire in the course of natural development, and that become habitual and ingrained in us; people who understand the difference between goods and preferred indifferents get rid of their passions, but many people never come to understand this difference. The passions, then, are the product of arrested rational development. It is not surprising that the beliefs underlying the passions are especially tenacious, even when they turn out (from the enlightened point of view of the sage) to be unreasonable.

10 Freedom from passion

The Stoics believe that their account of the passions justifies them in seeking to get rid of the passions, not simply to moderate them. Seneca sets out the dispute between Stoics and Peripatetics about the proper role of the passions in a virtuous person:

> It has often been asked whether it is better to have moderate passions or no passions. We Stoics expel them, whereas the Peripatetics temper them. I do not see how any moderate condition of a disease could be healthy or useful. Don't be afraid; I am not depriving you of anything that you do not want to be denied to you. (Seneca, *Ep.* 116.1; cf. 85.3)

Seneca insists, however, that the Stoic sages' freedom from passion (*apatheia*) does not leave them completely indifferent to the losses that provoke passions in other people. If they were completely indifferent and unconcerned, thinking there is no reason to prefer being healthy over being ill, they would be Cynics; but since they prefer to have some of the things that they sometimes

---

[62] This estimate of Aristotle's account of incontinence (for which see Irwin [680]) should be contrasted with the careful defence of an anti-Socratic interpretation by Charles [670].

lose, they are not unconcerned, even though they are free from passions (*Ep.* 9.2–5).

> The sage is self-sufficient, not in the sense that he wants (*vult*) to be without a friend, but in the sense that he can do without him. And when I say 'can', I mean that he bears it with his mind undisturbed (*aequo animo*).   (9.5)

The Stoics' task, then, is to describe both the positive and the negative side of the sage's attitude to passions, so that they can explain what is involved in being free of passion without being unconcerned by the situations that normally provoke passions.

The Stoics do not simply want the sage to be without passion. They want the sage to have 'good affections':

> And they say that there are three ways of being well affected, (*eupatheiai*) – joy, caution and wish. Joy is opposed to pleasure, being reasonable elation. Caution is opposed to fear, being reasonable avoidance; for the sage will not fear at all, but will be cautious. And wish is opposed to appetite, being reasonable desire . . . And they say that the sage is also unaffected, because he is not carried away. But another sort of unaffected person is the bad person, where 'unaffected' is equivalent to 'insensitive' and 'relentless'.
> (D.L. VII.115–16)

The Stoics appropriate the names of some apparent passions, and ascribe these states to the sage who, despite having them, is free from passion. They deny him pleasure, fear, and appetite, but allow him joy, caution, and wish. The sage entirely lacks the uncompromising tendency, based on anger, to insist that a criminal should be punished more than he deserves. He has no judgement that conflicts with a rationally justified judgement about preferred indifferents, and so he has no anger. When we recognise that passions involve this potential conflict, we must agree that the sage has no passions. The good affective states are the reasonable reactions to situations that provoke passions in other people.

The Stoics deny that the sage has passions, because a passion has several elements and anyone who lacks any of these elements lacks a passion, just as anyone who lacks any of the elements of wisdom is a fool.[63] But, just as some fools may have some important elements of wisdom, someone who is free of passion may have some important elements of a passion. The sage lacks passions because she lacks their constitutive false beliefs; what other elements of a passion does the sage retain? Are we to suppose that she simply makes correct assents, and is free of the especially immediate, urgent and insistent appearances leading to the 'immediate' assents that are

---

[63] This uncompromising Stoic attitude is explored by Brunschwig [919].

characteristic of passions? Or is there something like these present in the sage also?

According to Epictetus, the sage goes pale when he is in danger of ship-wreck:

> not because any belief in any evil has been accepted, but because of some rapid and unpremeditated movements that outrun[64] the function of mind and reason. Soon, however, that sage does not endorse – that is to say, does not assent to, and does not add his belief to, such appearances (*phantasias*), namely these frightening impressions (*visa*), but he rejects and repudiates them, and nothing in these appearances seems (*videtur*) to him to be some-thing to be feared (*metuendum*).

The sage's momentary reaction comes from an appearance without assent, which for a moment has the sort of effect on him that appearances have in non-rational animals. The difference between the sage and the fool is this:

> the fool supposes things to be really as harsh and severe as they appeared to him to be when his mind was first struck, and once he has received them, also endorses them with his assent and adds his belief to them, as though they were rightly to be feared . . . The sage, however, while he is changed in complexion and facial expression for a short time and to a limited degree, does not assent, but at once holds on to the strength of his opinion.
> (Aulus Gellius, *Noctes Atticae* XIX.1.17–18 = Epictetus fr. 9)

Similarly, Poseidonius' gout made him groan, even though he insisted that it was not bad. A sage may be moved to tears by an affecting scene in a play.[65]

These conditions are not passions, because they lack the crucial element of assent. But they have other elements of passions; in particular, they have the sorts of appearances that in other people contribute to passions.[66] The

---

[64] 'Praevertentibus'. Perhaps 'anticipate' or 'forestall'.

[65] The point that the sage's reaction involves a psychological state in which a preferred or non-preferred indifferent appears good or bad is also suggested by Seneca, *de Ira* II.3.1 = LS 65X. In II.4.1 Seneca distinguishes an involuntary movement (having the appearance) from the voluntary (*cum voluntate*) movement, which is (in the case of anger) the belief that I must retaliate. Cf. I.3.3–8; Cicero *Tusc.* II.61 (Poseidonius' gout); III.61, 72.

[66] Stoic accounts do not always distinguish different possible aspects of the sage's condition: (i) the appearance that this (shipwreck, for instance) is evil; (ii) the appearance that this is a non-preferred indifferent; (iii) the immediate ('fresh') opinion that this is evil; (iv) the immediate opinion that this is a non-preferred indifferent. It is clear that the sage does not have (iii) the immediate opinion that the shipwreck is evil; that is why Poseidonius said that however annoying (*molestum*) the pain (*dolor*) might be, he would never agree that it was bad (*malum*) (Cic. *Tusc.* II.61). It is equally clear that he has (ii) the appearance that it is a non-preferred indifferent. But it is not clear whether he has (i) the appearance that the shipwreck is evil; if he has it, then he clearly must avoid being taken in by the suggestion. Nor

Stoics do not suggest that appearances are totally plastic,[67] or that we can expect them to conform completely to correct assents. Though we can eliminate passions, because we can eliminate the weak and rash assents, the Stoics do not claim that we can eliminate the appearances that make the suggestions that we tend to assent to.[68]

Some of Epictetus' advice on dealing with appearances is instructive:

> As we exercise against sophistical questions, so we should exercise ourselves daily against appearances; for they also propose questions to us. 'So-and-so's son is dead.' Answer: Not chosen (*aprohaireton*); not evil. 'His father left so-and-so without inheritance. What do you think?' Not chosen; not evil. 'Caesar condemned him.' Not chosen; not evil. 'He was in pain at this.' A matter for choice (*prohairetikon*); evil. 'He has endured it nobly.' A matter for choice; good. And if we habituate ourselves this way, we shall progress. For we shall never assent to anything except what we get a grasping appearance of. 'His son is dead. What happened?' His son is dead.

is it clear whether the belief that it is a non-preferred indifferent is supposed to be an immediate belief, or similar to one in its psychological effects. Since these things are not clearly distinguished, it is not clear whether the sage in the storm at sea goes pale (a) because of an appearance of evil, which moves him despite his refusal of assent, or (b) because of his appearance that this is a non-preferred indifferent, which moves him despite his recognising that shipwreck is not an evil, or (c) because of his belief that this is a non-preferred indifferent. For simplicity, I have spoken as though (a) is the Stoic view, but the main points I make in defence of the Stoics could still be made with some adaptation if (b) or (c) were their view.

[67] They are, however, plastic to some degree. We cannot suppose that the sage has all the same appearances that other people have, and differs from other people simply in her assents. The Stoics believe that increased understanding modifies the character of our appearances, not simply our tendency to assent to them; the expert's appearances are different from the ordinary person's. See D.L. VII 51: 'Moreover some appearances are rational, some non-rational. The rational are those of rational animals, the non-rational those of non-rational animals. The rational ones are thoughts, the non-rational have no name [i.e. no special name of their own]. And some are expert (*technikai*), some non-expert. For we must admit that a picture is looked at in one way by an expert, and in another way by a non-expert.' Cf. Galen, *de Methodo Medendi* 7; Cicero, *Acad.* II.20; Epictetus II.15.23–4.

[68] Some of these cases might be regarded as purely physiological reactions, comparable to jumping at a loud noise even if we believe there is nothing really dangerous about it. (See Seneca, *de Ira* II.3.1: 'corporis hos esse pulsus'.) But they cannot all be explained this way. If the sage goes pale in a storm at sea, it is difficult to suppose that he does not anticipate shipwreck, and that this anticipation does not explain his going pale. See also *Ep.* 71.27: 'I do not remove the sage from among human beings, nor do I exclude feelings of distress (*dolores*) from him as from some rock that is incapable of any awareness (*sensus*).' The sage differs from other people because he has unshaken opinions. 'The sage will tremble and be distressed and grow pale; for these are all modes of awareness belonging to the body (*corporis sensus*). Then where is the calamity, where is the genuine evil? Clearly it happens if these things pervert his mind (*animus*)' (29). This aspect of Seneca's view is discussed by Inwood [850], 177.

'Nothing else?' Not a thing. 'His ship was lost. What happened?' His ship
was lost. 'He was imprisoned. What happened?' He was imprisoned. That
he has fared badly each man adds for himself.   (Epictetus III.8.1)[69]

Epictetus suggests that we have to be ready for the misleading suggestions
that we may receive from appearances, and so we have to attend to the fact
that the situations that appearances present in an unfavourable light are not
really bad. He tells us that 'against the persuasive aspects (*pithanotētas*) of
things we must have preconceptions evident, polished and ready to hand'
(1.27.6). We need to bring reason to bear to stop the outbreak of misguided
desire. If we do not do this, then the next time we get the corresponding
appearance, we shall be aroused more quickly to the desire (II.18.8–9). How
well we have brought reason to bear will be clear the next time a disturbing
(*taraktikē*) appearance arises (II.16.20).[70]

 We might be inclined to insist that if all this is true of sages, then they have
emotions, and it is pointless of the Stoics to insist that these conditions are
not really passions.[71] The Stoics seem to admit that suggestive appearances
can move us to some reaction even without any intervening assent, and if
they admit this, have they not described emotions? They answer that these
are not genuine emotions, but merely preliminaries to them; a passion
requires something further than a momentary inclination towards the
action suggested by an appearance, and anything more than a momentary
inclination requires assent. The sage lacks the crucial assent.

 Would it be desirable, whether or not it is possible, to remove the

---

[69] See also 1.28.31: tragic characters such as Agamemnon and Achilles are people
who followed their appearances too readily.

[70] Epictetus asks his interlocutor: when you meet an attractive woman, do you resist
the appearance (*antecheis tē(i) phantasia(i)*)? If your neighbour comes into money,
aren't you bitten by envy? (III.2.8). Sometimes Epictetus suggests that we have
some control over the character of our appearances; if, for instance, we realise it
would be bad to pursue the pleasure suggested by a particular appearance, then we
can avoid imagining (*anazōgraphein*) the actual enjoyment of the pleasure (II.18.16,
25). He does not suggest, however, that we can expect to eliminate the appearances
that make suggestions we need to resist. If appearances were totally plastic, then
sages would not need to be wary about their appearances, because their
appearances would make either correct suggestions or no suggestions. But
Epictetus does not suggest that the modification of our appearances can go so far
that we no longer need to be cautious about agreeing with them.

[71] This view that the Stoics attribute emotions to the sage is Augustine's view in *Civ.
Dei* IX.4. He paraphrases the passage from Aulus Gellius (quoted on p. 185 above) to
make it appear that the sage has passions, but does not assent to them ('ita ut
paulisper vel pavescat metu, vel tristitia contrahatur, tamquam his passionibus
praevenientibus mentis et rationis officium'. The difference between the sage and
the fool is that the fool's mind 'eisdem passionibus cedit adque accommodat mentis
adsensum', whereas the sage's mind does not assent). Where Gellius speaks of
appearances, Augustine speaks of passions.

suggestions that need to be resisted in our appearances? The Stoics do not say so, and they have no reason to say so. Our appearance that it is bad for us to be impoverished is not completely wrong, because impoverishment is in fact a non-preferred indifferent, and it is normally reasonable for us to try to avoid it.[72] Perhaps our best method for detecting preferred and non-preferred indifferents essentially involves selective and critical reliance on the appearances that make misleading immediate suggestions. It would be a bad thing to inhibit the immediate suggestion that it is bad to be tortured or impoverished, if such suggestions are the most effective way of making sure that we pay attention to these non-preferred indifferents.[73]

11 The emotional life of the sage

Our emphasis on the similarity of good affective states to emotions, and our claim that Stoics will justifiably attend to the suggestions made by appearances that they do not assent to, may seem to underestimate the austerity of the Stoic attitude to ordinary human concerns. In particular, we might be impressed by some well-known examples of the Stoics' apparently austere attitude to external goods. Epictetus advises us to think of the death of a child or friend as though it were the breaking of a pot or a jug. We might take him to be advising us to cultivate a careless attitude, treating the death of a child or friend as a trivial matter, not worth taking seriously. In that case, he can hardly agree that a sage has any reason to value the immediate and suggestive appearance that, in ordinary people, precedes grief.

We shall understand Epictetus better, however, if we remember that he assumes that we are already attached to external goods, and do not need to be persuaded that they have some value.[74] He assumes that we need to counter a

---

[72]   This argument for the cognitive usefulness of appearances is still easier to defend if the sage simply has the appearance that he is suffering a non-preferred indifferent. For this appearance is true, and he would be quite mistaken if he did not take it into account in his deliberation.

[73]   The cases of the sage in the shipwreck and of Poseidonius' gout indicate that the sage's assent to the suggestion that he suffers a non-preferred indifferent has some of the immediacy ('freshness') that also belongs to a passion. The Stoics recognise that a passion is not a conclusion of an argument, and that it is formed as a relatively immediate reaction to some particularly forceful stimulus. If this is a source of immediate assent, then the appearances of the sage may have the sort of immediacy that produces an immediate assent, even though they do not lead to passions.

[74]   Following Aristotle's advice to train people to avoid the extreme that they are naturally or temperamentally prone to (*EN* 1109b1–7), Epictetus assumes that he is dealing not with Cynics, but with people who are prone to passions towards external goods. He recommends the training (*askēsis*, III.24.84) that can be used to prevent the attachment to external goods from becoming misguided. Hence he says 'Don't give way to the appearance, and don't allow your expansion to go as far as it wants to, but pull against it and restrain it' (III.24.85).

tendency in our appearances to go too far, and that we can do this by taking account of features of the situation that a particular appearance tends to neglect. The appearances that underlie passions are selective; they tend to focus our attention on one aspect of a situation. That is why they are often valuable, in so far as they focus our attention in the right place, but often misleading, in so far as they divert our attention from other considerations that deserve attention. Epictetus wants to recall the other considerations that we are liable to overlook because of the appearance that underlies the passion.

He does not suggest, however, that we ought to get rid of the appearance that something non-preferred has happened when a friend dies. Nor does he suggest that it is as trivial as the breaking of a jug, or that we ought to care about it no more than we care about the breaking of a jug. The point of the comparison is to remind us of our conviction that good and ill fortune are no part of happiness, since they are no part of virtue. He warns us against confusing cases in which we lose an important preferred indifferent with cases in which life is not worth living because we are really deprived of happiness.

The Stoics, then, have every reason to agree with the claim that passions reveal important aspects of value to us, and they retain this cognitive function of the passions in the sage, in so far as they retain the appearances that make us vividly aware of preferred and non-preferred indifferents. They argue, however, that this aspect of passions is separable from the aspect that implies mistaken assent to the appearance suggesting that something good or evil is involved.

Would it be reasonable to answer that Stoic sages are inhuman because they do not treat indifferents as goods and evils and so do not care enough about them to have passions?[75] If we are convinced by Stoic arguments to show that happiness is the internal end, not the external objective, we cannot maintain that external goods are necessary for happiness. The Stoics, however, maintain that external goods contribute to the life in accordance with nature, and so they care about acquiring them. They share the responses of other people, in so far as they focus sharply and vividly on the preferred and non-preferred aspects of indifferents.

---

[75] This is the judgement of Striker: 'What has gone wrong here is not, I think, the suggestion that we could be without emotion, but that we should try to be. And the reason for this lies not in the Stoics' theory of emotion, but in their theory of what is good or bad, and consequently what should make us feel elated, what we should seriously wish for, and what we should make every effort to avoid' ([865], 68); 'in so far as the Stoics wanted to say that we ought not to be upset or excited about things that have no real value, we might perfectly well agree with them, but we should reject their "freedom from emotion" on the ground that it makes us indifferent to things we ought to appreciate. Far from being a necessary condition of virtue, Stoic *apatheia* actually seems to be incompatible with it' (p. 71).

A different sort of objection claims that the Stoics' lack of passions excludes the sort of sympathy with other people that might be taken to be an important source of our sense of community with other people. We might argue that if you are a Stoic sage and you see me suffering, you will not suppose that anything bad is happening to me, and so you will see no reason for sympathy or compassion. Moreover, since you are not subject to passions yourself, my suffering will not move you to any passion in response. If this is true, does it not support the charge that the Stoics separate themselves from human society?

The argument to show that the Stoic will not feel sympathy is perfectly correct, if sympathy is taken to require a passion. But it leaves out of account the ways in which the Stoic can react. Sages recognise that we are liable to suffer significant non-preferred indifferents, and they have vivid and insistent appearances of these sufferings in other people. These appearances give them a good reason for doing something to relieve the sufferings of others.[76] We suppose, rather plausibly, that in sharing emotions with other people we also have access to certain sorts of reasons for helping them. The Stoics have every reason to agree with us; but they insist that we have access to these reasons even if we have only the aspects of emotions that are allowed to the sage.

What, then, remains of the charge that the Stoics remove some essential element of virtue in denying that the sage has passions? It is not clear that we can support this charge convincingly from an Aristotelian point of view. For Aristotle also believes that the virtuous person has been trained to realise that the loss of external goods is not an occasion for being devastated, and that a blow to one's reputation does not threaten the most important aspects of one's happiness. When Aristotle tells us to form passions so that they harmonise with right reason, is he really telling us anything different from what the Stoics tell us when they require us to get rid of passions and to replace them with good affective states? For Aristotle does not mean that the virtuous person should retain some of the irrational and excessive reactions that are characteristic of other people's attitudes to external successes and failures. On the contrary, he thinks virtuous people's reactions should be proportionate to the value of the situations they react to, and that these reactions should never threaten our recognition of the supreme value of virtue.

These are just the sorts of reactions that the Stoics try to describe more clearly in their doctrine of preferred indifferents, and in its consequences for

---

[76] Epictetus may be recognising this point when he connects lack of *apatheia* with the recognition of obligations. He says that the sage should not be passionless (*apathēs*) like a rock, but should 'observe natural and acquired relations' in acknowledging duties (*kathēkonta*) (III.2.4).

the doctrine of good affective states. They suggest that once we consider how we are to follow Aristotle's advice to form passions in harmony with reason, we shall see that they must be what the Stoics regard as good affective states. Conversely, they reject the charge that if sages have no passions they cannot have the sorts of reactions that Aristotle recommends. This defence of the Stoic position does not disarm all reasonable criticism; but it suggests that if we are to criticise the Stoics for failure to take the non-rational components of virtue seriously enough, we must think more carefully about what those non-rational components are and why they are to be taken seriously. For if we accept one apparently Aristotelian and apparently plausible account of these components, we cannot fairly accuse the Stoics of failing to take them seriously enough.

12 The case for the Stoics

At the beginning of section 2 above we noticed that the Stoics defend two Socratic paradoxes, taking virtue to be sufficient for happiness, and knowledge to be sufficient for virtue. We have found that the Stoics defend these paradoxes rather resourcefully. They argue dialectically; they begin from premises that they can reasonably expect non-Stoics, and especially Aristotelians, to share, and they claim to show that these premises actually commit us to the Stoic positions. The Stoic defence also gives us some insight into the connections between the Socratic paradoxes. The two paradoxes are logically independent, but the Stoic arguments show that objections to one paradox can be answered by a defence of the other paradox. The view that the sage's attitude to indifferents is morally acceptable turns out to be more plausible once we see that a virtuous person ought not to have any passions; and the view that the virtuous person ought not to have any passions is more plausible once we see that we can value external goods as preferred indifferents once we abandon the mistaken belief that they are goods.

Reflection on the Stoic arguments also defuses the Socratic paradoxes, showing that the conclusions are not so paradoxical after all. Though we may initially suppose that the Stoic sage is completely unconcerned with indifferents and has no emotional life whatever, closer acquaintance with the Stoic position shows that it does justice to ordinary convictions without accepting them uncritically.

If this argument is right, it shows that Stoic dialectical argument provides a good answer to the charge of inhumanity. Its very success in answering this charge, however, may seem to expose it to the charge of triviality. Even if we are persuaded that, in the precise sense intended by the Stoics, virtue is happiness, external advantages and disadvantages are indifferents, and the virtuous person is free of passions, what do we learn from these Stoic doctrines if we understand them correctly? Do they not simply tell us, in other terms, what Aristotle tells us?

If we must choose, on the Stoics' behalf, between inhumanity and triviality, then we ought to choose triviality, if we focus on the dialectical side of their arguments. We ought not to grant, however, that inhumanity and triviality exhaust the options open to us. The Stoics take themselves to give a clear account and defence of claims that other people accept but cannot explain or defend. Once we combine Aristotle's different claims about virtue, happiness and ends, we find that they cannot all be correct. Once we combine his different claims about virtue and passion, we find that they cannot all be correct. To give the most plausible account of Aristotle's main claims, we must abandon his theory for the Stoic theory.

If this is true, then the Stoics can present a strong case to show that their doctrine of happiness, virtue, the indifferents and the passions introduces some distinctions that we need in order to justify some of Aristotle's principal doctrines; and if the Stoics are right about that, then they have given some good reasons for rejecting those Aristotelian doctrines that conflict with Stoicism. It is useful, therefore, to think seriously about the case that can be made for the Stoic doctrines on an Aristotelian basis. This approach certainly does not do justice to the whole scope of Stoic ethics, or to the variety of arguments that the Stoics have available to them; but it may suggest why some aspects of Stoic ethics are not refuted by general attacks on the Stoic system.[77]

[77] I am grateful to Suzanne Bobzien, Lindsay Judson and the editor of this volume for helpful comments.

8

Doing without objective values: ancient and modern strategies

JULIA ANNAS

I

Before doing philosophy, we tend to think that people, actions and institutions are good or bad, praiseworthy or deplorable. That we are wrong to have these beliefs is a point on which ancient and modern sceptics appear to agree. Ancient sceptical arguments about proof, say, or perception, are different from modern analogues, and in important respects less radical.[1] But when we read the arguments that Sextus Empiricus retails to the effect that nothing is by nature good or bad, they appear familiar.

The appearance is misleading, however; ancient and modern uses of, and reactions to, sceptical arguments about value are profoundly unalike. If this is so, then pointing it out is of more than historical interest; it alerts us to a number of interesting possibilities about value, and moral value in particular.

I shall begin by looking at the ancient arguments (few and easily survey-able, it turns out) which try to undermine our confidence that people and actions really are good or bad. I shall also look at the ancient sceptics' account of the benefits of having been convinced by these arguments. Then I shall consider what seem to have been the standard ancient objections to moral scepticism, and the strength of the sceptic's defence. Doing so will, I hope, bring out the radical difference between ancient and modern attitudes to sceptical arguments about moral value.

Discussions of ancient philosophy often stress the continuity of ancient concerns with ours, and sometimes it is felt that if no such continuity can be established, then studying the ancient texts loses its point. In this area, however, the reverse seems to be true. Modern moral philosophy has been rejuvenated by study precisely of discontinuities in moral concern, and of different understandings of morality. Why this should be so is rather a

---

[1] The importantly restricted scope of ancient scepticism is brought out by Burnyeat [45].

mystery. One's understanding of an essentially modern sceptical problem, such as scepticism about induction, is not necessarily furthered by realising the extent of the gap between it and ancient analogous but different problems, such as sceptical arguments about 'signs'. But in the area of moral value the problematic nature of the concepts involved makes awareness of differences often more fruitful than awareness of similarities.

II

Sextus Empiricus, our major source for ancient scepticism,[2] gives us our only extended accounts of ancient scepticism about values. He puts the topic at the end of both his shorter work, *Outlines of Pyrrhonism (PH)* and of his longer work, those sections of the *adversus Mathematicos (M)* that we number as VII–XI. This reflects the way that ancient sceptics gave their destructive attention to all the ancient divisions of philosophy in turn, logic, physics and ethics. One of the ten sceptical Modes which go back to the earlier sceptic Aenesidemus is also 'mostly concerned with ethics' (*PH* 1.145), and since there is clear over-lap between this Mode and some of Sextus' arguments (at least in *PH* III) it seems best to begin with it.

I call it the tenth Mode, following Sextus' order.[3] Sextus gives the fullest and most organised version, but the outlines of an already ordered argument are visible behind all three variants.

Sextus carefully distinguishes five factors which are relevant to our beliefs about values. These are

(1) Life-style (*agōgē*): the way one structures one's life either as an individual deliberately copying another individual, or as part of a community.

(2) Customs or habits (*ethē*): unwritten codes of behaviour that bring it about, for example, that even where there is no law about it, people just do not copulate in public (ancient writers seem obsessed with alleged public performance of this private act).

(3) Laws (*nomoi*): conventions that are backed by definite sanctions against those who break them.

(4) Mythical beliefs (*muthikai pisteis*) about various divine and fictional matters.[4]

---

[2] In this chapter I shall concentrate mainly on ancient Pyrrhonism, represented for us by Sextus. For the response of the Academic sceptics to similar problems, see my [925].

[3] We possess the Modes in three sources, Sextus *PH* 1.145–63, Diogenes Laertius IX.83–4 and Philo, *On Drunkenness* §§193–205. For translation and commentary on all the Modes, see Annas and Barnes [892]; the Tenth Mode is discussed in ch. 13.

[4] Philo omits these, understandably since he is employing the Modes in exegesis of a Jewish theme, for a Jewish audience.

(5) Dogmatic conceptions (*dogmatikai hupolēpseis*)[5] of which the examples are various abstract philosophical theories about the constitution of the universe and the providence of the gods.

How are these factors relevant to scepticism? None of our sources make this explicit. Diogenes Laertius just lists examples of laws which differ, customs which differ, and so on. Persians, he implausibly claims, marry their daughters, Massagetae have wives in common and Cilicians shamelessly enjoy piracy, but Greeks – we civilised Greeks, that is – do none of these things. Why, however, should this lead us to any kind of scepticism, rather than to complacency, since (we civilised) Greeks seem to have got it right? Sextus produces conflicts by systematically listing examples of a life-style clashing with a custom, a life-style clashing with a law, a custom clashing with a law; and so on, until we have gone through every possible combination of the five factors. However, while such clashes do occur, they also get resolved, whether by compromise, prosecution or whatever; it is still not clear how we get to scepticism.

The Tenth Mode, like the others, is an argument-schema into which examples can be put which will produce *conflicts of appearances*.[6] An appearance is just the way things appear to someone. Since things can appear in a wide variety of ways, appearances are not limited to just one type, such as sense-appearances. It can appear to me that a proof is sound, for example. The Tenth Mode is concerned with appearances of value, that is, with cases where people, actions, institutions, and the like appear to people to have positive or negative value. Take Sextus' third example (a hardy perennial in ancient sceptical texts, despite its falsity, like the false belief that sufferers from jaundice see everything yellow). Indians have sex in public; other nations not. This produces a conflict in that it implies that having sex in public appears acceptable and good to Indians, unacceptable and bad to other nations. This is a clash between customs; we can generalise, if we use a generic term, say 'persuasion', for all five factors, and say that the Mode gives us material with which to produce the following kind of conflict. One thing (action, practice, etc.) appears to have positive value (to be good, praiseworthy, etc.) to people of one persuasion. But the very same thing appears to have negative value to people of a different persuasion. And obviously both persuasions can't be right – the thing can't have both positive and negative value.

[5] Philo does not name these; but he clearly deals with them (§§198 ff.), making the transition by a rhetorical flourish of his own. He alters the structure of the Mode somewhat by giving so much stress to philosophical disagreement and by introducing arguments of his own.

[6] For a fuller account of this and other aspects of ancient sceptical reasoning, see Annas and Barnes [892].

The sceptic proceeds this way in order to shake our beliefs. For these often rest on our acceptance of our own persuasion; having been brought up in certain customs, I believe public copulation to be unacceptable, for example. When I encounter people who, having been brought up in other habits, do not think it wrong, my belief that it is wrong is challenged; for here are people who disagree, and who have just the same kind of grounds that I do, namely their persuasion. And why should I, rationally, be more impressed by my persuasion than by theirs? They are both the same kind of factor. The sceptic aims to get us to the stage of *isostheneia*, 'equipollence', the state where I can find no more to be said for than against the belief that public copulation is wrong. For if I get to this point, I shall suspend judgement about it; I shall lose all commitment to any belief in its wrongness. It may still, of course, *appear* to me to be wrong, and so I shall retain certain reactions to it. For my persuasion is still in place, having the same effects that it always did. But I shall have lost the belief that I had that it is wrong; for all I can point to in order to defend my belief is my persuasion; and I now see that rationally I have no grounds to prefer my persuasion to the other side's as being a source of justified beliefs. Suspension of belief, we should note, is not a conclusion of any inference; rather, pointing out differences in persuasion puts us in a position where we are led *in fact*, according to the sceptic, to find no more reason to hold our beliefs about value than their opposites, and hence, also as a matter of fact, led to suspend judgement.

Moral scepticism thus comes in as part of a wider sceptical strategy; differences of persuasion are employed to lead us to suspend judgement about values just as differences in distance, species, frequency, and so on are employed to lead us to suspend judgement about other features of the world. The sceptic regards people who believe things to be good or bad as misguided, and in need of correction; but this is achieved not by altering their beliefs, but by putting them in a position where they lose them. To do this, all the weight, in Diogenes and Sextus, is put on establishing the 'conflict of appearances': I believe that public copulation is wrong, because it appears to me a certain way; but there are others to whom it appears differently, and it is pointing this out that brings me to lose the belief.

Philo has two different arguments, which are isolated in ancient scepticism and may be his own contribution. One (§202) is that dispute is, where persuasions are concerned, chronic and hopeless. It is not just that uneducated people disagree – philosophers, who have given all their time and talent to it over generations, are still locked in apparently insoluble disagreement over questions like providence and the meaning of life; and this strongly suggests that their disagreement is, in fact, insoluble.

The other (§§196–7, §199) is that people's habits and upbringing differ so totally that they are bound to find that things appear differently to them, and that they disagree. 'This being so, who is so senseless and idiotic as to say steadfastly that such-and-such is just or intelligent or fine or advantageous? Whatever one person determines to be such will be nullified by someone else whose practice from childhood has been the contrary.' Philo is not entirely clear here, but it is reasonable to see here at least a proto-version of the argument, popular with modern sceptics, from preferred explanation. Disagreements over value correlate strongly with differences in persuasions. The sceptic claims that it is reasonable to explain the disagreements, not as genuine disagreements about real subject-matter, but as merely being the effects of the different persuasions. As a modern author puts it, 'Disagreement about moral codes seems to reflect people's adherence to and participation in different forms of life. The causal connection seems to be mainly that way round: it is that people approve of monogamy because they participate in a monogamous way of life rather than that they participate in a monogamous way of life because they approve of monogamy.'[7]

Philo's two arguments are interesting in that they are more limited than the conflict of appearances argument. They lead to a piecemeal scepticism; they apply only where conflict *is* chronic, only if and where disagreement *is* best explained by differences in persuasion. In any case they do not form part of the standard ancient strategy for moral scepticism: their force was probably unappreciated.

The arguments of the Modes can provide at most the first step. For a more reflective and sophisticated response is at hand. Once we realise the effects of our persuasions, we may none the less argue for our own beliefs about value on different grounds, namely by appealing to general principles which hold for people of diverse persuasions. Pressed to defend these principles, we shall end up appealing to moral theories, which are developed structures of rational thought on these matters. And so we find in *PH* iii and *M* xi strings of arguments 'against the moral philosophers'. These arguments aim to remove any reliance we might have had on the rational support that moral theories could give to a given action or practice. If this kind of support all collapses, then, since common sense has proved insufficient, we shall, promises the sceptic, revert to equipollence, and thence to suspension of judgement.

Sextus gives us rather little by way of specific arguments against particular ethical theories; unfortunately he is much less interested in ethics than in other parts of philosophy, and instead of arguments against Stoic,

---

[7] Mackie [958], 36.

Epicurean and Aristotelian ethical theory we merely find, apart from irrelevancies,[8] very general arguments to show us that ethical argument as such is in bad shape, and thus unable to save us from suspension of judgement.

In both the *PH* and the *M* passages Sextus points out that there is widespread disagreement over the definition of 'good' (and so of 'bad' and 'indifferent' – *PH* III.169–78, *M* XI.21–41). He spends some time on particular definitions of 'good', notably the Stoics', and retails some *ad hominem* objections, but the general sceptical objection is to hold against all purported definitions (*M* XI.35); its form is clearer in *M* than in *PH*. These definitions cannot give the essence or nature of good. A definition that did would put an end to controversy; but controversy has manifestly not ceased, so these definitions must have failed to make the essence of good clear. At most, claims that good is 'choiceworthy' or 'productive of happiness' and the like can tell us what happens to be true of good. In fact, though, they can't make a decent job even of that; for we can't be told informatively even what a thing happens to be until we know its nature. Therefore, defining good as, for instance, 'choiceworthy' tells us neither what good essentially is nor even what is contingently true of it. Therefore we should suspend judgement about our conception of good.

This argument is clearly exploiting the assumption that when a definition gives rise to disagreement, we have a conflict in the way things appear which cannot be rationally resolved. 'If what good is had been shown by the definitions mentioned, they would not have gone on fighting as though the nature of the good were still unknown' (*M* XI.37). Once we have started arguing over the definition, thinks the sceptic, we shall either just carry on uselessly, or end up suspending judgement because both sides have come to seem equally convincing.

Sextus goes on to claim that people disagree endlessly also over what things (people, actions) are good (bad, indifferent) (*PH* III.179–234, *M* XI.43–109). In *PH* III Sextus swamps us with a flood of examples, often overlapping with those of the Tenth Mode (199–234); in *M* XI he has got bored by all the publicly copulating Indians and incestuous Persians, and limits himself to typical examples (47–67, 90–5). But in both passages the core of the argument is quite simple (*PH* III.179–82, *M* XI.68–78): if anything were good by nature, as the philosophers claim, it should be good, and so positively

---

[8] Both passages have a long and tedious final section arguing against the Stoic 'skill in living' (*PH* III.239–279 and *M* XI.168–256) which concentrates on trivial points and wastes the chance to raise several central ethical issues. There are some arguments directed at particular ethical theories, but always as a by-product of a larger piece of argument (see, for instance, *PH* III.183–90, *M* XI.79–89; *PH* III.193–6, *M* XI.96–109).

motivating, for everyone. But in fact different people are differently motivated, and disagree over what is good. We can't accept all the claims, because they conflict; and conflict cannot be resolved. We can see the basic sceptical strategy at work. Every belief is countered, to produce a conflict, and argument pro is countered by argument con. The disagreement cannot be resolved; as a result, both sides end up appearing as convincing, and judgement is suspended; we cease to be able to commit ourselves to the original beliefs or to their denials.[9]

In *M* xi.69 Sextus introduces what looks like a different idea: what is by nature good should be common (*koinon*) to all.[10] Sextus presents the sceptic as denying this: nothing is good in a way common to all; rather things are good relative to particular agents' particular situations. Thus the sceptic makes the liberating discovery that what is good is always relative, not absolute (78, 114–18). This looks like what we call relativism, and if so, it is a bad, and surprising, mistake. For the claim 'this is good relative to me, though it might not be good relative to *you*' is a claim about moral reality, and so problematic for the ancient sceptic, even though it denies an absolute principle.

Possibly Sextus is at this point confusing moral realism with moral absolutism. If so, he is not the first or the last; this failing dogs discussion of moral and political norms since the fifth-century sophists, who often assume that if norms hold at all they must hold absolutely. Anyone who teaches moral philosophy will find that pupils depressingly often make the same assumption. But it is a confusion, and one that he could have been expected to avoid, for at least three reasons.

First, he goes on to argue that the offending belief (that there is a good common to all) is a source of troubling anxiety and perturbation, whereas the thought that it's only *my* good brings relief and mental equilibrium (*M* xi.118). But this is obviously wrong; however relative to me, *my* good is still my *good*, just as real and troubling a part of moral reality as any universal good. Secondly, it had already been clearly stated by at least one philosopher that even if values are relative to a group or individual, they are just as real (and therefore just as troubling) as any non-relative items. Polystratus the Epicurean[11] had claimed that it is a mistake to think that 'good' or 'just', even

[9] Diogenes brings this out economically at ix.101 (which derives from the same source as some of Sextus' arguments, since they share an example: pleasure appears good to Epicurus, bad to Antisthenes). People disagree about what is good; the arguments on either side are equally compelling; so we end up with suspension of judgement about the nature of the good.

[10] The word *koinon* occurs in Diogenes ix.101, which clearly derives from the same source (cf. the example of pleasure in both passages).

[11] Polystratus, *On Irrational Contempt for Popular Opinions*, ed. G. Indelli, chs. 6 and 7. Striker [915] points out the importance of this for the Modes as a whole.

if we concede that they are relative terms, refer to items that are any less real than the referents of non-relative terms. Thirdly, relativism is, in ancient terms, not a form of *scepticism* at all, for it leaves the agent holding beliefs. And, however narrowed-down the content of those beliefs – 'this is good in certain respects for me here now in this situation' – they are still beliefs; the relativist is a dogmatist, not a sceptic, for the sceptic aims to shed his beliefs by suspending judgement.

Sextus is certainly capable of confusing scepticism with some forms of relativism.[12] However, so gross and obvious an error here would be very surprising, and it may be preferable on grounds of method to interpret Sextus here as simply redescribing the sceptical claim, though in a possibly misleading way. In rejecting a 'common' good and holding merely a 'private' one, the sceptic is just repeating the point that she holds no beliefs about what is good, and therefore provides no objectively discussable justification for what she finds good and bad. The 'private' good is just the appearance of good that she is left with when she has lost her beliefs about value. This certainly renders Sextus consistent, though in view of the many and confusing ancient notions of 'relative' he could perhaps have chosen a better expression.[13]

How good are the ancient arguments? Philo's arguments, being atypical, can perhaps be left aside. In any case their effectiveness will have to be made out for each case, for we should not be ready to accept ahead of time that *all* chronic disagreement is, just as such, insoluble; or that differences of persuasion will always be a preferred explanation of disagreement about value; or indeed, that such explanation will render idle our initial assumption that the disagreement is genuine.

It is the conflicting-appearances argument which is the heart of ancient sceptical strategy; and here we may well raise queries at two stages. First, do the appearances really conflict? Even if persuasions differ as the sceptic says they do (and much of the ancient material is transparently fictional), must this be because people have conflicting appearances of value? What look superficially like disagreements over value can often be better interpreted as consensus over value coupled with difference over what particular means are appropriate. Thus the fact that Ethiopians tattoo their babies while Greeks do not reveals more community than difference in shared beliefs about attitudes to babies. Often the sceptic is at least taking a short cut.

---

[12] See Annas and Barnes [892], index of topics, s.v. 'Relativism' and 'Scepticism' for discussions of the various passages in the Modes (with reference to other passages in Sextus) where relativism and scepticism are, puzzlingly, confounded.

[13] For a defence of the view that Sextus is consistently sceptical here see McPherran [910] and [911].

But even where appearances do conflict, do we get to suspension of judgement? Only if we get to equipollence, if we are convinced that nothing tips the balance one way or the other, because either side is equally convincing. And here the ancient sources let us down. As they stand, few of the examples piled up in the Tenth Mode and *PH* III have the power to make us feel any uneasiness. Why should we care that Crates and Hipparchia, the Cynic philosophers, copulated in public, or that the early Stoics thought that there could be situations where incest and cannibalism would be all right? The obvious response is not to be shaken in our beliefs, but to conclude that Crates and Hipparchia were being deliberately shameless, and that Zeno and Chrysippus were not prescribing for the sort of situations that it would be reasonable to worry about. Indeed, we can find a certain tension, at least in Sextus, who plainly enjoys retailing examples of shocking and upsetting persuasions. For the more shocking an example, the *less* likely it is to undermine our belief that we are right to believe, and do, the opposite. Many of Sextus' examples would be more likely to reinforce than to weaken his audience's moral beliefs.

This is a weakness in Sextus, but not necessarily a weakness in the sceptical approach generally. Sextus is not bound to his examples. Indeed, since sceptical argument is always *ad hominem*, we should regard the Tenth Mode as merely a schema into which the sceptic will insert examples which will work for the audience he is addressing.[14] All we need to show that the Tenth Mode does have force is a set of examples which do produce convincing conflicts of values; if we find the ancient ones feeble, we need only turn to rich contemporary sources of such examples.

We find a further weakness in Sextus when we turn to the arguments about moral theory. For it is reasonable to think that here argument could settle matters in favour of one alternative over another; what we need, to get us to reject this idea, is a systematic demonstration that all available moral theories let us down because they all make effective criticisms of one another. Arguments of this form were certainly available in the ancient world; Cicero's *de Finibus*, for example, is a work in which there are detailed arguments for and against major ethical theories. The modern analogue would be a work which systematically put forward arguments for and against Kantianism, utilitarianism, virtue ethics and rights theory; and we can see from this that what Sextus should have done is complex and hard.

---

[14] Sextus at one point (*PH* III.280–1) says that the sceptic is like a doctor, who will use only the minimal level of treatment needed; thus if the opponent is convinced by feeble examples, or invalid arguments, then these will do, and someone who protests is merely showing that they need better examples and arguments to be convinced.

However, although he does the analogue for logic and physics, Sextus shirks the task for ethics, leaving a large gap in his argument. Unfortunately, where ethics is concerned he simply retains his general confidence that no argument is immune, that an equally powerful counter-argument can always be found. He shows no interest in the idea that ethical argumentation might be in any way special to the field, or that different theories and arguments might require careful attention. If anything he seems somewhat dismissive of ethical arguments: at *M* xi.77 he states as though obvious that arguments about the good convince only the committed within each philosophical school. Here he is just wrong; arguments do change people's positions in ethics, and ethical argumentation does require careful study. It is also disappointing to find him, at *PH* iii.233–4, urging us to be moved by *possible* conflicts of appearances if no actual ones are available. This is not peculiar to ethics – Sextus when in straits urges merely possible examples in other fields also (*PH* i.34, ii.143) – but in ethics is particularly weak. Whyever should I be shaken in my belief that some practice, say, is bad because, although nobody *has* brought an objection to it, somebody *might*? And if this will not even shake my belief, still less will it ever get me to equipollence on the subject, to the state of seeing no more to be said for it than against. Sextus exaggerates the ease of getting argument in ethics to balance out and leave us undecided. Even a moderately serious look at the subject shows us that some positions are such that equipollence about them would be extremely hard to obtain.

Nor is it clear why we should be shaken by the fact of continued disagreement about the meaning or definition of 'good'. Perhaps some progress has been made though disagreement remains – it makes a difference, after all, whether disagreement is widespread or limited, and some disagreement in a subject is a sign of healthy progress rather than of hopeless confusion. Or perhaps (and more likely) progress in moral philosophy was not to be found, in the first place, by trying to explicate the meaning or definition of 'good'. People are bound to disagree over a division as wide as that of good, bad and indifferent. They are not so likely to fall into chronic disagreement over the question of whether an action is generous, or a person cruel.

The ancient arguments are disappointing, then; they give up just where the discussion gets interesting, at the point where the sceptic has to cope with the opponent who thinks that there may well be a right answer in cases of moral disagreement, and that equipollence, and hence suspension of judgement, are not reached so quickly or so easily.

It should be obvious that, whatever they are worth, the ancient arguments are radically different from modern ones in the same area. To begin with, the point is to reach suspension of judgement about the objective existence of values. None of the arguments aim to show that there are no such things. For a conclusion that there are no objective values would be, not scepticism but negative dogmatism, the holding of beliefs, and this would be no improvement on the original common-sense positive dogmatism. (Why this should be so will become clearer later.)

Modern arguments, by contrast, aim to show that when we assume that actions and people are really good or bad, we are making a discoverable and correctable mistake. No ancient sceptic claims this, and thus it is no accident that there are no ancient analogues of 'error theory'. For ancient sceptics do not see themselves as preserving us from error by pointing out the true view; a project locating moral scepticism as part of a larger attempt to find out the truth about the world would be thoroughly dogmatic despite the negative nature of some of its conclusions. Ancient scepticism leads to suspension of judgement as the salvation from rashness and precipitancy; the enemy is not error but premature commitment to assertions that we have no warrant for (*PH* III.235, *M* XI.111).

Another important contrast is to be found in the absence, in the ancient sources, of any thought that scepticism about the existence of values is a healthy rejection of dubious items based on an equally healthy confidence in the reality of better-attested parts of the world. Scepticism about value is part of a *general* sceptical approach to *all* beliefs, not a localised choosiness resting on the soundness of beliefs in other areas.

Thus we find no analogue in the ancient sources to the common modern assumption that there is something too *queer* about values for them to be genuinely existing items. Mackie, in a passage that has become notorious because of the openness of this crucial assumption, declares that differences in moral beliefs *must* be explained entirely by differences in people's upbringing, etc., and not as being differing views of something objective, for *that* would demand 'queer' entities, 'utterly different from anything else in the universe' and known in a similarly distinctive way.[15] And the assumption has remained common, often in more sophisticated forms.

Of course the mere claim that objective values are queer has no force on its own; so are lots of things that we happily believe in. The reason why this kind of claim is thought to have force by opponents of moral reality is that the 'queer' entities are taken to be dubious and unacceptable by the standards of a world-view that we all share which certifies other kinds of entity as real. It is thought to be so obvious as not to need argument, merely pointing out, that moral values show up badly by comparison with other, more solid parts of our familiar world.

---

[15] Mackie [958], 38.

It may be claimed that this assumption, that there is an obvious contrast, to the disadvantage of value, *is* present in the ancient arguments. For in two places (*PH* III.179–82, *M* XI.68–78) Sextus presents the following argument: fire, which heats by nature, heats everyone alike, and snow, which chills by nature, chills all alike; nothing which affects us by nature does so in a non-uniform way. But what is good does not affect all similarly, as shown by the fact of continued disagreement; so there is nothing good by nature. This certainly looks like an attempt to contrast things in the world of nature, whose existence we confidently assume, with values, which are rejected by contrast with these. But a closer look dispels any apparent similarity.

First, the argument is feeble. Perhaps the variable effects of goodness are to be explained by our varying degrees of sensitivity to it, unlike our crasser responses to fire and snow. It has not been argued that they vary too much to allow the assumption of a core of common response 'by nature'. It is instructive that in 179 Sextus both admits that he will have to *establish* the fact of differing response and reports the view that it is *obvious*; it is not clear just how much we do differ in our responses to goodness.

Secondly, even if it held up, Sextus' rejection of values as not being 'by nature' is not presented as part of a firmly established world-view unfolding the truth about natural objects. Such a view is dogmatism, and Sextus, the sceptic, is not in his own person committed to it. He uses its premises only to get us to be sceptical about values. Thus he uses, for example, the notions of 'nature' (*phusis*) and 'by nature' (*PH* III.179) to the disadvantage of values here, but elsewhere he is equally scathing about the notion of nature itself, on the grounds of continued dogmatic disagreement about it.[16]

Partly this is because the ancient sceptic always regards arguments as *ad hominem* and so as tailored to need (*PH* I.35 and III.280–1), so that even rotten ones will do provided that they have the desired effect; once you have got to suspension of judgement, the arguments that got you there can be kicked away or purged out along with the harmful beliefs they removed.[17] But partly the sceptic's position results from the fact that ancient scepticism about values does not ride on the back of any commitment to the truth of beliefs in other areas.

Modern scepticism on this issue, however, does rely crucially on the sceptic's having a serious commitment to the reality of a contrast between values and some other preferred area of the world, and to there being a real basis for this preference.[18]

[16] *PH* I.98.

[17] Cf. *M* VIII.481, *PH* I.206, Diogenes IX.76 and Aristocles ap. Eusebius, *Preparation for the Gospel* XIV.762a–b. See McPherran [909].

[18] For disagreement on this point, see Bett [938].

This becomes clear from a (rapid) inspection of two kinds of ground commonly put forward for moral scepticism. One comes from the thought that moral values cannot be real because there is so much dispute about them and no clear way of resolving it. In morality we are always aware of the existence of alternative points of view; and unless we accept a very unrealistic theory like utilitarianism there is no decision-procedure for determining who is right. Moreover, there are no acknowledged experts in morality, and (connectedly) no cumulative and developing body of generally received results, no firm marks for what counts as progress in the subject. Someone impressed by these points will probably conclude that morality is a spurious enterprise, and that there is no real subject to be right or wrong about; morality has no genuine subject-matter, by contrast with subjects where there are clear guidelines for what constitutes successful argument and progress in discovery, and where accordingly there are acknowledged experts and received results. The reality of moral values is rejected because moral enquiry as an intellectual enterprise does not come up to the standards of those to which we unhesitatingly assign a genuine subject-matter.

It is not a necessary condition of accepting this line of thought that one be over-impressed by science (hence it is too simple to blame the rejection of moral realism on 'scientism'). However, it is undeniable that the preferred paradigm will be the empirical sciences, since nothing else will in fact fill the bill. (Disconcertingly, the model of mathematics does not fit at all.)[19] The norms of objectivity which morality is deemed to fail are to be found, if at all, in the natural sciences. The contrast can take two forms. One could work from the acknowledged successes of science, claiming that the sciences do in fact tell us – have already told us – about the world as that objectively is. But the contrast could also appeal to people who did not think science to be actually very successful at giving us an objective view of the world; for it might still be that the *procedures* and approach of science came nearer to giving us an objective view of the world than the procedures of ethical argument could do. Either way, modern arguments about value depend on a contrast: ethics is deemed incapable of giving us an objective view of the world such as is provided by science, either in practice or in principle.

This comes out in the fact that the person who suffers loss of confidence in the objectivity of science loses *pari passu* their grounds for impugning the

---

[19] In fact an influential modern school of *anti*-realists rests its arguments on the analogy with mathematics, though arguably this depends on an idiosyncratic view of mathematics. (For Plato the same analogy provides strong support for a *realist* view of morality.) My own view (which I merely state here, unargued) is that *any* view which assimilates moral reasoning to mathematical has got to be wrong; practical thinking is fundamentally different from theoretical.

objectivity of the other term of the contrast, morality. If one is convinced that disputes in science are not definitely resolvable, because scientists are (for example) too committed to incommensurable background frames of thought, one is left with no convincing contrast with the alleged inadequacy of moral argument. A firm conviction that moral values are, for the reasons suggested, not real requires a robust sense of the objectivity of the scientific world-view. If that crumbles, so does the crucial contrast which undermined the objectivity of morality. So one source of scepticism about values does require serious commitment to the objective nature of our enquiries into the natural world.[20]

Another source of modern moral scepticism springs from our conception of the subject-matter rather than our investigations of it. Values, it is claimed, are not real because they are not part of the world as that is independently of us. Values depend on there being people with various concerns, desires, and so on; but anything so dependent cannot be what *really* exists. Values, on this view, are like secondary qualities such as colours. Given our physical constitution, it is understandable that we see things as coloured, and also that we think that colours are really part of the world which we experience; but in fact they are only projections on to the objective world of what appears to us to be so in virtue of our own sensitivities. Of course we think that people are good, and pillarboxes red; but an objective account of how the world really is will include neither values nor colours, though it will include explanations both of why we see things as good and as coloured, and why we project these features on to a neutral reality.

Values are not objective, then, *if* the world as it really is, is like that: as it would be described from the non-human, absolute viewpoint. Here the moral scepticism rests crucially on the confidence that there is such a viewpoint, even if it is one that we have not attained and never shall. (And, again, it would be useless to deny that a part is played in this by the belief that this is what science actually or ideally aims at.) If one's confidence that this is the nature of reality is sapped, one has correspondingly less reason to exclude values from reality. If, for example, one comes to doubt that what actually does figure as explanatory in our accounts of the world is reality as seen from the absolute viewpoint, then one loses the corresponding reason to deny that values themselves can be explanatory of what we believe and do. Once more, the scepticism is local, and essentially local; the sceptical thought about values rides on the confidence, untouched by scepticism,

---

[20] It is relevant here that ancient science was so theoretical and speculative, with numbers of very general competing theories highly underdetermined by available evidence, and no accepted canons of empirical enquiry. It could strike no one as an example of the cumulative pursuit of secure results.

about the objective part of reality from which values are excluded. If this conception of objectivity goes, then the needed contrast goes.

Modern moral scepticism, then, is essentially local, a part of a globally unsceptical world-view which is likely to be scientifically based, with claims to explain the nature of the world, including us humans as part of that world. But ancient scepticism never takes this partial form: as a systematic approach it undermines the claims in turn of 'the logicians', 'the physicists' and 'the ethical philosophers', fighting a total war over the whole range of philosophy, and, if from dogmatic premises, always regarding them as occupied only provisionally and *ad hominem*. For the ultimate aim is a rejection of all beliefs, not a dogmatic retention of some after preliminary sifting.

III

I turn now to Sextus' account of the sceptic's reaction to his arguments. Leaving aside, as he would do, questions of their soundness, and concentrating only on their supposed power to convince, why would it be preferable to be led by them to suspension of judgement than to act in the conviction that things really are good or bad?

The account of the benefits of moral scepticism is much fuller in *M* than in *PH*. The main thought is: all unhappiness is produced by anxiety (*tarachē*). Happiness consists in the desirable state of relief from anxiety (*ataraxia*). But we shall never be free from anxiety as long as we believe that the things we pursue and avoid really are good or bad – that there really is something about, say, a course of action which genuinely produces motivation to do it (*M* xi.112–13). The sceptic alone is happy because he lacks this belief. He suspends judgement as to whether anything really is good or bad, and relief supervenes on this state without being positively sought for (*PH* i.28–9, cf. Diogenes ix.107). The sceptic is pleased by good things and pained by bad in so far as these are of an unavoidable nature (hunger, physical pains and pleasures). These are feelings over which reason has no power; one can't be persuaded not to be cold or hungry (*PH* i.29–30, *M* xi.148–9). But what most people regard as goods or evils are not like this, but depend crucially on belief. Sextus implicitly though not very clearly distinguishes two ways in which this happens. First, the belief that an object of pursuit is good will bring with it many subsidiary beliefs. If, for example, I think wealth good, I shall be harassed by many beliefs about its precariousness, my ability to get and keep it, others' desires to have it, and so on (cf. *M* xi.146–7). But also, and more fundamentally, the mere belief that an object is good brings with it an exposure to anxiety in its own right, consequences apart. Anxiety lurks in any commitment to an object's being good, as opposed to the agent's merely observing that it seems good to him.

Sextus never retails any argument for this fundamental point. And we may well say: why should detachment from values produce relief and commitment to them anxiety? Once we accept the claim, Sextus has no difficulty in showing us that no philosophical theory about value can help us. For to be persuaded that one type of behaviour is better than another is merely to have one's anxiety redirected, not removed, and to compare values is to compare degrees of anxiety without reducing it (*M* XI.130–40). Sextus points out acutely that from the sceptical point of view, the philosopher who recommends moderation of desires is not reducing anxiety but actually increasing it, since the agent now thinks his present aim *more* valuable than his previous one (*M* XI.137–8).[21] But none of this meets the fundamental point, why belief in objective values should bring anxiety rather than, say, a sense of security. (We shall return to this point.) Sextus does claim that anxiety comes from pursuing goods intensely (*suntonōs* – *M* XI.112, *PH* I.28); the sceptic is happier because less keen, more relaxed. But sceptical detachment, it will be claimed, does not preclude the agent from acting in a normal way, and the radical inner detachment from values that is recommended is supposed to be compatible with paying a normal amount of attention to one's aims. The sceptic is not claiming that in everyday life he will be conspicuously more laid-back or mellow than anyone else. Rather, he will be active in his profession (*PH* I.24). But then claims that he is free from the 'intensity' that torments the moral realist are just restatements of the claim that moral realism is *in itself* a source of anxiety, and therefore a hindrance to happiness.

In so far as the sceptic has an argument, it is not one that is peculiarly relevant to morality, or to practice in general. The anxiety latent in moral realism must simply be the possibility that arises in any area, of conflicting appearances with no way to decide between them. Moral realism is more exposed to this kind of anxiety than realism in, say, physics, only in that it is (supposedly) easier to find conflicting beliefs in the former than in the latter. (And in so far as this is not true of ancient physics, the contrast is further weakened.)

The sceptic about values, then, is happy because in suspending judgement about values, he is detached from them; he lives without the belief that anything is good or bad (*PH* III.235, *M* XI.144, 167 (which refer to *PH* I.23–39), *PH* II.246). He will act, both because some motives to action are unavoidable, and because in all matters something will always appear to be the better

---

[21] See Striker [916] for criticism of Sextus on this point. For replies to Striker see the chapter on scepticism in part 4 of my [71].

course, and will work on him accordingly. But 'he does not identify with the values involved'.[22]

This characterisation of the sceptic already looks very unlike anything in modern moral scepticism. But to bring out its full strangeness I shall first face it with an attack from our ancient sources; it is not merely twentieth-century thinkers who have baulked here.

Aristocles,[23] in his sustained attack on scepticism, makes a particular objection to scepticism in the area of morality. What kind of citizen, he says, or judge or counsellor or friend can the sceptic be – in fact, what kind of person? What evil things would he not dare to do, seeing that he thinks nothing to be really bad or shameful, just or unjust? It can't be said that sceptics can still be afraid of laws and penalties – how can they be, he sneers, when they claim to be so unaffected and unanxious (*apatheis* and *atarachoi*)?

The sceptic response to this attack, which is very obvious and must have been very frequent, is preserved most fully in Sextus (*M* xi.162–7, which refers to *PH* i.21–30).[24] The sceptic will act; following the way things appear good or bad he will behave accordingly. That is, he will follow 'the conduct of life' (*biōtikē tērēsis*). And there is no reason to think that it follows that he will act in a bad way when under pressure to do so – from a tyrant, for example. In such a case he will (perhaps) make his choice according to his intuitions, which are in accordance with the laws and customs he was brought up in. The sceptic has adequate reason for acting in the fact that things appear good or bad to him. And he will have moral intuitions that are the result of his upbringing, so there is no reason to think that he will do wrong because of immediate pressure to do so. The tyrant's threats produce some effect, but not necessarily as much as that produced by his upbringing.

Aristocles has no patience with this. He retorts: when they come out with the clever point that one should live following nature and habits but not assent to any belief, they are just being silly. For one would have to assent to *that* (the belief that one should so live) if to nothing else. And, if one has no knowledge and no means of judging, why should one live following nature and habits rather than not?

Aristocles' first point begs the question: Sextus, for example, goes to great

---

[22] Burnyeat [906]. Frede [907] argues for a more restricted interpretation of the sceptic's detachment, but it seems to me that his arguments apply to theoretical rather than practical beliefs; he admits (p. 127) that in ethics the sceptic's attitude to his beliefs cannot be that of the ordinary person, who in this area is dogmatic. See also Barnes [903].

[23] Aristocles of Messene, a second-century A.D. author of a history of philosophy, quoted extensively by Eusebius in his *Preparation for the Gospel* xiv; this passage is 758c–763d.

[24] Diogenes ix.108 is essentially the same, but unfortunately the text is a mess.

lengths in *PH* I to show that the sceptic is not someone who commits himself to the *truth* of scepticism, but someone to whom a certain attitude happens to recommend itself, so that he lives by appearances, not beliefs; scepticism is not a theory like others, but a detachment from all theory. It can, of course, be questioned whether this defence works; but it exists.

But the second point is not so easily dismissed. Why *should* the sceptic follow the moral intuitions he finds natural[25] because he has been brought up in them? The answer has to be: there is no *should* about it. He just does. They work on him and lead him to act in basically the same way as do feelings of hunger and cold. He regards himself as passive with respect to them in much the same way he does with respect to hunger and other bodily feelings. This is certainly the picture we get from *PH* I.23–4, where the handing-down of customs and laws (and the learning of skills) is explicitly put on a level with the constraints arising from our nature as sentient beings with desires (for food, for example) that we can do nothing about.

But this is a disturbing answer, and one which casts doubt on the claim that the sceptic lives an *ordinary* life, unaffected by his philosophy (*M* XI.165, Diogenes IX.105). For such a response to the tyrant's command, even if it results in the right action (and it might not; even Sextus adds 'perhaps'), is an essentially *uncritical* response. The sceptic *just does* what his intuitions tell him. He has no basis for considering alternatives, or for wondering whether this occasion might prove an exception. He might, of course, fail to follow his intuitions, because of the immediate fear, but this would not worry him, or present itself as a difficulty in decision, for he could not see it as his responsibility, something which concerns him because its origin goes back to his choosing self. The fear outweighed the moral intuitions – why should that be anything for him to worry about? For the intuitions themselves are only motives to acting which happen to be there, like hunger or thirst – not to be ignored, but not the kind of thing that can sensibly be questioned, either.

We do not think of moral choice this way, because we do not think of our moral intuitions and principles this way, as just happening to be there and working themselves out one way or another while we, so to speak, look on. Whatever he or she actually does in the end, the person threatened by the tyrant will identify with his or her moral outlook and intuitions; moral motivation is seen as part of the self, not as something external to the self from which one might be detached.

The radical nature of this detachment emerges if we ask, can the sceptic retain the notions of *laws* and *moral* intuitions? The notion of a

---

[25] For a discussion of the sceptical appeal to nature, see the chapter on scepticism in part 2 of my [71].

law one has been brought up to obey is precisely the notion of something with a justifiable sanction, something utterly unlike hunger or thirst. If the sceptic is right, my belief that something contrary to the law, say murder, is wrong is no more than a feeling that I happen to be stuck with as a result of my upbringing. But this is no good except as an initial move. It only pushes us back to the fact that the people who gave me that upbringing did not think of it that way; they thought that murder was *wrong*. They had a non-sceptical belief which was their basis for giving me my belief. The sceptic's response has to be: whether they realised this or not, their belief was no better grounded than mine is. It no more than mine can be relied on to correspond to anything in reality. But the problem here is obvious. If their belief is just a result of their upbringing, we push the question back again; and if we are never going to reach beliefs that are immune from the sceptic, we have to conclude that morality as a whole is a sham; for it presents itself as having a claim on us, while in reality it is just another appearance, like hunger or thirst, only perhaps more avoidable.

This *need* not be a reason for ignoring or despising morality; sophisticated moderns find biological or more likely sociobiological reasons why we say the moral things we do. All the same, this detached attitude to morality as a whole, while compatible with theoretical interest, precludes any half-way serious practical commitment to any moral project; and while the sceptic might accept this, he can hardly also claim that his conduct of life is 'non-philosophical' (*M* XI.165). If we really cannot hold our beliefs that there are values, then everyday moral life is not what we take it to be. For the moral world as it appears to us provides us with reasons of varying kinds for our moral responses, and we are engaged in our acceptance or rejection of those reasons. When we are led to suspension of judgement as to there being anything behind this appearance, we become detached both from the reasons and – more weirdly – from our own responses, which now become themselves nothing more than appearances: a desire to be generous, say, becomes merely a feeling that happens to present itself to me, but with nothing behind it. But then everyday moral life as it appears to us is indeed not what we take it for, and the sceptic is reduced to merely going through motions. Whatever the upshot of his motions, or the content of the utterances he produces, he is in an important sense not *in* them, not committed to them. Moral scepticism, then, is not, in its ancient version, a bland doctrine that can be held in insulation from everyday life; it is profoundly subversive of everyday life. Timon, a follower of the early sceptic Pyrrho, declared that he had not gone outside 'the customary' (*sunētheia*); but he was wrong.[26]

---

[26] Diogenes IX.103.

It is interesting that both objection and response here can be seen as a special application of a more general objection: that scepticism, in leading the sceptic to suspension of judgement about the truth of his beliefs, and thus to detachment from their content (since he cannot assert them as being true), renders him unable to act, since action requires commitment to the truth of some beliefs. This objection, the *apraxia* or inactivity argument, is highly interesting in its own right,[27] and too complex to be discussed here. I mention it in passing only to point out briefly one ancient rebuttal.[28] Action, the sceptic claims, does not require assent to the truth of any belief; it merely requires that the world appear to the agent in a certain way, and that movement be thereupon produced by an impulse in the agent. However, any impulse to action that is regarded by the agent as merely an impulse in him, detached from any beliefs, will leave it mysterious to him why that impulse should result in that action; he becomes the uncommitted spectator of his own actions and his own impulses. Moral scepticism merely gives us a special case of this; the agent notes his moral intuitions, their strength and their upshot in much the same way as he regards his hunger, or pains; they are all merely things that happen to and in him. What he does may look from the outside like what the ordinary person does; but on the inside it is completely different.

It was recognised in the ancient world that scepticism about value has very radical consequences. We find disagreement, however, as to how radical the changes will be in the sceptic's life as a result. One set of stories about Pyrrho, the prototypical sceptic, tells us that Pyrrho was rendered so indifferent to things by suspending judgement about values that his (non-sceptical) friends had to save him from dogs and from falling off precipices. These stories are obviously not true, but they illustrate the thought that suspension of judgement about value will leave the agent completely passive, 'denying life and suspending judgement, like some vegetable' (*M* xi.163). It is this interpretation which is the basis for the *apraxia* argument.

But there is also another set of stories about Pyrrho: he was a model citizen, who performed the duties of a high priest, and was publicly honoured by his city.[29] And behind this lies the view defended by Sextus: the sceptic who suspends judgement is left, not with a blank, but with his appearances, and this will produce someone who conforms with the tendencies of his upbringing, rather than somebody who weirdly flouts it. For

---

[27] The best treatment of the *apraxia* argument is Striker [912].

[28] Used by the Academic sceptic Arcesilaus: see Plutarch, *Against Colotes* 1122a–d.

[29] Diogenes Laertius ix.62, 64. It seems to have been Aenesidemus, who refounded Pyrrhonism in the first century b.c., who appealed to, or actually started, this tradition.

when the sceptic realises that there is nothing rationally justifying her belief, nothing beyond the persuasion that explains her holding it, this still leaves the persuasion; realising that she has only her culture and upbringing as backing for her view need not weaken the effect of that culture.

What the sceptic really needs, however, is neither of these pictures. For while scepticism in some ways claims to leave everything where it was, in some respects it is more positive: the sceptic tells us that becoming sceptics will make us happier.[30] So suspending judgement about values must make a difference; but if we are to be happy, it cannot be enough of a difference to leave us indifferent to falling off precipices. Losing our value beliefs leads to detachment from our values; can this be consistent with living a life that we would recognise as a desirable one? Sextus does not give us reason to think so.[31]

This ancient response to the experience of finding oneself convinced by arguments for moral scepticism is dramatically different from the modern one in at least three ways, all of which are illuminating for our understanding of either. The first two are perhaps more striking, but it is the third that is in the end philosophically fundamental.

The first emerges in the extreme oddity, to our minds, of the happiness that Sextus thinks will supervene on sceptical suspension of judgement. Sextus urges that moral scepticism is the only way to *ataraxia*, freedom from anxiety, and, as we have seen, assumes that commitment to moral realism is just in itself something that produces anxiety. But not only is this not argued for; it is the opposite of what modern sceptical theories find obvious. We have become used to the idea that assent to belief that things are good or bad by nature produces security, not anxiety; that it is responsible for moral laziness, not intensity and over-keenness; and that it brings about bad faith and refusal to face difficulties, rather than hazardous exposure to the conflicts in the world. For Sextus, the person who believes that his moral problem has an answer which is independent of his decision is foolishly letting himself in for all kinds of anxiety, whereas the person who realises that no objective answer is available is able to relax into relief. For us the matter tends to be presented as being the other way round; it is the moral sceptic who is commonly put forward as the intense one, alert to the seriousness of his or her plight in a world where there are no objective values to fall back on. Moral scepticism is presented as a *rejection* of security – indeed sometimes as a

---

[30] For fuller discussion on this aspect of the sceptic's claim, which is barely touched on in this chapter, see my chapters on scepticism in [71].

[31] But for a powerful and sophisticated defence of the claim that the inner detachment of Pyrrhonism is compatible with a life that can be called happy see McPherran [910] and [911].

course forced on one by mature consideration of the ways in which moral realism supposedly pre-empts one's moral decisions. The favoured image that we find over and over again in the twentieth century is that of the moral sceptic as the person who grows up, where this is taken to mean: who thoughtfully rejects comforting easy answers in order to grapple seriously and responsibly with the complexities of personal moral thinking. Undoubtedly this common picture is exaggerated, sometimes to the point of caricature, by naive and limited views of moral realism, but the fact remains: whatever one's reasons for being a moral sceptic in the twentieth century, a search for security is not among them.[32]

Secondly, the ancient sceptical response is a programmatically *passive* one: suspension of judgement as to things being really good or bad is followed by radical inner detachment from one's beliefs, which involves taking up a passive attitude to them, and treating them as items which just happen to be there given certain conditions.

A common modern reaction to the abandonment of the belief in objective values has been the extreme opposite from passive detachment: the thought that if I do not discover value then I actively create it. An influential introductory book, for example, is subtitled '*Inventing* Right and Wrong';[33] the sceptic invents or creates where there is nothing to discover. In line with this is the immense stress that has been laid on our alleged *freedom* in moral matters if there are no objective values – a totally creative, unconstrained freedom stressed in traditions as otherwise different as those of Sartre and early Hare.[34] This goes with the view that morality is essentially a matter of choice and deciding what to do, not in the humdrum sense of choosing between alternatives whose practicability depends on external factors, but in the more exciting sense of choosing what is to be valuable, deciding what is to count as a moral reason.[35] Indeed, in an exact reversal of the ancient picture, the person rejecting moral realism identifies with the purely active self rather than the purely passive, with the freely choosing, totally creative will. (Both pictures leave it equally mysterious how this 'real' self is related

---

[32] See the comments at the end of Striker [913] ([914]).   [33] Mackie [958].

[34] Cf. Hare [948], 2: 'We are free to form our own moral opinions in a much stronger sense than we are free to form our own opinions as to what the facts are.' Hare takes this freedom to be so strong as to set up a prima facie dilemma when coupled with the belief that 'the answering of moral questions is, or ought to be, a rational activity'. He thinks that this is just common sense, talking of 'this conviction, which every adult has, that he is free to form his own opinions about moral questions'. (Note the image of adulthood and maturity.) For refutations of the claim that this is common sense, see Taylor [974] and Warnock [976].

[35] Taylor [973] discusses this idea of radical choice and its relation to the agent's self and his or her notion of the self.

to the tediously obtrusive empirical self and the constraints that that imposes.)

Such a view is unavailable to the ancient sceptic. And it is worth asking what it is that makes the modern view not only available but so apparently compelling. Two quite different streams seem to me to have fed the current. One is the tradition which sees the alternative to the constraining existence of values as *personal* creation of value. The ancients were, after all, familiar with the idea that values might be the product of *society*, that justice might be rooted in political rather than natural fact. But this is quite distinct from the idea that *I* can unaided bring value into the world.[36] It is only in the last century and a half that we find such stress on the first person in ethics that we are frequently presented with the alleged dichotomy: either values are there in the world to make me act, or I decide what is to be a value. It is a further question, probably unanswerable, what brings into moral philosophy this stress on the isolated first person and the agent's ability to create from nothing.

The other stream derives from twentieth-century analyses of moral terms as being 'non-cognitive' or involving a 'non-descriptive' element. Such analyses have usually not been motivated by a desire to understand moral language, but have been by-products of analyses of language that have concentrated on 'scientific' statements and have had a narrow conception of what a descriptive term could be. All the same, they have had appeal within moral philosophy. For if moral language is not straightforwardly descriptive, it is tempting to think of it as having the 'real' form of imperatives or commands (or, in the ultra-crude version, of exclamations like 'Boo!' and so on). And such analyses reinforce the thought that in making a moral judgement I am not reporting on anything that exists independently of me, but am performing a more creative act, bringing something about that was not there before. That thought is powerfully supported by theories like emotivism and prescriptivism, which are both formally the products of an analysis of the meaning of moral statements which allots them no, or only partial, descriptive meaning. That analysis is a twentieth-century one, and so it is no surprise that there are no ancient analogues of emotivism or prescriptivism. It also seems to me that though such meaning-analyses have been highly influential in the formation of twentieth-century moral philosophy, they are not as fundamental an element as is sometimes claimed. The basic debate

---

[36] Interesting here is Timon fr. 70, quoted by Sextus at *M* xi.140. Anxiety about pursuit of things as being good or bad is to be allayed by the sceptic who conveys the lesson that there is nothing good or bad by nature – in Timon's words 'alla pros anthrōpōn tauta noōi kekritai'. Hirzel's emendation to *nomōi* has some appeal, but even if we reject it we do not find an appeal to the *individual*'s mind; it is the thoughts of *people* that are in question, not *my* thoughts.

between moral sceptic and moral realist is independent of whether moral language is judged to be 'non-cognitive' or not. Non-cognitivist analyses of moral language have at most facilitated the development of an existing tendency to see morality as creation rather than discovery, and I suspect that in future their role in the debate will be seen as a minor one.

The third major contrast can be seen in the fact that modern versions of moral scepticism do not so much as recognise the possibility of any *apraxia* argument.[37] There is not felt to be any conflict between accepting arguments that render one sceptical about morality, and yet acting on firmly held moral beliefs. Mackie, indeed, after an initial chapter claiming that 'there are no objective values', goes on to produce a book-length theory of ethics. Why is this assumed to be so unproblematic? If moral reality really is 'queer' and unacceptable, how can one continue to feel confidence in the commitment to values that everyday life requires?

Those modern forms of moral scepticism which avoid the cruder versions of the idea that moral judgement is merely sounding-off or expressing one's feelings are explicitly *insulated* from moral practice in a way that no ancient variety is. In so far as the sceptic retains the forms of everyday life (making what look like moral judgements, instead of explicitly prescribing or emoting), these are compartmentalised in a way which insulates them from his philosophical judgements on them. There are two ways in which this happens, and they tend to reinforce each other: one from the side of scepticism in general, one from that of moral philosophy in particular. On the one hand, modern scepticism itself is not taken to have any practical consequences; the sceptic about time, for example, does not regard himself as refuted by Moore's point that he knows that he had breakfast *before* lunch; this is taken to be simply irrelevant to the philosophical question.[38] Scepticism is taken to be neither established by everyday beliefs nor refuted by them. Hence the moral sceptic regards it as a confusion to challenge his consistency in holding that there are no objective values while passionately claiming that honesty is the best policy; this is a special case of a philosophical sceptical theory being insulated from everyday beliefs, answerable to them neither for support nor for disproof.

---

[37] See, however, Bett [904].

[38] See Burnyeat [895], to which I owe both the terminology of insulation and much in the way of understanding of the fundamental differences between ancient and modern forms of scepticism. Bett [42] argues that there are two relevant senses of 'insulation': (i) in the claim that our everyday beliefs and practices are insulated from scepticism because the latter relies on philosophical arguments, which can have no impact on our deep-seated everyday practices, and (ii) in the claim that sceptical arguments and their results are purely theoretical, and cannot be 'lived'. Bett claims that only (ii) divides ancient from modern philosophers.

This is reinforced by the (distinct) tendency to distinguish 'meta-ethics' from 'normative', common or garden ethics. Sceptical questions are taken to be questions about the meanings of ethical terms, and our conclusions here are on the 'meta-level', and have no effect on our employment of the terms in actual use. On different grounds we get the same result: there is nothing odd about committedly campaigning for the *best* candidate whilst giving an analysis of the meaning of 'good' which reveals it as a mere vehicle for the agent's sounding-off; these activities are supposed to take place at different levels.

It seems to me that neither of these insulating moves has the self-evident merits that are often assumed. But obviously I cannot argue that here; I am concerned only to show that it is the assumption of insulation that forms a large part of the difference between ancient moral sceptics, who took the *apraxia* argument seriously, and modern ones, who seem unaware of its force, and who avoid it by analysing it as a confusion either between the philosophical and everyday levels, or between meta- and normative ethics.

Two positions in particular are, by virtue of insulation, open to the modern moral sceptic but inconceivable to the ancient sceptic, who has no logical room for them.

One is that of the philosopher who holds a substantive moral theory but is comparatively indifferent as to whether it comes in a realist or a non-realist form. Two utilitarians, for example, can agree that they hold the same theory and discuss details and so on, although one holds that it is a fact that I ought to maximise utility, while the other holds that 'I ought to maximise utility' merely expresses the way I happen to feel about things. They regard themselves as having clearly more in common than either does with a deontologist. Here moral scepticism has become insulated at a level which cuts across different moral theories; it has in effect become a purely metaphysical theory about the basis of a moral theory, not a moral theory in its own right. The ancient sceptic, by contrast, regarded moral scepticism as a theory in its own right, with its own conception of the end that is desirable (freedom from anxiety) and of the means to get there.

The other position is that of the 'quasi-realist'.[39] This is the person who rejects moral realism on the grounds that there can be no such things as

---

[39] Quasi-realism is defended and developed by Blackburn [939], [940], [941]. It is, I think, the implicit view of many people who are anti-realists but turn out to wish to retain at least some of the intellectual attitudes associated with realism, rather than jettisoning them in favour of a totally 'creative' view of moral statements. For criticism of quasi-realism, and discussion of moral realism more generally, see McDowell [960], [961] and Brink [942], which contains a good bibliography.

objective moral values or moral facts bringing about, and explaining, our moral beliefs and actions. Nevertheless he does not see himself as forced to reject all the ideas that normally are held to depend on realism: he does not see moral thinking as unconstrained free choice, or moral language as essentially imperatival or expressive of feeling. He thus feels free to regard moral judgements as being such that we can say that they are true or false, discussable rationally, correctible and improvable by reflection, and so on – in fact, we can make free with all the intellectual attitudes and commitments of the realist. But we can not only have our cake, we can eat it too; for we can do all this while rejecting the actual existence of objective values which is the hallmark of realism.

Such a view clearly depends on insulation; for it takes the question 'Are there really objective values (moral facts, etc.)? to be isolable; it answers it negatively while taking this to leave unaffected the questions 'How can I act on what appear to me to be moral values?' and 'How can I be seriously committed to my practical beliefs?' Indeed, insulation has to be regarded by the quasi-realist as one of the *strengths* of his position. For he has to demarcate that position against the realist, who points to our irresistible feeling that values present themselves as really being there; and also against the kind of anti-realist who insists that the only alternative to accepting the existence of objective values is the view that moral language is, despite appearances, nothing but a vehicle for sounding-off. The quasi-realist accepts neither position; for he thinks that we can *both* reject the existence of values *and* be as serious as we ever were about our moral commitments. But this position is achieved only by insulating the question of moral values and our acceptance of them from practical moral concern – paradoxically, given what the quasi-realist wants to achieve. Once again the question about values has been transformed into a purely metaphysical question, with no intrinsic moral repercussions.

Quasi-realism is thus a position unavailable to the ancient sceptic, who refuses to separate moral beliefs from their practical import. For him, there can be no third way like quasi-realism, because, if we no longer assent to our beliefs about values, those beliefs lose the role they used to play for us; we are reduced to reporting the way values appear to us, and this makes a real difference.

This is important, both because some form of quasi-realism is the implicit view of most thoughtful people who reject extreme 'creative' views of moral language and because of the depth of the disagreement. For the ancient sceptic is not putting forward a *recommendation*, which one might accept or reject; he is not saying that, if we come to find realism false, we *should* cease to assent to the truth of our moral beliefs. Rather, he takes himself to be pointing to a *fact* about human nature: once we come to see that there is no more reason to think realism true than to think it false we *shall in fact* cease to assent to our moral beliefs. For he takes it as a deep but obvious fact about human nature that there is *no way* we can be motivated to go on acting according to moral beliefs once we have ceased to believe in the existence of values for those beliefs to be beliefs about; once that goes, our practical commitment, which depends on it, will simply wither. The possibility just does not occur that this might be avoided by insulating the rejection of realism and confining it to a harmless level with no practical effect. This is surely not due to lack of imagination or ingenuity. Rather, it comes from a conviction that this is not a human option, not a viable way of living. Thus a whole tradition of moral scepticism took it absolutely for granted that its upshot could not be conveniently avoided by insulating the effects of scepticism at a practically ineffective level. This makes it all the more remarkable that modern theories take the opposite for granted, assuming without defence that such insulation is not only a possible, liveable option, but easily available to all who reflect on the foundations of their moral convictions but want to go on having them.

IV

So both the sceptical arguments against the objective existence of values and the response to those arguments are quite different for the ancient and the modern philosopher, who perceive a different range of alternatives. It would be easy, and useless, to draw simplistic morals by siding with one or the other. We might dismiss the ancient lines of thought simply because they do not perceive the possibility of insulation, or the distinction of normative from meta-ethics; if these distinctions are themselves thought to constitute a philosophical advance, then philosophers who do not employ them will seem crude and blundering. On the other hand, it is equally possible to see the contrast as revealing the extent to which twentieth-century forms of moral scepticism have been formed by comparatively parochial twentieth-century concerns; and if so, one will be less inclined to think that now at last, as never before, we have the definitive answers to these problems. Certainly, if it is a fact that we can live with a position like quasi-realism, whereas the ancients thought it obvious that we could not, this is a deeply mysterious fact, and one that needs consideration, rather than just being taken for granted.

We cannot, of course, straightforwardly choose between these options, or give them comparative marks; it is not open to us to take on the ancient way of thinking, as though we could forget our own philosophical history and habits. But we can see both negative and positive ways in which it clarifies the modern approaches we find familiar; and what we need is not a ready-made alternative, but a deepened understanding of the options that we can and cannot make real to ourselves.[40]

40 This is a revised version of a chapter originally published in [723]. For that chapter I am grateful for help from comments and discussion from Myles Burnyeat, Tony Long, Gisela Striker and Terry Irwin. I owe especial gratitude to Jonathan Barnes for joint work on the Modes, particularly the Tenth Mode, and on ancient scepticism generally. In this version I have made the chapter more accessible in parts to a non-specialist audience, and have also taken account of subsequent work on ancient and modern scepticism about value, particularly by Mark McPherran and Richard Bett, which has caused me to think again about some of the issues which the chapter deals with.

9
Moral responsibility: Aristotle and after

SUSAN SAUVE MEYER

A morally responsible agent is someone who is properly subject to the demands, expectations and evaluations of morality. In practice, we subject only normal human adults to these expectations and evaluations. We exempt non-human animals, inanimate objects and the insane from them and we subject children to them only to a limited degree (a degree that increases, of course, as they grow older). While praise and blame are not restricted to agents who are morally responsible, only morally responsible agents *merit* praise or blame for their actions. It may be appropriate or useful to praise and blame (or reward and punish) agents who are not morally responsible – for example as a means to controlling or altering their behaviour or dispositions. But such attitudes and treatment are not merited or deserved by these agents. Only morally responsible agents merit praise and blame for what they do. The task of a philosophical account of moral responsibility is to explain why some agents merit praise and blame for their actions. To execute this task is to identify the criteria for inclusion in the moral community.

There is no expression in Classical or Hellenistic Greek that corresponds to the English expression 'moral responsibility'. However, the topic of moral responsibility was the subject of lively discussion and debate in the Classical and Hellenistic periods. For it was generally agreed by all major figures and schools that agents whose activity is properly evaluated in moral terms – that is, as virtuous or vicious – are distinguished by possessing the capacity of reason. And it was agreed that an agent who is subject to moral evaluation (for example praise or blame) for some particular activity must stand in an appropriate causal relation to that activity. This causal requirement was variously articulated as the requirement that we be in control (*kurioi*) of such actions, that they be 'up to us' (*eph' hēmin*) or 'depend on us' (*par' hēmas*), or that they be 'in our power' (*in nostra potestate*). I shall generally use 'up to us' to render the last three locutions.[1]

One of the central questions disputed in the Hellenistic period of Greek philosophy is whether our actions can be 'up to us' if they are completely determined by antecedent causes. This question continues to be debated in the present day, and is known as the question of whether moral responsibility is compatible with causal determinism. The two major positions in the current debate were well articulated and developed in the Hellenistic period (323–31 B.C.). The central dispute today is between compatibilists, who argue that moral responsibility is compatible with causal determinism, and incompatibilists – who argue for the contradictory thesis. Compatibilism as an explicit thesis dates back to the Stoics, and incompatibilism to the Epicureans.

Epicurus (341–271 B.C.) adopts the atomistic physical theory of the Presocratic philosopher Democritus, but with a significant modification. While Democritus claimed that everything happens as the necessitated result of the interactions of basic atoms, Epicurus claims that the atoms do not always interact of necessity (by their own weight and by the impact from collisions with other atoms). Sometimes, he argues, the atoms swerve off the course that has been determined by necessity (Cicero, *de Fato* (Cic. *Fat.*) 23; cf. Lucretius, *de Rerum Natura* (Lucret.) II.216–20). Epicurus appeals to this 'swerve' in order to solve various problems internal to his atomic theory. But he also maintains that this break in causal necessitation is necessary for our actions to be up to us in the way that morality requires. On the Democritean view, Epicurus complains, necessity is an 'overlord' (*despotis*) of everything, whereas:

> <We see that some things are necessitated,> others due to fortune, and others are up to us (*par' hemās*), since necessity is accountable to no one, and fortune is an unstable thing to watch, while that which is up to us, with which culpability and its opposite are naturally associated, is free of any overlord (*adespoton*). For it would be better to follow the mythology about gods than be a slave to the 'fate' of the natural philosophers: the former at least hints at the hope of begging off the gods by means of worship, whereas the latter involves an inexorable necessity.
>
> (Epicurus, *Letter to Menoeceus* (*Ep. Men.*) 133–4)

---

[1] Except for this rendering of *eph' hēmin, par' hēmas*, and *in nostra potestate*, my quotations of ancient texts are from the following translations. Quotations from Alexander of Aphrodisias are from Sharples [884]; those from Aristotle are my own; and those from all other authors are from Long and Sedley [719]. Where appropriate, I shall also indicate the section and passage number in which quotations occur in Long and Sedley (LS) [719], or in von Arnim [791].

It is not clear exactly how the swerve is supposed to make our actions up to us, on Epicurus' view.[2] But it is clear that he thinks the necessity avoided by the atomic swerve is incompatible with our actions being up to us. This view of Epicurus makes him an incompatibilist. In further deciding that, of the two incompatible theses, the thesis that our actions are up to us is true and the thesis of determinism false, Epicurus affirms a version of incompatibilism known today by the label 'libertarianism'.

In contrast with the Epicureans, the philosophers of the Stoic School founded by Zeno of Citium (334–262 B.C.) affirm and argue for a deterministic thesis. This is the thesis that every aspect of everything that happens is governed by a sequence of causes that they call 'fate' (*heimarmenē*).[3] According to this thesis, at any given time in the history of the world, the condition of the causes at that time contains within it everything that will occur in all subsequent time,[4] and whenever the same set of conditions obtains, the same result occurs.[5] Although the Stoics generally decline, for reasons we shall examine in section 5, to describe fated events as occurring of necessity,[6] they insist that the succession from cause to effect in this sequence is inescapable (*aparabatos*), inevitable (*adiadrastos*) and inflexible (*atreptos*).[7] Thus their thesis of fate is a thesis of determinism. The Stoics insist that human actions and choices, no less than any other occurrences, are inescapable consequences of the sequence of prior causes.[8] But they also insist that this fact is perfectly compatible with our actions being up to us in the way that moral responsibility requires.[9]

Like his successors in the Hellenistic period of Greek philosophy, Aristotle (384–322 B.C.), the latest major philosopher of the Classical period, was also interested in the topic of moral responsibility. Like his Hellenistic successors, he maintains that reason is the faculty that distinguishes normal human adults from agents whose behaviour cannot be evaluated in specifically moral terms (*Nicomachean Ethics* (Arist. *EN*) 1149b31–5; cf. 1145a25–7). And also like his Hellenistic successors, Aristotle insists that an agent can be subject to moral evaluation for an action only if he stands in the appropriate

---

[2] For different interpretations of the role of the swerve in preserving our responsibility, see D. J. Furley, 'Aristotle and Epicurus on the Voluntary', study 2 in [52]; Mitsis [760], ch. 5; and Sedley [787].

[3] SVF II.939/LS 55P; SVF II.944/LS 550; SVF II.945/LS 55N; SVF II.997/LS 55R; Cic. *Fat.* 20–1/LS 38E.   [4] SVF I.98/LS 46G; SVF II.1027/LS 46A; SVF II.921/LS 55L.

[5] SVF II.982/LS 62H.

[6] Cic. *Fat.* 39–43/LS 62C; Cic. *Fat.* 12–15/LS 38E5; Alexander, *de Fato* (Alex. *Fat.*) 176. 14–24/LS 38H.

[7] SVF I.98/LS 46G; SVF II.917/LS 55J; SVF II.997/LS 55R; SVF II.1000/LS 55K.

[8] SVF II.982/LS 62H; SVF II.1002/LS 62I; SVF II.1003/LS 62J.

[9] SVF II.998/LS 62F.

causal relation to that action. He introduces a discussion of voluntariness (*to hekousion*) into his accounts of virtue and vice of character in order to articulate this causal condition:[10]

> Since virtue and vice and their products are praiseworthy and blameworthy respectively (for one is blamed and praised not because of what happens from necessity or from chance or from nature but [because of] those things for which we are ourselves responsible – for what someone else is responsible for, he has both the blame and the praise), it is clear that virtue and vice concern those actions of which one is oneself the cause (*aitios*) and the origin. So we must identify the sorts of actions of which he is himself the cause and the origin. Now we all agree that he is the cause of his voluntary actions . . . and that he is not the cause of his involuntary ones.   (*Eudemian Ethics* (Arist. *EE*) 1223a9–18; cf. *EN* 1109b30–5)

Aristotle insists that praiseworthy and blameworthy activity is activity of which the agent is 'the cause' (*aitios*). Such an action, he explains, is one whose 'origin' (*archē*) is in the agent (or the agent *is* its origin); the action is 'up to' the agent (*ep' autō(i)*) to do and not to do; and the agent is in control (*kurios*) of whether the action occurs.[11] In insisting on this causal precondition of praise and blame, Aristotle appears to be articulating the precondition of moral responsibility whose compatibility with determinism was the subject of heated dispute in the Hellenistic period. But nowhere in his discussions of voluntariness (or elsewhere in his writings) does he address that disputed question explicitly.

Aristotle's silence on this question does not, of course, show that he would have no answer to the question were it posed to him explicitly. While we have no evidence that the Epicureans or Stoics raised the question of what position he would have taken on the disputed question, writers later in antiquity offered conflicting interpretations of Aristotle's position. Cicero (106–43 B.C.) includes Aristotle on his list of philosophers who, like the Stoics, subscribe to the doctrine of 'fate' (*heimarmenē*) (Cic. *Fat.* 39). Alexander of Aphrodisias, the great Aristotelian exegete of the third century A.D., criticises the Stoics, in his *de Fato*, from what he professes to be an Aristotelian perspective. He portrays Aristotle as a libertarian incompatibilist like Epicurus on the subject of moral responsibility (Alex. *Fat.* 164.13–15).

---

[10] I offer a full defence of the claim that Aristotle's enquiry into voluntariness investigates moral responsibility in my [642].

[11] The origin of action is in the agent: Aristotle, *EN* 1111a23, 1112b28; *EE* 1224b15. The origin is the agent: *EE* 1222b19–29; *EN* 1112b31–2, 1113b18, 1139b5. The action is up to the agent: *EN* 1110a17–18, 1112a31, 1113b7–8; *EE* 1223a2–9, 1225a9–33, b8. The agent is in control of the action: *EE* 1223a5–7; *EN* 1113b32, 1114a3. Aristotle indicates that these conditions are mutually entailing: *EE* 1223a2–9, *EN* 1110a15–17, 1113b18–1114a6.

I propose to show that Alexander's interpretation of Aristotle is mistaken. If we examine the moves and counter-moves in the Hellenistic debate over the compatibility of moral responsibility with determinism, and if we examine the Aristotelian texts on which Alexander appears to base his criticisms of Stoic determinism, we shall see that Alexander is wrong to suppose that Aristotle's views give him any reason to reject Stoic compatibilism. On the contrary, we shall see that Aristotle would find the Stoic position much more congenial than Alexander recognises. We shall be able to discover affinities between the Aristotelian and the Stoic positions on the question of compatibility, in spite of Aristotle's silence on the question, because the Stoics' defence of compatibilism depends on their views on other subjects – in particular, their views about causation and modality – and Aristotle's views on these subjects are relevantly similar to those of the Stoics.

The questions we shall pursue in this enquiry are not only of historical significance. For in seeing the resources that the Stoics have for responding to the sorts of criticisms put forth by Alexander, we shall be in a better position to appreciate what it would take to settle the ancient question of whether moral responsibility is compatible with causal determinism.

2 Fatalism versus determinism

It is generally agreed by all parties to the ancient dispute over the compatibility of moral responsibility and determinism, as well as by non-participants such as Aristotle, that action for which we are morally responsible must be action that we are in control of, action whose occurrence is up to us or depends on us. The general worry expressed by the incompatibilists is that the thesis of determinism (fate), if true, would rob us of this control. One way of expressing this worry is to complain that if everything we do and everything that will happen to us is already determined by prior causes, then there is no point in deliberating about what we should do, or in taking trouble to secure the outcomes we desire; for at the time at which we might deliberate or make an effort, the outcomes we hope to influence are already determined. Alexander offers a version of this complaint:

> But if we should do everything we do through some causes laid down beforehand ... what advantage comes to us, as far as action is concerned, from deliberating about what will be done? For [on this view] it is necessary for us, even after deliberating, to do what we would have done if we had not deliberated, so that no advantage comes to us from the deliberating beyond the fact of having deliberated itself. (Alex. *Fat.* 179.11–22; cf. Cic. *Fat* 28–9)

The Stoics label this type of argument the 'lazy argument' (*argos logos*), because it purports to show that the thesis of fate would license lazy behaviour (Cid. *Fat.* 28/LS 55s1). They respond to such arguments by pointing out that they depend on a mistaken premise: the assumption that if it is fated (determined) that *x* will occur, then *x* will occur regardless of whether I make any effort to bring it about, or deliberate about whether to bring it about, etc. The Stoic Chrysippus explains why this assumption is false. According to Cicero's report:

> Some events in the world are simple, [Chrysippus] says, others are complex. 'Socrates will die on such and such a day' is simple: his day of dying is fixed, regardless of what he may do or not do. But if a fate is of the form 'Oedipus will be born to Laius', it will not be possible to add 'regardless of whether or not Laius has intercourse with a woman'. For the event is complex and 'co-fated'. He uses this term because what is fated is *both* that Laius will have intercourse with his wife *and* that by her he will beget Oedipus. Likewise, suppose it has been said 'Milo will wrestle at the Olympic Games.' If someone replied, 'Will he then wrestle regardless of whether or not he has an opponent?' he would be mistaken. For 'He will wrestle' is complex, because there is no wrestling without an opponent. All fallacies of this kind, then, are refuted in the same way. 'You will recover, regardless of whether or not you call the doctor' is fallacious. For it is just as much fated for you to call the doctor as for you to recover.   (Cic. *Fat.* 30/LS 55s)

Chrysippus explains here that according to the Stoic thesis of fate, fated events are not determined to happen independently of the antecedent causes necessary to bring them about. Rather, they are 'co-fated' along with these antecedent causes. For example, in the sorts of cases relevant to the lazy argument, our decisions and actions are not fated to occur independently of the deliberations and efforts that are necessary to bring them about; rather, the deliberations and efforts are no less fated to occur than the decisions and actions they cause (cf. SVF ii.998/LS 62F). Hence, the lazy argument's assumption is wrong. If we did not make the effort or the deliberation we are fated to make, then the action we are fated to perform would not occur. Thus, even under the doctrine of fate, our deliberations and efforts do make a difference to our decisions and action. The lazy argument mistakenly supposes that if our actions are fated, then they are determined by causal chains that by-pass our own causal contribution. The Stoic response in effect points out that it is compatible with the thesis of fate that the causal chain that determines our actions passes through us and essentially includes these efforts and deliberations.

The Stoics' response to the lazy argument gives rise to their account of what makes things up to us. Those things are up to us whose causal chain passes through us (SVF ii.998/LS 62F). As Alexander reports the Stoic view, we are responsible for the things whose causal chain involves our impulse – the causal faculty human beings share with all animals – and this makes these things up to us:

> There is a certain movement that is in accordance with nature for animals too, and this is movement according to impulse; for every animal that moves *qua* animal is moved in a movement according to impulse brought about by fate through the creature. These things being so, and fate bringing about movements and activities in the world, some through earth, if it so happens, some through air, some through fire, some through something else, and some also being brought about through animals (and such are the movements in accordance with impulse), they say that those brought about by fate through the animals are up to the animals.
> (Alex. *Fat.* 182.5–13/SVF ii.979/LS 62G)

According to Alexander's report, the Stoic view is, roughly, that those things whose occurrence depends on our impulses, and are thus co-fated along with our impulses, are up to us (*eph' hēmin*). Thus things can be up to us even if they are completely determined by antecedent causes. They are up to us if our own impulses figure among these antecedent causes.

3 Up to us, desire and deliberation

Alexander criticises this Stoic account of what is up to us, claiming that not everything that happens through us is thereby up to us. According to Alexander, only those actions that happen both through us *and* by our reason are up to us:

> The voluntary and what is up to us are not indeed the same thing. For it is what comes about from an assent that is not enforced that is voluntary; but it is what comes about with an assent that is in accordance with reason and judgement that is up to us. And for this reason, if something is up to us, it is also voluntary, but not everything that is voluntary is up to us. For the irrational animals too, which act in accordance with the impulse and assent in them, act voluntarily; but it is peculiar to man that something of the things that are brought about by him is up to him. For this is what his being rational is, having in himself reason which is the judge and discoverer of the appearances that impinge and generally of the things that are and are not to be done.　　　　(Alex. *Fat.* 183.26–184.1)

Only the rational actions of human beings are up to them, Alexander claims, because the operation of reason frees the human agent's assent from determination by antecedent causes (184.1–11). Merely voluntary actions need not involve reason in this way; therefore, they need not be up to us.

Alexander, in offering this criticism of the Stoic view, purports to be giving Aristotle's own position. But in fact Aristotle's own account of what is up to us is strikingly similar to the Stoic position that Alexander here criticises in his name. When Aristotle describes the proper objects of deliberation, he claims that these are things that would occur through us, and indicates that such things are up to us:

> One does not deliberate about eternal things, for example, about the cosmos or about the diagonal and the side, that they are incommensurate. Nor does one deliberate about things in motion that are always occurring in the same way, whether by necessity or by nature or because of some other cause – for example orbits and risings [of the planets]. Nor does one deliberate about things that are sometimes one way, sometimes another – for example droughts and rains – or about what happens by chance – for example finding treasure. And not even concerning all human beings, for no Spartan deliberates about how best the Scythians might be governed. For none of these things might come about through us, while we deliberate about what is up to us and doable. And these things are the remainder. (Arist. *EN* 1112a21–31)

The examples Aristotle cites indicate that the distinction between things not up to us and things up to us is the distinction between things whose occurrence will not be affected by anything we do and those things to which what we do does make a difference (1112a21–9). While deliberation involves the use of reason, our deliberating does not make such things up to us; rather, we can deliberate about them fruitfully because they are already up to us (contra Alex. *Fat.* 178.28–179.12). Aristotle here does not license the conclusion that only those things happening through us *and* by use of our reason are up to us. Nor does he give any indication, here or elsewhere, that he agrees with Alexander that only some voluntary actions are up to us. He explicitly indicates that non-rational animals act voluntarily (*EN* 1111b7–8; cf. *de Motu Animalium* 703b3–4), and he regularly uses 'up to us' interchangeably with 'voluntary'.[12] This entails that the voluntary actions of animals are up to them, a suggestion he confirms in the *Physics*, where he indicates that if the natural motion of fire were like the self-moved voluntary movements of animals, that motion would be up to fire (Arist. *Physics* 255a5–11).

In insisting that actions are up to us only if they are due to our deliberation, Alexander appears to rely on an interpretation of another claim Aristotle makes about what is up to us. This is the thesis that, if an action is up to me to do, it is also up to me not to do (Alex. *Fat.* 169.15–18, 180.31–181.5). Aristotle articulates this claim as follows:

> In those cases in which it is up to us to act, so too is not acting up to us. And in cases in which no is up to us, so too is yes. So if acting, which is fine, is

---

[12] Arist. *EN* 1113b3–17; cf. 1110a15–17, *Magna Moralia* 1187a5–29, b31–4.

up to us, so too not acting, which is shameful, is up to us. So if it is up to us to do fine and shameful things, so too it is up to us not to do them. (Arist. *EN* 1113b7–13)

Call this the two-sided nature of what is up to us. Alexander appears to associate the two-sided nature of what is up to us with a distinction Aristotle draws in the *Metaphysics* (Arist. *Met.*) between rational and non-rational capacities (Alex. *Fat.* 169.6–18, 180.46–181.6). In Aristotle's view, rational capacities differ from non-rational capacities in being capacities for opposites:

> Some capacities are non-rational while others are rational. This is why all the crafts and productive sciences are capacities – for they are principles that cause change in another or in something *qua* other. All the rational capacities are the same capacity for opposite effects, while the non-rational capacities are for only one effect. For example, the hot is capable only of heating, while the medical craft is capable both of sickness and of health. The reason for this is that the knowledge is an account (*logos*), and the same account reveals both a thing and its privation.   (Arist. *Met.* 1046b1–9)

When the possessor of a non-rational capacity such as fire's capacity to heat is in the condition appropriate for the exercise of that capacity, it is necessarily exercised, Aristotle tells us. But with a rational capacity, a capacity for opposites, this is not the case:

> With [non-rational capacities], when the agent and patient draw near to each other in the way in which they are capable, it is necessary that the one act and the other undergo. But with [rational capacities] this is not necessary. For the former are all productive only of one thing, while the latter are productive of opposites, and so [if it is necessary], they will produce opposite effects simultaneously, which is impossible. So there must be something else which is in control – by this I mean desire or decision. For whichever of the two he desires properly, he will do this whenever he is present in the way he is capable and draws near to the patient. So with all rational capacity, it is necessary that whenever he desires that of which he has the capacity and in the way he has it, he will do this.   (Arist. *Met.* 1048a5–15)

Alexander supposes, reasonably enough, that the possession of rational capacities makes our actions up to us precisely because rational capacities need not be exercised in the conditions appropriate for their exercise. Something other than these conditions is in control of the exercise of such capacities. It is, however, mistaken of Alexander to infer from this that the rational activity of deliberation provides the relevant two-sidedness (Alex. *Fat.* 184.1–10). The type of reason that makes a capacity two-sided, on Aristotle's view, is reason that tells the agent 'how to' bring about either of a pair of opposite effects. It need only be the minimal amount of 'reason' involved in having some conception of the outcomes one might or might not bring about, depending on whether one desires to do so. Furthermore, the capacity that controls whether the rational capacity will be exercised is not reason but rather the desire on which the exercise of the capacity is contingent. Aristotle's account of two-sided capacities does not support Alexander's claim that only actions due to our deliberation are up to us. Aristotle's conception of two-sided capacities supports rather than contradicts the Stoic view that what is up to us is what happens through us.

4 External causes and control

Alexander invokes deliberation as the mechanism that makes our actions up to us because he thinks this operation of reason gives us the sort of control over our actions that non-rational animals lack. All voluntary action, Alexander claims, is preceded by an externally caused appearance (*prospesousa phantasia*). For example, the prey that wanders into the sight of the lion might cause the appearance in the lion as 'pleasant to eat'. Non-rational animals simply yield (*eixai*) to such appearances, and pursue the object that appears to them (183.24–184.1). By contrast, human beings can deliberate about the externally caused appearance, and will not follow it unless reason agrees that it is to be done. Thus human beings do not simply yield to the externally caused appearances:

> And for this reason the other animals, which yield to appearances alone, have the causes of their assents and of their impulses to action in accordance with these; but man has reason, a judge of the appearances which impinge on him from outside concerning things that are to be done, and using this he examines each of them . . . And if he finds in his reasoned enquiry that its reality is different from the appearance, he does not concede to it because it appears of a certain sort, but resists it because it *is* not also of that kind.   (Alex. *Fat.* 184. 1–8)

The metaphors of yielding to, following and resisting external causes express the incompatibilist's worry about action under determinism. On the determinist picture, the causal chain of our actions extends back to something external to us which causes us to have a certain 'appearance' of what to do – in the way that the entrance of the prey into the lion's field of vision inclines the lion to pursue it. Epicurus' metaphor of fate as a despot to which we are enslaved expresses the view that under determinism, external causes would control us (Epicurus, *Ep. Men.* 133–4, quoted above). Lucretius expresses a similar point when he likens externally caused action to action compelled by a stronger agent (Lucretius II.272–83/LS 20F3). Cicero expresses this worry in its general form:

> If all things come about through fate, all things come about through an antecedent cause. And if impulses do this, so do the things which are consequent upon impulse; therefore, so do acts of assent. But if the cause of impulse is not located in us, neither is assent itself in our power. If that is so, not even the results of impulse are in our power (*in nostra potestate*). Therefore neither acts of assent nor actions are in our power. The result is that neither commendations nor reproofs nor honours nor punishments are just. (Cic. *Fat.* 40/LS 62C4)

This formulation of the worry avoids the fallacy of the lazy argument, for it acknowledges that under determinism our actions result from causal chains that go through our impulse and assent. The worry is therefore not the unfounded worry that the causation of our actions by-passes our desires, choices and efforts. It is a worry that focuses on the fact that in such a causal chain there are external causes of impulse and assent: something external brings about the appearance, which in turn is followed by assent and impulse. According to the thesis of determinism, our assent and impulse are inescapable and inevitable results of their antecedent causes. And therefore the mere fact that our actions occur *through* our assent and impulse does not show that our actions are up to us – since our assent and impulse are themselves due to prior causes external to us.

The Stoics respond to this reformulated objection by distinguishing between the kinds of causes involved in the inexorable deterministic sequence. According to Cicero's report:

> 'Of causes', [Chrysippus] explains, 'some are complete and primary, others auxiliary and proximate. Hence when we say that all things come about through fate by antecedent causes, we do not mean this to be understood as "by complete and primary causes", but "by auxiliary and proximate causes".' (Cic. *Fat.* 41)

Chrysippus concedes that if the external precipitator of an action (the external object that produces the impression to which the agent assents) was the 'complete and primary' cause of the action, then the action would not be up to the agent. But if that external cause was simply the 'auxiliary and proximate' cause of the action, and the agent its 'complete and primary' cause, then the action would still be up to the agent. And the external cause is in fact merely the auxiliary and proximate cause of the action, while the agent is its complete and primary cause, Chrysippus claims.

He illustrates the application of this distinction between causes with the following analogy. Just as an agent's action will not occur unless prompted or precipitated by an externally caused impression, so too a cone or a cylinder will not move unless it receives a push from an external impetus. But how the agent acts in response to the externally caused impression is not determined by the external cause, just as the sort of movement to which the cone or cylinder is subject is not determined by the external push. For the same push would result in the forward rolling of the cylinder and the circular rolling of the cone. The external source of the impetus is not the 'complete and primary' cause of the cylinder's forward rolling because such a cause is no more a cause of forward rolling than of circular rolling. Similarly, the external cause of the agent's impression is no more the cause of the agent's acting the way he does rather than some other way. For example, the pot of gold that produces an impression in the agent is no more the cause of the agent's theft of the gold than of the agent's not stealing the gold. Which action results from the impression brought about by the gold depends on what the agent's dispositions and character are like. Even if the Stoic thesis of fate is true, and it is completely determined by antecedent causes that the agent will steal the gold, it is still up to the agent whether or not to steal the gold because the presence of the gold (the external object) still leaves it up to an agent to steal the gold or to leave it alone.[13]

Again, it is worth noting that the Stoic response to this objection is very Aristotelian. Aristotle too addresses the worry that the external stimuli of our actions compel us to act in a way that deprives us of responsibility for what we do:

> If someone were to say that pleasant and fine things force us, because they compel us from the outside, then everything would be forced for him, for everyone acts for the sake of these things.   (Arist. EN 1110b9–11)

And he responds to the worry by appeal to precisely the same features to which Chrysippus appeals in explanation of his distinction between causes:

> It is ridiculous to attribute responsibility to the externals, and not to oneself – for being susceptible to such things.   (Arist. EN 1110b13–14)

Aristotle does not, in this passage, invoke a distinction similar to Chrysippus' distinction between two types of causes in order to explain his claim that the agent rather than the externals should be attributed responsibility for the action. But, like Chrysippus, he indicates here that facts about the agent's character support his claim that the action originates in the agent, rather than the externals, and so is up to the agent. Moreover, he does in other contexts appeal to a distinction between causes (the distinction between accidental and intrinsic causes) to defend the claim that the origin of an

---

[13] Cic. *Fat.* 41–3/LS 62.5–10; Aulus Gellius, *Noctes Atticae* VII.2.6–13/LS 62D/SVF II.1000.

outcome goes back only so far. The causal factor operating antecedently to such an origin is only its accidental cause (Arist. *Met.* 1027a29–b16; cf. *de Interpretatione* (Arist. *Int.*) 18b5–25). In such contexts, Aristotle takes the existence of such accidental occurrences to disprove the thesis that 'everything happens of necessity' (*Met.* 1027a30–2; *Int.* 18b6), and Alexander interprets Aristotle's rejection of this thesis of necessity as a rejection of the thesis of determinism (Alex. *Fat.* 172. 17–173.28, 174.29–176.13). However, the sort of necessity Aristotle here rejects is much stronger than the variety of necessity involved in determinism. It is the necessity of essentialism rather than determinism, and not all determined events satisfy the criteria for essentialism.[14] Indeed, Aristotle himself allows that the deterministic necessity of Democritus' thesis is compatible with the existence of accidental occurrences (Arist. *Ph.* 198b16–32).[15]

A critic of compatibilism might well respond that the Stoics' distinction between causes (and Aristotle's too, if it serves the same function) proves too much to be an adequate account of what makes our actions up to us. The critic may charge that if this distinction between causes shows that the virtuous or vicious person's actions are up to him, it also shows that the cone's or cylinder's rolling is up to it. But surely the cone or cylinder is not morally responsible for what it does. Alexander articulates such a criticism (*Fat.* 182.31–183.21; cf. 179.15–17, 185.15–18). This criticism amounts to the charge that an account like the Stoics' account of 'up to *X*' does not succeed in identifying a causal relation in which only morally responsible agents can stand to their causal effects. But the Stoics (and Aristotle too) can accept this criticism without conceding that their account of what is up to us is faulty. For they need not (and do not) accept the critic's presupposition that having one's actions up to oneself is sufficient for moral responsibility; such a causal relation is only necessary, not sufficient for moral responsibility. While they accept that the class of entities whose actions are up to them extends more widely than the class of agents whose activity is subject to moral evaluation (Alex. *Fat.* 183.2–3), they claim that the morally responsible agents within this class of entities are distinguished by possessing the faculty of reason.[16] Much more, of course, needs to be said to explore the adequacy of such a criterion for moral responsibility.[17] But our present

---

[14] See Sharples [885].

[15] By contrast, the sceptic Carneades claims that the existence of accidental causes is inconsistent with the Stoic thesis of fate (Cic. *Fat.* 19–21). I explain how the existence of accidental occurrences is compatible with determinism in my [927].

[16] Seneca, *Epistulae* (Sen. *Ep.*) 124.13–14/LS 60H; Arist. *EN* 1149b31–1150a1; cf. 1116b30–1117a9, 1145a25–7.

[17] I explore the details of Aristotle's conception of moral responsibility in my [642].

project concerns the narrower and more manageable question of whether the Stoics are right to claim that even under determinism, our actions are up to us.

5 Fate, necessity and the ability to do otherwise

The Stoic distinction between causes succeeds in establishing that the external causes of our actions do not suffice to determine our actions, since our actions depend on us as well. However, their opponents can still complain that the event that determines our actions and decisions is one in which we are unable to decide to act otherwise than we do. For the Stoics think that given the agent's nature and character, and given the circumstances of the agent at the time (the '*periechon*'), the agent's decision and action are inevitable. Since in those circumstances it is inevitable that the agent decide and act as he or she does, the opponents may charge, the agent is unable to decide and act otherwise than he or she actually does. Since it is reasonable to claim that it is up to me to do something only if I am able to do it, the opponent might conclude that it is not after all up to me to do what I am fated to do. Alexander spells out this criticism in detail in *de Fato* xII.

In insisting, on Aristotle's behalf, that an action is up to me to do only if it is also up to me not to do, and that this entails that I am able both to do it and not to do it, Alexander is correctly reporting Aristotle's views (cf. Arist. *Ph.* 255a7–10). However, in claiming that the Stoic thesis of determinism rules out the requisite ability, Alexander goes beyond Aristotle's own stated position. Aristotle recognises a variety of different ways in which it would be true to say that an agent is unable (*mē dunasthai*) to do something, but in none of these ways would it follow from the Stoic thesis of determinism that the agent is unable to do otherwise than he or she actually does.

In *Met.* v.12, Aristotle identifies two general classes of conditions in which an agent is able to do something.[18] In the first class, the agent is able to do *X* depending on whether he or she possesses the requisite capacity, ability or condition (1019a33–b22). Within this general category there is wide variation. For example, in one way tone-deaf Socrates would be able to sing – in the sense that he can manage to warble something like a tune. But in another way, it would be proper to say that tone-deaf Socrates is unable to sing – in the sense that he cannot do so well (for example, 'He can't sing at all!') (1019a23–6, b11–15). So Aristotle identifies two ways in which it would be true to say that Socrates is unable to do *X*:

---

[18] The class of things which are *dunaton* described in *Met.* v.12 includes things that might be suffered or experienced, not just things one is able to do. I restrict my remarks to the latter subclass.

INABILITY I: Socrates lacks the capacity to do X.
INABILITY II: Socrates lacks the capacity to do X well.

Suppose that Socrates is not singing at a particular time. According to the Stoic thesis of determinism, if Socrates is not singing at a particular time, then it is determined by antecedent causes that Socrates not be singing then. But it does not follow from the thesis of determinism that Socrates lacks the ability to sing, or that he lacks the ability to sing well. So the Stoic thesis of fate does not entail Aristotelian inability either of variety I or of variety II.

According to the second general class of conditions identified by Aristotle in *Met.* v.12, an agent is able to do something provided that the opposite state of affairs is not necessary (1019b22–33). The sort of necessity Aristotle has in mind is the sort of necessity involved in a rectangle's diagonal not being commensurate with its side, or in a man's being an animal (b22–7). This is the necessity of essential connections. According to this notion of necessity, it is not necessary that a human being be walking, since there is no essential connection between being human and walking. Hence according to this general condition of ability and inability, Socrates is able to sing if there is no essential connection between being Socrates and not singing; that is, Socrates who happens not to be singing is able to sing if his nature does not preclude singing. So the third way in which Aristotle recognises that Socrates might be unable to do X is:

INABILITY III: Socrates' nature is incompatible with doing X.

The necessary connection that would make Socrates unable to sing, in this third sense of 'unable', is a connection between Socrates' nature and singing. It is not a necessary connection between circumstances antecedent to the time when Socrates is not singing, and the circumstances at the time when Socrates is singing. Socrates might be able to sing, in this third sense, even if it is causally determined by antecedent circumstances that he should not be singing at a particular time. So the Stoic's thesis of fate does not entail that Socrates is unable, in this third way, to do otherwise than he actually does.

In *Met.* IX.5, Aristotle might appear to identify a fourth and fifth variety of ability and inability. He insists there that if Socrates has the capacity to do something, this is not a capacity to do that thing in just any situation (*pantōs*), but rather only in certain conditions (*pote kai pōs*) (*Met.* 1047b35–1048a2, 15–21). The requisite conditions include the presence of necessary materials and the absence of any external impediment. Let us refer to these conditions as 'enabling conditions'. At 1048a15–16, Aristotle makes a remark that might mean: if these enabling conditions do not obtain, then the agent is unable to do the action in question. If this is the correct interpretation of his remark,[19] then there are two further types of circumstance in which Aristotle would allow that Socrates is unable to do X:

> INABILITY IV: Socrates lacks the appropriate materials for doing X.
> INABILITY V: Socrates is prevented by something external from doing X.

Socrates would be unable to sing if something external (for example a gag over his mouth) prevented him from singing. And a shoemaker would be unable to make shoes if he had no leather or nails with which to work. But the Stoic thesis of fate, although it entails that the shoemaker who is not making shoes at a particular time is determined not to be making shoes then, surely does not entail that the shoemaker lacks the relevant materials or is prevented from acting by an external obstacle. Quite generally, the thesis of fate does not entail that an agent who fails to be doing X at a particular time satisfies the conditions for either of these varieties of inability.

We have surveyed the various conditions in which Aristotle would agree that an agent is unable to perform a particular action that she happens not to be performing. We have seen that, contrary to Alexander's assumption, one of these conditions is a consequence of the Stoic thesis of fate. Indeed, if we examine the sorts of inability that the Stoics recognise, we shall see that their views are very much like Aristotle's on this subject. The Stoics define necessity and possibility as follows:

> Some propositions are possible (*dunata*), some impossible (*adunata*), and some necessary (*anankaia*), some non-necessary (*ouk anankaia*). Possible is that which admits of being true and which is not prevented by external factors from being true, such as 'Diocles is alive.' Impossible is that which does not admit of being true, [or admits of being true but is prevented by external factors from being true], such as 'The earth flies.' Necessary is that which is true and does not admit of being false, or admits of being false but is prevented by external factors from being false, such as 'Virtue is beneficial.' Non-necessary is that which both is true and is capable of being false, and is not prevented by external factors from being false, such as 'Dion is walking.' (Diogenes Laertius, *Lives of the Philosophers* (D.L.) VII.75/LS 38D)

These definitions of possibility and necessity show why the Stoics deny that their thesis of fate entails that everything happens of necessity, and why they think their thesis of fate does not entail that we are unable to do

---

[19] On the alternative interpretation of the remark, it means that if these enabling conditions obtain and the agent desires to do the action in question but he does not succeed in doing it, then he does not have the ability (*dunamis*) in question. That is, he would simply be invoking the account of a *dunamis* articulated in Plato, *Hippias Minor* 366b–c.

otherwise than we actually do. These definitions apply directly to possible and impossible propositions rather than to agents' ability and inability, but the connection between these two things is clear. Dion is able (*dunatai*) to walk if the proposition 'Dion is walking' is possible (*dunaton*), and Dion is unable (*mē dunatai*) to walk if the proposition 'Dion is walking' is impossible (*adunaton*).

Consider the case of Dion who remains seated while the others are walking around the stoa. According to the Stoic definitions of modality, Dion is able to walk if one of two conditions obtains. First of all, Dion is able to walk if the proposition 'Dion is walking' admits of being true. The proposition admits of being true (*endechomenon to alēthes*) if its subject, Dion, and predicate, walking, are not incompatible – that is, if Dion can be walking and yet still exist. For example, Dion does not admit of being non-human, and fire does not admit of being not hot because these properties belong to Dion and to fire in virtue of their natures and essence. So Dion would be unable to walk, according to this criterion, if:

STOIC INABILITY I: Dion's nature is incompatible with walking.

This type of inability is the same as the third type of inability Aristotle recognises. It is not entailed by the Stoic thesis of determinism.

The second set of conditions in which the Stoics would deny that Dion is able to walk are conditions in which something external prevents Dion from walking.

STOIC INABILITY II: Something external prevents Dion from walking.

That is, something external to the terms of the proposition, Dion and walking, must prevent Dion's walking now. Dion would be prevented from walking by such an external factor if he was tied to his chair, or (perhaps) if he lacked the ability to walk, or if he was not in a location suitable for walking (for example if he was perched on a small rock in the middle of the ocean). These conditions correspond to the first, fourth and fifth types of inability recognised by Aristotle. The presence of none of these conditions is entailed by the Stoic thesis of determinism. Like Aristotle, the Stoics can deny that the thesis of determinism entails that we are unable to do otherwise than we do.

Of course, Alexander can reply that the Stoics fail to recognise all the genuine varieties of inability. And, in support of this position, he might well point out that although Aristotle does not explicitly recognise a kind of inability that is a consequence of determinism, he is none the less committed to recognising it. For Aristotle, in other contexts, is willing to refer to the deterministic thesis of Democritus as a thesis according to which things happen of necessity (*Generation of Animals* 789b2–7; cf. *Ph.* 198b10–14). And in his articulation of the third kind of inability in *Met.* v.12, he claims that an agent is able to do X provided that the opposite state of affairs is not necessary. Clearly the sort of necessity Aristotle has in mind in that context is not the deterministic necessity invoked by Democritus. But he still might be committed to recognising a further type of inability, to be added to all the previous types he recognises: the inability to do otherwise than what we are determined to do.[20] Let us refer to this new type of inability as 'deterministic inability', and the corresponding type of ability as 'indeterministic ability'.

From a modern point of view, Alexander would seem to be quite reasonable to insist that the Stoics must admit that there is a type of inability to do otherwise than we do that is a consequence of the thesis of determinism. However, this does not settle the substantive question at issue between the Stoics and incompatibilist critics like Alexander. For Alexander needs to show that the deterministic inability to do otherwise than we do is a lack of the sort of ability that makes our actions up to us in the way that morality requires.

Faced with the multiplicity of types of ability and inability, we must find independent criteria to identify the sort of ability that moral responsibility requires. In our survey of the moves and counter-moves in the Hellenistic debate, we have seen that determinism, and hence deterministic inability, does not put us at the mercy of external circumstances, does not deprive us of the capacity of choice or of action, and does not keep us from deciding on the basis of what we value or of how we feel on the spur of the moment. All these things are compatible with deterministic necessity, and they are all important. An incompatibilist like Alexander must give some reason for supposing that the deterministic inability to do otherwise than we do is something that we have any reason to worry about, that it would undermine what we value in being morally responsible agents. The mere fact that under determinism we are 'unable' to do otherwise is insufficient to establish this point. For Alexander, being a good Aristotelian, should recognise that 'unable' is said in many ways (*pollachōs legomenon*).

---

[20] An alternative route to this conclusion might proceed via *Met.* v.5, which claims that all types of necessity are necessary because they do not admit of being otherwise. Given (a) the connection between 'necessary' and 'does not admit of being otherwise' in Aristotle's view, (b) his recognition that Democritean determinism is a type of necessity and (c) the view that 'what does not admit of being otherwise' is *adunaton* (*Met.* v.12), it would follow that Aristotle must recognise a type of inability co-ordinate with Democritean necessity.

6 Problems for the libertarian: Epicurus, Alexander, Carneades

To settle the dispute between the Stoics and their incompatibilist critics, one needs to enquire whether the kind of ability to do otherwise that would be secured by the failure of determinism is a sort that we have any reason to believe moral responsibility requires. A relevant question to ask is whether this kind of ability ('indeterminist ability') would not undermine rather than preserve that responsibility. The Stoics' general criticism of the Epicurean postulation of the swerve is that it introduces motion without a cause (*anaition kinēsis*). The agent's action, if it is produced by the swerve, which is uncaused, is itself ultimately uncaused. This means that nothing, including the agent, is responsible for it. Thus to deny determinism (fate), the Stoics charge, is to do away with responsibility altogether.

Alexander and the sceptic Carneades (214–129 B.C.) think that the libertarian can respond successfully to this Stoic charge. We need not claim that the agent's action is uncaused, Alexander claims, in order to deny that it is subject to determinism. We can claim that it is brought about by the agent's two-sided capacity for deciding what to do (*Fat.* xv). Carneades makes a similar proposal: the Epicurean need not invoke the swerve to guarantee responsibility, but need only maintain that the agent's action is caused by a voluntary motion of the mind. This motion is not uncaused, he claims, but due to the mind's nature:

> Of the atom itself it can be said that, when it moves through the void as a result of its heaviness and weight, it moves without a cause, in as much as there is no additional cause from outside. But here too, if we don't all want to incur the scorn of the natural philosophers for saying that something happens without a cause, we must make a distinction and say as follows: that it is the atom's own nature to move as a result of weight and heaviness, and that that nature is itself the cause of its moving in that way. Similarly for voluntary motions of the mind there is no need to seek an external cause. For a voluntary motion itself has it as its own intrinsic nature that it should be in our power to obey us. And this fact is not without cause: for the cause is that thing's own nature. (Cic. *Fat.* 24–5/LS 20E)

Both Carneades and Alexander maintain that, according to their respective proposals, the agent's action does not lack a cause; it simply lacks a cause external to the agent.

But surely, the Stoics can respond, Alexander and Carneades have not succeeded in defining a position that avoids both the determinism of the Stoic view and the uncaused motion of the Epicurean view. Their view, once it is made more precise, collapses into one or the other of these two positions. Both the Stoics and the Epicureans will want to ask Carneades (or Alexander) whether, given the mind's own nature (or its two-sided capacity for deciding) together with the external circumstances in which it produces the voluntary action, it is determined that the mind will produce this voluntary action rather than another. If he answers yes, then the Epicureans will complain that he has reintroduced precisely the deterministic thesis whose avoidance motivates the introduction of the swerve. But if he answers no, then the Stoics and the other critics of the Epicureans will be able to complain that he has reintroduced motion without a cause, for he denies that the circumstances antecedent to the agent's action are sufficient to determine the agent to perform this action rather than another. They may therefore reintroduce their charge that such a thesis precludes rather than guarantees responsibility. If Alexander and the other critics of Stoic compatibilism are to be justified in maintaining that agents are in fact responsible for what they do, then they must have a better response than the ones we have examined to the Stoic charge that determinism is not simply compatible with, but in fact necessary for, our responsibility.

Bibliography*

This bibliography is intended to provide a starting-point for further reading. It includes, in addition to the works cited in the essays, other books and articles which will be of use in exploring ancient views on ethics. It is by no means comprehensive, but the principles of discrimination were not such that inclusion should be taken to imply recommendation. Further reading on other aspects of Greek thought can be found in the bibliographies to the earlier volumes in this series, [17], [18] and [19].

General

The fullest introduction in English to Greek philosophy before the Hellenistic age is W. K. C. Guthrie's *A History of Greek Philosophy*:

[1] *The Earlier Presocratics and the Pythagoreans* (Cambridge, 1962)
[2] *The Presocratic Tradition from Parmenides to Democritus* (Cambridge, 1965)
[3] *The Fifth-century Enlightenment* (Cambridge, 1969)
[4] *Plato: The Man and his Dialogues: Earlier Period* (Cambridge, 1975)
[5] *The Later Plato and the Academy* (Cambridge, 1978)
[6] *Aristotle: An Encounter* (Cambridge, 1981).

An admirably informative and brief history of classical thought is

[7] T. H. Irwin, *Classical Thought* (Oxford, 1989).

The following contain articles about various periods and aspects of ancient philosophy:

[8] A. Alberti (ed.), *Logica, mente e persona* (Florence, 1990)
[9] J. P. Anton and G. L. Kustas (edd.), *Essays in Ancient Greek Philosophy* (Albany, 1971)
[10] J. P. Anton and A. Preus (edd.), *Essays in Ancient Greek Philosophy*, vol. 2 (Albany, 1983)
[11] R. Bambrough (ed.), *New Essays on Plato and Aristotle* (London, 1965)
[12] M. F. Burnyeat (ed.), *The Skeptical Tradition* (Berkeley/Los Angeles/London, 1983)
[13] H. Cherniss, *Collected Papers* (Leiden, 1977)

* I am grateful to Terry Irwin for very helpful suggestions on bibliographical material, and to Hugh Johnstone for supplying many references.

[14] E. M. Craik (ed.), *Owls to Athens: Essays on Classical Subjects presented to Sir Kenneth Dover* (Oxford, 1990)

[15] D. Depew (ed.), *The Greeks and the Good Life* (Fullerton, Calif., 1980)

[16] S. Engstrom and J. Whiting (edd.), *Rethinking Duty and Happiness* (Cambridge, 1996)

[17] S. Everson (ed.), *Epistemology* (Cambridge, 1990)

[18] S. Everson (ed.), *Psychology* (Cambridge, 1991)

[19] S. Everson (ed.), *Language* (Cambridge, 1994)

[20] M. I. Finley (ed.), *The Legacy of Greece* (Oxford, 1981)

[21] M. Frede, *Essays in Ancient Philosophy* (Oxford/Minneapolis, 1987)

[22] M. Frede and G. Striker (edd.), *Rationality in Greek Thought* (Oxford, 1996)

[23] J. Hankinson (ed.), *Method, Medicine and Metaphysics: Studies in the Philosophy of Ancient Science* (Edmonton, 1988)

[24] J. Harmatta (ed.), *Proceedings of the VIIth Congress of the International Federation of the Societies of Classical Studies* (Budapest, 1984)

[25] E. N. Lee, A. P. D. Mourelatos and R. M. Rorty (edd.), *Exegesis and Argument* (Assen, 1973)

[26] A. Loizou and H. Lesser (edd.), *Polis and Politics: Essays on Greek Moral and Political Philosophy* (Aldershot, 1990)

[27] D. Manetti, *Studi su papiri Greci di logica e medicina* (Florence, 1985)

[28] M. Nussbaum (ed.), *The Poetics of Therapy, Apeiron* 23 (1990)

[29] G. E. L. Owen, *Logic, Science and Dialectic: Collected Papers in Greek Philosophy* (London/Ithaca, 1986)

[30] R. Robinson, *Essays in Greek Philosophy* (Oxford, 1969)

[31] M. Schofield and M. C. Nussbaum (edd.), *Language and Logos* (Cambridge, 1982)

[32] P. A. Vander Waerdt (ed.), *The Socratic Movement* (Ithaca, 1994)

[33] G. Vlastos, *Studies in Greek Philosophy*, ed. D. W. Graham, 2 vols. (Princeton, 1995).

The following books and articles are concerned with more than one period of ancient thought:

[34] A. W. H. Adkins, *Merit and Responsibility* (Oxford, 1960)

[35] A. W. H. Adkins, 'The Greek Concept of Justice from Homer to Plato', *Classical Philology* 75 (1980), 256–68

[36] J. Annas, 'Plato and Aristotle on Friendship and Altruism', *Mind* 86 (1977), 532–54

[37] J. Annas, 'Naturalism in Greek Ethics: Aristotle and After', *Proceedings of the Boston Area Colloquium in Ancient Philosophy* 4 (1988), 149–71

[38] J. Annas, 'Self-Love in Plato and Aristotle', *The Southern Journal of Philosophy* Suppl. 27 (1988), 1–18

[39] J. Annas, 'Ancient Ethics and Modern Morality', *Philosophical Perspectives* 6 (1992), 119–36

[40] J. Annas, 'Scepticism Old and New', in [22], 239–54

[41] J. Annas, 'Prudence and Morality in Ancient and Modern Ethics' *Ethics* 105 (1995), 241–57

[42] R. Bett, 'Scepticism and Everyday Attitudes in Ancient and Modern Philosophy', *Metaphilosophy* 24 (1993), 363–81

[43] M. W. Blundell, *Helping Friends and Harming Enemies* (Cambridge, 1989)

[44] J. Brunschwig, 'The Cradle Argument in Epicureanism and Stoicism', in [723], 113–44

[45] M. F. Burnyeat, 'Idealism and Greek Philosophy: What Descartes Saw and Berkeley Missed', *Philosophical Review* 91 (1982), 3–40

[46] D. B. Claus, *Towards the Soul: An Inquiry into the Meaning of 'Psyche' before Plato* (New Haven/London, 1981)

[47] J. M. Cooper, 'Greek Philosophers on Euthanasia and Suicide', in [943], 9–38

[48] *Corpus dei papiri filosofici Greci e Latini* part 1, vol. 1 (1) (Florence, 1989)

[49] *Corpus dei papiri filosofici Greci e Latini* part 1, vol. 1 (2) (Florence, 1992)

[50] K. J. Dover, *Greek Popular Morality in the Time of Plato and Aristotle* (Oxford, 1974, reprinted Indianapolis, 1994)

[51] S. Engstrom and J. Whiting (edd.), *Rethinking Duty and Happiness: Aristotle the Stoics and Kant* (Cambridge, 1996)

[52] D. J. Furley, *Two Studies in the Greek Atomists* (Princeton, 1967)

[53] J. C. B. Gosling and C. C. W. Taylor, *The Greeks on Pleasure* (Oxford, 1982)

[54] F. Heinimann, *Nomos and Phusis* (Basle, 1965)

[55] T. H. Irwin, 'Prudence and Morality in Greek Ethics', *Ethics* 105 (1995), 284–95

[56] W. Jaeger, *Paideia: The Ideals of Greek Culture*, vol. 2, tr. G. Highet (Oxford, 1944)

[57] H. Lloyd-Jones, *The Justice of Zeus*, 2nd edn (Berkeley, 1983)

[58] A. Momigliano, *The Development of Greek Biography* (Cambridge, Mass., 1971)

[59] H. North, *Sophrosune* (Cornell, 1966)

[60] M. C. Nussbaum, *The Fragility of Goodness* (Cambridge, 1986)

[61] S. Panagiotou (ed.), *Justice, Law, and Method in Plato and Aristotle* (Edmonton, 1987)

[62] W. J. Prior, *Virtue and Knowledge* (London, 1991)

[63] A. O. Rorty, 'Plato and Aristotle on Belief, Habit and *Akrasia*', *American Philosophical Quarterly* 7 (1970), 50–61

[64] D. Sedley, 'Philosophical Allegiance in the Greco-Roman World', in [727], 97–119

[65] R. R. K. Sorabji, *Animal Minds and Human Morals* (London, 1993)

[66] G. Striker, 'Origins of the Concept of Natural Law', *Proceedings of the Boston Area Colloquium in Ancient Philosophy* 2 (1987), 79–94 and in her [730], 209–20

[67] G. Striker, 'Greek Ethics and Moral Theory', in her [730], 169–82

[68] C. C. W. Taylor, 'Popular Morality and Unpopular Philosophy', in [14], 233–43

[69] J. Walter, *Die Lehre von der praktischen Vernunft in der griechischen Philosophie* (Jena, 1874)

[70] B. Williams, 'Philosophy', in [20], 202–55

A major treatment of the ethical theories of Aristotle and the Hellenistic schools is

[71] J. Annas, *The Morality of Happiness* (Oxford, 1993).

This is reviewed in

[72] T. H. Irwin, 'Happiness, Virtue and Morality', *Ethics* 104 (1994), and is the
subject of two interchanges:

[73] N. Sherman, 'Ancient Conceptions of Happiness', *Philosophy and
Phenomenological Research* 55 (1995), 913–20

[74] J. M. Cooper, 'Eudaimonism and the Appeal to Nature in the Morality
of Happiness: Comments on Julia Annas' *The Morality of
Happiness*', *Philosophy and Phenomenological Research* 55 (1995),
921–8

[75] J. Annas, 'Reply to Commentators', *Philosophy and Phenomenological
Research* 55 (1995), 929–38,
and

[76] R. Crisp, 'Ancient Wisdoms', *Philosophical Books* 35 (1994), 233–40

[77] J. Annas, 'Response to Crisp', *Philosophical Books* 35 (1994), 241–5.

Presocratics and sophists

Texts and translations

The writings of the Presocratic philosophers survive only in fragments
cited by later writers. The standard collection of these fragments, together
with later ancient reports of Presocratic philosophy, is

[78] H. Diels and W. Kranz, *Die Fragmente der Vorsokratiker*, 10th edn (Berlin,
1960).

Translations of all the fragments within their doxographical context are
provided in

[79] J. Barnes, *Early Greek Philosophy* (Harmondsworth, 1987).

[80] R. D. McKirahan jr, *Philosophy Before Socrates* (Indianapolis, 1994)
provides a good selection of Presocratic fragments in translation together
with a commentary.

The following provide general accounts of the Presocratics:

[81] J. Barnes, *The Presocratics*, 2 vols. (London, 1979); revised in one volume
(London, 1982)

[82] H. Fränkel, *Early Greek Poetry and Philosophy*, tr. by M. Hadas and J. Willis
(Oxford, 1975)

[83] E. Hussey, *The Presocratics* (London, 1972)

[84] C .H. Kahn, 'Presocratic Greek Ethics', in [937]

[85] G. S. Kirk, J. E. Raven and M. Schofield, *The Presocratic Philosophers*, 2nd
edn (Cambridge, 1983).

For general accounts of the sophists, see

[86] G. B. Kerferd, *The Sophistic Movement* (Cambridge, 1981)

[87] J. De Romilly, *Les Grands Sophistes dans l'Athènes de Périclès* (Paris, 1988),
which is translated by Janet Lloyd as

[88] J. De Romilly, *The Great Sophists in Periclean Athens* (Oxford, 1992).
See also

[89] G. B. Kerferd (ed.), *The Sophists and their Legacy*, Hermes Einzelschrift 44
(1982), 92–108.

Two collections of articles on Presocratic philosophy are

[90] D. J. Furley and R. E. Allen (edd.), *Studies in Presocratic Philosophy*, 2 vols. (London, 1970, 1975)

[91] A. P. D. Mourelatos (ed.), *The Presocratics*, 2nd edn (Garden City, 1993). See also

[92] H. Fränkel, *Wege und Formen frühgriechischen Denkens*, 2nd edn (Munich, 1960).

[93] C. J. Classen (ed.), *Sophistik, Wege der Forschung* 187 (Darmstadt, 1976)

[94] G. B. Kerferd (ed.), *The Sophists and their Legacy* (Wiesbaden, 1981) are collections of essays on the Sophists.

Heraclitus

[95] C. H. Kahn, *The Art and Thought of Heraclitus* (Cambridge, 1979)

Democritus

[96] C. H. Kahn, 'Democritus and the Origins of Moral Psychology', *American Journal of Philology* 106 (1985), 1–31

[97] M. Nill, *Morality and Self-Interest in Protagoras, Antiphon and Democritus* (Leiden, 1985)

[98] J. F. Procopé, 'Democritus on Politics and the Care of the Soul', *Classical Quarterly* 39 (1989), 307–31

[99] J. F. Procopé, 'Democritus on Politics and the Care of the Soul: Appendix', *Classical Quarterly* 40 (1990), 21–45

[100] C. C. W. Taylor, 'Pleasure, Knowledge and Sensation in Democritus', *Phronesis* 6 (1961), 10–28

[101] G. Vlastos, 'Ethics and Physics in Democritus', in [33], vol.1, 378–50

Solon

[102] G. Vlastos, 'Solonian Justice', *Classical Philology* 41 (1946), 65–83, and in
[33], vol. 1, 32–56

Sophists

[103] A. W. H. Adkins, '*Arete, Techne*, Democracy, and Sophists', *Journal of Hellenic Studies* 93 (1973), 3–12

[104] J. L. Creed, 'Moral Values in the Age of Thucydides', *Classical Quarterly* 23 (1973), 213–31

[105] D. J. Furley, 'Antiphon's Case Against Justice', in [94], 81–91

[106] C. H. Kahn, 'The Origins of the Social Contract Theory in the Fifth Century B.C.', in [94], 92–108

[107] T. J. Saunders, 'Antiphon the Sophist on Natural Laws (B44DK)', *Proceedings of the Aristotelian Society* 78 (1977–8), 215–36

Socrates

Our major source of evidence for Socrates' views and his approach to philosophy is the early dialogues of Plato. Translations of these can be found in

[108] T. J. Saunders (ed.), *Early Socratic Dialogues* (Harmondsworth, 1987) as well as in [285] and [286].

The role of Socrates in these dialogues is examined in
[109] T. Penner, 'Socrates in the Early Dialogues', in [303], 121–69.

For doubts about the status of the early dialogues as reasonably direct evidence for Socratic views, see
[110] C. H. Kahn, 'Did Plato Write Socratic Dialogues?', *Classical Quarterly* 31 (1981), 305–20, and in [129], 35–52.
See also
[111] C. H. Kahn, 'Plato's *Charmides* and the Proleptic Reading of Socratic Dialogues', *Journal of Philosophy* 85 (1988), 541–9.

An important collection of texts is
[112] G. Giannantoni, *Socratis et Socraticorum Reliquiae*, 2nd edn, 4 vols. (Naples, 1990).

Two translations of individual dialogues, together with commentaries, are
[113] R. E. Allen, *Plato's Euthyphro and the Earlier Theory of Forms* (London, 1970)
[114] P. Woodruff, *Plato's Hippias Major* (Oxford, 1982).

General studies of Socratic thought include
[115] T. Brickhouse and N. D. Smith, *Plato's Socrates* (Oxford, 1994)
[116] A. Gomez-Lóbo, *The Foundations of Socratic Ethics* (Indianapolis, 1994)
[117] N. Gulley, *The Philosophy of Socrates* (London, 1968)
[118] G. Santas, *Socrates* (London, 1979)
[119] M. C. Stokes, *Plato's Socratic Conversations* (London, 1986)
[120] G. Vlastos, *Socrates, Ironist and Moral Philosopher* (Cambridge, 1991)
[121] G. Vlastos, *Socratic Studies* (Cambridge, 1994) as well as chs. 1–9 of [294].
There are several helpful reviews of [120], which include
[122] T. H. Irwin, 'Socratic Puzzles', *Oxford Studies in Ancient Philosophy* 10 (1992), 241–66
[123] C. H. Kahn, 'Vlastos' Socrates', *Phronesis* 37 (1992), 233–58
[124] R. Kraut, 'Review of G. Vlastos', *Philosophical Review* 101 (1992)
[125] A. Nehamas, 'Voices of Silence: On Gregory Vlastos' Socrates', *Arion* 2 (1992), 157–86.
See also
[126] A. Patzer, *Der historische Sokrates* (Darmstadt, 1987)
[127] A. A. Long, 'Socrates in Hellenistic Philosophy', *Classical Quarterly* 38 (1988), 150–71, and in his [805], 1–34.

Collections of essays on Socrates are
[128] G. Vlastos (ed.), *The Philosophy of Socrates* (Garden City, 1971)
[129] H. H. Benson (ed.), *Essays on the Philosophy of Socrates* (New York/Oxford, 1992)

[130] B. S. Gower and M. C. Stokes (eds.), *Socratic Questions: The Philosophy of Socrates and its Significance* (London, 1991).

Method

[131] H. H. Benson, 'A Note on Eristic and the Socratic Elenchus', *Journal of the History of Philosophy* 27 (1989), 591–9

[132] H. H. Benson, 'The Priority of Definition and the Socratic Elenchus', *Oxford Studies in Ancient Philosophy* 8 (1990), 19–65

[133] H. H. Benson, 'Misunderstanding the "What is F-ness" Question', *Archiv für Geschichte der Philosophie* 72 (1990), 125–42 and in [129], 123–36

[134] H. H. Benson, 'The Dissolution of the Problem of the Elenchus', *Oxford Studies in Ancient Philosophy* 13 (1995), 45–112

[135] J. Beversluis, 'Socratic Definition', *American Philosophical Quarterly* 11 (1974), 331–6

[136] T. C. Brickhouse and N. D. Smith, 'Vlastos on the Elenchus', *Oxford Studies in Ancient Philosophy* 2 (1984), 185–96

[137] T. C. Brickhouse and N. D. Smith, 'Socrates' Elenctic Mission', *Oxford Studies in Ancient Philosophy* 9 (1991), 131–60

[138] M. F. Burnyeat, 'Examples in Epistemology: Socrates, Theaetetus and G. E. Moore', *Philosophy* 52 (1977), 381–98

[139] T. H. Irwin, 'Coercion and Objectivity in Plato's Dialectic', *Revue Internationale de Philosophie* 40 (1986), 47–74

[140] G. Nakhnikian, 'Elenctic Definitions', in [128], 125–57

[141] R. Polansky, 'Professor Vlastos' Analysis of Socratic Elenchus', *Oxford Studies in Ancient Philosophy* 3 (1985), 247–59

[142] G. Vlastos, 'What did Socrates Understand by his "What is F?" Question?', in his [308], 410–17

[143] G. Vlastos, 'The Socratic Elenchus', *Oxford Studies in Ancient Philosophy* 1 (1983), 27–58, and in [121], 1–37

[144] G. Vlastos, 'Elenchus and Mathematics: A Turning Point in Plato's Philosophical Development', *American Journal of Philology* 109 (1988), 362–96, and in [120], ch. 4

The 'Socratic fallacy'

See, first,

[145] P. T. Geach, 'Plato's *Euthyphro*: An Analysis and Commentary', *Monist* 50 (1966), 369–82, reprinted in his [947], 31–44.

Geach's attribution to Socrates of this fallacy is discussed in

[146] J. Beversluis, 'Does Socrates Commit the Socratic Fallacy?', *American Philosophical Quarterly* 24 (1987), 211–23, and in [129], 107–22

[147] G. Santas, 'The Socratic Fallacy', *Journal of the History of Philosophy* 10 (1972), 127–41

[148] G. Vlastos, 'Is the Socratic Fallacy Socratic?', *Ancient Philosophy* 10 (1990), 1–16, and in [121], 67–86.

Socrates' own protestations of ignorance are discussed in

[149] S. Austin, 'The Paradox of Socratic Ignorance (How to Know that You Don't Know)', *Philosophical Topics* 15 (1987), 23–34

[150] J. H. Lesher, 'Socrates' Disavowal of Knowledge', *Journal of the History of Philosophy* 25 (1987), 275–88

[151] M. M. Mackenzie, 'The Virtues of Socratic Ignorance', *Classical Quarterly* 38 (1988), 331–50

[152] G. Rudebusch, 'Plato's Aporetic Style', *Southern Journal of Philosophy* 27 (1989), 539–47

[153] G. Vlastos, 'Socrates' Disavowal of Knowledge', *Philosophical Quarterly* 35 (1985), 1–31, which is revised in [121], 39–66.

Virtue, knowledge and akrasia

[154] J. Annas, 'Virtue as the Use of Other Goods', *Apeiron* 26 (1993), 53–66

[155] M. F. Burnyeat, 'Virtues in Action', in [128], 209–34

[156] G. R. F. Ferrari, '*Akrasia* as Neurosis in Plato's *Protagoras*', *Proceedings of the Boston Area Colloquium in Ancient Philosophy* 6 (1990), 115–40

[157] G. Nakhnikian, 'The First Socratic Paradox', *Journal of the History of Philosophy* 10 (1973), 1–17

[158] A. Nehamas, 'Socratic Intellectualism', *Proceedings of the Boston Area Colloquium in Ancient Philosophy* 2 (1986), 275–316

[159] T. Penner, 'Socrates on Virtue and Motivation', in [25], 133–51

[160] T. Penner, 'Desire and Power in Socrates', *Apeiron* 24 (1991), 147–201

[161] G. Santas, 'The Socratic Paradoxes', *Philosophical Review* 73 (1964), 147–64, and in his [118], ch. 6

[162] G. Santas, 'Socrates at Work on Virtue and Knowledge in Plato's *Charmides*', in [25], 105–32

[163] G. Santas, 'Socrates at Work on Virtue and Knowledge in Plato's *Laches*', *Review of Metaphysics* 22 (1969), 433–60, and in [128], 177–208

[164] G. Vlastos, 'Socrates on *Acrasia*', *Phoenix* 23 (1969), 71–88, and his [33], vol. 2, 43–59

[165] J. J. Walsh, 'The Socratic Denial of Akrasia', in [128], 235–63

Virtue as a technē

[166] J. Annas, 'Virtue as a Skill', *International Journal of Philosophical Studies* 3 (1995), 227–43

[167] G. Klosko, 'The Technical Conception of Virtue' *Journal of the History of Philosophy* 19 (1981), 98–106

[168] J. Kube, *Techne und Arete* (Berlin, 1969)

[169] G. Lesses, 'Virtue as Techne in the Early Dialogues' *Southwest Philosophical Studies* 13 (1982), 93–100

[170] D. L. Roochnik, 'Socrates' Use of the Techne-Analogy', *Journal of the History of Philosophy* 24 (1986), 295–310, and in [129], 185–97

[171] E. Warren, 'The Craft Analogy: An Argument', in [302], 101–16

The parts of virtue and the unity of virtue

[172] D. Devereux, 'The Unity of the Virtues in Plato's *Protagoras* and *Laches*', *Philosophical Review* 101 (1992), 765–89

[173] M. Ferejohn, 'The Unity of Virtue and the Objects of Socratic Inquiry', *Journal of the History of Philosophy* 20 (1982), 1–21

[174] M. Ferejohn, 'Socratic Thought-Experiments and the Unity of Virtue Paradox', *Phronesis* 29 (1984), 105–22

[175] C. H. Kahn, 'Plato on the Unity of the Virtues', in [309], 21–39

[176] T. Penner, 'The Unity of Virtue', *Philosophical Review* 82 (1973), 35–68, and in [129], 162–84

[177] G. Vlastos, 'Socrates on the "Parts of Virtue"', in [308], 418–23

[178] P. Woodruff, 'Socrates on the Parts of Virtue', in *New Essays on Plato and the Presocratics* (*Canadian Journal of Philosophy*, Suppl. 2 (1976)), 101–16

Virtue, pleasure and happiness

[179] T. C. Brickhouse and N. D. Smith, 'Socrates on Goods, Virtue and Happiness', *Oxford Studies in Ancient Philosophy* 5 (1987), 1–28

[180] T. H. Irwin, 'Socrates the Epicurean?', *Illinois Classical Studies* 11 (1986), ch. 6, and in [129], 198–219

[181] G. Klosko, 'Socrates on Goods and Happiness', *History of Philosophy Quarterly* 4 (1987), 251–64

[182] G. Rudebusch, 'Callicles' Hedonism', *Ancient Philosophy* 12 (1992), 53–71

[183] G. Santas, 'Socratic Goods and Socratic Happiness', *Apeiron* 26 (1993), 37–52

[184] G. Vlastos, 'Happiness and Virtue in Socrates' Moral Theory', *Proceedings of the Cambridge Philological Society* 30 (1984), 182–213

[185] D. Zeyl, 'Socrates and Hedonism', *Phronesis* 25 (1980), 250–69, and in [302], 5–26

[186] D. Zeyl, 'Socratic Virtue and Happiness', *Archiv für Geschichte der Philosophie* 64 (1982), 225–38

Courage (and the Laches)

[187] D. T. Devereux, 'Courage and Wisdom in Plato's *Laches*', *Journal of the History of Philosophy* 15 (1977), 129–41

[188] C. S. Gould, 'Socratic Intellectualism and the Problem of Courage: An Interpretation of Plato's *Laches*', *History of Philosophy Quarterly* 4 (1987), 265–79

[189] R. G. Hoerber, 'Plato's *Laches*', *Classical Philology* 63 (1968), 95–105

[190] C. H. Kahn, 'Plato's Methodology in the *Laches*', *Revue Internationale de Philosophie* 40 (1986), 7–21

[191] M. J. O'Brien, 'The Unity of the *Laches*', *Yale Classical Studies* 9 (1963), 131–47

[192] T. Penner, 'What Laches and Nicias Miss', *Ancient Philosophy* 12 (1992), 1–27

[193] M. T. Tatham, *Plato's Laches* (New York, 1966)

[194] W. T. Schmid, 'The Socratic Conception of Courage', *History of Philosophy Quarterly* 2 (1985), 113–30

Sophrosunē (and the Charmides)

[195] C. Chung-Hwan, 'On Plato's *Charmides* 165c4–175d5', *Apeiron* 12 (1979), 13–28

[196] M. Dyson, 'Some Problems Concerning Knowledge in Plato's *Charmides*', *Phronesis* 19 (1974), 102–11

[197] D. A. Hyland, *The Virtue of Philosophy: An Interpretation of Plato's Charmides* (Athens, Ohio, 1981)

[198] R. J. Ketchum, 'Plato on the Uselessness of Epistemology: *Charmides* 166e–172a', *Apeiron* 24 (1991), 81–98

[199] L. A. Kosman, '*Charmides*' First Definition: *Sophrosune* as Quietness', in [9], 203–16

[200] R. McKim, 'Socratic Self-Knowledge and "Knowledge of Knowledge" in Plato's *Charmides*', *Transactions of the American Philological Association* 115 (1985), 59–77

[201] W. T. Schmid, 'Socrates' Practice of Elenchus in the *Charmides*', *Ancient Philosophy* 1 (1981), 141–7

[202] W. T. Schmid, 'Socratic Moderation and Self-Knowledge', *Journal of the History of Philosophy* 21 (1983), 339–48

[203] G. T. Tuckey, *Plato's Charmides* (Amsterdam, 1968)

[204] R. R. Wellman, 'The Question Posed at *Charmides* 165a–166c', *Phronesis* 9 (1964), 107–13

Justice

[205] G. Vlastos, 'Socrates' Contribution to the Greek Sense of Justice', *Arkaiognosia* 1 (1980), 301–24

The Euthyphro *and piety*

As well as [113] and [145], see

[206] D. E. Anderson, 'Socrates' Concept of Piety', *Journal of the History of Philosophy* 5 (1967), 1–13

[207] S. W. Calef, 'Piety and the Unity of Virtue in *Euthyphro* 11E–14c', *Oxford Studies in Ancient Philosophy* 13 (1995), 1–26

[208] M. McPherran, 'Socratic Piety: In Response to Scott Calef', *Oxford Studies in Ancient Philosophy* 13 (1995), 27–36

[209] S. W. Calef, 'Further Reflections on Socratic Piety: A Reply to Mark McPherran', *Oxford Studies in Ancient Philosophy* 13 (1995), 37–46

[210] S. Candlish, '*Euthyphro* 6d-9b and its Misinterpretations', *Apeiron* 17 (1983), 28–32

[211] S.M. Cohen, 'Socrates on the Definition of Piety', *Journal of the History of Philosophy* 9 (1971), and in [128], 158–76

[212] R. Garrett, 'The Structure of Plato's *Euthyphro*', *Southern Journal of Philosophy* 12 (1974), 165–83

[213] R. G. Hoerber, 'Plato's *Euthyphro*', *Phronesis* 3 (1958), 95–107

[214] J. H. Lesher, 'Theistic Ethics and the *Euthyphro*', *Apeiron* 9 (1975), 24–30

[215] M. McPherran, 'Socratic Piety in the *Euthyphro*', *Journal of the History of Philosophy* 23 (1985), 283–309, and in [129], 220–41

[216] W. G. Rabinowitz, 'Platonic Piety: An Essay Toward the Solution of an Enigma', *Phronesis* 2 (1958), 108–20

[217] F. Rosen, 'Piety and Justice: Plato's "Euthyphro"', *Philosophy* 43 (1968), 105–16

[218] R. Sharvy, '*Euthyphro* 9d–11b: Analysis and Definition in Plato and Others', *Nous* 6 (1972), 119–37

[219] C. C. W. Taylor, 'The End of the *Euthyphro*', *Phronesis* 27 (1982), 109–18

[220] L. Versenyi, *Holiness and Justice: An Interpretation of the Euthyphro* (Washington, D.C., 1982)

[221] R. Weiss, 'Virtue without Knowledge: Socrates' Conception of Holiness in Plato's *Euthyphro*', *Ancient Philosophy* 14 (1994), 263–82

[222] R. Weiss, 'Euthyphro's Failure', *Journal of the History of Philosophy* 24 (1986), 437–53.
See also:

[223] M. McPherran, 'Socrates on Teleological and Moral Theology', *Ancient Philosophy* 14 (1994), 245–62.

Philia *(and the* Lysis*)*

[224] D. Adams, 'The *Lysis* Puzzles', *History of Philosophy Quarterly* 9 (1992), 3–17

[225] D. Bolotin, *Plato's Dialogue on Friendship* (Ithaca, 1979)

[226] D. K. Glidden, 'The *Lysis* on Loving One's Own', *Classical Quarterly* 31 (1981), 39–59

[227] G. Lesses, 'Plato's *Lysis* and Irwin's Socrates', *International Studies in Philosophy* 18 (1986), 33–43

[228] D. N. Levin, 'Some Observations concerning Plato's *Lysis*', in [9], 236–58

[229] D. B. Robinson, 'Plato's *Lysis*: The Structural Problem', *Illinois Classical Studies* 11 (1986), 63–84

[230] A. Tessitore, 'Plato's *Lysis*: An Introduction to Philosophical Friendship', *Southern Journal of Philosophy* 28 (1990), 115–32

[231] C. W. Tindale, 'Plato's *Lysis*: A Reconsideration', *Apeiron* 18 (1984), 102–9

[232] L. Versenyi, 'Plato's *Lysis*', *Phronesis* 20 (1975), 185–98

Two dialogues which are probably slightly later than the very early ones but in which recognisably 'Socratic' views are presented are the *Protagoras* and the *Gorgias*. For the dating of these works, see

[233] C. H. Kahn, 'On the Relative Date of the *Gorgias* and the *Protagoras*', *Oxford Studies in Ancient Philosophy* 6 (1988), 69–102

[234] M. L. McPherran, 'Comments on Charles Kahn, "The Relative Date of the *Gorgias* and the *Protagoras*"', *Oxford Studies in Ancient Philosophy* 8 (1990), 211–36

[235] C. H. Kahn, 'In Response to Mark McPherran', *Oxford Studies in Ancient Philosophy* 9 (1991), 161–8.

The Protagoras

A commentary on the Greek text is

[236] J. and A. M. Adam, *Platonis Protagoras*, 2nd edn (Cambridge, 1905).

A commentary on the dialogue in translation is

[237] C. C. W. Taylor, *Plato, Protagoras*, 2nd edn (Oxford 1991).

[238] Plato, *Protagoras*, tr. by S. Lombardo and K. Bell (Indianapolis, 1992), contains a helpful introduction by Michael Frede, and

[239] G. Vlastos (ed.), *Plato, Protagoras* (Indianapolis, 1956), one by Gregory Vlastos.

[240] A. W. H. Adkins, '*Arete, Techne*, Democracy and Sophists: *Protagoras* 316b–328d', *Journal of Hellenic Studies* 93 (1973), 3–12

[241] W. S. Cobb, 'The Argument of the *Protagoras*', *Dialogue* 21 (1982), 713–31

[242] J. Cronquist, 'The Point of the Hedonism in Plato's *Protagoras*', *Prudentia* 12 (1980), 63–81

[243] D. T. Devereux, 'Protagoras on Courage and Knowledge: *Protagoras* 351a–b', *Apeiron* 9 (1975), 37–9

[244] R. Duncan, 'Courage in Plato's *Protagoras*', *Phronesis* 23 (1978), 216–28

[245] M. Dyson, 'Knowledge and Hedonism in Plato's *Protagoras*', *Journal of Hellenic Studies* 96 (1976), 32–45

[246] D. Frede, 'The Impossibility of Perfection: Socrates' Criticism of Simonides' Poem in the *Protagoras*', *Review of Metaphysics* 39 (1986), 729–53

[247] M. Gagarin, 'The Purpose of Plato's *Protagoras*', *Transactions of the American Philological Association* 100 (1969), 133–64

[248] D. Gallop, 'Justice and Holiness in *Protagoras* 330–331', *Phronesis* 6 (1961), 86–93

[249] D. Gallop, 'The Socratic Paradox in the *Protagoras*', *Phronesis* 9 (1964), 117–29

[250] G. M. A. Grube, 'The Structural Unity of the *Protagoras*', *Classical Quarterly* 27 (1933), 203–7

[251] N. Gulley, 'Socrates' Thesis at *Protagoras* 358b–c', *Phoenix* 25 (1971), 118–23

[252] R. Hackforth, 'Hedonism in Plato's *Protagoras*', *Classical Quarterly* 22 (1928), 39–42

[253] C. H. Kahn, 'Plato and Socrates in the *Protagoras*', *Methexis* 1 (1988), 33–52

[254] G. Klosko, 'Towards a Consistent Interpretation of the *Protagoras*', *Archiv für Geschichte der Philosophie* 61 (1979), 125–42

[255] G. Klosko, 'On the Analysis of *Protagoras* 351b–360e', *Phoenix* 34 (1980), 307–22

[256] R. D. McKirahan, 'Socrates and Protagoras on *Sophrosune* and Justice (*Protagoras* 333–334)', *Apeiron* 18 (1984), 19–25

[257] R. D. McKirahan, 'Socrates and Protagoras on Holiness and Justice (*Protagoras* 330c–332a)', *Phoenix* 39 (1985), 342–54

[258] B. Manuwald, 'Lust und Tapferkeit: Zum gedanklichen Verhältnis zweier Abschnitte in Platons *Protagoras*', *Phronesis* 20 (1975), 22–50

[259] H. S. Richardson, 'Measurement, Pleasure, and Practical Science in Plato's *Protagoras*', *Journal of the History of Philosophy* 28 (1990), 7–32

[260] G. Rudebusch, 'Plato, Hedonism and Ethical Protagoreanism', in [302], 27–40

[261] G. Santas, 'Plato's *Protagoras* and the Explanations of Weakness', *Philosophical Review* 75 (1966), 3–33, and in [128], 264–98

[262] M. Schofield, 'Socrates versus Protagoras', in [130], 122–36

[263] J. P. Sullivan, 'The Hedonism in Plato's *Protagoras*', *Phronesis* 6 (1961), 9–28

[264] G. Vlastos, 'The Unity of Virtues in the *Protagoras*', in [308], 221–65

[265] J. Walsh, 'The Dramatic Dates of Plato's *Protagoras* and the Lesson of Arete', *Classical Quarterly* 34 (1984), 101–6

[266] J. Wakefield, 'Why Justice and Holiness are Similar: *Protagoras* 330–331', *Phronesis* 32 (1987), 267–76

[267] R. Weiss, 'Socrates and Protagoras on Justice and Holiness', *Phoenix* 39
       (1985), 334–41
[268] R. Weiss, 'Courage, Confidence, and Widom in the *Protagoras*', *Ancient
       Philosophy* 5 (1985), 11–24
[269] R. Weiss, 'The Hedonic Calculus in the *Protagoras* and the *Phaedo*', *Journal
       of the History of Philosophy* 27 (1989), 511–29
[270] R. Weiss, 'Hedonism in the *Protagoras* and the Sophist's Guarantee',
       Ancient Philosophy 10 (1990), 17–40

The Gorgias

A commentary on the Greek text is
[271] E. R. Dodds, *Plato's Gorgias* (Oxford, 1959).
       A commentary on the dialogue in translation is
[272] T. H. Irwin, *Plato, Gorgias* (Oxford, 1979).
[273] S. Berman, 'How Polus was Refuted: Reconsidering Plato's *Gorgias*
       474c–475c', *Ancient Philosophy* 11 (1991), 265–84
[274] J. M. Cooper, 'The *Gorgias* and Irwin's Socrates', *Review of Metaphysics* 35
       (1982), 577–87
[275] G. Calogero, '*Gorgias* and the Socratic Principle *Nemo sua sponte peccat*',
       Journal of Hellenic Studies 77 (1957), 12–17
[276] R. Duncan, '*Philia* in the *Gorgias*', *Apeiron* 8 (1974), 23–6
[277] R. W. Hall, '*Techne* and Morality in the *Gorgias*', in [9], 202–18
[278] C. N. Johnson, 'Socrates' Encounter with Polus in Plato's *Gorgias*', *Phoenix*
       43 (1989), 196–216
[279] K. McTighe, 'Socrates on Desire for the Good and the Involuntariness of
       Wrong-Doing: *Gorgias* 466a–468e', *Phronesis* 29 (1984), 193–236, and in
       [129], 263–97
[280] M. M. Mackenzie, 'A Pyrrhic Victory: *Gorgias* 474b–477a', *Classical
       Quarterly* 32 (1982), 84–8
[281] M. A. Principe, 'Restraint of Desire in the *Gorgias*', *Southern Journal of
       Philosophy* 20 (1982), 121–32
[282] W. H. Race, 'Shame in Plato's *Gorgias*', *Classical Journal* 74 (1979),
       197–202
[283] G. Vlastos, 'Was Polus Refuted?', *American Journal of Philology* 88 (1967),
       454–60
[284] N. P. White, 'Rational Prudence in Plato's *Gorgias*', in [305], 139–62

Plato

Translations of all the dialogues, by various hands, can be found in
[285] E. Hamilton and H. Cairns (edd.), *The Collected Dialogues of Plato*
       (Princeton, 1961)
       and
[286] J. M. Cooper and D. S. Hutchinson (edd.), *Plato: Complete Works*
       (Indianapolis, 1996).

Introductions

[287] I. M. Crombie, *An Examination of Plato's Doctrines*, 2 vols. (London, 1962,
       1963)

[288] J. C. B. Gosling, *Plato* (London, 1973)

[289] G. Grote, *Plato and Other Companions of Socrates* (London, 1865)

[290] R. Kraut, 'Introduction to the Study of Plato', in [303], 1–50

[291] J. E. Raven, *Plato's Thought in the Making* (Cambridge, 1965)

[292] C. J. Rowe, *Plato* (Brighton, 1984)

The following are wide-ranging studies of various aspects of Plato's thought:

[293] T. H. Irwin, *Plato's Moral Theory* (Oxford, 1977), which has been revised and expanded as

[294] T. H. Irwin, *Plato's Ethics* (Oxford, 1995)

[295] J. Moline, *Plato's Theory of Understanding* (Wisconsin/London, 1981)

[296] R. Robinson, *Plato's Earlier Dialectic* (Oxford, 1953)

[297] K. M. Sayre, *Plato's Analytical Method* (Chicago/London, 1969)

[298] P. Shorey, *What Plato Said* (Chicago, 1933)

[299] A. E. Taylor, *Plato, the Man and his Work* (London, 1926)

[300] N. P. White, *Plato on Knowledge and Reality* (Indianapolis, 1976).

The following contain articles on Plato:

[301] R. E. Allen (ed.), *Studies in Plato's Metaphysics* (London, 1965)

[302] J. P. Anton and A. Preus (edd.), *Essays in Ancient Greek Philosophy*, vol. 3: *Plato* (Albany, 1989)

[303] R. Kraut (ed.), *The Cambridge Companion to Plato* (Cambridge, 1992)

[304] J. Moravcsik (ed.), *Patterns in Plato's Thought* (Dordrecht, 1973)

[305] D. J. O'Meara (ed.), *Platonic Investigations* (Washington, D.C., 1985)

[306] G. Vlastos (ed.), *Plato*, vol. 1, *Metaphysics and Epistemology* (Garden City, 1971)

[307] G. Vlastos (ed.), *Plato*, vol. 2, *Ethics, Politics and Philosophy of Art and Religion* (Garden City, 1971)

[308] G. Vlastos, *Platonic Studies*, 2nd edn (Princeton, 1981)

[309] W. H. Werkemeister (ed.), *Facets of Plato's Philosophy*, *Phronesis*, Suppl. vol. 2 (1976).

The relative dating of the dialogues is discussed in

[310] G. E. L. Owen, 'The Place of the *Timaeus* in Plato's Dialogues', *Classical Quarterly* (1953), 79–95, in [301], 313–38 and in [29], 65–84

[311] H. Cherniss, 'The Relation of the *Timaeus* to Plato's Later Dialogues', *American Journal of Philology* (1957), 225–66, in [301], 339–78 and in his [13], 298–339

[312] L. Brandwood, *The Chronology of Plato's Dialogues* (Cambridge, 1990)

[313] L. Brandwood, 'Stylometry and Chronology', in [303], 90–120

[314] G. R. Ledger, *Re-Counting Plato: A Computer Analysis of Plato's Style* (Oxford, 1989).

The Meno

A commentary on the Greek text is

[315] R. S. Bluck, *Plato's Meno* (Cambridge, 1961).

[316] R.W. Sharples, *Plato: Meno* (Warminster, 1985) provides the Greek text, together with a facing translation and commentary.

[317] J. Brunschwig, 'Pouvoir Enseigner la Vertu?', *Revue Philosophique* 181 (1991), 591–602
[318] D. T. Devereux, 'Nature and Teaching in Plato's *Meno*', *Phronesis* 23 (1978), 118–26
[319] J. Barnes, 'Enseigner la vertu?', *Revue Philosophique* 181 (1991), 571–89
[320] K. V. Wilkes, 'Conclusions in the *Meno*', *Archiv für Geschichte der Philosophie* 61 (1979), 143–53
[321] H. Zyskind and R. Sternfeld, 'Plato's *Meno* 89c: "Virtue is Knowledge" a Hypothesis?', *Phronesis* 21 (1976), 130–4

The Republic

Translations of the *Republic* include
[322] Plato, *Republic*, tr. G. M. A. Grube (revised by C. D. C. Reeve) (Indianapolis, 1992)
[323] Plato, *The Republic*, with an English translation by P. Shorey, 2 vols. (Cambridge, Mass./London, 1935–7)
[324] Plato, *Republic*, tr. R. Waterfield (Oxford, 1993).

General and introductory studies include
[325] J. Annas, *An Introduction to Plato's Republic* (Oxford, 1981)
[326] R. C. Cross and A. D. Woozley, *Plato's Republic: A Philosophical Commentary* (London, 1964)
[327] N. R. Murphy, *The Interpretation of Plato's Republic* (Oxford, 1951)
[328] R. L. Nettleship, *Lectures on the Republic of Plato*, 2nd edn (London, 1901)
[329] C. D. C. Reeve, *Philosopher-Kings: The Argument of Plato's Republic* (Princeton, 1988)
[330] N. P. White, *A Companion to Plato's Republic* (Indianapolis, 1979).

Book I

[331] T. Y. Henderson, 'In Defence of Thrasymachus', *American Philosophical Quarterly* 7 (1970), 218–28
[332] C. H. Kahn, 'Proleptic Composition in the *Republic*, or Why Book I was Never a Separate Dialogue', *Classical Quarterly* 43 (1993), 31–42
[333] P. P. Nicholson, 'Unravelling Thrasymachus' Argument in the *Republic*', *Phronesis* 19 (1974), 210–32
[334] J. H. Quincey, 'Another Purpose for Plato, *Republic* I', *Hermes* 109 (1981), 300–15
[335] C. D. C. Reeve, 'Socrates Meets Thrasymachus', *Archiv für Geschichte der Philosophie* 67 (1985), 246–65
[336] S. G. Salkever, 'Plato on Practices: The *Technai* and Socrates' Question in *Republic* I', *Proceedings of the Boston Area Colloquium in Ancient Philosophy* 8 (1992), 243–67
[337] C. M. Young, 'Polemarchus' and Thrasymachus' Definitions of Justice', *Philosophical Inquiry* 2 (1980), 404–19

The good

[338] H. W. B. Joseph, *Knowledge and the Good in Plato's Republic* (Oxford, 1948)

[339] G. Santas, 'The Form of the Good in Plato's *Republic*, in [10], 232–63
[340] N. P. White, 'The Classifications of Goods in Plato's *Republic*', *Journal of the History of Philosophy* 22 (1984), 393–421
       See also:
[341] G. Santas, 'Aristotle's Criticism of Plato's Form of the Good: Ethics Without Metaphysics', *Philosophical Papers* 18 (1989), 137–60
[342] G. Fine, 'Knowledge and Belief in *Republic* v–vii', in [17], 85–115

The psuchē and motivation

[343] J. M. Cooper, 'Plato's Theory of Human Motivation', *History of Philosophy Quarterly* 1 (1984), 3–21
[344] A. Kenny, 'Mental Health in Plato's *Republic*', *Proceedings of the British Academy* 55 (1969), 229–53, and in his [954], 1–27
[345] G. Lesses, 'Weakness, Reason and the Divided Soul in Plato's *Republic*', *History of Philosophy Quarterly* 4 (1987), 147–61
[346] S. Lovibond, 'Plato's Theory of Mind', in [18], 35–55
[347] J. Moline, 'Plato on the Complexity of the Psyche', *Archiv für Geschichte der Philosophie* 60 (1978), 1–26
[348] T. Penner, 'Thought and Desire in Plato', in [307], 96–118
[349] T. Penner, 'Plato and Davidson: Parts of the Soul and Weakness of the Will', *Canadian Journal of Philosophy*, Suppl. 16 (1990), 35–74
[350] R. Robinson, 'Plato's Separation of Reason and Desire', *Phronesis* 16 (1971), 38–48
[351] R. F. Stalley, 'Plato's Arguments for the Division of the Reasoning and Appetitive Elements within the Soul', *Phronesis* 21 (1975), 110–28
[352] B. Williams, 'The Analogy of City and Soul in the *Republic*', in [25], 196–206
[353] M. J. Woods, 'Plato's Division of the Soul', *Proceedings of the British Academy* 73 (1987), 23–47

Justice, pleasure and happiness

[354] J. Annas, 'Plato and Common Morality', *Classical Quarterly* 28 (1978), 437–51
[355] J. M. Cooper, 'The Psychology of Justice in Plato', *American Philosophical Quarterly* 14 (1977), 151–57
[356] N. O. Dahl, 'Plato's Defence of Justice', *Philosophy and Phenomenological Research* 51 (1991), 809–34
[357] R. Demos, 'A Fallacy in Plato's *Republic?*', *Philosophical Review* 73 (1964), 395–8
[358] C. Kirwan, 'Glaucon's Challenge', *Phronesis* 10 (1965), 162–73
[359] R. Kraut, 'Reason and Justice in the *Republic*', in [25], 207–24
[360] R. Kraut, 'The Defence of Justice in Plato's *Republic*', in [303], 331–7
[361] R. Kraut, 'Return to the Cave', *Proceedings of the Boston Area Colloquium in Ancient Philosophy* 7 (1991), 43–62
[362] R. D. Parry, *Plato's Craft of Justice* (Albany, N.Y., 1996)
[363] D. Sachs, 'A Fallacy in Plato's *Republic*', *Philosophical Review* 72 (1963), 141–58, and in [307], 35–51
[364] M. C. Stokes, 'Some Pleasures of Plato, *Republic* IX', *Polis* 9 (1990), 2–51

[365] G. Vlastos, 'Justice and Happiness in the *Republic*', in [307], 66–95 and [308], 111–39

[366] N. P. White, 'Happiness and External Contingencies in Plato's *Republic*', in [972], 1–21
See also

[367] C. Gill, 'Plato and the Education of Character', *Archiv für Geschichte der Philosophie* 67 (1985), 1–26

[368] C. C. W. Taylor, 'Plato's Totalitarianism', *Polis* 5.2 (1986), 4–29.

The theory of Forms

[369] R. E. Allen, 'Participation and Predication in Plato's Middle Dialogues', *Philosophical Review* 69 (1960), 147–64 and in [301], 43–60

[370] D. Bostock, 'Plato on Understanding Language', in [19], 10–27

[371] G. Fine, 'Separation', *Oxford Studies in Ancient Philosophy* 2 (1984), 31–87

[372] J. C. B. Gosling, '*Republic* v: *Ta Polla Kala*, etc.', *Phronesis* 5 (1960), 116–28

[373] A. Nehamas, 'Participation and Predication in Plato's Later Thought', *Review of Metaphysics* 36 (1982), 343–74

[374] C. Stough, 'Forms and Explanation in Plato', *Phronesis* 21 (1976), 1–30

[375] R. Turnbull, 'Knowledge and the Forms in the Later Platonic Dialogues', *Proceedings and Addresses of the American Philosophical Association* 51 (1978), 735–58

[376] A. Wedberg, 'The Theory of Ideas', in [306], 28–52

[377] N. White, 'Plato's Metaphysical Epistemology', in [303], 277–310

The claim that Forms can be predicated of themselves is discussed in

[378] J. S. Clegg, 'Self-predication and Linguistic Reference in Plato's Theory of the Forms', *Phronesis* 18 (1973), 26–43

[379] J. Malcolm, 'Semantics and Self-predication in Plato', *Phronesis* 26 (1981), 286–94

[380] J. Malcolm, *Plato and the Self-predication of Forms* (Oxford, 1991)

[381] A. Nehamas, 'Self-predication and Plato's Theory of Forms', *American Philosophical Quarterly* 16 (1979), 93–103

[382] A. Silverman, 'Synonymy and Self-predication', *Ancient Philosophy* 10 (1990), 193–202

[383] G. Vlastos, 'On a Proposed Redefinition of "Self-predication" in Plato', *Phronesis* 26 (1981), 76–9 (which is a criticism of [381]).

[384] G. Fine, *On Ideas* (Oxford, 1993)
provides a thorough examination of Aristotle's discussion of the theory of Forms and thereby of the theory itself.

Statesman

[385] J. B. Skemp, *Plato's Statesman* (London, 1952)

Philebus

A commentary on the dialogue in translation is

[386] J. C. B. Gosling, *Plato, Philebus* (Oxford, 1975).

[387] J. M. Cooper, 'Plato's Theory of the Human Good in the *Philebus*', *Journal of Philosophy* 74 (1977), 714–30

[388] N. Cooper, 'Pleasure and the Good in Plato's *Philebus*', *Philosophical Quarterly* 18 (1968), 12–15

[389] D. Davidson, 'Plato's Philosopher', *Apeiron* 26 (1993), 179–94

[390] J. Dybikowski, 'False Pleasures and the *Philebus*', *Phronesis* 15 (1970), 147–65

[391] D. Frede, 'Rumpelstiltskin's Pleasures', *Phronesis* 30 (1985), 151–80

[392] D. Frede, 'Disintegration and Restoration: Pleasure and Pain in Plato's *Philebus*', in [303], 425–63

[393] J. C. B. Gosling, 'False Pleasures: *Philebus* 35c–41b', *Phronesis* 4 (1959), 44–54

[394] J. C. B. Gosling, 'Father Kenny on False Pleasures', *Phronesis* 5 (1960), 41–5

[395] C. Hampton, 'Pleasure, Truth and Being in Plato's *Philebus*: A Reply to Professor Frede', *Phronesis* 32 (1987), 253–62

[396] C. Hampton, *Pleasure, Knowledge and Being: An Analysis of Plato's Philebus* (Albany, 1990)

[397] A. Kenny, 'False Pleasures in the *Philebus*: A Reply to Mr. Gosling', *Phronesis* 5 (1960), 45–52

[398] O. Letwin, 'Interpreting the *Philebus*', *Phronesis* 26 (1981), 187–206

[399] T. Penner, 'False Anticipatory Pleasures', *Phronesis* 15 (1970), 166–78

[400] R. A. H. Waterfield, 'The Place of the *Philebus* in Plato's Dialogues', *Phronesis* 25 (1980), 270–305

Aristotle

A complete translation of Aristotle's surviving work is

[401] J. Barnes (ed.), *The Complete Works of Aristotle: The Revised Oxford Translation*, 2 vols. (Princeton, 1984).

Two useful selections of Aristotelian texts are

[402] J. L. Ackrill (ed.), *A New Aristotle Reader* (Oxford, 1987)

[403] T. H. Irwin and G. Fine (edd.), *Aristotle: Selections* (Indianapolis, 1995).

Introductions

Two short introductions to Aristotle's thought are

[404] J. L. Ackrill, *Aristotle the Philosopher* (Oxford, 1981)

[405] J. Barnes, *Aristotle* (Oxford, 1982).

Longer introductions include

[406] I. Düring, *Aristoteles: Darstellung und Interpretation seines Denkens* (Heidelberg, 1966)

[407] J. D. G. Evans, *Aristotle* (Brighton, 1987)

[408] J. Lear, *Aristotle: The Desire to Understand* (Cambridge, 1988)

[409] G. E. R. Lloyd, *Aristotle: The Growth and Structure of his Thought* (Cambridge, 1968)

[410] W. D. Ross, *Aristotle* (London, 1923).

[411] T. H. Irwin, *Aristotle's First Principles* (Oxford, 1988) provides a systematic account of Aristotle's thought and method.

The following are anthologies of articles on various aspects of Aristotle's thought:

[412] *Autour d'Aristote: Recueil d'études offert à Mgr Mansion* (Louvain, 1955)

[413] J. Barnes (ed.), *The Cambridge Companion to Aristotle* (Cambridge, 1995)

[414] J. Barnes, M. Schofield and R. Sorabji (edd.), *Articles on Aristotle*, vol. 1, *Science* (London, 1975)

[415] J. Barnes, M. Schofield and R. Sorabji (edd.), *Articles on Aristotle*, vol. 3, *Metaphysics* (London, 1979)

[416] J. Barnes, M. Schofield and R. Sorabji (edd.), *Articles on Aristotle*, vol. 4, *Psychology and Aesthetics* (London, 1979)

[417] E. Berti (ed.), *Aristotle on Science: The Posterior Analytics* (Padua/New York, 1980)

[418] I. Düring and G. E. L. Owen (edd.), *Plato and Aristotle in the Mid-fourth Century* (Gothenburg, 1960)

[419] D. J. Furley and A. Nehamas (edd.), *Aristotle's Rhetoric: Philosophical Essays* (Princeton, 1994)

[420] J. M. E. Moravcsik, *Aristotle* (Garden City, 1967 and Oxford, 1968)

[421] D .J. O'Meara (ed.), *Studies in Aristotle* (Washington, 1981)

[422] M. C. Nussbaum and A. O. Rorty (edd.), *Essays on Aristotle's De Anima* (Oxford, 1992)

[423] A. O. Rorty (ed.), *Essays on Aristotle's Rhetoric* (Berkeley and Los Angeles/ London, 1996)

[424] M. A. Sinaceur (ed.), *Penser avec Aristote* (Toulouse, 1991).

Translations of the *Nicomachean Ethics* include

[425] T. H. Irwin, Aristotle, *Nicomachean Ethics* (Indianapolis, 1985)

[426] W. D. Ross, *The Nicomachean Ethics of Aristotle* (London, 1954).

Commentaries on the Greek text are

[427] J. Burnet, *The Ethics of Aristotle* (London, 1900)

[428] F. Dirlmeier, *Aristoteles Nicomachische Ethik*, 2nd edn (Berlin, 1969)

[429] R. A. Gauthier and J. Y. Jolif, *Aristote: L'Ethique à Nicomaque*, 2nd edn (Paris/Louvain, 1970)

[430] J. A. Stewart, *Notes on the Nicomachean Ethics of Aristotle* (Oxford, 1892).

See also

[431] A. Grant, *The Ethics of Aristotle* (London, 1885)

[432] L. H. G. Greenwood, *Aristotle: Nicomachean Ethics Book VI* (Cambridge, 1909)

[433] H. H. Joachim, *Aristotle: The Nicomachean Ethics* (Oxford, 1955)

[434] G. Rodier, *Aristote: Ethique à Nicomaque, livre X* (Paris, 1897).

A commentary on the *Eudemian Ethics* is

[435] F. Dirlmeier, *Aristoteles Eudemische Ethik*, 2nd edn (Berlin, 1969).

A commentary on part of the *Eudemian Ethics* in translation is

[436] M. J. Woods, *Aristotle's Eudemian Ethics, Books I, II, and VIII*, 2nd edn (Oxford, 1992).

The relation between the *Nicomachean* and the *Eudemian Ethics* is discussed in

[437] C. J. Rowe, 'The *Eudemian* and *Nicomachean Ethics*: A Study in the Development of Aristotle's Thought', *Proceedings of the Cambridge Philological Society*, Supplement no. 3 (1971)

[438] A. Kenny, *The Aristotelian Ethics: A Study of the Relationship between the Eudemian and the Nicomachean Ethics of Aristotle* (Oxford, 1978)

[439] A. Kenny, 'The Relationship Between the *Eudemian* and *Nicomachean Ethics*', in his [457], 113–42. [438] is reviewed by

[440] D. Charles in *Journal for Hellenic Studies* 100 (1980), 224–5

[441] J. M. Cooper in *Nous* 15 (1981), 381–92

[442] T. H. Irwin in *Journal of Philosophy* 77 (1980), 338–54.

The authenticity of the *Magna Moralia* is a matter of great controversy. A commentary on the Greek text is

[443] F. Dirlmeier, *Aristoteles: Magna Moralia*, 2nd edn (Berlin, 1969), which defends its authenticity, as do

[444] I. Düring, 'Review of F. Dirlmeier, *Aristoteles: Magna Moralia*', *Gnomon* 33 (1961), 547–57, and

[445] J. M. Cooper, 'The *Magna Moralia* and Aristotle's Moral Philosophy', *American Journal of Philology* 94 (1973), 327–49. For doubts, see

[446] D. J. Allan, '*Magna Moralia* and *Nicomachean Ethics*', *Journal of Hellenic Studies* 77 (1957), 7–11

[447] P. L. Donini, *L'Etica dei Magna Moralia* (Turin, 1965)

[448] C. J. Rowe, 'A Reply to John Cooper on the *Magna Moralia*', *American Journal of Philology* 96 (1975), 160–72

[449] R. Walzer, *Magna Moralia und aristotelische Ethik* (Berlin, 1929).

General studies of Aristotle's ethics include

[450] G. Anagnostopoulos, *Aristotle on the Goals and Exactness of Ethics* (Berkeley and Los Angeles/London, 1994)

[451] S. Broadie, *Ethics with Aristotle* (Oxford, 1991)

[452] S. R. L. Clark, *Aristotle's Man* (Oxford, 1975)

[453] J. M. Cooper, *Reason and Human Good in Aristotle* (Cambridge, Mass., 1975)

[454] T. Engberg-Pedersen, *Aristotle's Theory of Moral Insight* (Oxford, 1983)

[455] R. A. Gauthier, *La Morale d'Aristote* (Paris, 1958)

[456] W. F. R. Hardie, *Aristotle's Ethical Theory*, 2nd edn (Oxford, 1980)

[457] A. Kenny, *Aristotle on the Perfect Life* (Oxford, 1992)

[458] R. Kraut, *Aristotle on the Human Good* (Princeton, 1989) (which is reviewed in

[459] T. H. Irwin, 'The Structure of Aristotelian Happiness', *Ethics* 101 (1991), 382–91)

[460] J. O. Urmson, *Aristotle's Ethics* (Oxford, 1988)

[461] S. A. White, *Sovereign Virtue: Aristotle on the Relation between Happiness and Prosperity* (Stanford, 1992). See also:

[462] T. H. Irwin, 'Ethics in the *Rhetoric* and in the *Ethics*', in [423], 142–74.

Collections of articles on Aristotelian ethics include:

[463] J. P. Anton and A. Preus (edd.), *Essays in Ancient Greek Philosophy* 4: *Aristotle's Ethics* (Albany, 1991)

[464] A. Alberti (ed.), *Studi sull'etica di Aristotele* (Naples, 1990)

[465] J. Barnes, M. Schofield and R. Sorabji (edd.), *Articles on Aristotle*, vol. 2, *Ethics and Politics* (London, 1977)

[466] R. Heinaman (ed.), *Aristotle and Moral Realism* (London, 1995)

[467] P. Moraux and D. Harlfinger (edd.), *Untersuchungen zur Eudemischen Ethik* (Berlin, 1971)

[468] C. Müller-Goldingen, *Schriften zur aristotelischen Ethik* (Hildesheim, 1988)

[469] A. O. Rorty (ed.), *Essays on Aristotle's Ethics* (Berkeley/Los Angeles/London, 1980)

[470] J. J. Walsh and H. L. Shapiro (edd.), *Aristotle's Ethics: Issues and Interpretations* (Belmont, Calif., 1967).

Aristotle's method

[471] J. Barnes, 'Aristotle and the Methods of Ethics', *Revue Internationale de Philosophie* 34 (1980), 490–511

[472] E. Berti, 'Il metodo della filosofia pratica secondo Aristotele', in [464], 23–63

[473] R. Bolton, 'The Objectivity of Ethics', in [463], 7–28

[474] T. H. Irwin, 'Aristotle's Methods of Ethics', in [421], 193–224

[475] L. J. Jost, '*Eudemian* Ethical Method', in [463], 29–40

[476] S. Klein, 'An Analysis and Defence of Aristotle's Method in *Nicomachean Ethics* I and x', *Ancient Philosophy* 8 (1988), 63–72

[477] S. Klein, 'The Value of *Endoxa* in Ethical Argument', *History of Philosophy Quarterly* 9 (1992), 141–57

[478] C. Natali, 'Fino a che punto rispettare le opinioni in Etica: Aristotele e gli *endoxa*', in *Emmeneutica e filosofia pratica*, ed. N. De Domenico, and A. Di Stefan (Puglisi, 1990), 191–201

[479] T. D. Roche, 'In Defence of an Alternative View of the Foundation of Aristotle's Moral Theory', *Phronesis* 37 (1992), 46–84

[480] A. M. Wiles, 'Method in the *Nicomachean Ethics*', *The New Scholasticism* 56 (1982), 239–43

Moral epistemology

[481] W. W. Fortenbaugh, 'Aristotle's Conception of Moral Virtue and its Perceptive Role', *Transactions of the American Philological Association* 95 (1964), 77–87

[482] R. J. Hankinson, 'Perception and Evaluation: Aristotle on the Moral Imagination', *Dialogue* 29 (1990), 41–63

[483] T. H. Irwin, 'First Principles in Aristotle's Ethics', *Midwest Studies in Philosophy* 3 (1978), 252–72

[484] R. B. Louden, 'Aristotle's Practical Particularism', *Ancient Philosophy* 6 (1986), 123–38, and in [463], 159–78

[485] J. D. Monan, *Moral Knowledge and its Methodology in Aristotle* (Oxford, 1968)

[486] C. D. C. Reeve, *Practices of Reason* (Oxford, 1992)

[487] T. Upton, 'Aristotle's Moral Epistemology', *The New Scholasticism* 56 (1982), 169–84

[488] M. J. Woods, 'Intuition and Perception in Aristotle's Ethics', *Oxford Studies in Ancient Philosophy* 4 (1986), 145–66
See also

[489] J. M. Cooper, 'Ethical-political Theory in Aristotle's *Rhetoric*', in [418], 193–210

[490] S. Halliwell, 'Popular Morality, Philosophical Ethics and the *Rhetoric*', in [418], 211–30

[491] S. Lovibond, 'Aristotelian Ethics and the "Enlargement of Thought"', in [466], 99–120.

The good

[492] J. L. Ackrill, 'Aristotle on "Good" and the Categories', in [465], 17–24

[493] H. Flashar, 'The Critique of Plato's Theory of Ideas in Aristotle's Ethics', in [465], 1–16

[494] W. W. Fortenbaugh, '*Nicomachean Ethics* i, 1096b26–9', *Phronesis* 11 (1966), 185–94

[495] C. Kirwan, 'Logic and the Good in Aristotle', *Philosophical Quarterly* 17 (1967), 97–114

[496] C. Korsgaard, 'Aristotle and Kant on the Source of Value', *Ethics* 96 (1986), 486–505, and in her [955], 225–48

[497] S. MacDonald, 'Aristotle and the Homonymy of the Good', *Archiv für Geschichte der Philosophie* 71 (1989), 150–74

[498] H. A. Prichard, 'The Meaning of *Agathon* in the *Ethics* of Aristotle', in his *Moral Obligation: Essays and Lectures* (Oxford, 1949), 40–53

[499] H. Richardson, 'Degrees of Finality and the Highest Good in Aristotle', *Journal of the History of Philosophy* 30 (1992), 327–52

[500] G. Santas, 'Desire and Perfection in Aristotle's Theory of the Good', *Apeiron* 22 (1989), 75–99

[501] T. M. Tuozzo, 'Aristotle's Theory of the Good and its Causal Basis', *Phronesis* 40 (1995), 293–314

[502] N. P. White, 'Good as Goal', *Southern Journal of Philosophy*, Suppl. 27 (1988), 169–93

[503] B. Williams, 'Aristotle on the Good – A Formal Sketch', *Philosophical Quarterly* 12 (1962), 289–96

The fine

[504] D. J. Allan, 'The Fine and the Good in the *Eudemian Ethics*', in [467], 63–72

[505] T. H. Irwin, 'Aristotle's Conception of Morality', *Proceedings of the Boston Area Colloquium in Ancient Philosophy* 1 (1985), 115–43

[506] C. Korsgaard, 'From Duty and for the Sake of the Noble: Kant and Aristotle on Morally Good Action', in [16], 203–36

[507] J. Owens, 'The *Kalon* in Aristotelian Ethics', in [421], 261–78

Eudaimonia

[508] J. L. Ackrill, 'Aristotle on *Eudaimonia*', *Proceedings of the British Academy* 60 (1975), 339–59, and in [469], 15–34

[509] J. Annas, 'Aristotle on Virtue and Happiness', *University of Drayton Review* 19 (1988–9), 7–22

[510] J. L. Austin, '*Agathon* and *Eudaimonia* in the *Ethics* of Aristotle', in [419], 261–96 and in his [936], 1–32

[511] R. Crisp, 'White on Aristotelian Happiness', *Oxford Studies in Ancient Philosophy* 10 (1992), 233–40

[512] R. Crisp, 'Aristotle's Inclusivism', *Oxford Studies in Ancient Philosophy* 12 (1994), 111–36

[513] H. J. Curzer, 'Criteria for Happiness in *Nicomachean Ethics* 1.7 and x.6–8', *Classical Quarterly* 40 (1990), 421–32

[514] H. J. Curzer, 'The Supremely Happy Life in Aristotle's *Nicomachean Ethics*', *Apeiron* 24 (1991), 47–69

[515] D. Devereux, 'Aristotle on the Essence of Happiness', in [421], 247–60

[516] J. C. Dybikowski, 'Is Aristotelian *Eudaimonia* Happiness?', *Dialogue* 20 (1981), 185–200

[517] W. F. R. Hardie, 'The Final Good in Aristotle's *Ethics*', *Philosophy* 40 (1965), 277–95

[518] W. F. R. Hardie, 'Aristotle on the Best Life for a Man', *Philosophy* 54 (1979), 35–50

[519] R. Heinaman, '*Eudaimonia* and Self-sufficiency in the *Nicomachean Ethics*', *Phronesis* 33 (1988), 31–53

[520] R. Heinaman, 'Rationality, *Eudaimonia*, and *Kakodaimonia* in Aristotle', *Phronesis* 38 (1993), 31–56

[521] A. Kenny, 'Happiness', *Proceedings of the Aristotelian Society* 66 (1965–6), 93–102 and in [465], 25–32

[522] C. Kirwan, 'Two Aristotelian Theses about *Eudaimonia*', in [464], 149–91

[523] R. Kraut, 'The Peculiar Function of Human Beings', *Canadian Journal of Philosophy* 9 (1979), 467–78

[524] R. Kraut, 'Two Conceptions of Happiness', *Philosophical Review* 88 (1979), 167–97

[525] J. McDowell, 'The Role of *Eudaimonia* in Aristotle's Ethics', *Proceedings of the African Classical Association* 15 (1980), and in [469], 359–76

[526] J. McDowell, 'Eudaimonism and Realism in Aristotle's Ethics', in [466], 201–18

[527] D. Wiggins, 'Eudaimonism and Realism in Aristotle's Ethics: A Reply to John McDowell', in [466], 219–231

[528] T. Nagel, 'Aristotle on Eudaimonia', *Phronesis* 17 (1972), 252–9, and in [469], 7–14

[529] C. Natali, 'Due modi di trattare le opinioni notevole. La nozione di felicità in Aristotele, *Retorica* 1 5', *Methexis* 3 (1990), 51–63

[530] R. Renehan, 'Aristotle's Doctrine of the Proper End of Man: Some Observations', *Proceedings of the Boston Area Colloquium in Ancient Philosophy* 6 (1990), 79–102

[531] M. Ring, 'Aristotle and the Concept of Happiness', in [15], 69–90

[532] T. D. Roche, 'The Perfect Happiness', *Southern Journal of Philosophy*, suppl.
       vol. 27 (1988), 103–25

[533] C. J. Rowe, 'The Good for Man in Aristotle's *Ethics* and *Politics*', in [464],
       193–225

[534] F. Siegler, 'Reason, Happiness and Goodness', in [470], 30–46

[535] M. Wedin, 'Aristotle on the Good for Man', *Mind*, 90 (1981), 243–62

[536] N. P. White, 'Conflicting Parts of Happiness in Aristotle's Ethics', *Ethics*
       105 (1995), 258–83

[537] S. A. White, 'Is Aristotelian Happiness a Good Life or the Best Life?',
       Oxford Studies in Ancient Philosophy 8 (1990), 103–43

[538] M. H. Wörner, '*Eudaimonia* in Aristotle's *Rhetoric*', *Proceedings of the
       Boston Area Colloquium in Ancient Philosophy* 8 (1992), 1–33
       See also

[539] D. Charles, 'Aristotle and Modern Realism', in [466], 135–72

[540] S. Everson, 'Aristotle and the Explanation of Evaluation: A Reply to David
       Charles', in [466], 173–99

[541] S. Engstrom, 'Happiness and the Highest Good in Aristotle and Kant', in
       [16], 102–38

[542] D. Keyt, 'The Meaning of *Bíos* in Aristotle's *Ethics* and *Politics*', *Ancient
       Philosophy* 9 (1989), 15–21

[543] C. M. Young, 'Virtue and Flourishing in Aristotle's Ethics', in [15], 138–56.

Human nature and the 'ergon' argument

[544] D. Achtenberg, 'The Role of the *Ergon* Argument in Aristotle's
       Nicomachean Ethics', *Ancient Philosophy* 9 (1989), 37–47 and in [463],
       59–72

[545] G. Anagnostopoulos, 'Aristotle on Function and the Attributive Nature of
       the Good', in [15], 91–137

[546] P. Glassen, 'A Fallacy in Aristotle's Argument about the Good',
       Philosophical Quarterly 66 (1957), 319–22

[547] A. Gomez-Lobo, 'A New Look at the Ergon Argument in the *Nicomachean
       Ethics*', *Proceedings of the Society for Ancient Greek Philosophy* (1988)

[548] A. Gomez-Lóbo, 'The Ergon Inference', in [463], 43–58

[549] M. C. Nussbaum, 'Aristotle on Human Nature and the Foundations of
       Ethics', in [931], 86–131

[550] T. D. Roche, '*Ergon* and *Eudaimonia* in *Nicomachean Ethics* I: Reconsidering
       the Intellectualist Interpretation', *Journal of the History of Philosophy* 26
       (1988), 175–94

[551] B. Suits, 'Aristotle on the Function of Man: Fallacies, Heresies and Other
       Entertainments', *Canadian Journal of Philosophy* 4 (1974), 23–40

[552] J. Whiting, 'Aristotle's Function Argument: A Defense', *Ancient Philosophy*
       8 (1990), 33–48

[553] K. V. Wilkes, 'The Good Man and the Good for Man in Aristotle's Ethics',
       Mind 87 (1978), 553–71, and in [469], 341–58
       See also

[554] T. H. Irwin, 'The Metaphysical and Psychological Basis of Aristotle's
       Ethics', in [469], 35–54

[555] J. McDowell, 'Two Sorts of Naturalism', in [952], 149–80

[556] T. D. Roche, 'On the Alleged Metaphysical Foundations of Aristotle's *Ethics*', *Ancient Philosophy* 8 (1988), 49–62.

Contemplation

[557] A. W. H. Adkins, '*Theoria* versus *Praxis* in the *Nicomachean Ethics* and the *Republic*', *Classical Philology* 73 (1978), 297–313

[558] R. Burger, 'Wisdom, Philosophy, and Happiness: On Book x of Aristotle's *Ethics*', *Proceedings of the Boston Area Colloquium in Ancient Philosophy* 6 (1990), 289–307

[559] J. M. Cooper, 'Contemplation and Happiness: A Reconsideration', *Synthèse* 72 (1987), 187–216

[560] P. Defourney, 'L'Activité de Contemplation dans les *Morales* d'Aristote', *Bulletin de l'Institut Historique Belge de Rome* 18 (1937), 89–101 and, in English translation, in [465], 104–12

[561] T. B. Eriksen, *Bios Theoretikos: Notes on Aristotle's Ethica Nicomachea* x, 6–8 (Oslo, 1976)

[562] D. Keyt, 'Intellectualism in Aristotle', in [10], 364–87

[563] J. Moline, 'Contemplation and the Human Good', *Nous* 17 (1983), 37–53

[564] A. O. Rorty, 'The Place of Contemplation in Aristotle's *Nicomachean Ethics*', *Mind* 87 (1978), 343–58 and, revised, in [469], 377–94

[565] M. J. White, 'Aristotle's Concept of *Theoria* and the *Energeia/Kinesis* Distinction', *Journal of the History of Philosophy* 18 (1980), 253–65

[566] J. Whiting, 'Human Nature and Intellectualism in Aristotle', *Archiv für Geschichte der Philosophie* 68 (1986), 70–95

External goods

[567] J. M. Cooper, 'Aristotle on the Goods of Fortune', *Philosophical Review* 94 (1985), 173–96

[568] T. H. Irwin, 'Permanent Happiness: Aristotle and Solon', *Oxford Studies in Ancient Philosophy* 3 (1985), 89–124

Virtue

[569] M. F. Burnyeat, 'Aristotle on Learning to be Good', in [469], 69–92

[570] H. J. Curzer, 'A Defense of Aristotle's Doctrine that Virtue is a Mean', *Ancient Philosophy* 16 (1996), 129–38

[571] W. W. Fortenbaugh, 'Aristotle's Distinction Between Moral Virtue and Practical Wisdom', in [463], 97–106

[572] E. Garver, *Aristotle's Rhetoric: An Art of Character* (Chicago, 1994)

[573] W. F. R. Hardie, 'Aristotle's Doctrine that Virtue is a "Mean"', *Proceedings of the Aristotelian Society* 65 (1964–5), 183–204, and, amended, in [465], 33–46

[574] M. Homiak, 'The Pleasure of Virtue in Aristotle's Moral Theory', *Pacific Philosophical Quarterly* 66 (1985), 93–110

[575] R. Hursthouse, 'A False Doctrine of the Mean', *Proceedings of the Aristotelian Society* 81 (1980–1), 57–72

[576] D. S. Hutchinson, *The Virtues of Aristotle* (London, 1986)

[577] A. M. Ioppolo, 'Virtue and Happiness in the First Book of the *Nicomachean Ethics*', in [464], 119–48

[578] T. H. Irwin, 'Disunity in the Aristotelian Virtues', *Oxford Studies in Ancient Philosophy*, suppl. vol. (1988), 61–78

[579] R. Kraut, 'Comments on "Disunity in the Aristotelian Virtues" by T. H. Irwin', *Oxford Studies in Ancient Philosophy* suppl. vol. (1988), 79–86

[580] T .H. Irwin, '"Disunity in the Aristotelian Virtues": Reply to Richard Kraut', *Oxford Studies in Ancient Philosophy* suppl. vol. (1988), 87–90

[581] C. Korsgaard, 'Aristotle on Function and Virtue', *History of Philosophy Quarterly* 3 (1986), 259–79

[582] L. A. Kosman, 'Being Properly Affected: Virtues and Feelings in Aristotle's Ethics', in [469], 103–16

[583] R. Kraut, Aristotle on Choosing Virtue for Itself', *Archiv für Geschichte der Philosophie* 58 (1976), 223–39

[584] S. Peterson, '"Horos" in Aristotle's *Nicomachean Ethics*', *Phronesis* 33 (1988), 33–50

[585] G. Santas, 'Does Aristotle have a Virtue Ethics?', *Philosophical Inquiry* 15 (1993), 1–32

[586] N. Sherman, *The Fabric of Character* (Oxford, 1989)

[587] N. Shermam, 'The Role of Emotions in Aristotelian Virtue', *Proceedings of the Boston Area Colloquium in Ancient Philosophy* 9 (1992), 1–33

[588] E. Telfer, 'The Unity of Moral Virtues in Aristotle's *Nicomachean Ethics*', *Proceedings of the Aristotelian Society* 91 (1989–90), 35–48

[589] J. O. Urmson, 'Aristotle's Doctrine of the Mean', *American Philosophical Quarterly* 10 (1973), 223–30, and in [469], 157–70

[590] M. J. White, 'Functionalism and the Moral Virtues in Aristotle's Ethics', *International Studies in Philosophy* 11 (1979), 49–57

[591] S. A. White, 'Natural Virtue and Perfect Virtue in Aristotle', *Proceedings of the Boston Area Colloquium in Ancient Philosophy* 8 (1992), 135–68

[592] B. Williams, 'Acting as the Virtuous Person Acts', in [466], 13–23

[593] R. Hursthouse, 'The Virtuous Agent's Reasons: A Reply to Bernard Williams', in [466], 24–39

See also

[594] J. M. Cooper, 'An Aristotelian Theory of the Emotions', in [423], 238–57 (which is a revision of

[595] J. M. Cooper, 'Rhetoric, Dialectic and the Passions', *Oxford Studies in Ancient Philosophy* 11 (1993), 175–98).

[596] W. W. Fortenbaugh, *Aristotle on Emotion* (London, 1975)

[597] D. Frede, 'Mixed Feelings in Aristotle's *Rhetoric*', in [423], 258–85

[598] S. R. Leighton, 'Aristotle and the Emotions', *Phronesis* 27 (1982), 144–74, and in part in [423], 206–37

[599] G. Striker, 'Emotions in Context: Aristotle's Treatment of the Passions in his *Rhetoric* and his Moral Psychology', in [423], 286–302

[600] J. E. Whiting, 'Self-love and Authoritative Virtue: Prolegomenon to a Kantian Reading of *Eudemian Ethics* viii 3', in [16], 162–99.

Virtues

[601] N. Cooper, 'Aristotle's Crowning Virtue', *Apeiron* 22 (1989), 191–205

[602] H. Curzer, 'A Great Philosopher's Not So Great Account of Great Virtue: Aristotle's Treatment of "Greatness of Soul"', *Canadian Journal of Philosophy* 20 (1990), 517–38

[603] H. Curzer, 'Aristotle's Much Maligned *Megalopsuchos*', *Australasian Journal of Philosophy* 69 (1991), 131–51

[604] W. F. R. Hardie, '"Magnanimity" in Aristotle's Ethics', *Phronesis* (1978), 63–79

[605] E. Schütrumpf, 'Magnanimity, *Megalopsuchia* and the System of Aristotle's *Nicomachean Ethics*', *Archiv für Geschichte der Philosophie* 71 (1989), 10–22

[606] S. R. Leighton, 'Aristotle's Courageous Passions', *Phronesis* 33 (1988), 76–99

[607] D. Pears, 'Courage as a Mean', in [469], 171–88

[608] C. M. Young, 'Aristotle on Temperance', *Philosophical Review* 97 (1988), 521–42, and in [463], 107–26

[609] C. M. Young, 'Aristotle on Liberality', *Boston Area Colloquium in Ancient Philosophy* 10 (1994), 313–34

[610] J. Hare, '*Eleutheriotes* in Aristotle's *Ethics*', *Ancient Philosophy* 8 (1988), 19–32

[611] J. S. Zembaty, 'Aristotle on Lying', *Journal of the History of Philosophy* 31 (1993), 7–30

Justice and equity

[612] H. Jackson, Peri dikaiosunes: *The Fifth Book of the Nicomachean Ethics of Aristotle* (London, 1879)

[613] P. Aubenque, 'The Twofold Natural Foundation of Justice According to Aristotle', in [466], 35–47

[614] T. Engberg-Pedersen, 'Justice at a Distance – Less Foundational, More Naturalistic: A Reply to Pierre Aubenque', in [466], 48–60

[615] R. Bambrough, 'Aristotle on Justice: A Paradigm of Philosophy', in [11], 159–74

[616] J. Brunschwig, 'Rule and Exception: On the Aristotelian Theory of Equity', in [22], 115–55

[617] C. Georgiadis, 'Equitable and Equity in Aristotle', in [61], 150–72

[618] H. Kelsen, 'Aristotle's Doctrine of Justice', in [470], 102–19

[619] P. Keyser, 'A Proposed Diagram in *EN* v 3, 1131a24–b20 for Distributive Justice in Proportion', *Apeiron* 25 (1992), 15–44

[620] D. Sachs, 'Notes on Unfairly Gaining More: *Pleonexia*', in [952], 209–18

[621] R. Shiner, 'Aristotle's Theory of Equity', in [61], 173–9

[622] B. Williams, 'Justice as a Virtue', in [469], 189–200

Phronēsis

[623] D. J. Allan, 'Aristotle's Account of the Origin of Moral Principles', *Actes du XIe Congrès International de Philosophie* 12 (1953), 120–7, and in [465], 72–8

[624] P. Aubenque, *La Prudence chez Aristote* (Paris, 1963)

[625] S. Broadie, 'Nature, Craft and Phronesis in Aristotle', *Philosophical Topics* 15 (1987), 35–50

[626] R. Kraut, 'In Defence of the Grand End', *Ethics* 103 (1993), 361–74
[627] W. Leszl, 'Alcune specifità del sapere pratico in Aristotele', in [464],
       65–117
[628] D. K. W. Modrak, 'Aristotle on Reason, Practical Reason and Living Well',
       in [463], 179–92
[629] C. Natali, 'Virtu o scienzia? Aspetti della *Phronesis* dei *Topici* e delle *Ethiche*
       di Aristotele', *Phronesis* 29 (1984), 50–72
[630] C. J. Rowe, 'The Meaning of *Phronesis* in the *Eudemian Ethics*', in [467],
       73–92

Voluntariness and responsibility

[631] J. L. Ackrill, 'An Aristotelian Argument about Virtue', *Paideia* 7 (1978),
       133–7
[632] S. Broadie, 'On What Would Have Happened Otherwise: A Problem for
       Determinism', *Review of Metaphysics* 39 (1985/6), 433–54
[633] R. Curren, 'The Contribution of *Nicomachean Ethics* III.5 to Aristotle's
       Theory of Responsibility', *History of Philosophy Quarterly* 6 (1989),
       261–77
[634] S. Everson, 'Aristotle's Compatibilism in the *Nicomachean Ethics*', *Ancient
       Philosophy* 10 (1990), 81–104
[635] D. J. Furley, 'Aristotle on the Voluntary', in [465], 47–60 (excerpted from
       his [52])
[636] W. F. R. Hardie, 'Aristotle and the Free Will Problem', *Philosophy* 43
       (1968), 274–78
[637] R. Heinaman, 'The *Eudemian Ethics* on Knowledge and Voluntary Action',
       Phronesis 31 (1986), 128–47
[638] R. Heinaman, 'Compulsion and Voluntary Action in the *Eudemian Ethics*',
       Nous 22 (1988), 253–81
[639] P. M. Huby, 'The First Discovery of the Free Will Problem', *Philosophy* 42
       (1967), 353–62
[640] R. Hursthouse, 'Acting and Feeling in Character: *Nicomachean Ethics* 3.1',
       Phronesis 29 (1984), 252–66
[641] T. H. Irwin, 'Reason and Responsibility in Aristotle', in [469], 117–56
[642] S. Sauvé Meyer, *Aristotle on Moral Responsibility* (Oxford, 1993)
[643] J. Moline, 'Aristotle on Praise and Blame', *Archiv für Geschichte der
       Philosophie* 71 (1989), 283–302
[644] J. Roberts, 'Aristotle on Responsibility for Action and Character', *Ancient
       Philosophy* 9 (1989), 23–36
[645] M. Schofield, 'Aristotelian Mistakes', *Proceedings of the Cambridge
       Philological Society* 19 (1973), 66–70
[646] R. Sorabji, *Necessity, Cause and Blame* (London, 1980)

Choice, desire and deliberation

[647] J. Annas, 'Aristotle and Kant on Morality and Practical Reasoning', in
       [16], 237–58
[648] G. E. M. Anscombe, 'Thought and Action in Aristotle', in [11], 143–58, in
       [465], 61–71, and in [934], 66–77
[649] A. Broadie, 'Aristotle on Rational Action', *Phronesis* 19 (1974), 70–80

[650] S. Broadie, 'The Problem of Practical Intellect in Aristotle's *Ethics*',
       Proceedings of the Boston Area Colloquium in Ancient Philosophy 3 (1987),
       229–52
[651] D. Devereux, 'Particular and Universal in Aristotle's Conception of
       Practical Knowledge', *Review of Metaphysics* 39 (1986), 483–504
[652] D. S. Hutchinson, 'Aristotle on the Spheres of Motivation: *De Anima* iii',
       Dialogue 29 (1990), 7–20
[653] T. H. Irwin, 'Aristotle on Reason, Desire, and Virtue', *Journal of Philosophy*
       72 (1975), 567–78
[654] A. Kenny, *Aristotle's Theory of the Will* (London, 1979)
[655] J. McDowell, 'Deliberation and Moral Development in Aristotle's Ethics',
       in [16], 19–35
[656] A. Mele, 'Aristotle on the Roles of Reason in Motivation and Justification',
       Archiv für Geschichte der Philosophie 66 (1984), 124–47
[657] A. Mele, 'Aristotle's Wish', *Journal of the History of Philosophy* 22 (1984),
       139–56
[658] A. Mele, 'Choice and Virtue in the *Nicomachean Ethics*', *Journal of the
       History of Philosophy* 19 (1981), 405–24
[659] H. Richardson, 'Desire and the Good in the *De Anima*', in [421],
       381–400
[660] N. Sherman, 'Character, Planning and Choice in Aristotle', *Review of
       Metaphysics* 34 (1985), 83–106
[661] A. D. Smith, 'Character and Intellect in Aristotle's Ethics', *Phronesis* 41
       (1996), 56–74
[662] R. Sorabji, 'Aristotle on the Role of Intellect in Virtue', *Proceedings of the
       Aristotelian Society* 74 (1973–4), 107–29, and in [469], 201–20
[663] D. Wiggins, 'Deliberation and Practical Reason', *Proceedings of the
       Aristotelian Society* 76 (1975–6), 29–51, and revised in [469], 221–40

The practical syllogism

[664] D. J. Allan, 'The Practical Syllogism', in [412], 325–42
[665] A. Mele, 'The Practical Syllogism and Deliberation in Aristotle's Causal
       Theory of Action', *The New Scholasticism* 55 (1981), 281–316
[666] D. K. W. Modrak, '*Aisthesis* in the Practical Syllogism', *Philosophical
       Studies* 30 (1976), 379–92
[667] M. C. Nussbaum, *Aristotle's De Motu Animalium*, 2nd edn (Princeton,
       1985)
[668] R. Shiner, '*Aisthesis, Nous,* and *Phronesis* in the Practical Syllogism',
       Philosophical Studies 36 (1979), 377–87

Action

[669] J. L. Ackrill, 'Aristotle on Action', *Mind* 87 (1978), 595–601 and in [469],
       93–102
[670] D. O. M. Charles, *Aristotle's Philosophy of Action* (London, 1984)
       (which is reviewed by
[671] T. H. Irwin, 'Aristotelian Actions', *Phronesis* 31 (1986), 68–89, and
[672] M. Wedin, 'Critical Study: David Charles, "Aristotle's Philosophy of
       Action"', *Ancient Philosophy* 6 (1986), 161–7)

[673] D. Charles, 'Aristotle: Ontology and Moral Reasoning', *Oxford Studies in Ancient Philosophy* 4 (1986), 121–43

[674] C. A. Freeland, 'Aristotelian Actions', *Nous* 19 (1985), 397–414

[675] C. T. Hagen, 'The *Energeia/Kinesis* Distinction and Aristotle's Theory of Action', *Journal of the History of Philosophy* 22 (1984), 263–80

Moral psychology and akrasia

[676] J. Cook Wilson, *On the Structure of Book Seven of the Nicomachean Ethics* (Oxford, 1912)

[677] J. M. Cooper, 'Some Remarks on Aristotle's Moral Psychology', *Southern Journal of Philosophy* 27 Suppl. (1988), 25–42

[678] N. Dahl, *Practical Reason, Aristotle, and Weakness of the Will* (Minneapolis, 1984)

[679] J. C. B. Gosling, 'Mad, Drunk, or Asleep? – Aristotle's Akratic', *Phronesis* 38 (1993), 98–104

[680] T. H. Irwin, 'Some Rational Aspects of Incontinence', *Southern Journal of Philosophy* 28 Suppl. (1988), 49–88

[681] A. Kenny, 'The Practical Syllogism and Incontinence', *Phronesis* 11 (1966), 163–84

[682] G. Lawrence, '*Akrasia* and Clear-Eyed *Akrasia* in Nicomachean Ethics 7', *Revue de la Philosophie Ancienne* 6 (1988), 77–106

[683] J. McDowell, 'Comments on T. H. Irwin's "Some Rational Aspects of Incontinence"', *Southern Journal of Philosophy* 28 Suppl. (1988), 89–102

[684] J. McDowell, 'Incontinence and Practical Wisdom in Aristotle', in [957], 95–112

[685] A. Mele, 'Aristotle on *Akrasia* and Knowledge', *The Modern Schoolman* 58 (1981), 137–59

[686] R. D. Milo, *Aristotle on Practical Knowledge and Weakness of Will* (The Hague, 1966)

[687] R. Robinson, 'Aristotle on Akrasia', in [465], 79–91

[688] A. O. Rorty, '*Akrasia* and Pleasure: *Nicomachean Ethics* Book 7', in [469], 267–84

[689] G. Santas, 'Aristotle on Practical Inference, the Explanation of Action, and Akrasia', *Phronesis* 14 (1969), 162–89

[690] J. J. Walsh, *Aristotle's Conception of Moral Weakness* (New York, 1963)

[691] D. Wiggins, 'Weakness of Will, Commensurability and the Objects of Deliberation and Desire', *Proceedings of the Aristotelian Society* 79 (1978–9), 251–77, in [469], 241–66, and in his [978], 239–68

[692] M. J. Woods, 'Aristotle on *Akrasia*', in [464], 227–261

Pleasure

As well as [53], see

[693] J. Annas, 'Aristotle on Pleasure and Goodness', in [469], 285–300

[694] D. Bostock, 'Pleasure and Activity in Aristotle's Ethics', *Phronesis* 33 (1988), 251–72

[695] F. J. Gonzalez, 'Aristotle on Pleasure and Perfection', *Phronesis* 36 (1991), 141–59

[696] P. Gottlieb, 'Aristotle's Measure Doctrine and Pleasure', *Archiv für Geschichte der Philosophie* 75 (1993), 31–46

[697] G. E. L. Owen, 'Aristotelian Pleasures', *Proceedings of the Aristotelian Society* 72 (1971–2), 135–52, in [465], 92–103, and [29], 334–46

[698] F. Ricken, *Der Lustbegriff in der Nikomachischen Ethik des Aristoteles*, *Hypomnemata* 46 (Göttingen, 1976)

[699] A. O. Rorty, 'The Pleasure in Aristotle's *Ethics*', *Mind* 83 (1974), 481–93

[700] J. O. Urmson, 'Aristotle on Pleasure', in [419], 323–33
See also

[701] J. L. Ackrill, 'Aristotle's Distinction between *Energeia* and *Kinesis*' in [11], 121–42

[702] D. Graham, 'States and Performances: Aristotle's Test', *Philosophical Quarterly* 30 (1980), 117–30

[703] R. Heinaman, 'Activity and Change in Aristotle', *Oxford Studies in Ancient Philosophy* 13 (1995), 187–216

[704] M. T. Liske, '*Kinesis* und *Energeia* bei Aristoteles', *Phronesis* 36 (1991), 161–78

[705] T. Penner, 'Verbs and Identity of Actions', in [963], 393–460

Friendship and altruism

[706] A. Alberti, '*Philia* e identità personale in Aristotele', in [464], 263–301

[707] J. Annas, 'Aristotle on Friendship and Altruism', *Mind* 86 (1977), 532–54

[708] J. Benson, 'Making Friends: Aristotle's Doctrine of the Friend as Another Self', in [26], 50–68

[709] J. M. Cooper, 'Aristotle on the Forms of Friendship', *Review of Metaphysics* 30 (1977), 290–315

[710] J. M. Cooper, 'Friendship and the Good in Aristotle', *Philosophical Review* 86 (1977), 290–315

[711] J. M. Cooper, 'Aristotle on Friendship', *Philosophical Review* 86 (1977), 290–315, and in [469], 301–40

[712] W. W. Fortenbaugh, 'Aristotle's Analysis of Friendship: Function and Analogy, Resemblance and Focal Meaning', *Phronesis* 20 (1975), 51–62

[713] D. McKerlie, 'Friendship, Self-love, and Concern for Others in Aristotle's *Ethics*', *Ancient Philosophy* 11 (1991), 85–101

[714] G. E. L. Owen, '*Philia* and *Akrasia* in Aristotle', in [424]

[715] A. D M. Walker, 'Aristotle's Account of Friendship in the *Nicomachean Ethics*', *Phronesis* 24 (1979), 180–96

[716] J. E. Whiting, 'Impersonal Friends', *Monist* 75 (1991), 3–29

Hellenistic philosophy

A good brief introduction to Hellenistic philosophy can be found in:

[717] A. A. Long, *Hellenistic Philosophy*, 2nd edn (London/Berkeley/Los Angeles, 1986).

[718] E. Zeller, *Stoics, Epicureans, and Skeptics*, tr. O. Reichel (London, 1880) remains a worthwhile account of the Hellenistic schools.

Most of the writings of the Hellenistic philosophers survive only in fragments – either as reported by writers whose work has survived in full or, especially in the case of Epicurus and later Epicureans, on invariably damaged rolls of papyrus. A recent collection of key fragments and testimonia is

[719] A. A. Long and D. Sedley, *The Hellenistic Philosophers*, 2 vols. (Cambridge, 1987), of which the first volume contains the translations and commentary and the second the original texts.

A shorter collection of texts in translation is

[720] B. Inwood and L.P. Gerson (edd.), *Hellenistic Philosophy: Introductory Readings* (Indianapolis, 1988).

The following contain articles on different aspects of Hellenistic thought:

[721] M. Schofield, M. Burnyeat and J. Barnes (edd.), *Doubt and Dogmatism: Studies in Hellenistic Epistemology* (Oxford, 1980)

[722] J. Barnes, J. Brunschwig, M. Burnyeat and M. Schofield (edd.), *Science and Speculation: Studies in Hellenistic Theory and Practice* (Cambridge/Paris, 1982)

[723] M. Schofield and G. Striker (edd.), *The Norms of Nature: Studies in Hellenistic Ethics* (Cambridge/Paris, 1986)

[724] J. Barnes and M. Mignucci (edd.), *Matter and Metaphysics* (Naples, 1987)

[725] J. Brunschwig and M. C. Nussbaum (edd.), *Passions and Perceptions* (Cambridge, 1993)

[726] A. Laks and M. Schofield (edd.), *Justice and Generosity: Studies in Hellenistic Social and Political Philosophy* (Cambridge, 1995)

[727] J. Barnes and M. Griffin (edd.), *Philosophia Togata* (Oxford, 1989)

[728] H. Flashar and O. Gigon (edd.), *Aspects de la philosophie hellénistique.* Fondation Hardt, *Entretiens sur l'antiquité classique* 32 (Vandoeuvres Geneva, 1986)

[729] J. Brunschwig, *Papers in Hellenistic Philosophy* (Cambridge, 1994)

[730] G. Striker, *Essays in Hellenistic Epistemology and Ethics* (Cambridge, 1996).

The most accessible account of Hellenistic ethics is probably that to be found in [71]. See also

[731] M. C. Nussbaum, *The Therapy of Desire* (Princeton, 1994), and the review of [723]:

[732] C. C. W. Taylor, 'Hellenistic Ethics', *Oxford Studies in Ancient Philosophy* 5 (1987), 235–46.

The Cyrenaics

The fragments can found in

[733] G. Giannantoni, *I Cirenaici* (Florence, 1958)

[734] E. Mannebach, *Aristippi et Cyrenaicorum Fragmenta* (Leiden/Cologne, 1961), as well as [112].

For their ethical views, see [71], ch. 11, and

[735] T. H. Irwin, 'Aristippus against Happiness', *Monist* 74 (1991), 55–82

[736] A. A. Long, 'Cyrenaics', in [937], 236–8

[737] V. T. McKirahan, 'The Socratic Origin of the Cynics and the Cyrenaics', in [32], 367–91.

Epicurus

The most comprehensive edition of Epicurus, including the papyrus fragments, is

[738] G. Arrighetti, *Epicuro opere* (Turin 1960; 2nd edn, 1973), which has an Italian translation and commentary.

[739] C. Bailey, *Epicurus. The Extant Remains* (Oxford, 1926) does not contain papyrus fragments but does have an English translation.

[740] B. Inwood, L. P. Gerson and D. Hutchinson, *The Epicurus Reader: Selected Writings and Testimonia* (Indianapolis, 1994) provides a useful collection of Epicurean texts and doxographical reports in English translation.

[741] M. Isnardi Parente, *Opere di Epicuro* (Turin, 1974) has an Italian translation of and commentary on the surviving works and the more important testimonia.

For those with Greek

[742] H. Usener, *Epicurea* (Leipzig, 1887) remains an essential collection of texts and reports of Epicurean doctrines.

Editions of papyrus fragments of the important *de Natura* can be found in

[743] G. Leone, 'Epicuro, *Della Natura*, libro xiv', *Cronache Ercolanesi* 14 (1984), 17–107

[744] C. Millot, 'Epicure *de la Nature* Livre xv', *Cronache Ercolanesi* 7 (1977), 9–39

[745] D. Sedley, 'Epicurus, *On Nature* Book xxviii', *Cronache Ercolanesi* 3 (1973), 5–83.

Book xxv is discussed in

[746] S. Laursen, 'Epicurus, *On Nature* Book xxv', *Cronache Ercolanesi* 17 (1987), 77–8

[747] S. Laursen, 'Epicurus *On Nature*, Book xxv (Long–Sedley 20, B, C and J)', *Cronache Ercolanesi* 18 (1988), 7–18.

Apart from what survives of Epicurus' own work, our principal source for Epicurean philosophy is Lucretius' Latin poem, *de Rerum Natura*, written in the first century B.C. The standard edition of Lucretius is still

[748] C. Bailey, *Titi Lucreti De Rerum Natura Libri Sex*, 3 vols. (Oxford, 1947).

[749] W. H. D. Rouse, *Lucretius De Rerum Natura*, revised with new text, introduction, notes, and index by M. F. Smith (Cambridge, Mass. and London, 1975) provides a text and translation.

The relation between Epicurus and Lucretius is discussed in

[750] D. Clay, *Lucretius and Epicurus* (Ithaca/London, 1983), and that between Epicureanism and scepticism is discussed in

[751] M. Gigante, *Scetticismo e Epicureismo* (Naples, 1981).

For discussion of Philodemus, another important first-century Epicurean and source of Epicurean views, see Supplementary Essay 1 of

[752] P. and E. De Lacy, *Philodemus, On Methods of Inference* (Naples, 1978), and

[753] M. Gigante, *La Bibliothèque de Philodème et l'épicurisme romain* (Paris, 1987)

[754] M. Gigante, *Philodemus in Italy: The Books from Herculaneum*, tr. D. Obbink (Ann Arbor, 1995).

A perhaps surprising source of Epicurean doctrine is the second-century A.D. Diogenes of Oenoanda, who had his writings inscribed on a public colonnade in Turkey. A full critical text of the fragments of this text, together with translation and commentary, is provided by

[755] M. F. Smith, *The Epicurean Inscription* (Naples, 1993).

An introduction to Epicurus' philosophy is

[756] J. M. Rist, *Epicurus: An Introduction* (Cambridge, 1972).

The fullest study of Epicurus' epistemology and philosophy of science is

[757] E. Asmis, *Epicurus' Scientific Method* (Ithaca/London, 1984).

A valuable collection of essays is

[758] *SYZETESIS: Studi sull'Epicureismo Greco e Latino offerti a Marcello Gigante*, 2 vols. (Naples, 1983).
See also

[759] J. Bollack and A. Laks (edd.), *Etudes sur l'épicurisme antique*, in *Cahiers de Philologie* 1 (1976).

A general study of Epicurean ethics is

[760] P. Mitsis, *Epicurus' Ethical Theory: The Pleasures of Invulnerability* (Ithaca/London, 1988).
See also

[761] J. Bollack, *La Pensée du plaisir. Epicure: textes moraux, commentaires* (Paris, 1975)

[762] C. Diano, *Epicuri Ethica et Epistulae* (Florence, 1946)

[763] J. M. Guyau, *La Morale d'Epicure et ses rapports avec les doctrines contemporaines* (Paris, 1886).

Pleasure

As well as [53], see

[764] J. Annas, 'Epicurus on Pleasure and Happiness', *Philosophical Topics* 15 (1987), 5–21

[765] G. Arrighetti, 'Devoir et plaisir chez Epicure', in [24], 385–91

[766] G. Giannantoni, 'Il piacere cinetico nell'etica Epicurea', *Elenchos* 5 (1984), 25–44

[767] D. Glidden, 'Epicurus and the Pleasure Principle', in [15], 177–97

[768] M. Hossenfelder, 'Epicurus – Hedonist Malgré Lui', in [723], 245–64

[769] A. A. Long, 'Pleasure and Social Utility', in [728], 283–324

[770] S. E. Rosenbaum, 'Epicurus on Pleasure and the Complete Life', *Monist* 73 (1990), 21–41

[771] M. C. Stokes, 'Cicero on Epicurean Pleasures', in [890], 145–70

[772] G. Striker, 'Epicurean Hedonism', in [725], 3–17, and her [730], 196–208

Friendship

[773] B. Farrington, 'Lucretius and Manilius on Friendship', *Hermathena* 83 (1954), 10–16

[774] P. Mitsis, 'Epicurus on Friendship and Altruism', *Oxford Studies in Ancient Philosophy* 5 (1987), 127–53

[775] D. O'Connor, 'The Invulnerable Pleasure of Epicurean Friendship', *Greek, Roman and Byzantine Studies* 30 (1989), 165–86

[776] J. Rist, 'Epicurus on Friendship', *Classical Philology* 75 (1980), 121–9

[777] A. Tuilier, 'La Notion de *philia* dans ses rapports avec certains fondaments sociaux de l'épicurisme', in *ACGB 1968* (Paris, 1969), 318–29

Justice

[778] N. Denyer, 'The Origins of Justice' in [758], 133–52

[779] P. A. Vander Waerdt, 'The Justice of the Epicurean Wise Man', *Classical Quarterly* 37 (1987) 402–22
See also

[780] A. Alberti, 'The Epicurean Theory of Law and Justice', in [726], 161–90

Free will

As well as Study 2 of [52], see

[781] P. Conway, 'Epicurus' Theory of Freedom of Action', *Prudentia* 13 (1981), 81–9

[782] W. Englert, *Epicurus on the Swerve and Free Action*, American Classical Studies 16 (Atlanta, 1988)

[783] D. Fowler, 'Lucretius on the *Clinamen* and Free Will', in [758], 329–52

[784] D. Furley, *Two Studies in the Greek Atomists* (Princeton, 1967)

[785] P. M. Huby, 'The Epicureans, Animals and Free Will', *Apeiron* 3 (1969), 17–19

[786] T. Saunders, 'Free Will and the Atomic Swerve in Lucretius', *Symbolae Osloenses* 59 (1984), 37–59

[787] D. Sedley, 'Epicurus' Refutation of Determinism', in [758], 11–51
See also

[788] J. Annas, 'Epicurus on Agency', in [725], 53–71.

Death

[789] F. D. Miller, Jr, 'Epicurus on the Art of Dying', *Southern Journal of Philosophy* 14 (1976), 169–77

[790] P. Mitsis, 'Epicurus on Death and the Duration of Life', *Proceedings of the Boston Area Colloquium on Ancient Philosophy* 4 (1988), 295–314

The Stoics

The fragments of the Stoics are collected in

[791] H. von Arnim, *Stoicorum Veterum Fragmenta*, 3 vols. (Leipzig, 1903–5); vol. 4, indexes by M. Adler (Leipzig, 1924).

A much more comprehensive collection of fragments of Stoic dialectic (which included language, logic and epistemology) is

[792] K. Hülser, *Die Fragmente zur Dialektik der Stoiker – neue Sammlung der Texte mit deutscher Übersetzung und Kommentar*, 4 vols. (Stuttgart/Bad Cannstatt, 1987–9).

For the work of Poseidonius, see
[793] L. Edelstein and I. G. Kidd, *Poseidonius*, 3 vols. (Cambridge, 1972, 1988).

A useful, if critical, source of Stoic doctrine is
[794] P. H. De Lacy (tr. and ed.), *Galen: De Placitis Hippocratis et Platonis* (Berlin, 1978–80).

The following are introductions to Stoic thought:
[795] E. Brehier, *Chrysippe et l'ancien stoïcisme*, 2nd edn (Paris, 1951)
[796] J. Christensen, *An Essay on the Unity of Stoic Philosophy* (Copenhagen, 1962)
[797] L. Edelstein, *The Meaning of Stoicism* (Cambridge, Mass., 1966)
[798] M. Pohlenz, *Die Stoa. Geschichte einer geistigen Bewegung*, 2nd edn (Göttingen, 1959)
[799] J. M. Rist, *Stoic Philosophy* (Cambridge, 1969)
[800] F. H. Sandbach, *The Stoics* (London, 1975, repr. Indianapolis, 1994).

The following contain articles on various aspects of Stoic philosophy:
[801] J. Brunschwig (ed.), *Les Stoïciens et leur logique* (Paris, 1978)
[802] R. Epp (ed.), *Spindel Conference 1984: Recovering the Stoics* (*Southern Journal of Philosophy* 23 suppl., 1985)
[803] W. W. Fortenbaugh (ed.), *On Stoic and Peripatetic Ethics. The Work of Arius Didymus* (New Brunswick/London, 1983)
[804] A. A. Long (ed.), *Problems in Stoicism* (London, 1971)
[805] A. A. Long, *Stoic Studies* (Cambridge, 1996)
[806] J. M. Rist, *The Stoics* (Berkeley/Los Angeles/London, 1978)
[807] A.-J. Voelke (ed.), *Le Stoïcisme* (*Revue Internationale de Philosophie*, forthcoming).

For a discussion of contemporary interpretations of the Stoics, see
[808] J. M. Rist, 'Stoicism: Some Reflections on the State of the Art', in [802], 1–11.

Useful monographs on Stoic philosophy are
[809] M. Frede, *Die stoische Logik* (Göttingen, 1974)
[810] J. Gould, *The Philosophy of Chrysippus* (Leiden, 1971)
[811] B. Inwood, *Ethics and Human Action in Early Stoicism* (Oxford, 1985)
[812] B. Mates, *Stoic Logic* (Berkeley/Los Angeles, 1953)
[813] M. Mignucci, *Il significato della logica Stoica*, 2nd edn (Bologna, 1967)
[814] M. A. Reesor, *The Nature of Man in Early Stoic Philosophy* (London, 1989).

General ethical studies and collections

[815] A. Bonhöffer, *Epictet und die Stoa* (Stuttgart, 1890)
[816] A. Bonhöffer, *Die Ethik des Stoikers Epictet* (Stuttgart, 1894)
[817] A. Dyroff, *Die Ethik der alten Stoa* (Berlin, 1897)
[818] M. Forschner, *Die stoische Ethik: über die Zusammenhang von Natur- Sprach - u. Moralphilosophie im altstoischen System* (Stuttgart, 1981)

[819] W. W. Fortenbaugh (ed.), *On Stoic and Peripatetic Ethics: The Work of Arius Didymus* (New Brunswick/London, 1983)

[820] O. Rieth, *Grundbegriffe der stoischen Ethik* (Berlin, 1933)

[821] G. Rodier, 'La Cohérence de la morale stoïcienne', in *Etudes de philosophie grecque* (Paris, 1926, repr. 1957)

[822] D. Tsekourakis, *Studies in the Terminology of Early Stoic Ethics* (Wiesbaden, 1974)

[823] N. P. White, 'Stoic Values', *Monist* 73 (1990), 42–58
See also

[824] A. A. Long, 'Arius Didymus and the Exposition of Stoic Ethics', in [803], 41–65

[825] J. B. Schneewind, 'Kant and Stoic Ethics', in [16], 285–301.

For the Stoics' relation to their predecessors, see

[826] J. Annas, 'The Hellenistic Versions of Aristotle's Ethics', *Monist* 73 (1990), 80–96

[827] A. M. Ioppolo, 'La dottrina Stoica dei beni esterni e i suoi rapporti con l'etica Aristotelica', *Rivista Critica di Storia della Filosofia* 29 (1974), 363–85

[828] A. A. Long, 'Aristotle's Legacy to Stoic Ethics', *Bulletin of the Institute of Classical Studies* 15 (1968), 72–85

[829] F. H. Sandbach, 'Aristotle and the Stoics', *Proceedings of the Cambridge Philological Society* Suppl. 10 (1985)

[830] G. Striker, 'The Platonic Socrates and the Stoics', in [32], 241–51, and [730], 316–23.

Happiness

[831] J. M. Cooper, 'Eudaimonism, the Appeal to Nature, and "Moral Duty" in Stoicism', in [16], 261–84

[832] T. H. Irwin, 'Stoic and Aristotelian Conceptions of Happiness', in [723], 205–44

[833] A. A. Long, 'Stoic Eudaimonism', *Proceedings of the Boston Area Colloquium in Ancient Philosophy* 4 (1988), 77–101, and in his [805], 179–201

The good and goods

[834] R. Alpers-Gölz, *Der Begriff Skopos in der Stoa und seine Vorgeschichte* (Hildesheim, 1976)

[835] M. Forschner, 'Das Gute und die Güter, Zur Aktualität der stoischen Ethik', *Aspects de la philosophie hellénistique* Entretiens Hardt 32 (1986), 325–60

[836] A. Graeser, 'Zur Funktion des Begriffes "Gut" in der stoischen Ethik', *Zeitschrift für Philosophische Forschung* 26 (1972), 417–25

[837] H. Hunt, 'The Stoic and Antiochean Definitions of the Good', in [888], 116–21

[838] B. Inwood, 'Goal and Target in Stoicism', *Journal of Philosophy* 83 (1986), 547–56

[839] A. A. Long, 'Carneades and the Stoic Telos', *Phronesis* 12 (1967), 59–90

[840] M. Reesor, 'On the Stoic Goods in Stobaeus *Eclogae* 2', in [803], 75–84

[841] A. Reiner, 'Zum Begriff des Guten (Agathon) in der Stoischen Ethik',
       Zeitschrift für Philosophische Forschung 28 (1974), 228–34
       See also
[842] I. Kidd, 'Stoic Intermediates and the End for Man', in [804], 150–72
[843] M. Reesor, 'The "Indifferents" in the Old and Middle Stoa', *Transactions
       and Proceedings of the American Philological Association* 82 (1951), 102–10.

Virtue

[844] T. H. Irwin, 'Virtue, Praise and Success: Stoic Responses to Aristotle',
       Monist 73 (1990), 59–79
[845] G. Lesses, 'Virtue and the Goods of Fortune in Stoic Moral Theory' *Oxford
       Studies in Ancient Philosophy* 7 (1989), 95–127
[846] A. A. Long, 'The Harmonics of Stoic Virtue', *Oxford Studies in Ancient
       Philosophy*, Suppl. Vol. (1991), 97–116 and in his [805], 202–23
       See also
[847] K. Algra, 'Chrysippus on Virtuous Abstention from Ugly Old Women
       (Plutarch, *SR* 1038e–1039a)', *Classical Quarterly* 40 (1990), 450–8.

Moral psychology

[848] M. Frede, 'The Stoic Doctrine of the Affections of the Soul', in [723],
       93–110
[849] J. Gosling, 'The Stoics and *Akrasia*', *Apeiron* 20 (1987), 179–202
[850] B. Inwood, 'Seneca and Psychological Dualism', in [725], 150–83
[851] G. B. Kerferd, 'Two Problems concerning Impulses', in [803], 87–98
[852] A. C. Lloyd, 'Emotion and Decision in Stoic Psychology', in [804], 233–46
[853] J. M. Rist, 'The Stoic Concept of Detachment', in [806], 259–72
       See also
[854] G. B. Kerferd, 'The Search for Personal Identity in Stoic Thought', *Bulletin
       of the John Rylands University Library of Manchester* 55 (1972), 177–96.

Oikeiōsis

[855] C. O. Brink, '*Oikeiosis* and *Oikeiotes*: Theophrastus and Zeno on Nature in
       Moral Theory', *Phronesis* 1 (1955–6), 123–45
[856] T. Engberg-Pedersen, 'Discovering the Good: *Oikeiosis* and *Kathekonta* in
       Stoic Ethics', in [723], 45–84
[857] T. Engberg-Pedersen, *The Stoic Theory of Oikeiosis: Moral Development and
       Social Interaction in Early Stoic Philosophy* (Aarhus, 1990)
[858] H. Görgemanns, '*Oikeiosis* in Arius Didymus', in [803], 165–89
[859] S. G. Pembroke, '*Oikeiosis*', in [804], 114–49
[860] M. Pohlenz, 'Die Oikeiosis', *Grundfragen der stoischen Philosophie Abh. d.
       Gesellschaft d. Wissenschaften zu Göttingen, Philol.-hist. Klasse*, third series,
       N. 6, 11
[861] G. Striker, 'The Role of *Oikeiosis* in Stoic Ethics', *Oxford Studies in Ancient
       Philosophy* 1 (1983), 145–68, and in her [730], 281–97

Nature and the grounding of ethics

[862] E. Grumach, *Physis und Agathon in der alten Stoa* (Berlin, 1932, repr.
       Berlin/Zurich/Dublin, 1966)

[863] A. A. Long, 'The Logical Basis of Stoic Ethics', *Proceedings of the Aristotelian Society* 70 (1970–1), and in his [805], 134–55 (which is discussed in

[864] A. Graeser, 'Zirkel oder Deduktion? Zur Begründung der stoischen Ethik', *Kant Studien* 63 (1972), 213–24)

[865] G. Striker, 'Following Nature', *Oxford Studies in Ancient Philosophy* 9 (1991), 1–73, and in her [730], 221–80

[866] N. P. White, 'Nature and Regularity in Stoic Ethics', *Oxford Studies in Ancient Philosophy* 3 (1985), 289–305

[867] N. P. White, 'The Role of Physics in Stoic Ethics', *Southern Journal of Philosophy* 23 (1984), Spindel Conference Supplement, 57–74

[868] N. P. White, 'The Basis of Stoic Ethics', *Harvard Studies in Classical Philology* 83 (1979), 143–78

Individual Stoics

[869] H. Hunt, 'The Ethical System of Antiochus', in [888], 89–97

[870] I. G. Kidd, 'Poseidonius' Methodology and the Self-sufficiency of Virtue', in [728], ch. 1

[871] G. Striker, 'Antipater, or the Art of Living', in [723], 185–204, and in her [730], 298–315

[872] M. Schofield, 'Ariston of Chios and the Unity of Virtue', *Ancient Philosophy* 4 (1984), 83–96

[873] J. Brunschwig, 'On a Book Title by Chrysippus', *Oxford Studies in Ancient Philosophy*, Suppl. Vol. (1991), 81–95

[874] G. B. Kerferd, 'Cicero and Stoic Ethics', in J. R. C. Martin (ed.), *Cicero and Virgil* (Amsterdam, 1972), 60–74

[875] H. von Arnim, *Hierokles, Ethische Elementarlehre* (Berlin, 1906)

[876] B. Inwood, 'Hierocles: Theory and Argument in the Second Century A.D.', *Oxford Studies in Ancient Philosophy* 2 (1984), 151–84

[877] A. A. Long, 'Hierocles on *Oikeiosis* and Self-perception', in his [805], 250–63

[878] P. Hadot, 'Une clé des Pensées de Marc Aurèle: les Trois *Topoi* philosophiques selon Epictète', *Etudes Philosophiques* 33 (1978), 65–83

[879] I. G. Kidd, 'Poseidonius' Methodology and the Self-sufficiency of Virtue', in [728], ch. 1

[880] E. Asmis, 'Seneca's *On the Happy Life* and Stoic Individualism', in [28], 219–56

[881] P. Mitsis, 'Seneca on Reason, Rules, and Moral Development', in [725], 285–312

The Peripatetics

[882] W. W. Fortenbaugh, 'Arius, Theophrastus and the Eudemian Ethics', in [803], 203–23

[883] P. Huby, 'Peripatetic Definitions of Happiness', in [803], 121–34

[884] R. W. Sharples, *Alexander of Aphrodisias: De Fato* (London, 1983)

[885] R. W. Sharples, 'Aristotelian and Stoic Conceptions of Necessity in the *De Fato* of Alexander', *Phronesis* 20 (1975), 247–74

[886] R.W. Sharples (ed.), Alexander of Aphrodisias, *Ethical Problems* (London, 1990)

[887] R. W. Sharples, 'The Peripatetic Classification of Goods', in [803], 139–59

Cicero

[888] H. Hunt, *The Humanism of Cicero* (Melbourne, 1954)

[889] P. MacKendrick, *The Philosophical Books of Cicero* (London, 1989)

[890] J. G. F. Powell (ed.), *Cicero the Philosopher* (Oxford, 1995)

[891] M. R. Wright, 'Cicero on Self-love and Love of Humanity in *De Finibus* 3', in [890], 171–96

The sceptics

General accounts of ancient scepticism can be found in

[892] J. Annas and J. Barnes, *The Modes of Scepticism* (Cambridge, 1985)

[893] J. Hankinson, *The Sceptics* (London, 1994)

[894] V. Brochard, *Les Sceptiques grecs*, (2nd edn Paris, 1923)

[895] M. F. Burnyeat, 'The Sceptic in his Place and Time', in [969], 225–54, and in [896]

[896] M. F. Burnyeat and M. Frede (edd.), *The Original Sceptics* (Indianapolis, 1997)

[897] G. Giannantoni (ed.), *Lo scetticismo antico*, 2 vols. (Rome, 1981)

[898] M. dal Pra, *Lo scetticismo Greco*, 2 vols., 2nd edn (Rome/Bari, 1975)

[899] D. Sedley, 'The Motivation of Greek Scepticism', in [12], 9–30

[900] C. Stough, *Greek Skepticism* (Berkeley/Los Angeles, 1969).

A valuable general discussion of Sextus is

[901] K. Janáček, *Sextus Empiricus' Sceptical Methods* (Prague, 1972). See also

[902] W. Heintz, *Studien zu Sextus Empiricus* (Halle, 1932).

Relevant papers on scepticism are

[903] J. Barnes, 'The Beliefs of a Pyrrhonist', *Elenchos* 4 (1983), 5–43, and in [896]

[904] R. Bett, 'Scepticism as a Way of Life and Scepticism as "Pure Theory"', in *Homo Viator: Essays in Honour of John Bramble* (Bristol, 1986)

[905] R. Bett, 'Carneades' Distinction Between Assent and Approval', *Monist*, 73 (1990), 3–20

[906] M. F. Burnyeat, 'Can the Sceptic Live his Scepticism?', in [721], 20–53, in [12], 117–48, and in [896]

[907] M. Frede, 'The Skeptic's Beliefs', in [21], 179–200 and in [896]

[908] R. J. Hankinson, 'Values, Objectivity and Dialectic; The Skeptical Attack on Ethics: Its Methods, Aims and Success', *Phronesis* 39 (1994), 45–68

[909] M. McPherran, 'Skeptical Homeopathy and Self-refutation', *Phronesis* 32 (1987), 290–328

[910] M. McPherran, '*Ataraxia* and *Eudaimonia*: Is the Sceptic Really Happy?', *Proceedings of the Boston Area Colloquium in Ancient Philosophy* 5 (1989), 135–71

[911]   M. McPherran, 'Pyrrhonism and the Arguments Against Value',
        Philosophical Studies 60 (1990), 127–42
[912]   G. Striker, 'Sceptical Strategies' in [721], 54–83, and in her [730], 92–115
[913]   G. Striker, 'Über den Unterschied zwischen den Pyrrhoneern und den
        Akademikern', *Phronesis* 26 (1981), 153–71, which is translated as
[914]   G. Striker, 'On the Difference between the Pyrrhonists and the
        Academics', in her [730], 135–49
[915]   G. Striker, 'The Ten Tropes of Aenesidemus' in [12], 95–115, and in her
        [730], 116–34
[916]   G. Striker, '*Ataraxia*: Happiness as Tranquillity', *The Monist* 73 (1990),
        97–110, and in her [730], 183–95.

Non-ethical works cited

[917]   J. Annas, *Hellenistic Philosophy of Mind* (Berkeley, 1992)
[918]   D. Bostock, 'Plato on "is not"', *Oxford Studies in Ancient Philosophy* 2
        (1984), 89–120
[919]   J. Brunschwig, 'The Conjunctive Model', in his [729], 72–91
[920]   J. Brunschwig, 'L'Argument d'Epicure sur l'immutabilité du tout', in
        [962], 127–50; translated as 'Epicurus' Argument on the Immutability of
        the All', in his [729], 1–20
[921]   S. Everson, 'Psychology', in [413], 168–94
[922]   S. Everson, *Aristotle on Perception* (Oxford, 1996)
[923]   M. Frede, 'On the Original Notion of Cause', in his [721], 213–49 and his
        [21], 125–50
[924]   A.-M. Ioppolo, *Opinione e scienzia: il dibattito tra Stoici e Academici nel III e II
        secolo a.c.* (Naples, 1986) (which is reviewed in
[925]   J. Annas, 'The Heirs of Socrates', *Phronesis* 33 (1988), 100–12)
[926]   C. H. Kahn, 'Language and Ontology in the *Cratylus*' in [25], 152–76
[927]   S. Sauvé Meyer, 'Aristotle, Teleology and Reduction', *Philosophical Review*
        101 (1992), 791–825
[928]   G. E. L. Owen, 'Logic and Metaphysics in Some Earlier Works of Aristotle',
        in [418], 163–90, [415], 13–32 and [29], 180–99
[929]   D. Sedley, 'Two Conceptions of Vacuum', *Phronesis* 27 (1982), 175–93
[930]   D. Sedley, 'Epicurean Anti-Reductionism', in [724], 295–327

Modern works cited

[931]   J. E. J. Altham and R. Harrison (edd.), *World, Mind and Ethics* (Cambridge,
        1995)
[932]   G. E. M. Anscombe, *Intention*, 2nd edn (Oxford, 1979)
[933]   G. E. M. Anscombe, 'Modern Moral Philosophy', *Philosophy* 33 (1958),
        1–19 and in her [935], 26–42
[934]   G. E. M. Anscombe, *From Parmenides to Wittgenstein: Collected Philosophical
        Papers I* (Oxford, 1981)
[935]   G. E. M. Anscombe, *Ethics, Religion and Politics: Collected Philosophical
        Papers III* (Oxford, 1981)
[936]   J. L. Austin, *Philosophical Papers*, 3rd edn (ed. J. O. Urmson and G. J.
        Warnock) (Oxford, 1979)
[937]   L. Becker (ed.), *Encyclopedia of Ethics*, vol. 1 (New York/London, 1992)

[938] R. Bett, 'Is Modern Moral Scepticism Essentially Local?', *Analysis* 48 (1988), 102–7

[939] S. Blackburn, 'Truth, Realism and the Regulation of Theory', *Midwest Studies in Philosophy* 5 (1980), 353–72

[940] S. Blackburn, 'Rule-following and Moral Realism', in [951], 163–90

[941] S. Blackburn, 'Errors and the Phenomenology of Value', in [950], 1–22

[942] D. Brink, *Moral Realism and the Foundations of Ethics* (Cambridge, 1989)

[943] B. Brody (ed.), *Suicide and Euthanasia* (Dordrecht, 1989)

[944] P. Foot, 'Morality as a System of Hypothetical Imperatives', in her [945], 157–73

[945] P. Foot, *Virtues and Vices, and Other Essays in Moral Philosophy* (Oxford, 1978)

[946] P. Foot, 'Does Moral Subjectivism Rest on a Mistake?', *Oxford Journal of Legal Studies* 15 (1995), 1–15

[947] P. T. Geach, *Logic Matters* (Oxford, 1972)

[948] R. M. Hare, *Freedom and Reason* (Oxford, 1963)

[949] R. M. Hare, *Moral Thinking* (Oxford, 1981)

[950] T. Honderich (ed.), *Morality and Objectivity* (London, 1985)

[951] S. Holtzman and C. M. Leich (edd.), *Wittgenstein: To Follow a Rule* (London, 1981)

[952] R. Hursthouse, G. Lawrence and W. Quinn (edd.), *Virtues and Reasons* (Oxford, 1995)

[953] I. Kant, *Foundations of the Metaphysics of Morals*, tr. L. W. Beck (Indianapolis, 1959)

[954] A. Kenny, *The Anatomy of the Soul* (Oxford, 1973)

[955] C. Korsgaard, *Creating the Kingdom of Ends* (Cambridge, 1996)

[956] G. Lawrence, 'The Rationality of Morality', in [952], 89–148

[957] S. Lovibond and S. Williams (edd.), *Essays for David Wiggins: Identity, Truth, Value* (Oxford, 1996)

[958] J. L. Mackie, *Ethics* (London, 1977)

[959] J. McDowell, 'Are Moral Requirements Hypothetical Imperatives?', *Proceedings of the Aristotelian Society* Suppl. Vol. 52 (1978), 13–29

[960] J. McDowell, 'Non-cognitivism and Rule-following', in [951], 141–67

[961] J. McDowell, 'Values and Secondary Qualities', in [950], 110–29

[962] *Permanence de la philosophie: Mélanges Offerts à Joseph Mareau* (Neuchâtel, 1977)

[963] G. Pitcher and O. P. Wood (edd.), *Ryle* (Garden City, N.Y., 1970)

[964] H. Putnam, 'The Meaning of Meaning', in his [965], 215–71

[965] H. Putnam, *Mind, Language and Reality: Philosophical Papers Volume 2* (Cambridge, 1975)

[966] J. Rawls, 'The Sense of Justice', *Philosophical Review* 72 (1963), 281–305

[967] T. Reid, *Essays on the Active Powers of the Human Mind*, ed. B. Brody (Cambridge, Mass., 1969)

[968] A. O. Rorty (ed.), *The Identities of Persons* (Berkeley/Los Angeles/London, 1976)

[969] R. Rorty, J. B. Schneewind and Q. Skinner (edd.), *Philosophy in History* (Cambridge, 1984)

[970] H. Sidgwick, *The Methods of Ethics*, 7th edn (London, 1907)

[971] A. Smith, *The Theory of the Moral Sentiments*, edd. D. D. Raphael and A. L. Macfie (Oxford, 1976)

[972] W. C. Starr and R. C. Taylor (edd.), *Moral Philosophy* (Milwaukee, 1989)

[973] C. Taylor, 'Responsibility for Self', in [968], 281–300

[974] C. C. W. Taylor, Review of [948], in [975], 47–71

[975] G. Wallace and A. Walker (edd.), *The Definition of Morality* (London, 1970)

[976] G. Warnock, 'On Choosing Values', *Midwest Studies in Philosophy* 3 (1978), 28–34

[977] D. Wiggins, 'Truth, Invention, and the Meaning of Life', in his [978], 86–137

[978] D. Wiggins, *Needs, Values, Truth* (Oxford, 1987)

[979] B. Williams, *Ethics and the Limits of Philosophy* (London, 1985)

Index of names

Index of passages discussed[*]

---

[*] 'D–K' refers to the fragments cited in Diels Kranz [78], 'LS' to the passages cited in Long and Sedley [719], and 'SVF' to those given in von Arnim [791].

Index of subjects

ability, 234–8; *see also* capacities
absolutism, 199
action, 80, 212, 223
adultery, 70
advantages, 28, 163, 164–5, 170, 173, 175–6,
    182, 183, 191
agathon, 27–8; *see also* good, goods
agent-centred moral theories, 18–24
aidōs, 37
aischron, 27, 52; *see also* disgraceful
akrasia, 43, 45, 126–7; *see also* incontinence
altruism, 8, 27, 130
anger, 36, 66, 156, 181, 184
animals, 74, 94–5, 107, 136, 160–1, 179, 221,
    227, 228, 230
anxiety (*tarachē*), 207, 208, 213, 215n36
apatheia, see freedom from passion
aponia, 129–30
appearance (*phantasia*), 179–81, 185–8, 189,
    190, 200, 210, 211, 230–1; *see also*
    impressions
conflicts of appearances, 195–6, 200–1,
    202
appetite, 35, 66, 72, 117, 182, 184; *see also*
    desire, *orexis*
appropriate actions (*kathēkonta*), 174–5
apraxia 212, 216
aretē 31, 52; *see also* excellence, virtue
arguments, 201–2, 204
arrogance, 31
art, 103; *see also* crafts, *technē* , skill
assent, 178–82, 184, 185–7, 209, 212, 213,
    218–19, 227, 230–1
ataraxia 129, 207, 213

beauty, 30, 92
beliefs, 13, 58, 178–83, 207–13, 218–19; *see*
    also cognitions
benevolence, 27, 71
blame, 2, 178, 221
body, bodies, 132–3, 138–9, 144
bouleusis, see deliberation

cannibalism, 201
capacities, 229–30, 234–5; *see also* ability

categorical reasons, 9, 12
causes, 171, 222, 223–4, 225, 226–7, 230–4,
    239
character, 2, 3, 14, 16–17, 24, 32, 107, 124,
    232, 234
cheerfulness (*euthumiē*), 34, 36
children, 91–3, 105, 179, 221
choice, 107, 108–9, 186, 223, 231, 238
Christianity, 3
cleverness, 12
cognitions, 12, 56–9, 67; *see also* beliefs
colour, 56
compatibilism, ch. 9 *passim*
concepts, 55
conciliation (*oikeiōsis*), 160–1, 164, 165, 167,
    175
contemplative life, 125–6
continence, 126, 128
contracts, 148
convention, 52–4, 194; *see also nomos*
courage, 11, 17, 24, 36, 52, 54, 59, 62, 64,
    65, 67–8, 72–4, 149
cowardice, 148
Cradle Argument, 136–8
crafts, 60–1, 165–8, 229; *see also* skill, *technē*
cult, 32
customs (*ēthē*), 194, 209

death, 29–30, 32, 47, 147, 188
decision (*prohairēsis*), 171n39
definition, 17–18, 24–6, 54–7, 198, 202
deliberation, 13, 21, 105–6, ch. 5 *passim*, 169,
    225–30
desire, 1, 9, 12, 20, 23, 58, 61, 66–7, 69, 81,
    130, 156, 178, 182, 184, 208, 210, 231;
    see also appetite
determinism, 222, 223, 225, 231–40
dikaiosunē, 7–8, 27, 49; *see also* justice
disgraceful, 120; *see also aischron*
dogmatic conceptions, 195
duty, 2n3, 18, 27

education, 64, 67, 73
egoism, 5–7, 27, 50, 131
elenchus, 45